Home: Autobiographies, Etc.

Also by William Heyen

POETRY

Depth of Field (1970)
Noise in the Trees: Poems and a Memoir (1974)
The Swastika Poems (1977)
Long Island Light: Poems and a Memoir (1979)
The City Parables (1980)
Lord Dragonfly: Five Sequences (1981)
Erika: Poems of the Holocaust (1984)
The Chestnut Rain (1986)
Brockport, New York: Beginning with "And" (1988)
Pterodactyl Rose: Poems of Ecology (1991)
Ribbons: The Gulf War (1991)
The Host: Selected Poems 1965-1990 (1994)
Crazy Horse in Stillness (1996)
Diana, Charles, & the Queen (1998)
The Rope (2003)
Shoah Train (2003)

PROSE

Vic Holyfield and the Class of 1957: A Romance (1986)
Pig Notes & Dumb Music: Prose on Poetry (1998)
The Hummingbird Corporation: Stories (2003)
Titanic & Iceberg: Early Essays & Reviews (2004)

ANTHOLOGIES

A Profile of Theodore Roethke (1971)
American Poets in 1976 (1976)
The Generation of 2000: Contemporary American Poets (1984)
September 11, 2001: American Writers Respond (2002)

Home: Autobiographies, Etc.

by

William Heyen

William Heyen
Brockport, NY / 2022

For the Seymour Library

MAMMOTH books
DuBois, Pennsylvania

First Edition

ISBN: 0-9718059-3-8

MAMMOTH books
is an imprint of MAMMOTH press inc.
7 Juniata Street
DuBois, Pennsylvania 15801
www.mammothpressinc.org

Cover painting: "Shooting Flamingoes" (1857), a 19"x26½" oil on canvas by
George Catlin (American, 1796-1872), is reproduced by permission of the
Memorial Art Gallery of the University of Rochester and the Marion Stratton
Gould Fund.

Cover design by Mary Kay Stoddard
e-mail: mks107@graphic-designer.com

Production by Offset Paperback Manufacturers, Inc.

Note

Many of William Heyen's poems included in these essays first appeared in periodicals and then in four collections published by Time Being Books of Saint Louis: *Erika: Poems of the Holocaust, Pterodactyl Rose: Poems of Ecology, The Host: Selected Poems 1965-1990,* and *Ribbons: The Gulf War.* Copyright 1991, 1994 Time Being Press, Inc.; also in *The Rope: Poems,* published by MAMMOTH Books (DuBois, PA, 2003) and *Shoah Train,* published by Etruscan Press (Silver Spring, MD, 2003). Grateful acknowledgement for their use in *Home.*

The poem "Iwo Dahlia" first appeared in *Artful Dodge* (2002).

Many thanks to Bernice Graham and Karen Renner for their considerable help with the manuscript of *Home.*

I'm grateful, too, to poet-publisher Antonio Vallone—decades of friendship, and now this act of faith.

I'd like to dedicate this collection to the memory of my dear friend William B. Ewert (1943-2001) of Concord, New Hampshire, an educator and bibliophile who was also, for almost thirty years, one of America's pre-eminent fine-press publishers. Because of his love, his passion, and his art, Bill's limited editions will continue to give of themselves in unlimited ways.

W.H.

Contents

Poetry of the American Dream:
Arthur Miller's *Death of a Salesman*

Nothing about *Death of a Salesman*, once I step away from it, strikes me as quite believable, quite intelligent, quite intelligible, quite interesting. Characters, plot, even the language that so often falls into the poetry of romantic cliché, will not quite bear scrutiny. Reviewing the play in 1949, one irritated critic objected to its "speciousness." "The play," this reviewer said, "with its peculiar hodge-podge of dated materials and facile new ones, is . . . an ambitious piece of confusionism, such as in any other sphere would probably be called a hoax, and which has been put across by purely technical skills not unlike those of a magician or an acrobat." A hoax! Now, this is pretty strong and pretty silly. But, once I give the play some distance, almost everything about it irritates me or makes me laugh. But *Salesman* is much more than the sum of its parts. Once the curtains part, a flute begins to play and I am caught up in the poverty and dream and bitter bliss of the Lomans.

There is no question but that the play is elusive. As Miller himself has said, "*Death of a Salesman* is a slippery play to categorize because nobody in it stops to make a speech objectively stating the great issues which I believe it embodies." The play does not mirror, or reflect, or state; it embodies, and often puts us at a loss to enunciate the ideas and feelings it calls forth. That's the thing about *Salesman*: it reverberates, echoes, resonates. Its rhythms roll deep down toward and into American desires and delusions. Fear, pity, a sense of loss for what might have been, a qualified joy for Willy's happiness as he commits suicide—these are the inescapable and elusive feelings experienced during the play. There are a hundred ways to see the play, as Miller himself knew, bogus ways and true ways. We can smile when Miller tells us that as one audience left the play he heard a man, probably a salesman, tell another that New England always was a lousy territory. But something about the play strikes deep now, and

---

Delivered as a lecture at Tübingen University in June 1972. Subsequently published in *Amerikanisches Drama und Theater im 20 Jahrhundert*, eds. Alfred Weber and Siegfried Neuwiler (Göttingen: Vanderhoeck and Ruprecht, 1975). Reprinted in *Arthur Miller's* Death of a Salesman, ed. Harold Bloom (New York: Chelsea House, 1988).

did in 1940, and will. This something is the poetry of the play, not something that can be isolated in particulars, but the way the whole play ranges out from its center which is Willy, the way it echoes far past its own American images, the way it demands a hearing for its own sentimentality and exaggeration. The great issues the play embodies are human issues brought to a focal point on the American continent. We've had enough formal criticism of *Salesman*, and I have little or nothing to add of that. But I want to tell how the play feels and smells and looks to me. To do this, I've got to range all over and throw out nets and come up with whatever butterflies or fish I can. To do this, I have to take the sorts of risks that Miller took in writing such a simple and absurd and beautiful and true play.

It seems to me that a key Miller strategy has been to place his characters, most of whom have lost the old faiths, on a search for what will suffice. Little of consequence is decided for them ahead of time. They are out taking their chances (and sometimes, like Willy, spending for vast returns), within the world of the play, and finding out what it is that they believe in as they enact their own lives. It is a terrestrial morality they are looking for and trying to justify.

One of Miller's most dead-end characters is Joe Keller of *All My Sons* (1947). Joe sells faulty engine-heads to the American Army during World War II and is responsible for the deaths of twenty-one pilots. He commits this act not because his business, which he spent forty years building up, might be lost if he admits the flaws in the engines. He commits this act, as twisted as this seems, to keep his family together. He thinks he cannot maintain the family without money, property. When he finds out that his son Chris hates him for what he has done, when he finds out that the dead pilots and the boys who died under Chris's command were all his sons, Joe shoots himself. He labored in the wilderness, made his error in a moral wilderness. He didn't have anything of real value to give his family, or if he did, he didn't know what it was. Joe Keller's awakening, if that is what we should call it, occurs during only the last few minutes of his life.

Neither does Willy Loman have anything of real value to give his family, but he learns this earlier than Joe Keller, and his death, his suicide, a joyous one for Willy, is more complex than Keller's. Willy, to be sure, has been a great lie, a walking emptiness, a breathing delusion. He gives, in effect, only flawed ideas and desires to his sons. In Miller's world, what is unspoken but assumed and hinted at is a morality that holds that there can be no such thing as happiness, no such thing as love, without honesty. A painful self-knowledge is what Joe Keller and Victor and Walter Franz of *The Price* (1968) come to; Willy Loman, and Eddie Carbone of *A View from the Bridge* (1955), never admit to their families or their audience who they are and why they have done what they've done. Both die lying, and there may be nothing more upsetting for us as we witness a play than a character who never learns what we and the author know he has to learn. The dramatic irony holds to the end. Carbone and Willy die lying, but surely there is a different quality to their lies. Willy will not quite be explained as easily as Eddie can be. After all, Willy chooses to lie. Eddie never believes the truth about himself, but Willy does: he asks Bernard, for example, "What-what's the secret?" But, in effect, he turns away from the secret in rage and fierce joy.

Eddie Carbone's lie is an individual one, one of special circumstances. The gripping thing about Willy's lie is that it is so huge and hopeful. It is so pervasively American. He will not part with it. He dies with it and for it, and parting is all he knows of heaven. He dies happy, certain (no, but talking, talking, convincing himself) that his whole life will bear the fruit of his son's greatness. Willy is an incurable yea-sayer, painting everything rosy, prophesying empire and dominion for the Lomans, day after day for his whole life feeding his ego, breathing in the promises and lies. He is insatiable. He so much needs to believe in his dream.

And, day after day, dying, and knowing this, too. He asks his sons: "Where are you guys, where are you? The woods are burning!" We would like to help him, to console him. We love him. He is our father.

Willy Loman (bless him, damn him) will not let truth get the best of him. We will not hold to his failure. Admission of failure would have led to suicide the same way as his enduring dream led to suicide, so it is not admission that the play urges. Willy saw the truth. He knew he didn't have Ben's courage, Charley's good business sense, Dave Singleman's personality, his own father's fortitude and ingenuity. But Willy chose, and this is what I see and hear and feel in the play, to continue dreaming even unto death.

Again and again, when replying to reviewers and critics upset by *Death of a Salesman*'s darkness, Miller has insisted that the play is not unrelievedly black. He is right, certainly, but we are in no sense conditioned to hear of any kind of suicide as an act of affirmation. But for Willy it is. This is Willy's terrible beauty. Willy chooses meaning over meaninglessness, bless him. No, no, shout critics, give us more light. But what a man Willy is. I am thankful for him, I think. At least I am glad of the way he went out, forsaking my pity, doing it his way. He chose, in effect, to insist that he had lived, to defend his life as it was, to act so that his vision could become a reality. But he confuses us, that lovable old madman and humbug. He is a salesman! He's trying to sell us the wrong dreams! We can't hold him down to a generalization, can't pin him down, don't know how we ought to feel about him. Is he lost or found? He is lost. He is found. He is both. Willy is a dramatic experience that we cannot conceptualize, like a flight of birds in a poem by Richard Wilbur: words are no net to hold them, and the speaker of the poem learns "By what cross-purposes the world is dreamt" ("An Event"). Eleanor Clark said that it's a bit irritating not to know whether or not the insurance money is ever paid out to Willy's family after his suicide. What is behind this sort of irritation is the desire for a perfectly round play, a conventional play with all the answers. The insurance money matters not at all. Whatever Willy says before he drives off for the last time, it wasn't money that he gave to Biff. Willy gave Biff an undying illusion and, perhaps, the possibility of happiness. The question, too, of whether or not Biff's final statement that he knows himself is the truth or is the play's central irony becomes academic. At least he can live, at least he has some garment of even dull glory to wear during the meaningless passing of his days. Both Biff and Happy still head for the territory of dream, if in different directions. They at least have something. The salesman is dead. Long live the salesman. Nor does it matter what Willy is selling. That he does not mention Willy's line is not an oversight on Miller's part. Willy is selling himself, himself says Miller. Leslie Fiedler has said, in fact, that only one thing is sold in all of America. Indeed, Fiedler observes:

> There is only a single industry in the United States, which its bewilderingly and misleadingly various subdivisions tend to disguise even from its managers—though not from the consumers it serves who really determine the nature of its production. What that industry produces are not things—for things are old and do not interest the young of all ages who control the market—but dreams disguised as things: poor vulgar dreams they seem sometimes, but what can one expect of a population descended from the culturally dispossessed of all nations of the world?

Death of a Salesman is a play of great yearning. Willy says, in effect, "I've got to have something. I'm a failure, my sons are failures. I've lost the great elms that grew out front, and a man can't grow even a carrot around here. I've got to have something." So Willy justifies all those days spent shining the Chevy with Biff and Happy by committing suicide. It is the only way he can keep his dream intact. To save his life, he has to kill himself. Should he deny himself, it would be as though he did not live. Willy intimated the way better even than he knew. Miller has given us a man. We've not been brought up to attend his funeral; but, as Linda says, attention must be paid. And, as Charley says over Willy's grave, "Nobody dast blame this man." It's not that we have to praise him. It's probably as senseless to praise him as it is to condemn him. But we must acknowledge his presence and the stake we have in his state of mind at the moment of his death.

The enlightenment of tragedy, Miller says in his 1949 essay "Tragedy and the Common Man," lies in "the discovery of the moral law. . ." In the same essay he defines the moral law as "the indestructible will of man to achieve his humanity." This means pride, power, endurance. This means, first, an acceptance of the worst, and then an indomitable will, if only the will to believe what is felt not to be true. Allow me to quote part of Quentin's last speech in Miller's *After the Fall* (1964):

> I swear to you, I could love the world again! Is the knowing all? To know, and even happily, that we meet unblessed; not in some garden of wax fruit and painted trees,

that lie of Eden, but after, after the Fall, after many, many
deaths. Is the knowing all? And the wish to kill is never killed,
but with some gift of courage one may look into its face when it
appears, and with a stroke of love—to an idiot in the house—
forgive it; again and again . . . for ever?

Miller wrote this about fifteen years after *Death of a Salesman*. There is a sense in
which Quentin is a Willy Loman come back from the dead. Willy and Quentin,
the one loving and loving and dying with a dream of Eden on his lips; the other
knowing the death of love and the desire to kill but holding to the will to forgive
forever. These are two characters who will be asking us for a long time how we
must live in the world. Their presence, their humanity as they strain to realize
themselves, is staggering.

    I know that this is a personal, impressionistic talk. I'm trying to suggest
how I feel when I see or read *Salesman*. I'm trying to demonstrate my own
confusion and enlightenment. Now I ask: what's bothering Willy, what does he
want, just what has happened to him? What is the play's position? What are its
American rhythms, echoes, and reverberations? I have to start talking anywhere.

    For one thing, I think, Willy comes from the beginning. Listen to D.H.
Lawrence in *Studies in Classic American Literature* (1923):

> I can remember, when I was a little boy, my father used
> to buy a scrubby yearly almanac with the sun and moon and
> stars on the cover. And it used to prophesy bloodshed and
> famine. But also crammed in corners it had little anecdotes and
> humorisms, with a moral tag. And I used to have my priggish
> laugh at the woman who counted her chickens before they were
> hatched and so forth, and I was convinced that honesty was the
> best policy, also a little priggishly. The author of these bits was
> Poor Richard, and Poor Richard was Benjamin Franklin, writing
> in Philadelphia well over a hundred years before.

Lawrence goes on to say that he never got over those tags, those tight little
moralisms: "I rankle with them still." Intellectual history in America went in two
major directions during the eighteenth century. There was Jonathan Edwards, who
wanted souls at white heat, who wanted a great and continuing awakening, who
was driven to assimilate a new science into orthodox Puritan doctrine. And there
was Benjamin Franklin. Benjamin Franklin's practical moralism had the most
appeal, was most in step with the times, and Willy Loman's America is Benjamin
Franklin's America, certainly, not Edwards'. Ben Franklin, Lawrence said, created
a god convenient enough to allow him to pursue his own heart's desire. Virtue
would bring a man money, said Ben. Money was nothing to be ashamed of: in
fact, it was a manifestation of virtue. Gold coins were God's smiles. The man of

means would be likely to find, too, that he had enough love and respect. Not necessarily in Europe: for two centuries now Europeans have been shocked and embarrassed by frank American discussions of incomes and profits and costs. But to Ben the way to get it all, the practical way and perfect way and virtuous way, was to go after it, go after it, go after it convinced that it was your destiny and God's will for you to get it. Play it clean and straight, of course, as far as this was possible, as long as this didn't prove too inconvenient.

Now, Willy Loman has never heard of Jonathan Edwards, and has never read Benjamin Franklin. But his is Benjamin Franklin's dream, and Willy's brother Ben—it doesn't matter whether the name is coincidence or intention—is a walking talking Franklin, son of a Ghost of America's Past that Willy calls up. Miller knows: Ben says to Biff, "Never fight fair with a stranger, boy. You'll never get out of the jungle that way." Why, even Ben Franklin's wife was primarily a convenience for him. Franklin was the sort of man who would borrow a book from you and never read it and return it with great thanks and then know that you would be on his side because people like people they can do something for. Willy's brother Ben laughs lustily when he hears that Biff has been stealing lumber. And Willy himself is seen as straining constantly to justify himself and his life and his sons to Ben. But next to Ben and next to Ben Franklin Willy is, of course, an innocent, and so are his sons. At one point Ben trips Biff and stands over him, "the point of his umbrella poised over Biff's eye." Still, just before he kills himself Willy is saying "Ben! Ben, where do I . . .? Ben, how do I . . .?" These are gestures and words of great depth. Indeed, how can Willy reach out and take hold of happiness and meaning? For Ben has retreated into the past and left Willy behind with only a dream of being respected and successful and loved. Nothing helps, not even those moral tags with which Willy is filled, those tags that Lawrence wanted to spit out. "Never leave a job till you're finished," says Willy. "Be quiet, fine, and serious. Everybody likes a kidder, but nobody lends him money," says Willy. "Personality always wins the day," says Willy. "Moral America!" exclaims Lawrence. Lawrence saw Willy Loman coming to die. Willy is Ben's boy, and as I watch or read the play I know and feel this, and I'm hurt by it. This is one thing.

Another thing is that in *Salesman* what we could call details of the American landscape explode for me. Willy's lost elms, the horrible tearing scene in which he attempts to plant seeds, Biff's desire to work out in the open with his shirt off, the picture of Willy's father banging around the country in a horse drawn wagon—these are truths of the American heart. These may be exaggerations, but if so Miller exaggerates the way St. Jean de Crevecoeur exaggerated with his picture of the farmer plowing the heavenly dreamground of America. Truths reside in these exaggerations.

The American dream is rural, not urban, and the perfect world is out there somewhere, and when we can't find it out there ahead of us, we go back to the elm shaded past. The only trees in the play are those Willy tells us he sees when he's driving above Yonkers before the play begins. Listen to him:

> I was driving along, you understand. And I was fine. I was even observing the scenery. You can imagine, me looking at scenery, on the road every week of my life. But it's so beautiful up there, Linda, the trees are so thick, and the sun is warm. I opened the windshield and just let the warm air bathe over me. And then all of a sudden I'm goin' off the road! I'm tellin' ya, I absolutely forgot I was driving. If I'd've gone the other way over the white line I might've killed somebody. So I went on again—and five minutes later I'm dreamin' again, and I nearly—*He presses two fingers against his eyes.* I have such thoughts, I have such strange thoughts.

Yes, Willy has such strange thoughts. As we witness his drama we can almost enunciate these thoughts. Almost. There are a thousand poignant melodies Willy has heard and communicates to me, like this one from Thomas Wolfe's novel *The Web and the Rock* (1939):

> And everywhere, through the immortal dark, something moving in the night, and something stirring in the hearts of men, and something crying in their wild, unuttered blood, the wild unuttered tongue of its huge prophecies—so soon the morning, soon the morning: O America.

Or, this simple sentence from a story by Hamlin Garland: "The river was very lovely, curving down along its sandy beds, pausing now and then under broad basswood trees, or running in dark, swift, silent currents under tangles of wild grape vines, and drooping alders, and haw trees."

Or this from William Faulkner's story "Delta Autumn":

> two spans running out together, not toward oblivion, nothingness, but into a dimension free of both time and space where once more the untreed land warped and wrung to mathematical squares of rank cotton for the frantic old world people to turn into shells to shoot at one another, would find ample room for both of the names, the faces of the old men he had known and loved and for a little while outlived, moving again among the shades of tall unaxed trees and sightless brakes where the wild strong immortal game ran forever before the

tireless belling immortal hounds, falling and rising phoenix-like to the soundless guns.

Or this reminiscence by Halvdan Koht:

> This song [Stephen Foster's 1848 "Oh! Susanna," with the chorus "Oh! Susanna! Oh! don't you cry for me, / I've come from Alabama with my banjo on my knee"] we are told, was often sung by the foreign immigrants to enliven the long hours of travel through the country. From the immigrants it wandered back to the old countries, and there the tune was used for a new song, adapted for the events and hopes of the year of composition. In the new text, the chorus ran:
> Oh! Susanna! Oh! cry no more for me,
> I am going to California and digging gold for thee.
> I have seen a reference to this song in Sweden in the 1860's, and I have heard it in my own childhood in the far north of Norway in the 1890's. California had become virtually a symbol of America. There was to be found rehabilitation for everyone for whom life had gone wrong in Europe.

And listen to this characterization of Washington Irving's Rip Van Winkle by the critic Philip Young:

> Considering the universality of his fame, it is a wonder that no European, say, has pointed gleefully to this figure as a symbol of America, for he presents a near-perfect image of the way a large part of the world looks at us: likeable enough, up to a point and at times, but essentially immature, self-centered, careless and above all—and perhaps dangerously—innocent. Even more pointedly Rip is a stereotype of the American male as seen from abroad, or in some jaundiced quarters at home: he is perfectly the jolly overgrown child, abysmally ignorant of his own wife and the whole world of adult men—perpetually "one of the boys," hanging around what they are pleased to think of as a "perpetual men's club"; a disguised Rotarian who simply will not and cannot grow up. In moments of candor we will probably admit that a stereotype with no germ of truth in it could not exist: some such mythic America, some such mythic American, exist both actually and in the consciousness of the world. Rip will do very well as their prototype.

It is to some depth of mythic reverberation that the salesman takes us. Miller forces me to complete Willy's few words and meager strivings with everything American I have lived and read. I think that we all have a stake in him as he drives off to joyous death "riding on a smile and a shoeshine," as Charley said. Willy is both what we have to be thankful for and what we must regret.

How beautiful the land was, and it was as big as a man's spirit. A man could fulfill himself. What might have been . . . . For at the same time that *Salesman* gives me the dreams again, it takes them away from me and gives me nothing in return but the will of a few men to fulfill themselves no matter what. But, as I have said, *Salesman* is not a dark play: Willy chooses life instead of a living death. At the same time, *Salesman* is a very dark play. It tells us, as starkly and directly as Theodore Dreiser told us in *Sister Carrie* (1900), that happiness comes not in the fulfilling of dream but in ever believing in it and reaching for it. Drouet, the drummer, first exploring, testing, becoming Willy's real father, opening up territories of dream and trafficking in prostitution, and wearing himself out, getting older and no wiser. Carrie herself ends up with money, fame, everything she thinks she wanted. But she is not happy: at the end of the novel Dreiser hopes that she will dream such happiness as she will never feel. Willy Loman, and this his new and peculiar dimension, ends up dying happily, ecstatically, because he holds to the dream of meaning, holds to his sort of spiritual Franklinism. Dreiser places Carrie where she is through a series of accidents. Miller makes us feel that Willy chose his place, decided, but could not, of course, see what the consequences of his decisions would be. Miller is not preaching here, and this is why one critic's charge that the play is weak because it "is ambiguous in its attitude toward the business-success dream" is a non-criticism. "Miller has written a confused play," says the critic, "because he has been unwilling or unable to commit himself to a firm position with respect to American culture." We must understand that it is not Miller's job to commit himself to a firm position on American culture. It is not his job to commit himself to anything except, perhaps, the truths of the human heart, the truths of his own heart. It is not Miller's job to make, as the same critic warns, a "judgment on America." It is only Miller's job to write a play and to give his characters as much depth and reality as he can. Any man with an absolutely firm position on the American business-success dream is no friend of mine. "By what cross-purposes our lives are dreamt," says Richard Wilbur.

But the play's confusions and ambiguities and flutterings have, in the end, a distinct shade: we are hurt for Willy. We are hurt, at least all of us who don't care to spend our time wondering whether or not Willy Loman is a tragic character or whether *Death of a Salesman* is a tragedy, are hurt. We are elated that Willy died happily deluded, but we are hurt and assess our own contribution to the death of a man all of us know. *Salesman* is not a bible, a constitution, a bill of rights. It is drama with the sounds and rhythms and cycles of dream. What is the play's position? Do we have to be hit over the head? How does Miller himself feel about Willy, who is committed, to be sure, to the dream of business and power? Lawrence tells us how Hawthorne and Melville felt about Hester Prynne and Captain Ahab: ambiguously. Neither author could give mental allegiance to his protagonist's morality, but each identified passionally with his character's humanity. *Salesman* makes Willy neither saint nor villain. But I think the play clarifies our world for us as a place of infinite gradations of the moral values of our actions. We sympathize with Willy, and in so doing play out the endless play of our lives on this planet by giving and forsaking ourselves to the same perhaps fateful and unavoidable dream of knowledge and power and purity. At one point Biff says, "I tell ya, Hap, I don't know what the future is. I don't know—what I'm supposed to want." This is where Miller leaves us, nowhere except in dilemma. In his story version of "The Misfits" (1957), Miller's Perce says, "I don't want nothin" and I don't want to want nothin." "That's the way, boy," says Gay. But they do want something. Both of them need: love, money, a man's job to do. And so does Willy. And so do we. And so does anyone who is not manic depressive. America. America.

Enough of this. The play tears me back and forth and around, and a play ought to. But it has a center. I am hurt for Willy. Whether or not my sympathy condemns me to his sort of hell, I am hurt for the American dream salesman who buys his own dreams, and this is the play's complex position.

A Memoir of John Berryman

John, at least here
I hold you in mid-air.

In 1964 I was teaching at SUNY College at Cortland. One of my colleagues was Jerome Mazzaro. One day Jerry came back from somewhere with a copy of *77 Dream Songs*, which had just appeared. I remember thinking the dust jacket very striking. I borrowed the book and read it, or tried to. It was difficult going. I hadn't read Berryman before this, but soon looked up *Homage to Mistress Bradstreet,* which I studied. Now that, I felt until a couple of years ago, was a language to envy.

It was about this time that Jerry and I drove to Syracuse University to hear a reading by W. D. Snodgrass, who began by reciting several of the *77 Dream Songs* of the man who had been his teacher. Snodgrass' high-pitched voice carried Berryman's voices through their levels of irony and pain and humor perfectly. From that time on, although I never felt able to write anything on Berryman (except for a brief review for *Southern Review* of Berryman's *Sonnets* when it appeared in 1967), few days went by when I did not read at least a little while from one of his books. I became convinced that he was one of the great ones that he was so determined to be.

Against my real will and better judgment, I became Director of the Writers Forum at SUNY College at Brockport in 1970. My first thought was to write to John Berryman. I was to take over the Forum beginning that September, but I wrote Berryman in late April or early May. I don't have my letter, or subsequent ones, but I have his. The first note from him is postmarked May 9, 1970: "Dear Mr. Heyen" it goes, "How do you get to Brockport, from Kennedy airport? I travel a good deal but hate it. Could somebody pick me up? The first Wednesday in November would be best for me." I must have written back, and very happily, simply to tell him either to fly into Buffalo, just an hour's drove away, or into Rochester, just twenty minutes away, where I could pick him up. Kennedy is a seven hour drive from Brockport. His next note is dated 6 June: "I've been in hospital five weeks & I'm afraid my doctors have forbidden

The Ohio Review (Winter 1974). Revised for *First Person Singular: Writers on Their Craft,* ed. Joyce Carol Oates (Princeton: Ontario Review P, 1983).

anything until next Spring. Perhaps we can arrange something later." I'm not sure whether or not I answered right away. I know that his next note came as a surprise. No doubt, he'd forgotten he'd just written me. This note is dated 18 June 70: "I'm just home after a long spell in hospital & my doctors advise against any more trips this year. Could your attractive invitation be extended to some time next Spring?" That was fine with me, certainly. I must have written him back to tell him I would hold onto the $1,000 of our budget that I'd offered him until he could appear for a spring reading and television interview.

A surprise note dated 19 Aug 70 arrived: "I'll be at Loyola College in Montreal from mid-Sept. to mid-Dec, more convenient to you than here. If you want to propose a date or dates, do. Peter Stitt wd. be fine for the interview." I'd thought of flying Peter Stitt in from Vermont for the interview—I felt it best, when possible, to ask one of the poet's friends to co-interview: Allen DeLoach helped me interview Allen Ginsberg, and Jerry Mazzaro helped make James Wright comfortable—but Stitt's visit didn't work out. In any case, I wrote back to Berryman and proposed some dates. His next note makes it clear that he still expected to be in residence at Loyola in the fall: "Oct 7th sounds all right, if Loyola schedules me Mon-Tues as I suggested—but this is tentative: you haven't stated a fee yet ever, have you? My soc. sec. no. is 104-20-1374, and I'll look out a photograph." His next note is from 7 Sept 70: "I'm on Mohawk flight #196 arriving (fr. Buffalo) at Rochester 5:52 p.m. Wed. Oct 8th. That gives time for dinner—anyway, can't anyone who wants to meet me do so at a party somewhere (or just at a coffee shop or bar) after the reading?"

The problem here was that Wednesday was October 7, not 8. I wasn't sure what day he was arriving, and needed to know for television studio and room, program, and dinner arrangements. I wrote him. No answer. I had to call, and dreaded it. I hated the phone, and I hated to bother him. My memory blurs. I had to talk to him two or three times. It was incredible and baffling, but one of our conversations ended when he hung up immediately after saying he would fly into Kennedy. Another one left me with the feeling that he'd be flying to Pittsburgh (perhaps mistaking our Forum for the International Poetry Forum). But I never ascribed any of these confusions to his drinking. I felt that a man as brilliant and sensitive as Berryman ought to be distracted. I felt sure that if I had not been so awed and flustered and embarrassed on the phone, I could have made things clear.

Somehow things became settled. October 7 it would be. Worrying about J.B.'s visit, I hadn't slept well in weeks. I was particularly worried about the television tape, and hoped he would be easy to interview. The morning arrived. Around noon, my wife got a call from Berryman from the Minneapolis airport. I got back from school and he called again. He was drunk, and had missed his plane, and would try to charter one, etc., etc. I said that if he could get to Brockport, even too late for the reading, we could schedule him for the next day. He was relieved. He said fine, because he hated to miss an engagement, and he'd see what he could do. We talked on the phone three or four times. Then he didn't call. At eight in the evening, still hoping that he would descend on us like a miracle, I drove over to the college and announced to a couple of hundred people that the poet had not arrived. I invited lots of friends over to my house for drinks and consolation. We sat around. Some of us played poker. Our hopes were dwindling when J.B. called to say he was in Buffalo. I was elated and told him to sit tight, that Jerry Mazzaro would be there to pick him up within a half hour. I called Jerry, who was standing by at his house in Buffalo. I began drinking in earnest and losing at poker and didn't care. All of us waiting for the man. At about the time I hoped Jerry would be pulling into my driveway, a call came through from Berryman from the airport. He'd seen Mazzaro, but Mazzaro, it seems, had left him! I told him to sit tight, that Jerry must only have gone to the bathroom. I was afraid Berryman and Mazzaro had had an argument. Somehow, I began winning at poker. At one in the morning I heard a crash outside. Jerry had hit a boulder that edges my driveway. Yes, I saw a silhouette on the other side of the front seat. Berryman had made it to Brockport.

The two days of his visit remain central to my life in ways I can only hope to suggest. It was not just that Berryman's visit, at mid-week, had all the qualities of the proverbial lost weekend. This had something to do, once and for all for me, with the reality of poetry in this life. This had something to do with Berryman's presence as a presence committed to the life of poetry. I kept feeling that Berryman was spending for vast returns, was driving himself toward the next poem in a necessary frenzy, and that he had been born to do this. He was always noting lines, sounding out lines, pulling one of his new short poems from one of his pockets. His moods were mercurial, and he always wrenched me with him. Lawrence Lieberman has described Berryman's voice as a "superarticulate mental wail." He was brilliant, dazzling, this man who had met Yeats and had written *Homage*, the *Sonnets*, and *The Dream Songs*. I still feel that he was the only genius I've ever met. (In the Emersonian sense, Genius as opposed to Talent, inspired form as opposed to the somewhat pedestrian ability to make meters and rhymes.) It is my feeling that he came to this Genius at the end of his life in *Love & Fame* (1970) and *Delusions, Etc.* (1972), that we will find this out, and that this will take a long time.

In his essay on Whitman, Randall Jarrell quotes some lines and says that either someone with a tin ear and no art at all wrote those lines, or someone with an incredibly sensitive ear. We know the truth by now. In the same way, I feel that those poems of *Love & Fame* and *Delusions, Etc.*, received with general suspicion and dislike, need us to catch up to them. Their sounds are odd. We will have to tune up to them, and it will take some doing. As Berryman wrote of Stephen Crane's poems, "They are not like literary compositions. They are like things just seen and said, *said for use.*" Those late Berryman poems are deceptively excellent. He was making a violent break, and wanted to trust himself (that constant protesting "Isn't that good?" "Isn't that good?"), but was at the same time caught up in a horror of suspicion that his alcoholism had already destroyed his ability to function without delusion. He was shedding the self in these poems, dealing directly with his life in order to get away from it. He wanted to be of use. And he began to find God, even in "a motor hotel in Wallace Stevens' town," as he said in "The Facts & Issues."

We were up all the night that Berryman arrived in Brockport. We made the television tape the next morning, had lunch at the college and dinner at my house that day, and Berryman read that evening. We were up all night long again and he left by plane that morning. As his plane took off, I cried. Exhaustion and relief. I'd never been through anything like that before. I know that I felt, after he left Brockport, that he would not live for long, and I began to write out some impressions and memories of his visit. I felt a sense of history in his presence. Some of these notes are now embarrassing or naive or otherwise silly. For better or worse, here is what I wrote:

> He said at dinner that when he left a town everyone went to sleep and he checked into a hospital. We laughed. How long could he last? For two days, 48 sleepless hours, I wondered about his heart, miraculous machine: kept him going through fifty-six years, his chain-smoking, alcoholism, insomnia, rages and crying jags and a memory that would not let the dead die. His heart. Hard as a fist. Himself seeming to be all bone. What it must be like to live inside his head. Dream as the panorama of the whole mental life: in one of his four or five calls from the Minneapolis and Buffalo airports on Wed. as he was missing his reading here he spoke of the latest dream: a snake curled in a gold box that was half of his mother-in-law's French door. "What do you think it means," he asked me. I said, could you get to Syracuse? Sunday morning: his wife just called saying she does not know where he is, she is trying to retrace his steps. I told her I put him on a plane Friday morning at 9:00 to New York where he was going to meet Robert Giroux and have lunch, and spend the afternoon with friends, and fly back to Minneapolis at night, because he could not miss a talk he had to give in St. Paul on Saturday morning. Kate said she would call again. She said he did call her Friday night but she did not know where he was calling from. My wife just emptied out one of his ashtrays of Herbert Tarreyton butts. His lips would snap the cigarette with each drag, forced, hurried, driven. He left one of his shirts here with, like his others, cigarette burns and holes along its left side. Too absent-minded now to drive he said, and too absorbed ever to use an ashtray. Sugar that my daughter spilled and his ashes now to vacuum from our shag rugs. All of

this, the sleeplessness, an effort to murder time. His marriage is
what he had to have it, a storm, he said. He kept telling me that
he had one very fine piece of advice for me: to focus on my
wife, write about her, but to see her from someone else's
perspective, his, perhaps. This was the key. Wms. must have
been much the same in both ways: incredible physical stamina
and need to talk and write, living the 24 hr. day; to focus on his
wife through 3 novels and many poems culminating in "Of
Asphodel." I wanted, Friday morning to send him to
Minneapolis and not New York: he replied: "No. I will negotiate
from a position of strength, not weakness." The last time he had
called her (5 in the morning) her line was busy. He believed she
had taken it off the hook. He screamed, even to himself when I
left him alone in the living room for a minute: "She'll get out of
the house. Out. I will not live with her." "She hates me." "She
cannot bear my fame." "She is waiting for me to die." He kept
telling me he could not convince her that he loved her. He
arrived, finally, from Buffalo with Jerry Mazzaro, at midnight
on Wednesday. Fifteen or 20 of us at my house. He took over.
Wanted, at first, only to talk to my wife and Sis Rock. Shut the
rest of us out. I played cards with Bill Rock, Ned Grade, Allen
DeLoach, Mirko. Won $125. Kept going into the living room to
talk to him. He did not see the rest of us. Did not look like the
pictures on *His Toy, His Dream, His Rest*. Beard trimmed, hair
not as wild, or high. Glasses on. More professorial, academic.
Charming, disputatious, dominating, brilliant. What it must be
like to live in his head, to walk drunk into a living room filled
with strangers halfway across the country, and to talk.
Magnificent conceit. We were awed. "I won that round" after
destroying someone trying to be friendly. He had a bad foot,
pinched or displaced nerve. Went shoeless. Raged as we were
going down steps into the television studio, saying he had not
contracted to go up and down steps. Disdained a hand or
shoulder to lean on . . . . He disliked Jerry though Jerry tried to
be kind, flattered him, showing him his rare *The Dispossessed*
bought with money from a poetry prize which Jerry spent on
those books important to him. Shrug. He liked me, did not even
hear me when I said I would have knocked his block off had he
insulted and attacked me the way he did a student at the
Thursday night party. Said the student had condescended to him.
Egads. Sunday morning: I just called Mrs. Berryman to find out
whether she has found him yet. She said he was in Minneapolis
all the time. I was stupid enough to say I was glad things were

all right. She said, well, things weren't all right: he had to go to the hospital again. But, at least, he was safe. There were people talking in the background, friends, no doubt, who got hold of him and checked him in. In my easy chair Friday morning, stretched out straight, he seemed unreal, his clothes much too big for him, or so it seemed, as though there were nothing under his clothes. And when before the reading he came out of the bathroom shirtless, all bone, I thought of Ezra Pound as I'd seen him in photos. He was cute. The last thing my wife said to him at the airport was: Mr. Berryman, your pants are open. And he laughed and zipped his fly. He cried twice: early Thursday morning, over Dylan Thomas; Thursday afternoon over R. P. Blackmur and Auschwitz & Belsen & Dachau. The reading Thursday night: incredible, powerful, he said later he hadn't done so well in a long time, that he had people in the audience he liked and wanted to read to. He went on past where he usually quits, he said. The six dream songs he read knocked me over. He's better than Thomas. Imagine, to have written *The Dream Songs*, and *Homage*. He asked me, Wed. night-Thurs. morning, where I lived. I said do you mean here, in my house, or spiritually. Yes, he nodded. I said someday I hope to write a poem as fine as *Homage*. He said: "I want you to." I said that stanza beginning "It is Spring's New England . . ." choked me up. He said it was the best in the poem. Yes. He was "hot as a pistol" these days, writing like hell. Explained the Dickinson origin of his new style, the unrhymed quatrains he's been writing w. a short 4th line. I realize as I write this he is in the hospital, probably in a dead sleep. What it must be like to live in his head. He stuck the $1000 check in his jacket pocket without opening the envelope. Dream Song #282 was his current favorite. He said God must have spoken to him when he wrote that one. Yes. He liked Dickey. Jerry told him, on their drive from Buffalo, that Dickey didn't know what to do with detail. He disliked Jerry. Told me on the phone, when he'd wandered away from Jerry, that he couldn't imagine Mazzaro wd. write another book on Lowell. His love-hate for Lowell always apparent. Screwed up all my plans for the tape. I threw away my notes as soon as we started or, rather, didn't get to use them. Read, to begin, "The Song of the Tortured Girl." Best single reading of any poem I've ever heard. Impossible to interview. Sometimes 15 second pauses and then continuing, interrupting our next question; once saying we'd have to ask him a question. His obliviousness: to cigarette ashes; to being in one back-straight position at the party for 6 hrs; to traffic as we crossed streets; to anything but poems. When he 1st got here he gripped my hand long & hard. The "strain" and "torsion" in his work is the man. We did get him to eat: a cup of chicken soup Wed. night; a ham & cheese sandwich Th. noon; a decent dinner Thurs. night. Constant bourbon, water, no ice. "Mr. Heyen, I'm an alcoholic. I'd like another drink." I'd say sure. Betrayer, I suppose. He wrote my wife a poem out, which we'll frame: "After you went to bed, / Your tall sweet husband and I talked all night, / until there was no more to be said." Jerry went to bed in Kristen's room around 6 Thurs. morning. J. B. gripped my wrist hard, told me what I had to do to join the great ones: focus on my wife, write sonnets, suffer. Told me I was a late starter. Said he read my book and didn't like it. I don't think he read it—he talked as though he'd read something by a beat. We talked in the car as I tried to drop him off at the motel, about Wilbur. Wilbur said one of his new poems was "low voltage." He respected Wilbur. "No one" had done the perfect the way Wilbur had. "Walking to Sleep" a very great poem, he said. I asked him how Henry was: O.K.—hard to leave him behind . . . . When he sat down he did not want to move. He wanted to talk and drink. He was content talking for hours. His rage at the television taping was not that he was to be interviewed, but that they didn't start quickly enough for him and that he would be cued, told when to begin. This he couldn't bear, but once we did begin he would have been content to sit and talk and say poems for ten hours. This is no exaggeration. Swore on the phone to kiss my wife's left ear when he saw her, and he hadn't done this, he said, since 1940. It was too powerful. Angry at his own body—the brilliant mind having to be borne by the dying animal, the clumsy partner. Now, I'm a famous man, was his usual preface to a story. Now it is three days after he left and I can't get over him. Told me he had been unfaithful only once in his nine years of marriage, but that Kate didn't trust him, hated him, envied him, wanted him dead. In the same breath admitted he was a masochist, and smiled. Tortured himself into poems. Had to stay hot as a pistol. "I haven't finished my coffee. Sit down." Late to everything but lucky to get anywhere. And a little child shall lead them as Kristen led him to dinner. Mr. Berryman talks silly, she said. He has a daughter my son's age. Billy was very quiet. . . . When he broke into an imitation of Maurice Chevalier, Kristen said: "Mr. Berryman, are you talking or singing?" Han remembers that he cried a third time:

Wed. night when he called up an Yvonne, read his new poem to her, and, apparently, she didn't like it. About 6:30 Thurs. morning I drove him to the motel, had to come back for his suitcase, drove him there again, drove him back to my house again when he found there was no phone in his room. He told the woman: "Know that your accommodations are totally unsatisfactory." She winked at me as we left. / Two weeks later I travel to Rochester to hear John Logan read: before dinner, over drinks, Anthony Hecht says that he heard a great Berryman story from Bill Merwin: it seems that a couple of weeks before, Berryman was at the Minneapolis airport and couldn't remember whether he was supposed to go to Pittsburgh or Buffalo and . . . . Nov. 5: I travel to Buffalo to hear Robert Bly read. Later, at a party, Allen DeLoach says that Merwin and someone else *were* waiting in Pittsburgh for Berryman. A postcard arrives from Berryman in the hospital: he seems happy, has written 12 or 15 poems, promises to send *Love and Fame* when copies are available, remembers Patti Hancock "beautiful and serene," sends us all his love. I have written all this out of love.

I kept in loose touch with him after his visit, but never saw him again, except on the television tape we made. I sent him books and programs of his reading to sign. I have a letter from August 21, 1971, that ends: "I hope you both, & the kids, are flourishing. I am." And there's a postscript: "Reading in Rotterdam *1st* wk. in June, back for new baby due *2nd* wk. June. So it goes." I thought he was healthy and happy again and I was glad.

By September of 1971 I was walking the streets and woodpaths of a suburb of Hanover, Germany, where I'd gone for a year as a Fulbright lecturer. I was with my family, but I felt lost, gloomy. A whole year stretched darkly in front of me. I wrote to J.B. and asked him to write out a poem. A card arrived dated 16 Oct 71: "You think *you-all* are lonely. Listen to this poor guy I invented in Wisconsin & NYC & back here last Dec." He wrote out "Old Man Goes South Again Alone" which would appear posthumously in *Delusions, Etc.* (1972). Even though he is heading for the beaches of exotic Trinidad, the old man of the poem is sad "without the one // I would bring with me . . . ." Berryman knew that his own solitary trips tore him apart. He was telling me that I had enough not to be lonely. The *you-all* was emphatic. It was the same message he'd given me that night when he told me to focus on Han, study her, write about her, lose myself in her—love was the only way out of the lonely reaches of the ego.

The high ones die. He chose the frozen Mississippi. I received this telegram from Al Poulin, Jr. Han and I knew what it meant. I walked for miles through the woods that day, trying to will him back to life, playing mental tricks, trying to wake up earlier in the day than the telegram had arrived, often fighting back tears and losing, trying to believe his death. Over the next days, clippings came from friends.

This death struck/strikes us hard. We are still hurt. We cannot *understand* why he died. His suicide has deepened every question I have asked myself about poetry. W. D. Snodgrass once said to me that he would rather be happy than write great poems. I suspect that Berryman would not have said this, that he felt, although in the Brockport interview he denies this, that intense suffering led to the greatest poetry, and, certainly, he wanted nothing less than to write masterpieces. His horrible admission in the *Paris Review* interview that perhaps he needed something like cancer to get on with his writing, confirms this. "I hope to be nearly crucified," he says. I say *No* to this. *No.*

And now we have *Recovery* (1973), a powerful reading experience, certainly, for those who knew him. It lays bare the terrible dimensions of the battle Berryman fought against the forces that finally killed him. That he could not, or *would not* (I have to say this: if it is a delusion, it is a necessary one) cure himself and finish the book—this says something chilling about the death of art, and about where several other poets a decade younger than Berryman was when he died are now headed. Berryman's suicide, for me, has cast a pall over much of his work, the darkest and most painful of it. It may be true, as Lionel Trilling said of Robert Frost, that it takes a poet who terrifies us to satisfy us. But, I would think, there exists a line between truth-telling and morbidity. For Roethke, finally, the dead seemed to help.

I have come to feel that as magnificent as *The Dream Songs* is, it is a great death-flower, held in full bloom by Berryman's elegiac genius. I read the songs saying to myself, "Yes, yes, but poetry does not have to be what this is. It can be, but it does not have to be." I turn for comfort to Stevens and Wilbur: Stevens, who wrote at the end of his life about the "planet's encouragement," and Wilbur, to whom Sylvia Plath's "brilliant negative" is, finally, "unjust." I have come to feel that I have to find my own life in Stevens and Wilbur. There are lives of obsession and frenzy, and there are lives of gentleness and grace and control. And it may be that our lives are can sometimes be what we wish and will them to be. Stevens, Wilbur, William Stafford. This is one of Stafford's "Stories to Live in the World With":

> At a little pond in the woods
> I decided: this is the center of my life.
> I threw a big stick far out, to be
> all the burdens from earlier years.
> Ever since, I have been walking
> lightly, looking around, out of the woods.

In the *Paris Review* interview, Berryman says that he has absolutely no observation of nature. Observation of nature, he says, "makes possible a world of moral observation for Frost, or Hopkins." Nature as the measure, and comfort, whether or not it ought to be, whatever the truth of the matter. All those burdens from earlier years never left Berryman. I have to try to believe that this is more than a matter of chemistry, that he could have turned his back and gone about a different business. In "Dream Song #265" he says "next time it will be nature & Thoreau." Henry admits to loving "the spare, the hit-or-miss, / the mad." Robinson Jeffers would have told Berryman, as he wrote to the American Humanist Association, "most of our time and energy are necessarily spent on human affairs; that can't be prevented, though I think it should be minimized; but for philosophy, which is an endless research of truth, and for contemplation, which can be a sort of worship, I would suggest that the immense beauty of the earth and the outer universe, the divine 'nature of things,' is a more rewarding object. Certainly it is more ennobling. It is a source of strength; the other of distraction." It may be that this goes too far. It may be, in fact, that Jeffers himself so loved and was so concerned with man that, in Hyatt H. Waggoner's words, Jeffers' single real theme was "his desperate effort to teach the heart not to love." I do not mean to oversimplify a very complex matter of balance. I mean to say that during the many years while he was writing The *Dream Songs*, Berryman did not dwell on those things that could have been sources of strength for him.

Many people were much closer to John Berryman than I was. But, as someone said, we can love even a stranger known for only a few moments, and grieve at his death, because the soul does not keep time. I loved/love him, and cherish him, and will always count it among the privileges of my life that I met him. But I realize, also, that I am often afraid of him, that the bad angels also hovered around him, that the God he turned to at the end did not rescue this rare man from his despair. Unless, and I will keep trying to find out, this is exactly what happened.

Erika

They were points of transit, they offered impressions whose essence could not be held steady, was always vanishing, and when I inquire what there is about them that cannot be stressed and found valuable, to give a firm position in the topography of my life, I keep on coming up against what keeps retreating from me, all those cities become blurs, and only one place, where I spent only one day, remains constant.

Peter Weiss

Buchenwald: a beech wood, a soft word shining with sunlight falling through yellow leaves. A name, a place of terror. *Ravensbrück*: bridge of the ravens, a word out of the medieval gloom. *Dachau, Auschwitz*: words with no, so far as I know, particular root meanings, but words that leave us confounded and inconsolable. And *Bergen-Belsen*. The name whines like a missile or jet engine. It is a name from which there is no escape. And it is impossible to imagine what happened at Belsen.

It happens that my earliest memories are of 1945. I was five. We lived in Woodhaven, on Long Island. My father worked in the shipyards, building against the Axis. I remember the green gate in front of our house and what the houses on our street looked like and how close together they were. I remember a trellis that leaned against one side of our garage. I remember, though I did not know what it was at that time, the persecution we suffered because we were Germans, the swastikas my father scraped from our windows or painted over when they appeared suddenly in the mornings on our steps or doors. 1945. At Belsen, as the trees began to leaf that spring, Jews and other dissidents were being murdered by the thousands. I remember the day in 1945 that Franklin Roosevelt died. I remember that day because my brother and I were getting ready to go to the movies when my mother came outside and said we couldn't go because the President had died and the movies were closed. I remember that day because I was

---

Strivers' Row 1 (Spring 1974). Revised for inclusion in *The Swastika Poems* (NY: Vanguard P, 1977). Reprinted in *Erika: Poems of the Holocaust* (NY: Vanguard Press, 1984; St. Louis: Time Being Books, 1991).

bitterly disappointed. And that day, because Roosevelt had died, down in his Berlin bunker Hitler was pounding his fist on a table and assuring himself that God had sent him a sign, that Roosevelt's death meant the Third Reich would now rise from the rubble. And that same day, children no older than I was were being put to death at Belsen.

Belsen is forty miles north of Hannover, out of the way, and was meant to be. You are not likely to visit the place, but if you do, if you find the signs to *Gedenkstatte Bergen-Belsen* and find the place and park in the lot outside the grounds, you will walk under pines past a caretaker's apartment to which the central building, a square and simple affair of glass and stone, is attached. From the outside it looks like a small art gallery, perhaps, or a gymnasium. You will pause outside its glass doors to read a sign whose legend outlines the camp's history.

In 1940 Belsen, an already existing barracks, became a prisoner-of-war camp, Stalag 311. Russian captives were quartered there when a massive epidemic of spotted fever swept the camp. April of 1943 saw the establishment of the so-called Detention Camp Bergen-Belsen; Jews began to be collected there. In March of 1944 people who were no longer able to work were transferred to Belsen from other camps. In October and November of 1944 eight thousand women arrived from Auschwitz-Birkenau. A month later, the latter camp's *SS* Commandant, Joseph Kramer, took charge at Belsen. The camp grew rapidly, apace with his ambition. Within a year after Kramer's arrival the camp grew from fifteen thousand to sixty thousand prisoners, many of whom came from camps too near the front.

Belsen's last year was absolute hell. Nine thousand were executed there during the first two weeks of April 1945. In the middle of that April the British arrived to liberate the camp, but despite their best efforts conditions were such that an additional nine thousand died during the next two weeks. Eighteen thousand died during that terrible April. While I was playing in the Woodhaven streets, six hundred people a day died at Belsen. The sign outside the memorial building concludes with the estimate that at least fifty thousand had been murdered at the camp. Anne Frank, who wrote that she needed only sunlight to hope, was one of them.

You are not likely to visit the place, but if you do, and if you are there in December, as I was, you will walk inside into a single big room. The room will be dark and cold. You will find no bones, hair, teeth, lampshades made of tattooed skin there, and for this you will be thankful. But you will see a map that locates what were German concentration camps and their surrounding cells and satellites. The map is a spiderweb of camps, stations, deployment centers. Then you will see the photographs that cover the stone walls, images you've seen so often before: the mummified bodies, the Lugers held against the temples of old men, the huge eyes, the common graves from which arms and legs sprout like mushrooms. But this time these photographs are of the very place where you are standing; this is a dimension you have not entered before.

In one photograph smoke rises from the center of the camp above barbed wire and shacks and pines. In another, you will see only the backs of seven women who stand above their graves for a last few seconds of life as the photographer trips his shutter. These are young women who must not have been at the camp for long: their hair seems luxurious, and they are not thin. Their tresses seem to billow slightly behind them, their hair seems slightly blown back from a wind blowing toward the camera. Now, as the seven women stand there above that ditch, their hands bound behind their backs, they can see dozens of bodies below them, perhaps the bodies of their husbands and children. For a few seconds, as the photographer arranged his equipment or simply brought his camera into focus, the women may have glanced up at the sky. They may have spoken to one another. They must have prayed. A few seconds after they stood up in the light and air and wind for a last time, they fell forward into the darkness. They are still falling.

On another wall in this room you will see blow-ups of newspaper descriptions of the conditions the British troops found here in the spring of 1945. They had to burn the place to the ground as quickly as possible because they feared an epidemic. Corpses were hanging out of windows. The dead had to be buried in a hurry. There was no time for more than cursory identification procedures. The machine of the camp had run down as the British had advanced. Records were no doubt being destroyed, no doubt the German officers and guards were making their own plans, no doubt the murder of the last nine thousand they had time to murder those first two weeks in April was an inconvenience. This was Nazi *Kultur*.

You will walk outside past the mass graves. Each grave has a concrete marker: *Hier Ruhen 800 Tote April 1945; Hier Ruhen 1,000 Tote April 1945; Hier Ruhen 2,000 Tote April 1945.* The graves are banked at their bases by a band of about two feet of stone, and then the earth curves and slopes upward, rising as high as your head. The mounds are shaped something like loaves of bread, but squarer, flatter. You might say to yourself: *They are really here. I am at Belsen, and these are the graves of people who were murdered here. This is the camp at Belsen.*

You will see that the graves are covered, as is the whole area, with Erika. Erika, bell-heather, *heide*, a heath plant, wild and strong. Wild and strong, and beautiful. When not in bloom Erika is green, a deep green. There is a poem by the German poet Hermann Löns, who died at Verdun, that begins: "Grün ist die Heide, / Die Heide ist grün." In December, Belsen is green, a dark green. But in early fall, I am told, Erika blooms a reddish blue or bluish red, and then Belsen must be very beautiful, the sun perhaps occasionally breaking through the cloud cover, a warmer wind perhaps rustling the stiff blooming Erika over the graves, the *heide's* billions of flowerlets veiling the open spaces in shifting mauves and orchids and blue-purple shadows. It must be very beautiful and very terrible at Belsen when each fall the Erika blossoms. I do not think I will ever live a fall day when I do not think of Belsen. I will be driving to work, or opening a window, or playing cards with friends, or reading, and I will think of Erika blowing green or blooming violet-red over the dead at Belsen. And whenever I see a starling, or crow, I will remember the crows that stroke their black wings against the wind at Belsen.

Bergen-Belsen is not a big place, and it isn't old: what happened there happened shortly before mid-century. And it isn't a complicated place. It is very simple. At the edge of the camp there is a shaft of white marble. The words incised on it are simple and direct, and eloquent. Its fifth and sixth words are painted blood-red: Israel and the World *Shall Remember* Thirty Thousand Jews Exterminated in the Concentration Camp of Bergen-Belsen by the Hands of the Murderous Nazis." And further down on the stone: "Earth Conceal Not the Blood Shed on Thee!" Bergen-Belsen is a simple place, but it is more eloquent than the cathedral at Köln. It is a simple place, and it is easy to remember: there may be just a few days a year when the Erika is covered with snow, but in the early fall it blooms in the shades of lilac, the blossom of memory.

And I will always remember speaking to the caretaker at Belsen. He said that he still finds things there. When spring breaks he tills the soil or replaces a brick along a walk or transplants a tree or rakes through the Erika and finds

> a rusty spoon,
>   or a tin cup,
> or a fragment of bone,
>
> or a strand of barbed wire,
>   or a piece of rotten board,
> or the casing of a bullet,
>
> or the heel of a shoe,
>   or a coin,
> or a button,
>
> or a bit of leather
>   that crumbles to the touch,
> or a pin,
>
> or the twisted frames of someone's glasses,
>   or a key,
> or a wedding band.

Home

In Hanover, West Germany, in February of 1972, two months after visiting Bergen-Belsen, I was reading for review the galley proofs of Theodore Roethke's notebooks, *Straw for the Fire*. One slight entry, not even a complete sentence, has been with me since: "The exhausting fight against the inner fatigue, the soul sickness." I ended my review: "There is no doubt in my mind that our best poets have won this fight."

Every day over the years I was writing *The Swastika Poems*, and now that I am writing a long poem called *The Chestnut Rain*, I've had moments that have troubled me. I've wanted to leave the earth. I've wanted to die. I've not been sure of the origins of these moments of death-wish. Sometimes, certainly, realizations of human cruelty or suffering (and my communion with this history); sometimes, certainly, the blight seeming to overwhelm the earth, the radioactive wastes seeping into our oceans and the acid, industrial rains falling on our forests, the knowledge that even at home away from heavy industry I can't be sure that the trees I've planted will not sicken and die from poisons pouring from chimneys a hundred miles away. Experience, and intimations of what is coming. Several times a day the space under my breastbone empties, and I want not to exist, not to witness. These moments have become more frequent, and have intensified. I've thought, of course, that they've evidenced my own "inner fatigue, the soul sickness."

I don't know how to describe these moments. They are not moments of *Weltschmerz,* melancholy sorrow. They are filled with longing, and fear is mixed in, and abandonment, and surrender. I've wanted to tell myself that these moments are not only unhealthy, but unnatural, and that it would be dangerous to live within them for long.

Often these moments seem to have their origins in news that is always the same: yesterday, Palestinian terrorists attacked along a coastal highway in Israel and killed or wounded more than a hundred people; yesterday, neo-Nazis replete with banners and swastika-bedecked shields held a demonstration in St. Louis; yesterday, the papers reported that surveys are being made in western New York State that may be the first steps in locating deep salt beds that may be used

Manassas Review I, 3-4 (Summer-Fall 1978).

to store radioactive wastes from around the world, and that President Carter is kindly disposed toward the location of such a depository in the United States. Such events seem always to overwhelm the happiness upwelling from love of family and friends, the glow that builds for me day by day. They seem to overshadow what Archibald MacLeish called "the shine of the world." They are, surely, completely out of my control.

During these moments that I've thought of as my own soul sickness, I've lost faith in poetry. How, I've wondered, can I possibly go on until the end of my life caring for literature, believing in it as necessary for our survival, as the tongue of our central being? In *Three Philosophical Poets* George Santayana remarks that "The sole advantage in possessing great works of literature lies in what they can help us to become," but I've sometimes been afraid that I will become only someone for whom literature seems to be talk without action or possibility.

As I've felt, during these difficult moments, that I've wanted to give up poetry, I've felt, too, that I've wanted to give up the earth. These impulses, of course, are very close to one another. The earth must always be poetry's body. I suppose I've always believed that we have only this earth to cherish, for now, and I've believed that during moments when I've wanted to die, I've lost out to the inner fatigue, have given up. I've always felt that God must be known here, through earthly things, and wanting to die, I've thought, is my own soul-rot. Whatever the earth has been, or is, or will be, it must be my home. I've come to this in many poems. This one, "The Elm," will some day end a book:

> Last night, heat
> lightning branching
> the blue-black sky,
> alone on our back lawn,
> when I closed my eyes for the right time,
> when I knelt within the nimbus
> where the elm I loved
> lived for a hundred years,
> when I touched the loam fill over the elm's stump,
> its clusters of tiny noctilucent mushrooms,
> I saw through them
> into the ground, into the elm's dead
> luminous roots, the branches of heaven,
> to my home, my lightning lord,
> my home.

"The Elm" is a prayer of thanks, I suppose, to the lord of lightning and dead but luminous elm roots. Within this poem, I know where I am, and I'm glad to be home for the poem's duration, out of chaos. The moments I've tried to describe in this essay have not been at all, I've thought, like the moments of the self I am in "The Elm." I've worried about losing that self who calls the earth his home.

But I've been reading Donald Goddard's *The Last Days of Dietrich Bonhoeffer*. Goddard follows the German pastor from his arrest by the Gestapo in 1943 to his execution and the burning of his body and last manuscript at Flössenburg on the 8th of that terrible April of 1945. It is a beautiful and moving book, testament to one of the whole men of this century. Just before Christmas in 1943, writing from prison to his friend Eberhard Bethge, Bonhoeffer says something profoundly simple, something that should enable me not only to live with myself and those moments that have worried me, but to mature, to become a man. Bonhoeffer writes:

> God will see to it that the man who finds Him in his earthly happiness and thanks Him for it does not lack reminder that earthly things are transient, that it is good for him to attune his heart to what is eternal, and that sooner or later there will be times when he can say in all sincerity, 'I wish I were home.'

I found God in earthly beauty when I was a boy, in pond scrum and water lilies, and I've never lost the sense of ongoing, moment-by-moment miracle, the sense of my own abiding transience. I used to wish that everyone on earth would die so that nature could revive itself before it was too late. Those moments that I believed to be my own intensifying soul sickness are not that at all. I will do what little I can, loving my family and friends, writing the poems I'm able to write, caring for an acre of trees, but sooner or later, as Bonhoeffer says, there will be times when even the happy man who believes in and thanks God will feel his heart yearning for the eternal and will say, "I wish I were home."

The Swastika Poems: An Interview
(Conducted by Stan Rubin)

SR: Bill, *The Swastika Poems* has been out now for a little over a year, and it has begun its life—its life as literature, and the consensus is in that it is an important book—but for you it began a long time ago; you wrote this over a period of some ten years. I wonder, where did the book come from? How did it grow for you?

WH: As you say, Stan, it's been out about a year. We're here now in March of 1978. I remember that the book was about finished by the end of 1975, and I've been doing many different things since and feel some distance from the book. Now, hopefully, I have an objective sense of it. I should say, in fact, that the things I'll say during this tape are, of course, after-the-fact; I don't know if during the time I was writing the book I knew all the things I might say about it now. This seems important to me to mention. We often get to where we are through blunder, naiveté, intuition, luck, rather than through lucid planning.

My first book, *Depth of Field*, was the kind of book that first books often are. I wrote about literary subjects and about things I thought poets wrote poems about—Loch Ness, the imagined drowning of a son, dead animals. I still care for and believe in that book, but it may be true that with my second book, *Noise in the Trees*, which concerned my pastoral childhood on Long Island and the loss of that world, I began to deal in my poetry with things more genuinely important to me.

The Swastika Poems. . . . My parents were both German immigrants. My father came to this country before the Second World War and two of his brothers stayed over there and died on the German side. It happens that my wife was born in Germany in Berlin and came to this country when she was twelve. Her father was a Nazi captain who was captured at Stalingrad and died later in a war camp. I was brought up around German-speaking people, and it happened that I spent a year in Germany on a Fulbright lectureship, wandered the country, sort of deepened my feelings about the things that are in this book. I've always been haunted, I think, by the Third Reich and the Second World War, and I like to think that these poems came along naturally, that I'm not exploiting a sensational subject. Well, anyway, that's the background of *The Swastika Poems*.

Manassas Review I, 3-4 (Summer-Fall 1978).

I never really thought that I would bring all of these poems together into a book. I would write one and then not want to dwell within its misery and then go on to something else. But then something—maybe a dream, or something I'd read or seen—would begin another one, and I'd write it and put it aside. I didn't send the poems out. Then one day I took out of a drawer the poem "Letter to Hansjörg Greiner," and I read it—this was maybe three years after I'd written it—and it struck me hard, and I realized that as a *poem* it was good, whatever else it was, whatever other worries I had about it. And then I began pulling out things and seeing how much material I had and the book at that point began to come together as a book.

SR: In other words, you weren't writing these as poems; when you wrote them, you didn't think of them as poems? You were doing other work . . .

WH: As William Stafford says, it's important for a writer not to know something about a lot of things, and one of the important things for him not to know much about is how to write. So we never think of things we're writing as poems, maybe. We want to get away from this idea of thinking about *genre* when we write. But it's true, with these poems as opposed to a lot of other things I've written, that a lot of them appeared in kind of an emotional flow that just went past any idea of audience or anything else. A few of them were labored over, but many were written out very quickly. I remember, after a dream, writing "The Trench" straight out, and "Simple Truths" was written in maybe fifteen minutes, after, of course, feeling things and being hurt into poetry, this poem, for years. When I skim the book now, I can't remember writing all those poems, can't quite believe that I did.

SR: When did you decide actually to publish them as a book?

WH: Probably in 1974 or 1975. I'd read a few at readings and for a long time I juggled the different poems to see what kind of collection they could make. The subject matter is so forbidding that I guess for a long time I held off from conceiving of a book that I probably thought would only serve to depress people. Who would really want to dwell inside the misery of a dark book for very long, or return to it?

   The psyche behind the book, the speaker, its consciousness, I think, tries to lift the whole experience, if that's at all possible. In "The Swastika Poems," for example, the sign of the hooked cross becomes the Jewish star of soft light. *Ewige Melodien* even suggests an afterlife. And a poem done too late for the book, one I'm anxious to add to it, "The Jewish Children," also captures a kind of dark affirmation.

SR: Were some of the poems considerably harder to write than others?

WH: Well, some of them were worked over. Some of the poems are metrically tight and rhymed. I imagine that I dwelled on these the longest.

One of the problems—we've talked about this other times—is that it's always difficult to end any poem. Maybe ending a poem about the Holocaust is even more difficult. Some of these poems waited around in notebooks for a year or two or three before I went back to them and found some way to end them.

SR: Did the presence of this strain or this vision in your work during those years when you were writing these influence your other work, or vice-versa? I know, for example, you were doing a lot of Viet Nam poems during that "dark time."

WH: Well, I did write many poems about Viet Nam and published many in quarterlies and in the *Nation* and the *New York Times*. But looking back on those poems now, looking back when I was putting together *The Swastika Poems* to see if any of them might be useful, I realized that they weren't any good. They just weren't. I suppose that whatever talent I had, whatever true feelings for human suffering or for the Nazi mentality, could come through in *The Swastika Poems* and not in my poems about Viet Nam because the Second World War was somehow more personal and obsessive for me. I took part in protests during Viet Nam, but maybe that period was for me not as overwhelming as the Holocaust. As involved as I was, and as many bad dreams as I had about Viet Nam, maybe my imagination didn't have the time to transform the material coming from newspapers and television every day.

SR: Stanley Plumly, writing in *American Poetry Review*, said that the first part of the book is where you take risks. I think the entire book is obviously full of risks, personally and aesthetically, but in the first part you do engage in a lot of direct address to your relatives, to your father-in-law, and even to the Fuehrer at the end, in "Darkness." How did you come to handle that material?

WH: I don't know. My writing has to satisfy me, and I try to find out if it does by reading it over and over hundreds, even thousands of times, trying to *hear* it. It's not easy really to hear what we've written, to know what we've written. Poems of direct address, of course, have to know what they're doing if they hope to be convincing, and they cannot forget the presence of another listener besides the person being addressed.

As I see the poems now, whether I'm talking to my wife's dead father or to my father's dead brothers or to Hitler, they are primarily about the speaker. My interest is in him, as I read the poems now. During the course of the book he strains to find out who he is. As a reader of the book, I know that he *has* to talk to these ghosts, and I'm interested in what he finds out about his own being. Come to think of it, even with a poem like "The Baron's Tour," though a German nobleman speaks that poem, I think of it in truth as being an invention of the consciousness that is the "I" of the book.

SR: You raised the issue of what is sometimes called "the aesthetics of the Holocaust," or the whole issue of Holocaust literature; maybe the touchstone is Adorno's line that "to write poetry after Auschwitz is barbarism." George Steiner says that "this whole experience lies outside of language, uniquely outside of language" and you're obviously very sensitive to this. How do you approach it?

WH: What I'm worried about is that, as a human being, I'm becoming less sensitive. The speaker in "Darkness" is worried that he will be forgetting the camps. So, there's that. And wouldn't the Holocaust be forgotten if people didn't write and talk about it?

     Still, I think that if I had been more conscious of the issues during the time I was writing these poems, I probably wouldn't have gotten far. Now I realize that just as many people say that it also would be barbarous *not* to write poetry after Auschwitz. You see, both propositions are probably true. Many things are involved. First of all, art, no matter its subject, gives pleasure. Maybe it's Picasso's *Guernica*, but in some way maybe there is a kind of dark joy that we feel even contemplating a painting or a poem about human misery. And maybe, in regard to the Holocaust, the dimensions of which are so huge and incredible to behold, maybe this is one subject that all art ought not try to deal with so that the subject will not lose its ineffability in some sort of pseudo-resolution. Art in some way manages to resolve things at the expense, perhaps, in this case, of a subject matter that is absolutely beyond resolve.

     Also, there's this: as a writer, I'm trying to say things as sharply as I can, as clearly as I can. And there's a sense in which writing is always an egotistical activity and involves manipulation. There's a sense in which writing is a performance, too—we don't want it to seem artificial, but there are many coldly-reasoned considerations of effect. And writing is like an athletic contest, as Robert Frost implies, and it's important to win. With these sorts of artistic considerations, then, on this side, and then again the theme of the Holocaust on the other side, writing *poetry* can make the writer feel as though he's engaging in a kind of obscene activity. I know that when I write other poems on other subjects, when I finished and published *Noise in the Trees*, I was happy! I felt good about things in general. I do not feel the same way about *Swastika* although I am glad, selfishly glad, that the book exists, that making my feelings into the objects that are poems has relieved me. And I'm glad, probably again selfishly, that I didn't know more about these things at the time when, from time to time, I would turn to the poems, and what would become the book was growing.

SR: You mean you weren't really aware of the dimensions of the debate about whether one should write about this or not?

WH: I wasn't, except maybe subconsciously. How could I possibly do justice to the history, the suffering, the psychology?—this question, of course, made me just put the poems away after I wrote them. This question kept me from sending most of the poems out. And to write a bad poem about the Holocaust seemed/seems to me somehow worse than writing a bad poem about something else. There's so much more, too, various pressures I was feeling even if I didn't articulate them. Language never lies, and what if my poems revealed me better than I knew and inhuman sympathies that I'd later regret surfaced? And does poetry have a moral function?—what the hell, I didn't have to worry about this with *Noise in the Trees*. However fashionable it is not to feel this way, I felt I had to be responsible in this book.

There have been bad moments, too. Once, reading "Erika" aloud to an audience for the first time, and "Erika" seems to me to be a piece of obvious sympathy and sadness, someone jumped up and yelled, "He's a Nazi." And when, about a year before *Swastika* came out, I did send some of the poems out and sent "Darkness," "The Uncertainty Principle," and others to *Poetry*, the editor at that time sent them back with a note saying, "Dear Mr. Heyen, I do not believe in writing light verse about the Holocaust." However drunk and stupid this editor might have been, I was hurt and confused, of course. But, near the end, there was crucial support from poets, too, and other friends.

SR: Do you feel that your language shows some of the strain of the subject, or that your language changed to handle this, the pressure of the material, in any way that you can comment on?

WH: Well, the poems were written over so long a period of time that they seem to me, now, from my vantage point years past their individual problems, very different. For one thing, each seems to make its own adjustments. The reason I'm uncomfortable reading only a few of the poems at readings is that each poem slants in on part of the world, while I like to feel that the book as a whole becomes a whole world.

Another worry I have, of course, is that I'm not Jewish, and no doubt I'm not able to appreciate the Jewish experience. Even Jews who were not there, of course, have the same worry. All I can say is that I didn't *decide* to write the poems, but that somehow I did write them, not even, in truth, wanting to write them or knowing what to do with them.

Well, anyway, one of my hopes is that—and I think this is going to be true—that many Jews who haven't fully entered their own heritage are, because of *The Swastika Poems*, going to do just that. Sandra McPherson mentioned in her essay in *American Poetry Review* that she was surprised, and I hadn't thought about this either, that there hadn't been a book of poems on the Holocaust. And why shouldn't there have been, really? Maybe that's the central question!

SR: Why, I was going to ask, had Berryman made an attempt which he abandoned? Is there anything else in American literature like *The Swastika Poems* that's willing to confront head-on the Holocaust as a fact, as the pressing central fact of modern imagination?

WH: Well, Berryman wrote a few poems, and powerful ones, toward what he thought would become a book to be called *The Black Book*. He said he had to abandon the project, that he couldn't take it, that it would have driven him insane. And he once told me, weeping, that he thought of publishing a book that would have, simply, the name of one of the camps on each page, that this would be enough. All his life he was haunted by the Holocaust. My book was able to come to be not because I was stronger than Berryman but because of the way it was written, sporadically. He couldn't imagine not devoting himself to a project and then working at it for twenty hours a day until it was finished! I never, in fact, until near the end, had a project in mind.

In a general sense, you know, art and this kind of topical-historical reality are supposed to be opposed to one another. I can't think, right now, of a book of poems that has as its central ground a historical event as *Swastika* has, at least this directly. I'm probably ignorant or forgetful, but what is there since *Drum Taps*? There have been, of course, many books by American poets largely concerned with one or another of our wars, and the fact that mine is, page after page direct and obsessive the way it is, means nothing of itself. I do feel that in poems like "Men in History" and "The Tree," such different poems, I've managed to get history into them without their becoming frozen into some kind of notation or reportage. Their central materials, after long brooding, somehow underwent the chemical change that enabled them to become poems.

SR: Do you feel that, in some way, a writer living at this time since WWII, should in some sense, have come to terms with this experience, rather than by absence negate it, by the fact that it doesn't appear in his or her work at all?

WH: It seems to me that the Holocaust is at the center of everything I know and feel about the century, about myself within human history. This is where everything that I've ever learned comes together, if it does. This is what I know about human nature and what tempers, in subtle ways, the way I see the maples and ash that grow on my property.

How is it that we can read the collected poems of Robert Frost and never know that the man lived through the First World War and the Second World War? It never comes up, never. There's one little poem about a bullet going through a meadow, and I think cutting a stalk, something like that. There's nothing there. There's nothing in Theodore Roethke, a poet I've loved, nothing. But think of Yeats and Whitman! Both were hurt into poetry by war. We have had many poets, and wonderful poets, who have never entered history directly, but, I think, finally, that if I were pressed I would say that this is a weakness and a failure in Frost and Roethke, for example. This limits, finally, my sense of their wholeness as sensibilities on this planet as I read their collected poems. This is complex, of course, and maybe idiosyncratic, and I would have to think about the assumptions behind my statement for a long time.

SR: In his book *The Holocaust and the Literary Imagination*, Lawrence Langer talks about the inevitable form and dignity which is art, which is any art. But he says that the role of the "literature of atrocity" is to make us, through the imaginative, confront the real. This leads me to a perception about your book. Maybe we can move on to discussing the book as a structure because Langer's contention really is that the "literature of atrocity" combines historical fact and really grotesque imagination in a way that makes us, as I said, confront the fact through the imaginative. It seems to me that that can be turned around in terms of *The Swastika Poems*, because once you establish the kind of personal reality and personal family connection that you have to these events, very carefully establish your distance and your connection in the first part, then you try to confront it more directly, but nevertheless you don't, it seems to me, as certain other writers do, go into surrealism or an intense grotesque nightmare world. You seem almost to force yourself to face fact or the facts; and where you do not know, you don't seem to wish to imagine or invent, or you will only do so if you incorporate eyewitness testimony, stories from people who were in camps. It seems that this is a task you set for your imagination: to discipline itself to truth. The history must mean something to you.

WH: It's probably true that I could have dealt with these things in all sorts of oblique ways, but the kind of poetry I happen to like—this may or may not have anything to do with goodness or badness—the kind of poetry I happen to like keeps its feet on the ground.

I was reading something last night: Louis Simpson was interviewed by *The Ohio Review*, and he was drawing distinctions between his own poetry, in which he was interested in dealing with the common and readily-apprehensible world, as opposed to what he saw to be developing in Robert Bly's poetry. I certainly care for and even believe in the poetry that Simpson is describing. In other words, my poems, these poems want to bring in the look of the Bunker and the Chancellery. They want to bring in the steps painted with swastikas. They want to bring in the look of the Erika that I saw over the graves at Bergen-Belsen. I would have rendered my apprehensions of the Holocaust in other ways, but the poems as they stand, within the recognizable historical world embody, I suppose, the kind of poetry I most care for and believe in.

SR: The "Erika" section is, in fact, in the middle; almost a resting point, in a sense. I think "rest" is really the wrong word, but it's a center in the three-part structure. It's a brief prose memoir of a visit to Belsen, full of facts—what it's like to look at the maps of Nazi camps, statistics, figures and, at the same time, nature, the Erika plant growing over the graves. . . . How did you come to this structure? What do you have to say about the presence of that prose memoir at that point?

WH: I think, well, several things occur to me now, and again, I don't know what I knew at the time, but I know I struggled very hard with the arrangement of the book. It went on for months, even when everything was done. It seemed to me that I was making morally important choices each time in regard to which poem followed which poem.

In general, the first section of poems in the three-part structure has to do with experiences here in America. The first poem gets my father over here on the boat. The other poems make it clear that even though he got away from Europe, and avoided the war his brothers fought, he really didn't avoid the war and neither did anybody else here. But all those poems in the first section are about consciousness here in America. "Darkness" ends that section, a dream of embrace, a terrible descent that must remain within the consciousness of the book, it seems to me, as it and its reader progress. The second section seems to me to be a relief from the rhythms of "Darkness." And it's a bridge. It's about a visit to Bergen-Belsen; it gets the book's ground to Europe, and all of the poems in the third section, then, as I hear them, even if like the title poem seeming to be about events of a Brooklyn childhood, have voice and consciousness arising from the other side of that bridge.

SR: Were they all in fact written after your visit to Germany?

WH: No, no. I went to Germany in 1971 and 1972. If I had to make a chart I'd have to say that about half the poems were written before then, and a few during that year—including "Erika," which was part of a journal—and the rest after.

SR: What about the third part, which has the title "The Numinous"? That's very suggestive.

WH: That's a word that just blooms for me. Its root meanings have to do with the spirit of place; and the consciousness there again is trying to find out something about the spirit of this soil. This comes up in poems like "The Liberation Films," "The Baron's Tour," "The Numinous," and that little prose poem "The Spire," in which the dreaming voice is somehow within the bell tower at Freiburg thinking *I've always been here, always, always.* . . .

SR: It also has suggestions of the sacred words. In a kind of literary criticism way, there are three themes that I would like to ask you about, one of which is suggested by "The Numinous." In that section are several poems—"Blue," "A

Visit to Belzec," "Simple Truths"—which deal explicitly with the notion of a God, a Creator, Our Father—"if he is our father"—watching these events. I guess this approaches that question of possible transcendence through art, or possible transcendence through any other means, that so many people raise in terms of the Holocaust; I mean, can it in any way be transcended by art, by faith, by history, by anything? What can you say about the presence of these moments, these very tense moments?

WH: I don't know. I'd like to know more about this as it develops in the book. I can see that in a few of the poems the speaker accuses a Lord who witnesses but does nothing else. That attitude, of course, is almost a naturalistic cliché, and I hope that the poems go further. I don't know what the book says as a whole in regard to the presence of Lord or Cause. That it is myriad? Maybe it is just dropped as being too baffling or too fearsome a subject to deal with squarely.

"The Numinous": I was reading a testimony the other day by a man, a young Jew, who with his wife had been planning to stop in Germany as part of a European tour and couldn't get out of the car once he got there.

SR: A second motif—and I hate to use that term, it seems to reduce what we're talking about here—but there is this related question of your response to the presence of nature, for instance the Erika, the plant itself, in this scene covering the graves, and the first entry in the third part is a prose poem called "The Tree," the Lidice section, and then there is the end of the Belzec poem. There is this nature imagery and nature is going on; there's no solace in it. It's almost irredeemably stained with these corpses that are now part of it; but it's out there, it has its own order.

WH: Yes, and I was just thinking of "Lines to My Parents," because the speaker is stunned that the same things were happening in the German woods— rabbits bursting across his path as they did at home—as happened before the full impact of such terrible history reached him.

Stephen Crane, most obviously, deals with this again and again: how is it that the birds can go on singing while the soldier's corpse rots in the woods?

By the way, in that poem "Lines to My Parents" the speaker actually comes across an iron soldier in the German woods. This happened to me. In different places across Germany you can enter the woods and all of a sudden come upon a memorial, a monument of some kind to the German soldier, maybe an iron soldier laid out at rest. There's one that I saw at Stocken, outside of Hannover, and it absolutely knocked me over. It was just a concrete bier and there was a helmet on the bier, you know, the German helmet. Well, I turned it into, I guess, the German soldier in that poem, within a grove of oaks. You see, my speaker is always wondering, I'm always wondering, what if I were there, had been there, what would I have done? Is there any escape, is there a possible way to escape from the propaganda around us? My father-in-law worked for Goebbels in the Propaganda Ministry, and we have at home still some of these obscene anti-Semitic books that are just incredible to behold. They're all dedicated to the Fuehrer, and have his color photograph in front, and they have bibliographies at the back of them that are extremely extensive. For young people brought up in that climate, it was impossible to avoid being brainwashed, or almost impossible. So that's one of the things, as I see it, always underneath the consciousness of the book. The same kind of confrontation with a German soldier occurs in "The Trench." "And only one of us will live. . . ." But, again, the book is as much the reader's now as it is mine. I'm just trying to mention some of the things that I see going on in it, and no doubt I've forgotten many of the things on my mind as I was putting the book together.

SR: I was thinking of the lines at the end of "Simple Truths"—"fortune that you and I were not the victims, this / luck that you and I were not the murderers,"—which are almost a certain attitude toward fortune and luck that makes me think of the default of God, if that's what it is.

WH: When I look at those lines in the cold light of rationality I might want to do something else with them; the poem ends, "as we kill them all, as we killed them all." In other words, it's an ongoing thing going on here. But that particular poem was written in a rush, and just as it may be true that if you don't know how to spell a word, your first choice may be the right one, I was sort of hard-headed and determined when I was done writing that one ought not to tear it apart and put it together and tear it apart and put it together again. What it is is what happened to it in the great rush of it as I was writing that poem. So, any poem is about the consciousness of its speaker trying to find out what he or she knows, what will suffice for a little while. I remain interested in the consciousness of that poem. It intrigues me, and is far from simple. The poem begins clearly, logically, and then seems to become almost hysterical. It's a self I was during the minutes when I was writing that poem out, I guess. . . .

SR: That gets me to the third theme I wanted to at least raise with you, one that arises, for instance, at the end of "A Visit to Belzec." The question of poetry itself, which is not a major theme in the book, but it's one that the book raises for anyone. We've talked about it in terms of the Holocaust-aesthetics question, and you say, "Reader, all words are a dream. / You have wandered into mine." And then you tell this little anecdote:

> This happened only once, but happened:
> one Belzec morning, a boy in deathline
> composed a poem, and spoke it.
> The words seemed true, and saved him.

The guard's mouth fell open to wonder.

Is this in fact a true story as you know it?

WH: It is a true story, but one, I believe, that happened at Auschwitz, not Belzec; I changed the ground, but not its truth, I trust.

I was reading Theodore Roethke's notebooks again a week or two ago, and thinking about a notation that really struck me: "The exhausting fight against the inner fatigue, the soul-sickness." And I hope that I can maintain to the end of my life a belief in literature, a belief in art as something important, although forces seem to overwhelm it occasionally. Yes, the art theme comes up in that poem, and is followed by my translation of Rilke's famous poem on the archaic torso of Apollo, a poem that suggests that when you see a work of art, a real work of art, and when its luminousness reaches out to every part of you, you will know that you must change your life. I'd like to believe that about art.

SR: A question of what poets can ever do in terms of history is raised in a general way, as well as the question of confronting the Holocaust. . . .

WH: Sometimes I think that poetry can do everything, and sometimes I think that . . . I don't know.

SR: That it makes nothing happen?

WH: Yes. But I have a wonderful friend on Long Island, Vincent Clemente, and once in a while I express my doubts to him and he says, "But, Bill, a poem can change somebody's life!" He says, "I've seen it happen, it happens all the time!" So, I need that kind of support, reassurance.

SR: How do you feel reading the poems to audiences?

WH: Well, I don't know. I sometimes feel that once I read one, I then have to go through the whole reading doing just these poems—you see the worry again: how can I read just a few of them and then go on to something else? Or sometimes I've not read any, and this didn't feel right either.

And there's another problem, of course. What right do I have to be at the center of the circle of attention, as I am right now, in regard to subject matter like this? How should I feel when people congratulate me on the poems? I said to myself about a year ago that I just wouldn't read them again. But then I did. . . . In regard to reading in general: when I'm reading one of my poems and I'm thinking about it and entering its experience, then I feel fine, true to myself and the audience. But when I go wandering off into other things, as happens, daydream, then I don't feel very good about it. After every reading that I've ever given I feel all right, but I also feel a little bit ashamed, dirty. Many poets feel the same way. I don't know what is within the nature of the public reading experience itself that leads to that feeling.

SR: Have you heard from any survivors who have read the book?

WH: Yes. I've received many moving letters. And a rabbi in Cincinnati, Albert Goldman, asked me to read from *Swastika* at a Friday night service. A few people had to leave as I read. I didn't speak to the man, but Rabbi Goldman told me about one of the many survivors who were there: he still had his uniform. He called the camp clothes his "Treblinka tuxedo." Imagine the human pain in *that* poetry.

SR: Will this book let you go? I know that you have written, since this was published, more poems that belong to *The Swastika Poems* sequence.

WH: For a while I thought I was done with the subject completely, that I'd written all I knew and felt. Then, just about the time I received the proofs, and too late to get anything else into the book, I had a dream and wrote a poem, "The Jewish Children." I think it's the kind of book that could be improved by adding other poems to it. It's that kind of book because there are for me always "buts," and maybe if I can take care of a few "buts" in my own mind by wedging in other poems and other experiences . . .

SR: One sees that in the choice between remembering and forgetting there is really no choice; it has to be remembered by poets as by everyone else.

WH: I was just going to say that, as you know, I use as an epigraph to *Swastika* something from Susan Sontag, something that buoyed my courage as I put the book together. She talks about "the moral function of remembering."

SR: People have forgotten Viet Nam already; I mean, we have a will to forget these days.

WH: In "The Numinous" the speaker knows that "only those with blue / numbers along their wrists / can truly imagine," but concludes by knowing, at least: "Beautiful blue-gray pigeons. / We will always remember."

Essay Beginning and Ending with Poems for Whitman

I

The Traffic

Red lights pulse and weave in
toward an accident ahead.
Trying to leave Smithtown,
I'm stopped dead,

here, where Whitman trooped
to tally the eighth-month flowers' bloom.
Diesels jam their bumpers together in a long line,
gas and rubber heat wafts in like soup.

A truck's exhaust curves up beside me
like a swan's neck. I sigh,
make a mistake, and breathe deep.
Concrete, signs, and cars cloud:

Lilacs utter their heart-shaped leaves,
locusts spell their shade. The Jericho's air
creaks with cartwheels, a carriage
moves with the certainty of mirage.

The Widow Blydenburgh flows to church,
stoops to admire an iris, and to smell.
A pigeon bends the slim branch of a birch.
The Widow plucks the iris for her Bible.

Walt Whitman: The Measure of His Song, eds. Jim Perlman, Ed Folsom, and Dan Campion (Minneapolis: Holy Cow! Press, 1981).

Horns soon blare me out of this.
Trailing a plume of smoke,
the trucker grunts his rig ahead.
I accelerate past a cop

directing traffic around the wreck.
He asks if I'm all right. I nod
and close the lane. Glass sparkles,
a splash of blood still shines

on the pavement, and time's itself again.
Pressed against the porch of Whitman's school,
the Dairy Freeze is booming, winks
its windows tinted green, and cool.

II

Walt Whitman was born on Long Island, moved with his family to Brooklyn when he was four, attended public schools there, worked from 1830 to 1836 at various jobs in Brooklyn and New York, and then returned to Long Island to teach and work on Island newspapers for several years before returning to Brooklyn. "In 1851," says Gay Wilson Allen, "he was operating a small printing office and bookstore on the first floor of the three-story house he had built at 106 Myrtle Avenue."

I was born in Brooklyn, spent my first years in a house on Myrtle Avenue. We then moved to Woodhaven (which was anything but wooded), near Jamaica, then to the wilds of Hauppauge in Suffolk County when I was four or five, and then further east outside Smithtown to Nesconset where I began, I believe, third grade. "O World so far away! O my lost world!" says Theodore Roethke. But Roethke knew, as did Whitman, that those worlds would always live inside him, that poems would flow out of those "lost" worlds.

Long Island to Brooklyn in Whitman's case, Brooklyn to Long Island in mine, both of us children of carpenter fathers. Now and then, I tremble with connections. It's an ongoing privilege for me to feel so close, physically close, to the great world poet. At the same time, in any case, time and space avail not, as he says, and that New Jersey country pond he bathed in and wrote so beautifully about in *Specimen Days* (and even gave credit for his recovery to) is one of the ponds of his old Island, too.

By school bus, or riding with my parents, or hitchhiking, or, as a senior in 1957 driving my brother's Plymouth—he was in the service—to high school on New York Avenue in Smithtown, I would pass through Smithtown Branch, under the huge locusts, past the Blydenburgh house. The Smithtown schoolhouse where

Whitman taught in 1837-38 is just off the Jericho Turnpike in the area across from the old Presbyterian Church where 25A begins its winding to St. James, and Route 111 angles left to Hauppauge. Though it is half hidden by a drive-in dairy food store, you can see it from the Jericho. Last I knew, it housed a lawyer's office. When I think of Smithtown, I first think of that place, that confluence.

I didn't know anything about Whitman. When I remember myself as I was, I picture a boy wading Gibbs Pond in Nesconset, and other ponds in Lake Grove, St. James, Hauppauge, Ronkonkoma, the natural world bending in to him, as it did. I spent so much time at ponds, that this is the most enduring image I have of myself as a youngster, and now I know that Whitman saw me, and now I know that the *presence* I felt when I was otherwise alone at a pond or walking through woods or, later, clamming at St. James Harbor, was his, as he is abiding spirit, as he is the miraculous confluence of space and time within a human voice.

Working on my poem "The Traffic," I was thinking of that busiest block of Bull Smith's town—in 1660 the Nissequoque Indians gave Smith, in exchange for trinkets and cattle and guns, as much land as he could encircle between sunrise and sunset while riding bareback on a bull. My speaker, "Trying to leave Smithtown," is stuck in traffic, "here, where Whitman trooped / to tally the eighth-month flowers' bloom." He is dizzied by a truck's fumes, and falls back into the past world of this same place:

> *Lilacs utter their heart-saped leaves,*
> *locusts spell their shade. The Jericho's air*
> *creaks with cartwheels, a carriage*
> *moves with the certainty of mirage.*
>
> *The Widow Blydenburgh flows to church,*
> *stoops to admire an iris, and to smell.*
> *A pigeon bends the slim branch of a birch.*
> *The Widow plucks the iris for her Bible.*

At the end of the poem, his head clear again, he glances to his right:

> *. . . and time's itself again.*
> *Pressed against the porch of Whitman's school,*
> *the Dairy Freeze is booming, winks*
> *its windows tinted green, and cool.*

What is the true traffic? I am far from this poem now. It is as much any reader's as mine, as I try to hear it.

The irony seems heavy, and intended, but I wonder if I was writing more than I knew. Earlier in the poem the speaker had compared a truck's exhaust pipe to a "swan's neck," and now, it seems to me, the Dairy Freeze windows, "green and cool," remind him bitterly of another world, the world of the sea and of ponds that we know is a part of his sensibility, in this one poem, or in the book *Long Island Light* in which this poem appears. But I wonder if the poem, with its lines juxtaposing Whitman's school and the Dairy Freeze pressed against it, isn't more, doesn't, somehow, find a kind of solace in the present traffic, doesn't somehow, trust the "booming" future, as Whitman did. I notice, now, the cop's concern, the healing influence of the speaker's vision of the past, his humor, the blood-like body of the experience ("Red lights pulse and weave in"). I see now that "Glass sparkles," and now know—I don't know if I did when I wrote the poem—Whitman's poem "Sparkles from a Wheel" "Where the city's ceaseless crowd moves on the livelong day" with "Myself effusing and fluid, a phantom curiously floating . . . ." On Island ground, having been everywhere, part of the traffic river flowing up against and through Whitman's world, my speaker may be curiously at home with himself.

III

As a child and young man, I had heard Whitman's name in grade school and high school. I remember that about the same time that we were reading Longfellow's "Evangeline" in seventh or eighth grade, we also read "O Captain! My Captain!," and it was from this same time that "I Saw in Louisiana a Live-Oak Growing" embedded itself behind my eyes. But, in general, I didn't read Whitman, but knew him, as any Island resident (even someone who has not read him) must know him when alone but feeling, in Whitman's word, some "impalpable" presence ("The impalpable sustenance of me from all things at all hours of the day" of "Crossing Brooklyn Ferry"). Sometimes Whitman says, as he does here in "Whoever You Are Holding Me Now in Hand," that we must be alone with him to know him:

> (For in any roof'd room of a house I emerge not, nor in company,
> And in libraries I lie as one dumb, a gawk, or unborn, or dead,)
> But just possibly with you on a high hill, first watching lest
>   any person for miles around approach unawares,
> Or possibly with you sailing at sea, or on the beach of the sea
>   or some quiet island,
> Here to put your lips upon mine I permit you . . . .

But alone or with others, impalpable, but tending toward him, all earthly *things* suffuse the power that sustains him, the physical world not only an emblem of benevolent spirit presiding and blessing, but spirit itself, indwelling, undivided soul and body of all being.

It seems to me that sometimes Whitman protests too much, tries in strained keys to "show that there is no imperfection in the present, and can be none in the future" ("Starting from Paumanok")—that overwhelming well-being I recently felt in the room in the Old Manse in Concord where Emerson, at white heat, wrote *Nature*. There is a bloated, declarative, Santa Claus quality in the unrealized work. But I care for Whitman all the more for this, his great humanity breaking through as he yearns to comfort and, often with sweep and subtler music, does. What he turns to, the force that will integrate all, solve all, resolve the knots of contrariety is, of course, love.

> (Were you looking to be held together by lawyers?
> Or by an agreement on a paper? or by arms?
> Nay, nor the world, nor any living thing, will so cohere.)
>
> ("Over the Carnage Rose Prophetic a Voice")

Not "any living thing" will cohere without love, he says, in so many ways. Cells at the centers of things, atoms at the centers of cells, whole nations at the centers of cells are held together by love. Whether or not this is true, great poetry has never depended on literal, empirical Truth, but on a rhythmical and imagistic passion of voice that involves us in and makes us, at least while we are in its presence, believe its truth. *Leaves of Grass* itself coheres because the poet's love—variously diffuse, teasing, specific, all-encompassing, wrenching, erotic, quietly transfiguring, pounding, disguised, blatantly passionate—draws it together, despite our ignorance, despite contrary aesthetics coming toward it to tear it apart, despite the singer's heartbreak or even his beloved nation's Civil War. Whitman never wrote a poem that was not, at its center, a poem of love.

IV

Whitman is the poet, finally, who comes full circle, who includes everything, but he will not be forced. I think of *Leaves of Grass* as a necklace gradually becoming visible for me as I grow older, the necklace of "The glories strung like beads on my smallest sights and hearings" of "Crossing Brooklyn Ferry," each poem, perhaps, a bead of different size on the necklace, the necklace and the beads themselves, of course, shifting shapes in time and changing light.

No single bead will be forced. Its facets and lines gradually impress themselves on me. I stare at them as Yeats in "Lapis Lazuli" stares at the stone, "Every discoloration of the stone, / Every accidental crack or dent," until he sees "a water-course or an avalanche, / or lofty slope where it still snows . . . ." When I think of a single Whitman line, and repeat it to myself, one like "Fog in the air, beetles rolling balls of dung" of that fathomless bead "Song of Myself" (a line prophesying the modern world, a line the angelic forefather of Eliot's dolorous

"Her drying combinations touched by the sun's last rays" in "The Waste Land"), I can only shake my head in amazement and gratitude. When I roll one of the great shorter beads on my tongue, I know it will give of itself for as long as I live. When I think of *Leaves of Grass*, the necklace itself . . .

V

Just northeast of the confluence I've described is/was an estate of 37 acres, the Rockwell estate. Bull Smith obtained the land three centuries ago, and it was passed down through nine generations to Charles Embree Rockwell, sixty-one as of June 12, 1978, the date of a *Newsday* article sent me by a friend.

Unable to afford twentieth-century property taxes, Rockwell sold 26 acres to The Point of Woods Construction Company of Massapequa. He donated one and one-half acres to the Town of Smithtown. And then he signed a contract of purchase for the remaining nine and one-half acres with Gordon and Jack Real Estate and Developers of Huntington. He plans to leave Long Island.

Rockwell once came into my father's woodworking shop on the Jericho with a walnut log from one of his trees fallen in a storm. Rockwell loved his trees, my father told me. He could tell this by the man's eyes and voice. Rockwell wanted to know what could be made out of the walnut log. It turned out that much of it was rotten, but my father pieced together enough of it for a table pedestal.

Rockwell's son Charles, asked how he felt when he was told that the land had been sold, said, "Well, it's as if I had been told someone in the family had died."

I don't know the details of what is happening/will happen to that land. The two-story family house, built about 1750, is on the plot donated to the town. Near it is a large red barn built in 1850, and next to it a carriage house where "rows of cobwebbed carriages lie under decaying white dust covers." The *Newsday* article says that the town plans to move the family house but that the Smithtown Historical Society is against it, maintaining that its original site is the town's most historically important. Widow Blydenburgh's tavern stood on this land, too, and it was here that George Washington, on April 21, 1790, stopped, to feed his horses and to thank Island residents for their support during the Revolution. The town may build a parking lot for the town library, if the Rockwell home is moved. It's interesting to think that people wanting to check out a book by Whitman, of course, will need a parking space. Says Town Historian Virginia Malone, "I consider that to turn into a blacktop parking lot the place where the first president of the United States once greeted the residents of Smithtown, [would be] a desecration of the land."

This complex story goes/will go on and on. Its repetition across American does not make it any easier to understand. No one knows what it means, not Rockwell or the Town Historian or the lawyers in Whitman's school. But as the farms are lost, as the maples, elms, walnut, oak, locust, hickory are lost, the blackberry brambles and honeysuckle and laurel, the dogwoods and lilac and wild roses, the deer and smaller animals, those of us in the traffic flow in the intersections of new and old Island, that Island that is everywhere, bear witness with the center of our lives. There is no answer. I am not sure of the question. But we will come away from the Island with what we need for eternity. The undiminished poet insists that we open ourselves to the new day, and that we are forever able to reciprocate, to conduct the current. "Dazzling and tremendous how quick the sunrise would kill me / If I could not now and always send sunrise out of me." Despite whatever deaths we suffer, there will be compensation, in our knowledge of Whitman and Whitman's light.

VI

Witness

We'd walked into the small warm shed
where spring lambs lay in straw
in the half-dark still smelling of their birth,
of ammonia, the damp grass, dung,
into this world in the middle of a field
where lambs bleating soft songs lifted
their heavy heads toward their mothers,
gentle presences within their wool clouds.
Later, outside, as I watched,
Wenzel wrapped his left arm around a sheep's neck
and struck her with the sledge in his right hand.
The dying sheep, her forehead crushed, cried out,
past pain, for her mortal life. Blood flowed
from her burst skull, over her eyes, her black nose.
Wenzel dropped her to the grass.
When I ran home, I struck my head
on a blossoming apple-bough.
Where was the dead sheep?
What did I hear?
Where is the witness now?

I was nine or ten.
Her cry was terror,
so I lay awake to hear her,
to wonder why she didn't seem to know
her next manger, her golden fields.

Her odors drifted through my screen—
the hay at the roots of her wool,
her urine, the wet graindust under her chin,
her birth fluids hot and flecked with blood.
I could hear her bleat
to her last lamb, hear her heartbeat
in the black air of my room.
Where was the dead sheep?
Why did she cry for her loss?
Where is the witness now?

Not to accept, but to awaken.
Not to understand, to cry terror, but to know
that even a billion years later, now,
we breathe the first circle of light,
and the light curves into us, into the deer's back,
the man's neck, the woman's thigh,
the cat's mouse-mossed tongue, all the ruby
berries ripening in evening air.
The dead elms and chestnuts are of it, and do not
break the curve. The jeweled flies sip it,

and do not break the curve.
The great named and nameless comets do not break the curve.
The odorous apple-blossom rain does not break the curve.
The struck ewe's broken brainpan does not break the curve.
Wenzel nor this witness breaks the curve.

In the shed's dusk where spring lambs
sang to their mothers, in my dark room
where the dead ewe's odors drifted my sleep,
and now, within these cells where her forehead blood
flows once more into recollection,
the light curves. You and I bear witness, and know this,
and as we do the light curves into this knowledge.
The struck ewe lives in this light,
in this curve of the only unbroken light.

48

Milkweed

In "The Lilies," my favorite Wendell Berry poem, the speaker tells us that chance, patience, and prayer may sometimes take us into the presence of these flowers, but there are no guarantees, except for one:

> I found them here at first without hunting,
> by grace, as all beauties are first found.
> I have hunted and not found them here.
> Found, unfound, they breathe their light
> into the mind, year after year.

Around a back corner of my boyhood home in Nesconset on Long Island, there was a small circle of calla lilies. Their white spikes reached up from thick green leaves to my waist. They held such a pure whiteness, not the off-white of peonies or yellowish-white of cabbage butterfly wings seen close. I don't know whether they are still there, reappearing each spring, or whether they've been uprooted, replaced, asphalted or cemented over by now. But I still have them, and they often appear to me when I'm not hunting them. I believe that our whole cosmos evolves from such thought, beyond death, outside our usual limited conception of death. Berry says "the" mind, not "a" mind or "my" mind.

There's a small and a beautiful painting by George Braque called "Peonies." I've seen it twice, eighteen years apart, at the National Gallery in Washington. Now, I think of it, too, its petals of swirled multi-colored but whitish paint, the plants all foreground and rendered with thick applications of color. I also see myself standing in front of it, my selves. The me that sees my selves holds me steady, and will, and is my soul.

In one of his essays Berry says that the most important lesson nature had to teach him was that he could not learn about her in a hurry. "What is to be known," he says, "is always there. When it reveals itself to you, or when you come upon it, it is by chance. The only condition is your being there and being watchful." Lilies, or paintings, or books have to be seen and "read" this way too, we come to realize.

Upstate (April 3, 1983).

At ponds when I was a boy, watching frogs or trying to catch them I'd seen thousands jump and disappear into the silt commotion of their jumps. But one day, by luck and chance, I saw a leopard frog strike the water, do a 180° turnabout, and burrow under mud and weeds back almost to the spot it leaped from. After that, knowing what to look for, I followed other frogs as they did the same thing. From this and from other intelligence that came by way of staring and by way of chance, I think I know more about the brain of a frog, and maybe more about the interstices of the brain of a crane, or a raccoon, than do most people, and I'm glad I do. One of my poems might want to jump, disappear into its own commotion, turn underwater 180°, and hide back where it jumped from.

Berry's "The Lilies," his love for Chinese poetry and Thoreau, his understanding of things I have myself tried to learn in my own slow way about place, about the land, about reading and writing, lead me here to a recent poem I followed until it revealed its subject, its meanings, to me as I wrote it. It begins as the eye of the poem, the "I," places himself on his one acre in a shifting world of moral decision and dilemma. It leaps, I think, into the unconscious, and then into another sphere where bodiless lilies and milkweed and our unborn children wait for us. I'm not certain yet whether to call this "The Unborn" or, simply, "Milkweed," about which I was thinking as I began to write:

> One acre, for now, to hold to. Entrusted
> (these days that thought is almost dead).
> Most is wooded—ash, maple, some small elm
> which live, for now, but may be last of their kind
> despite my prayer that this acre be the elm's home.
>
> There's one corner I've wanted to clear
> to plant giant sunflowers there—
> I picture them in their meditation
> bending their necks about my head, gold-
> petaled eyes seeing everything before
>
> autumn pecks them blind—but milkweed took over:
> I can plant sunflowers somewhere else, and will,
> but still the unborn souls of those
> not planted in the milkweed corner
> come toward me, some knee-, some genital-, some
>
> heart-, some brain-high. . . . But the milkweed
> now deepen into green;
> later, their stems will flutter
> orange and umber monarchs
> that lay their eggs only on them. . . .

50

What are, where are the children I didn't have,
anyway? . . . Maybe biding in time where all
the disincarnate dwell, while I walk earth
in their places, doing what I can
to sense, love, and name them.

When they are two or three inches long, milkweed pods look like tiny green squash. But I like best (though all their stages are one in Time and I should not discriminate) their earlier, purple-blossom stage, bees buzzing among the big blooms. A few spring evenings each year when I walk through my backyard Brockport darkness, their scent stops me beside them and I breathe their purple fragrance, look up at leaves, moon, and stars, place myself. Until they do, I never anticipate that the milkweed will stop me, so preoccupied am I by the day's habits of thought. The milkweed, almost invisible there in the darkness, make me breathe deep, and remind me that they will come to this every year in body, and that they will always be here in other ways, no matter what, if I pay attention and come to learn the only thing, in the end, that matters.

In another of his essays the poet-teacher-farmer tells of coming for the first time to a woods floor strewn with bluebells. "Though I had been familiar for years with most of the spring woods flowers, I had never seen these and had not known they were here. Looking at them I felt a strange loss and sorrow that I had never seen them before. But I was also exultant that I saw them now—that they were here." My own poem tapped for me something that I didn't know I knew until the writing, the finding. In the writing, apparently, I found and made a context that led to the leap between the last two stanzas. Autobiographical facts feed into the realization that the speaker would like to have had more children, and I could talk about this for a long time, but this doesn't matter. What matters is that something was waiting for me to find it and say it, to bring it to the light of words by way of these milkweed.

Talking about his bluebells, Berry continues: "For me, in the thought of them will always be the sense of joyful surprise with which I found them—the sense that came suddenly to me that the world is blessed beyond my understanding, more abundantly than I will ever know." We come upon poems as Berry comes upon lilies in his poem and bluebells in his essay. Truly inside our poems as we write, we come upon ourselves, often in mysterious and unexpected ways. Poems, too, are our children—we do what we can, while we can, to sense, love, and name them.

Within a Poem By MacLeish: "Companions"

The flowers with the ragged names,
Daffodils and such,
Met us on the road we came,
Nodded, touched.

Now, the golden day gone by,
We walk the other road:
They throng the evening grass beside,
Touch us . . .
               nod.

Archibald MacLeish's lyric "Companions" is memorable, is so easily memorized. As I was looking, it found me. Two or three readings and it had me by heart, for always.

MacLeish was there in Amherst when Robert Frost was eighty and said that all he'd hoped to do was to lodge a few poems where they'd be hard to get rid of. That humble sentiment impressed MacLeish. Well, on this score, certainly, MacLeish himself can rest assured. In a few hundred years, even should the anthology of twentieth-century American poetry spiral down to only a few dozen poems, a few of them will be his.

I want to say at the outset that "Companions" is so simple a poem that I almost hesitate to surround it with words, enter it, allow my tongue to try to be an eye, in Wallace Stevens' image. What I'll try to do is to follow naturally where the poem takes me, to allow myself to go along with it. I may sometimes go too far, sometimes not far enough.

On its simplest, most apparent level, the poem is an observation by a speaker who has gone somewhere on what he calls a "golden day" and now,

Delivered May 7, 1982, at a symposium held at Greenfield Community College in Massachusetts to mark Archibald MacLeish's 90th birthday. The poet died just weeks before this event. Published in *The Proceedings of the Archibald MacLeish Symposium, May 7-8, 1982*, eds. Bernard A. Drabeck, Helen E. Ellis, and Seymour Rubin (Lanham, MD: U P of America, 1988).

perhaps, returns. I say perhaps because "the other road" may be a second road, angling off elsewhere, rather than the return road that the circular nature of the poem seems to suggest. In one sense, of course, a return road *is* the same road, walked in a different direction, curving back finally, in a curved universe, on itself. In any case, at least one other person has been with him (or *her*, but I'll assume a masculine speaker as I talk about the poem). Coming and going, he has noticed that the roadside flowers nodded and touched, touched and nodded. He uses the word "road" twice, and it seems to me that the poem, on first reading, comes dangerously close to the poetry of romantic cliché, of the conventional sublime, of the "path of life" syndrome. But a poem is often successful because it takes risks and gets away with them, as this one does, and it may be that, immediately, enough mystery and understatement are present to save it from turning sticky-sweet on the page: the "companions" of the title are never definitely identified (in fact, we may think of ourselves as the speaker's companions), and the phrases "ragged names" and "and such" offhandedly undercut the full-blown roses and redolent phrasings of ultraromantic poetry.

On another level, of course, the poem reverberates and suggests things underneath the actual denotative saying. Poetry uses words to get at the shadings of feelings beyond words. We hear "Companions" as the speaker's summary— this is not a poem discovering what it knows, I think, as are many other MacLeish poems, but a poem spoken by someone who knows what he has seen and what he is going to say—the speaker's summary of his, our, whole life. Outside the text, we have the poem within a book, *The Wild Old Wicked Man* (1968), in which the theme of old age and the death of friends predominates. Inside the poem, "the road we came" and "the golden day gone by" suggest, of course, birth and approaching death. The speaker is condensing his life's going and coming into the one image of a walk along a country road. He is a man who is able, in Thomas Hardy's poignant phrase, "to notice such things," and "Companions," as we move closer to it, has to do, centrally, with the action that went on/is going on around him. This little poem reminds me of some of the brief deathbed poems of the Japanese Zen masters. A poem by Bunan (1602-76) reads:

> The moon's the same old moon,
> The flowers exactly as they were,
> Yet I've become the thingness
> Of all the things I see!

Hakuin (1685-1768) says: "Past, present, future: unattainable. . . . / But the moonlit window smells of plum." "Companions" is in no sense world-denying, or even afterlife-denying, but creates a time that many Zennists would care for, the now that always exists, a new time made from but beyond our old concepts of past and present tense. I have just heard myself hearing that the speaker is old and near the end of his life on this planet, but also, of course, he is speaking from the middle of his whole life, and seems just now to be setting out to complete the other half of the endless circle.

Perhaps this is a good time to mention, too, that the poem may be read as a poem for the poet's wife, the celebration of a marriage begun in 1916. In his interview with Bill Moyers, speaking of his good fortune, MacLeish says, "I have the kind of marriage that . . . about which you can't say anything. It's just a wonderful marriage. It's existed for about 60 years. It'll go on as long as we're around . . . as long as there is us to be married. And perhaps even after that." The flowers in "Companions" may be felt as part of the "perhaps even after that," so unassuming but omnipresent and trans-substantial do they seem. I know that for MacLeish, as he says in his 1938 essay "In Challenge, Not Defense," "Poetry can have no elsewhere. Poetry is art, and, being art, committed to this earth . . . ." He says that the church solves "the difficult arithmetic of this hard world by writing the equations on a blackboard somewhere else." Still, and I sense no contradiction here, "Companions" may also be read, I think, as though spoken by someone who is "dead," who is already walking the other world, remembering companions of his earthly life, joyfully touched by them again here when they illuminate his path again. Wherever its world, this poem is still grounded in what we, in MacLeish's phrase, "can see and sense and know."

"Companions" becomes for us illumination as its speaker recounts what was for him a discovery that now gives him comfort and peace. We notice in the poem that the speaker never mentions just where he's been, or what he did there. These aren't the important, the crucial things. The most crucial thing is that, golden day to evening shadow, daffodils and other common flowers (in "ragged" there may be a suggestion of ragweeds) have somehow not just waved in the wind dumbly apart from us but have acknowledged his/their/our presence. When they met us as we came, they nodded and touched (there is perhaps the primary suggestion in the first stanza that they touched each other rather than us—if so, the second stanza will become an intensification and expansion, and if the flowers come to suggest the human community, as I hope to discover here, the slight changing in the touching and nodding will be especially moving). Nodding is a movement up and down, a "yes," and also foreshadows old age because of the associations we make in our minds with uses such as "nodding off to sleep," uses lending a certain dreaminess and disembodiment, a going gentle through the evening. "Touched," of course, gives us both physical touching and the use suggesting that the speaker and whoever is with him have been emotionally moved, touched. As they met us at evening (and now, on the other road, there seem to be more of these companions—they *throng*), they touch us and nod. They are there along that spiritual road. They are almost human, touching, nodding, and the first meaning of "throng" is "a multitude of people." We hear the repeated "th" sound, the suggestion of thronging: "*th*e o*th*er road, / They *th*rong *th*e . . . ." In numbers, they seem to witness, and seem to say yes, and seem to accompany us into the future darkness. Though the golden day has gone by, through eight lines our companions seem to carry its yellow, its daffodil colors even unto evening. I'm reminded again of a MacLeish statement during the Moyers interview: "these people one sees and one admires . . . all have their own sufferings and their own sorrows. The delight of life is so much greater than the sorrow of it because the sorrow does eventually become part of the delight. It is a deep enrichment." Imagine the senses in which even the death of a loved one often becomes part of the joy, the joy of having loved and still loving, the joy of memory—it is some such dimension of joy that Yeats called *gaiety*. Here, "daffodils" and "golden" are the two words that seem to establish the poem's color, one undimished, even, but somehow modified by our image of "evening grass." I can't help recalling that in his essay "Mark Van Doren" in *Riders on the Earth* (1978), MacLeish says of his old friend, "He never accepted the dark night of the soul which has been a standard literary property for so many dwindling years." In fact, MacLeish concludes his essay by quoting a Van Doren poem which reads, in part:

> O world, my thought's despair,
> My heart's companion, made by love,
> So intimate, so fair,
> Stay with me till I die. . . .

It is as though MacLeish's "Companions," a poem that *does* keep the world with us until we die, and maybe even after, is a gift to Van Doren, and remembers him in the daffodil-gold of its enduring.

Our speaker, then, has seen as central to his/our lives a gesture of the natural world that seems to him to be the evidence and truth of everything. "Companions," heard whole, is a poem about what Nathan A. Scott, Jr., in *The Wild Prayer of Longing* (1971) sees as "the great thrust of the imagination toward that standpoint from which reality may be seen to be a thing of flow and dance . . . a drive toward rediscovery of a dimension of holiness in the quotidian." We have in so many ways lost the world. We have increasingly felt ourselves to be separate from evening grass and daffodils and our fellow man. On June 20, 1836, Ralph Waldo Emerson walked in a storm. The next day he wrote in his journal: "And truly in the fields I am not alone or unacknowledged. They nod to me & I to them." Emerson worried that "We distrust and deny inwardly our own sympathy with nature . . . ." Today, the assembly line, Verdun and the Holocaust and Viet Nam, Jonestown and acid rock and acid rain, office buildings whose occupants can't even open a window, media of overkill and frenzied fad—these things have jaded or insensitized us to the point where for us the great romantic dream of the essential existence of all heaven in a blade of grass, of the cosmos as a reality of interdependencies is near death. The result is, as Scott says, that "we crave assurances and manifestations that our world, for all of its radical contingency, is nevertheless shot through and through with holiness, with a sacred reality." This is what MacLeish imagines and makes real for us. The sacred reality of MacLeish's poem is that the natural (including human) worlds care and acknowledge, are abiding presence for us, that everything is One in a musical reciprocity. Theodore Roethke has talked about the necessity of long staring: "a thing perceived finally . . . looked at out of love . . . until you become the object and it becomes you . . . is an extension of consciousness . . . ." This poem, "Companions," telescopes this process. The feeling I have is not just of the speaker's accidental glimpsing, coming and going, but of ongoing seeing, even during the lifetime between the stanzas, during which he has realized the companionship of the flowers. When I am within this gentle, quiet, indirect poem, I am persuaded and assured of the things I sense, during my moments of deepest clarity and understanding, to be true. I'm not sure of this, but does the word "met" primarily suggest to us plan, a kind of foreshadowing? We seem to have to qualify the concept to say otherwise, as in "a chance meeting." In "Companions," the flowers "met us on the road we came." They do seem to know us, and connect with us. I also notice that fully ten of the poem's thirteen long vowel sounds (and most of us would agree that long vowel sounds are more emotional than short vowel sounds) are in the first three lines of the second stanza, lines that sweep us into such poignant knowledge and recognition. This poem makes a music that means.

Somehow, though "Companions" is in some ways about time, the poem treats time casually, matter-of-factly. The poem suggests that there is only one essential season, this present during which companions accompany us. The word "Now" at the beginning of the second stanza directs us to what matters, nowness, isness, and the gestures of the flowers tell us that all time is circular . . . . On the evening of May 7, 1888, four years before Archibald MacLeish was born, Horace Traubel visited Walt Whitman in his room on Mickle Street in Camden and they spoke of such things as these. Walt says, "I don't feel as if I wanted to disparage this world in favor of any other—the worlds are continuous—one opens into another: there is no start or stop. . . ." And he says, when Traubel asks him whether he ever goes back to the war days, "I do not need to. I have never left them. They are here, now; while we are talking together—real, terrible, beautiful days!" Traubel notes that Walt was in a very quiet mood. He kissed Walt goodnight and left. Very much time, and no time at all goes by between the two stanzas of "Companions." Everything within our lives is effortlessly carried into the second stanza.

Every time I'd ever said the poem to myself, I'd had the feeling that "Companions" had come quickly, intuitionally to the poet. In the *Paris Review* interview (1974) MacLeish says, "I am sure—I mean I am not sure at all but I believe—the master poets must come at their poems as a hawk on a pigeon in one dive. I can't. I chip away like a stone mason who has got it into his head that there is a pigeon in that block of marble." But "Companions" just never felt to me to be this kind of poem, one chipped away at, or built by fits and starts. Thinking about my talk today, feeling great unplanned and unconscious and even irrational depth in the poem, I wrote my friend and asked him about the composition of

"Companions." He replied: "It was a friend to me from the start. It came like an evening bird call—its whole self together." Yes, it is one of those rare poems, too, as he says about his "Words in Time" in *Poet's Choice* (1962) that "know more about their own business than the man who wrote them and go on thinking about it longer than he ever did." As he says, "this poem is writing me."

All of time is in the mind of the speaker of "Companions," and there is no separation here: this is not about a road less traveled by, but about one we all must take, or are on now. Walking the other road seems natural, unforced. We have come to the throngs of blooming flowers as a matter of course, as though in answer to the questions posed in MacLeish's much sadder "Rainbow at Evening" when "the heart is out of mind" (MacLeish himself pointing to a dissociation of sensibility, certainly): "show me, *arc-en-ciel*, bright bow, / where the gold is hidden now." "Companions" again and again in its eleven "d" sounds, it seems to me, grounds us, keeps us from floating away past the knowledge of death. At the same time, maybe in the speaker's mind (and deep in the mind of MacLeish writing), the daffodils and such embody those he sometimes *thought* were apart from him before this apprehension of time as One—there is his brother Ken among companions thought to be lost at war, there are Mark and Estlin and Ernest, there is (for the biographical future exists in the timeless present for the poet, too) his son Ken, there is his beloved wife. I will not take this thought further. MacLeish's roads in this poem traverse his deepest heart, and I/we through his simple, unpretentious artistry, accompany him. We do not need to know precise biographical detail. It is the poem's strategy, in fact, to avoid this, but its music carries everything we know, and enters us. It is a poem that came quickly to a poet who earned it by caring for language for so many decades, and by living a life of service and love. Maybe we will realize that the poem itself will become a companion for us, as some poems do, during this golden day, May 7, 1982, and after.

The Dragonfly

1. What does the future hold for poetry?
2. In what forms is it likely to be cast in the next two decades?
3. What techniques are likely to dominate the art?
4. What subjects will poets most likely choose?
5. Are there current trends which will continue?
6. Do you anticipate any new movements or schools?
7. Are there purposes it will serve that it doesn't now serve?
8. Are there breakthroughs which must be made?
9. What other art forms will most likely affect it?
10. What technological and/or scientific innovations will affect it?

      I've decided to devise my own question. This is it: Why do the questions sent to me by the editor of *Seems* make no sense to me, or matter to me?

      The older I get, despite whatever increased recognition there may or may not be of my books, poetry becomes more and more personal to me. I don't mean that the poems I write are not *things*. I hope they are, that they stand by themselves, that they don't need me. I mean that there is only one way for me to write. I must stay home, mind my business, not see a great many books of criticism or periodicals (I happen to see the *NYTBR* maybe once a year), and write. All that apparent achievement out there makes me nervous. The hype makes me glum. The theories about what poetry must be and do, or will be and do, should have no influence at all on the poem presently rising to me. What I must do is keep myself open, avoid critical entanglements that prohibit the flow I'm fortunate enough on occasion to experience. And when I've drafted a poem, what I must do, simply, is read it to myself again and again, hundreds of times, and try actually, truly to hear it. When the poem is at the point where it seems to me to be some part of what I am, seems to make an inevitable music, when I've revised it and am unable to hear any longer what seem to me to be false notes, distortions, when the poem seems true to itself (even true to its own idiosyncrasies), then it is done, and I'm pleased to let it go. I must, of course, work on a poem and hear it in the context of what I have come to feel about poetry, not in the context of theory. I

Seems 14 (1981).

don't want to be stupid, and read a great deal—poetry, biography, farm journals, history—but do want to come into my own poems intuitively, want to filter them from my self.

What do I care about where poetry is headed? What do I care about current trends? I've only got a few decades more to pursue this art (hoping it finds me, of course), and if in that time my soul is so lackluster, as it may well be, that I am writing tired poems within tired conventions I cannot now recognize, then I'll be out of luck, and should be. But it would be pure stupidity for me to try to put inside my poems something I anticipate the future might be interested in. I can only finish the kind of poem I care for. I must develop an honest relationship with my own language. I can't worry about poetry's "purposes," or worry about "breakthroughs," or how science will affect it. Poems are not written with ideas. The best ones do not prejudge the world, but build upon themselves, line by line. The poetry world floods me every day—advertisements, magazines, solicitations. It would be madness to pay much attention. I read poets I have come to care for, I try to mind my business, I write the poem I'm lucky enough to have come to me.

The other morning I was walking to my cabin across the acre of meadow and trees here in Brockport I'm lucky enough to have, when a blue dragonfly buzzed to the front of me and then, slowly, circled around me. For a second I didn't realize what had happened. The dragonfly disappeared. Then I knew. I was reminded of a little poem of mine, one within a winter sequence, about this same place.

> Bowing,
> I address the door,
> pray, once more,
> for that opening to everywhere,
> and enter.

And now another composed itself:

> A blue lord
> dragonfly circled
> completely around me,
> turned me completely
> around.

I just want to be open to these things, and recognize them when they come. I'd guess that the surest way for for me to stop whatever poetry I may have within me from turning with that dragonfly would be for me to come to any conclusions about the questions asked.

Preface

*Henry James . . . had come since to regard Whitman as the
greatest American poet . . . . Edith Wharton, hearing James
read "Lilacs," . . . . found "a new proof of the way in which,
above a certain level, the most divergent intelligences walk
together like gods."*

Justin Kaplan

For several years now I've attempted to define for myself that generation
of American poets to which I might belong. I've not been successful in any clear
way, have again and again caught myself contradicting myself or being
contradicted by a particular poet's life or work. But I've kept making these
attempts, I've realized, because I've needed to feel part of something, not
necessarily a "movement" or "group" or "school" with cloned characteristics, but
of a community of those poets of my approximate age who began writing and
publishing when I did, who will lose the earth approximately when I will and who,
for this reason among others, are now deepening into their lives and poetry in
many of the ways I am.

In one of his notebooks Theodore Roethke refers to "the exhausting fight
against the inner fatigue, the soul sickness." I connect Roethke's struggle, one felt
by most poets, with the fact that poetry is a lonely activity in this America in
which the life of the spirit itself seems increasingly to be in danger of obliteration,
and when I've read and/or heard and/or met the contributors to this book, I've felt
the kinship I've needed to feel. The generation is in the poems themselves, of
course, or it is nowhere. Underneath the various voices, underneath the various
subject matters that serve in the best poems to reach into what all true poetry has
always been about, I believe that what I've called "The Generation of 2000"
reveals itself here. I know it as I feel it. I feel it as I enter the poems.

There is a very limited audience for quality poetry in America. The best
work seldom reaches the shelves of the dominant fast-book chains now fixtures in
shopping malls built on what were once farms across the country. Television sells

---

The Generation of 2000: Contemporary American Poets, ed. William Heyen
(Princeton: Ontario Review P, 1984).

books now, but (perhaps fortunately) the poet is still felt to be too trivial or uninteresting or unbalanced or esoteric to appear on talk shows. Poetry does not make it into the "Books in the Media" displays at the mall stores, and if there is a poetry section, it consists of leatherette gilt-edged gift books or the latest insipid collection by some sweet singer, maybe a relative that a publisher decided to make famous. But genuine poetry will always guard its own integrity fiercely, and will always be necessary. It will not dilute itself to sell itself. In the most important sense, it is not for sale, and won't be. Nor will it condescend to us. We will have to reach up to it to discover its very real abilities to sustain us. In his essay included here, Wendell Berry quotes William Carlos Williams: "It is difficult / to get the news from poems / yet men die miserably every day / for lack / of what is to be found there." . . .

After I edited *American Poets in 1976*, one of the poets included wrote to me to say that another poet in the book was "the enemy," and that if he'd known "the enemy" was going to be in my anthology, he himself would have refused inclusion. I don't understand this kind of thinking. I have my own preferences, have a feeling myself for the poetry I most care for—some of the poets here write the kinds of poems I would most like to write, and some do not—but an anthology is a gathering, to my mind, of various aesthetics. Each poem here, I believe, whatever musics I prefer among them, is a work of language-integrity, and this is an eclectic book. Its aim is to reach that level where "the most divergent intelligences," both of readers and contributing poets, may come together.

What I feel poetry to be will, of course, be embodied in my poems and in the poems by others that I've chosen, and not in what I may come to say about them. But I'll hazard one observation now. If there is an editorial slant that helped form this wide-ranging collection, it is one against the kind of quasi-surrealist poem that Wallace Stevens made fun of when he said that "To make a clam play an accordion is to invent, not to discover." It is understandable but tragic that there is so much distracting silliness and indulgence in poetry during this critical point in human history, a time when all life on earth is threatened. Earlier, to suggest what I feel to be the rooted concerns of the poets of this generation I most believe in, I used the phrase "lose the earth" rather than the simple word "die." The poets *2000* brings together are not dadaists or faddists or stand-up comics, and they are not aestheticians tripletalking ethereal voices, but are poets of long-staring at the things of this world. Poetry's language is not overtly didactic, of course, does not beat us over our heads with blunt sticks. It discovers what it knows and feels as it comes to be itself, as it unfolds itself during its own present language again and again. But, as Stevens says, "Poetry has to be something more than a conception of the mind. It has to be a revelation of nature . . . ." It will be this in myriad ways, certainly, but not by the sort of false wit whereby bivalves play "Lady of Spain." At the same time, this is not a book of what Louis Simpson calls "deadly solemnity." The contributors here (and I as editor) take chances, I believe, endorse that necessary "wildness" that Emerson called for in the American poet . . . .

It may be that by the year 2000, because of accelerating economic and technological pressures that are forcing students overwhelmingly into business/computer/scientific fields, we will have a nation of imbalance, one in which the leavening qualities of the humanities to help us know ourselves and our earth, to help us laugh and curse and sing and pray, to help us order our priorities in life-giving ways will be seriously compromised. In its own small way, this anthology hopes to be a counterweight to that tendency. There are poems here that can help us realize, as Whitman says in "To Think of Time," "that the purpose and essence of the known life, the transient, / Is to form and decide identity for the unknown life, the permanent." During a time when we have been numbed by hourly exposure to news of unimaginable tragedies around the globe, there are poems here to help us imagine again, and feel, and become human again, soul-restoring poems. This anthology hopes to be an edge that cuts away at cant and complacency all the way to 2000 and beyond. This most recent generation of American poets will bear out the faith we place in it now. This anthology is dedicated to the faithful reader.

The Moon in the River

Several autumns ago I was walking to school on a windy Brockport morning when horse chestnuts were dropping from their trees at the end of my street. Unopened burs were falling, and the nuts themselves that had already broken out of their burs. I stood near that horse chestnut rain for a time, and then filled one of my pockets with the nuts. During the rest of my walk to school, I fingered one, and then others, brought different ones to light, thought about them.

During my undergraduate poetry workshop that day, hearing myself talk about some of the things Theodore Roethke meant when he talked about the necessity of staring at objects ("By all the things that are, I've come to be," as he says in "The Changeling"), on impulse I told my circle of about twenty students to close their eyes and open their palms, that I had something I wanted them to touch, feel, smell, think about. But they were not to open their eyes. To help us relax, I turned off the ceiling lights. I placed a nut in each student's hands. I told them to think hard about the object they held, to experience it, to dream their way into it, to meditate on it. Then we were silent for about twenty minutes. I told them to open their eyes, but still to be silent as they wrote something, anything, about the object. Fifteen minutes later, we went around the circle and heard the writings. These ranged all the way from straight notation to surreal journey. Some were hackneyed and boring (not one, though, without somewhere to begin again), some opened up into forests of horse chestnut trees or galaxies of chestnut moons and stars. Some recounted the *story* of what we'd done from their first touch to the opening of their eyes, while others flowed in present tense stream-of-consciousness images. My students were happy with what they'd done, and happy to hear what I'd done. We had some time left—this was a ninety-minute class—and stared again at our objects, and free associated. Then I asked them to exchange nuts with the person to their right, and to stare at that object. Then I asked them to get their own nuts back again and to exchange them with the person to their left. Then I kept the nuts moving in one direction. There were cries of loss! Finally, I gathered all the nuts and asked the students to pick their own from my cupped hands. All of them knew their own, and wanted their own back, such is our affection for/identification with an object we have brought into our world. . . . By now, a few of those horse-chestnuts are saplings, or real poems. I don't want to

Poet and Critic XIV, 3 (1983-84).

surround this experience, an experience with body, with ideas, but we live in a time when things of this world are too often inert to us, buttons to push, cans to open. Our minds are not, despite Wallace Stevens' feeling to the contrary in "Poems of Our Climate," "never-resting" enough. In the poets I most admire, and in the universe that communicates itself to me during my moments of clarity, objects shimmer with a kind of reciprocity, tend inward to me as I tend outward to them. A poetry workshop, it seems to me, has to evoke a kind of opening in many students, a willingness to stare into something of the outer world, or their poems will be endless analyses, in vitiated language, of states of feeling, poems of inner-weather only. My experiment, when I thought about it, was a moral one with ongoing implications. It was an indication of our willingness to allow a horse chestnut its life—and most of our writings did—even as we completed ourselves through them.

Maybe a child is astonished outright, and our condition as adults in this media-blitzed society has taken us past that as fast as our cars take us past trees. Maybe, now, to begin again, to create, we must sometimes move through seeing to feeling and astonishment, even to love, again, and once there, perhaps, we'll be less willing to destroy. This will not, of course, be a willed thing, but maybe we must learn to be receptive again, as we once were. Thomas Hardy wanted to be remembered as "A man who used to notice such things," "who had an eye for such mysteries" ("Afterwards"). I know that when I was a child I *saw*. Later, years of lethargy and academic strain and blur went by for me, especially during graduate school. Now, I am to some extent awake again, but need help, the help always around me. (As I write this, I am pressing a horse chestnut against my forehead.)

Some of the resulting poems, or prose poems, pleased my class more than any other writing they'd ever done. Their pieces had, sometimes for the first time, a grounding, a noticing of the world's weight. This is Bruce Agte's poem begun during that class, finished some time later:

Chestnut Days

Maybe we all live like this:
days brightening into darkness,
leaves and rain falling on chestnuts.

We become what is around us.
In the fall there are bare trees.
In the mind there are branches as well.

Today I gathered chestnuts
outside. What are these days to me?
These chestnuts must be dead or dreaming

and now I know they are neither.
The more I look at them in open air
the more I begin to know nothing at all.

Bruce wrote me this note about his poem: "This is the poem that grew out of the 'chestnut class.' I remember holding the chestnut in my right hand that day: one moment it was a hollow, weightless shell and contained nothing, or contained a dream, or the spirit of the tree itself. Then it had weight and substance, all the life and summer lushness of the tree compressed into a dense and dark star, a shape within my palm able at any moment to burst back into its mother shape, an eighty-foot tree. . . ."

I once carried a bag of horse chestnuts to Pittsburgh, and put one of Tom Murphy's high school classes at Shady Side Academy through the same exercise. Here are a couple of results, as they were later published in *Egerian*, the school literary magazine. The first is by David Garrett, and the second by Catherine Vodrey.

Blankets

Chestnut trees
at July noon:
apples
in a sun-filled
bedroom

The Game

The floor is chill
like her grave

I tremble,
sight stolen by the dark
and widen my eyes to hear
life, breathing all around me

Don't be shy,
this is her eye

more than a peeled grape,
caressing my palm

Have no fear,
this is her ear

more than a buckeye,
smooth as skin.

In passing I drop it
and with the round echo,
gasps accuse me
breathing deep and quick.

    I don't usually spend class time in actual writing, but maybe I should repeat that exercise, or similar ones, several times in every workshop, using stones, leaves, shells, bullets, feathers, coins, lengths of dental floss, potatoes, whatever. I'm sure I've only been discovering the wheel here, that many creative writing teachers have been doing such things while I've shunned all "gimmicks" and have become a little ill when I've glanced at manuals of such "tricks" or when I've been unlucky enough, as I have been a few times, to be in audiences when someone is lecturing on how to teach creative writing, and plays games. But this chestnut sense-and-mind work this merging of language with object (or a filtering through it) (with, perhaps, a certain necessary "wildness" and "abandonment" as Emerson says in "The Poet") seems to be important for any writer, a way to connect. The exercise itself means that the writer must transcend habitual patterns of sensing and thinking. During the act of writing, when it is going well, at best there will be an association of sensibility, and this made possible by the period of contemplative reception. Such a classroom exercise, too, enables us all to talk freely, grounded in a common experience, about the process of writing itself.

    What if the object were not in hand? Maybe this is the next step. On a subsequent day, now, I will ask the students simply to think hard about *something*, not an incident or emotion, but about a frog or apple or postage stamp or piece of furniture or mountain they know well, to sense it in as many dimensions as they can, and then to allow their language to come toward it in the rhythms their experience with it has given them. This is essentially what I did years ago with these two poems about what was biographically the same fish. One piece begins with the fish, moves away from it, and returns to it. The other finds it after a search. When I read these two poems of mine, as tethered as they are to something I saw and felt, I'm as interested in the movement of the grasping mind behind them, of course, as I am in the particular object that generates their speech.

Pickerel

Green body flowing yellow,
horizontal flame
lit under padshadow,
among bending lily stems,

gills fanning
rings, ripples, water-
lights—now its pond
is dead. How many years?

My eyes its amber
to hold it. It disappeared,
but hovers,
here.

The Return

I will touch things and things and no more thoughts.
Robinson Jeffers

My boat slowed on the still water,
stopped in a thatch of lilies.
The moon leaned over the white lilies.

I waited for a sign, and stared
at the hooded water. On the far shore
brush broke, a deer broke cover.

I waited for a sign, and waited.
The moon lit the lilies to candles.
Their light reached down the water

to a dark flame, a fish: it hovered
under the pads, the pond held it
in its dim depths as though in amber.

Green, still, balanced in its own life,
breathing small breaths of light, this
was the world's oldest wonder, the arrow

of thought, the branch that all words
break against, the deep fire, the pure poise
of an object, the pond's presence, the pike.

I suppose that these two poems are companion pieces, both using "hovers" or "hovered," both using the image of amber. Unconsciously, I had held that "arrow of thought" with me all of my life from the time I saw it until it declared itself in language. It may again. It *will* again, if I enter it again, down through water and past lily pad, as though I held it, as, essentially, I do.

From horse chestnuts to bullets, I've mentioned common things as objects to place in students' hands. My friend the English poet and novelist Martin Booth visits various schools to do workshops and carries along with him what he calls his "image box." More than in my horse chestnuts, there is an immediate voltage in the objects he hands to his pupils and tells them about: a vial of soil from D. H. Lawrence's grave in Taos, N.M.; a stone from the vent of Mt. Vesuvius; a talisman against toothache from a tribe in the Sahara; a tiny cage used by Chinese gamblers to keep their fighting crickets in; a pickled baby flatfish; a thistle head from the temple of Apollo in Delphi; a stone-age bead; the necklace from a Roman mummy from about 2,200 B.C.; a stone from the courtyard at Dubrovnik, Yugoslavia, where Richard the Lion-Hearted was allowed to exercise as a prisoner during the Crusades; a pair of WWII *Luftwaffe* cufflinks; etc. He asks the students to free-associate on paper, to feel the love or violence or history or nothingness given off by their objects.

In my own life, I cannot bring myself to throw out, as Thoreau did, all the pieces of limestone that gather dust on my shelves. I've some wonderful, magical objects around, and I suspect that most writers do. I suppose I believe more in our beginning with common objects, and am worried about our minds casting about for what we assume to be (basing our assumptions on a false aesthetic) poetical subjects. But a beginning with "electrical objects" may be necessary for some. In the end, whether an exercise begins with a common object or one with a story already trembling with connections, our hope is to do what the most memorable poems have always done, to pay attention again, to see, to grow back into language that holds and feels what it talks about. I keep thinking of the Zen image of serenity, a moon reflected in the flowing water of a river. Poetry is the changing water, certainly, but any true poem in its language has always also been the moon, bodiless, itself changing but somehow grounded at the same time.

Walt's Faith

John Burroughs tells us that he last saw his friend Walt Whitman the day after Christmas, 1891, just three months before the poet's death. "Though he had been very near death for many days," says Burroughs, "I am sure I had never seen his face so beautiful. There was no breaking-down of the features, or the least sign of decrepitude, such as we usually note in old men. The expression was full of pathos, but it was as grand as that of a god. I could not think of him as near death, he looked so unconquered." During any given moment of his long disability those last years of his life, Walt could be discouraged, glum, plaintive, resigned to the curve toward death, but there was something inside himself that steadied him, illuminated his words and face. This was the Whitman, the "Kosmos" he had made and become, or become and made, who said in "Song of Myself" that "The minute that comes to me over the past decillions, / There is no better than it and now," who noticed in "Crossing Brooklyn Ferry" that there were "fine centrifugal spokes of light round the shape of my head in the sunlit water" and identified all of us in our particular embodiments as being "struck from the float forever held in solution." Because his view of the world was always the widest possible, and because he was no poseur but believed what he said of the eternal now, of the golden aura around us, of the soulful cosmos from which we come, momentarily incarnate, Whitman, "Almost alone among the major American writers," concludes Justin Kaplan in his 1980 biography, "achieved in his last years radiance, serenity and generosity of spirit."

It seems to me that many readers do not realize or do not want to come to terms with the dimensions of Walt's optimism, the power of affirmative belief that enabled him to move toward death with a "yes" for all of us, with peace for himself. When he was young, earthly objects at once shimmered with transcendence, and became part of him forever, as he said directly in "Starting from Paumanok" and many other poems; he knew Emerson's *Nature* (1836) early and almost by heart, and his whole being assented when his mentor said that "Man is conscious of a universal soul within or behind his individual life," that we and our world exist "to the soul to satisfy the desire of beauty." He knew "the sea of torment, doubt, despair and unbelief," as he says in "Song of Myself"—one of his

Newsday (April 25, 1982).

first sights at Fredericksburg in 1862 was "a heap of amputated feet, legs, arms, hands, &c., a full load for a one-horse cart"—but knew there would be an afterlife, that what comes afterward "will in its turn prove sufficient, and cannot fail":

> It cannot fail the young man who died and was buried,
> Nor the young woman who died and was put by his side,
> Nor the little child that peep'd in at the door, and then drew back
>   and was never seen again,
> Nor the old man who has lived without purpose, and feels it
>   with bitterness worse than gall,
> Nor him in the poor house tubercled by rum and the bad disorder,
> Nor the numberless slaughter'd and wreck'd . . . .

The universal soul took everything into account, and would reward, and sustain. In 1888 Walt said to his friend Horace Traubel, "Oh! I feel how empty everything would seem if I was not full of this faith—if this faith did not overflow me: how useless all things would be if they led on to nothing but what we see—to nothing but what we appear to wind up in here." The poet didn't feel it was important to define the exact nature of the beyond. It could remain a tantalizing mystery. (In *Walden* Thoreau asks, "Should not every apartment in which man dwells be lofty enough to create some obscurity overhead, where flickering shadows may play at evening about the rafters?") Our task, Walt felt, is to perfect our "human social body" now, to contribute to the upward evolution.

Walt's cosmic optimism, then, takes into account our personal fears, natural disasters, even the Holocaust. Here, I am just talking, of course, and cannot sway anyone toward a like faith, but caught up in the musical and imagistic power of Walt's best poems, the cynical reader may find new life. I've witnessed transformations, assent suddenly or gradually given to the fact of the Whitman presence. Walt believed that poetry could make everything happen, and so beautiful, luminous, transparent is his best work, that there will no doubt always be readers who take on his rhythm, his life, complete themselves in him.

Reacting to Walt's didactic presence, Pablo Neruda has gone so far as to call him "the first totalitarian poet: his intention was not just to sing, but to impose on others his own total and wide-ranging vision of the relationships of men and nature." But Neruda loves this vision, and adds, "in Walt Whitman's work one never finds the ignorant being humbled, nor is the human condition ever found offended." Still, Whitman is not for everyone, and he knew he would not be. He always knew that the masses would have to catch up to him, and he said that he was waiting somewhere. In a late prose note, "Splinters," he said that strange as it perhaps sounded for a democrat to say so, he was convinced "that no free and original and lofty-soaring poem" could be written by any poet "who has largely in his thought the *public* . . . ." He wrote as deeply as he could, aiming to "arouse from its slumber that eligibility in every soul for its own true exercise!"

In the magnificent 44th section of "Song of Myself" Walt integrates his history with the history of the universe, from "the first huge Nothing" to the guiding of generations before his mother gave birth to him. He concludes, "All forces have been steadily employed to complete and delight me, / Now I stand on this spot with my robust soul." Walt's is a singing voice that apprehends the universe faithfully as a place where vast and indwelling laws of compensation abide, where the divine within each of us awaits the full recognition that will lead us to peace and love at last.

Memorial Day: The Voices

I

June 6, 1984 (Brockport, New York)

I'm back here in my Brockport cabin on a shining morning forty years of mornings after D-Day. I have with me a folder of newspaper clippings, a thermos of coffee, and the mug my brother-in-law brought me back from Viet Nam, where he was a Marine pilot. Under its gold rim the heavy porcelain mug carries the American eagle of his air wing, and the legend "Chu Lai RVN." All these years, Ken has been silent about Viet Nam. I sip coffee from the mug this morning, as I have so often for almost twenty years, trying to put a few thoughts and feelings together.

Memorial observances of the Allied invasion of 1944 have been on television steadily these days. A little while ago, I saw President and Mrs. Reagan at Utah Beach. They will visit the American cemetery at Omaha Beach this afternoon with other heads of state. There are twenty-seven Allied and German cemeteries along fifty miles of coastline at Normandy where 150,000 Allied troops fought their way ashore on that day now so hard to imagine.

I've seen, again, the documentary made when President Eisenhower, General "Ike," returned to those beaches twenty years after he commanded the invasion. Near the end, speaking to Walter Cronkite, looking out over endless rows of crosses, Ike says, simply, "We must find some way to work for peace, to gain an eternal peace for the world."

There have been reunions and ceremonies this day, church services, recreations of parachute drops and cliff-scalings by Rangers, but the personal moments have been most poignant. On television, I see a woman who was married to a soldier for just eleven days before he shipped off for D-Day, when he was killed, visit his grave for the first time. A veteran kneels at another grave, sprinkles soil on it, says, "Oh Bobby, here you are, here you are. Here's some dirt from where you were born, Bobby." I've choked back tears often, have turned the

Chaminade Literary Review 14-15 (Spring-Fall 1994).

television off, have sat quietly in my study or have gone for a walk or bike ride to try to surface.

But what has been deep in my mind, deeper than even the fathomless graves at Normandy, has been that black, polished stone in Washington, D.C. I sometimes feel as though that stone has my name on it. I know that when I stand in front of it, as I do each day no matter where I am, I can see myself reflected in it.

On May 29th of this year, at Arlington National Cemetery, the Unknown Soldier of Viet Nam received the Medal of Honor and was laid to rest, as we say, between his brothers, as we say, from Korea and WWII. Looking to his left at the Soldier's flag-draped coffin, President Reagan was visibly moved by his own words as he prayed that this latest "dear son" would be "Cradled in God's loving arms."

Earlier, there was the solemn parade, precise military units shining, seeming invincible as Roman legions, accompanying the Unknown Soldier to an afterlife of marble and ceremony. But a unit of Nam vets, the 101st Infantry, had asked for and received permission to march. The fifty or so men, those not crippled or in wheel chairs, kept roughly in step. Some were bearded, some wore chain jewelry, most had long hair, their fatigues were mismatched, some wore bandannas, their sneakers or boots flapped. Other Nam vets, I heard, fell in behind the Soldier's coffin itself. These men and their dead comrade on his way at last to an American grave were the soul of this parade. They were what we had become, in all our mixed emotions, because of Viet Nam . . . .

Most of the veterans were a few years younger than I was at the time they shipped out or flew to Viet Nam, willingly or unwillingly; I was in graduate school in Ohio. By the time America sent troops in large numbers to Southeast Asia, my wife and I had a young son. Then we had a daughter. The draft took others, always others. Others had to make the decisions that would haunt them all their lives as this war turned out to be unlike any other that Americans had ever fought. Those men in the Memorial Day parade who had been to Viet Nam and back, the marchers who had survived and the dead Soldier who represented so many, were selves of mine. I know that this is easy for me to say, or could be, but I say it.

Of their time, of their place, drafted, I would have gone to Viet Nam, I know. I would not have had the background or inner resources to do otherwise. I knew nothing very substantial about the war, was a part of no underground. I would not have burned my draft card. As I went to war, I would have been afraid, and had misgivings, but would have felt that my country and I were doing the right thing. I might have survived, as did these marchers, or might have been buried by now in Hawaii where so many Americans are, or near my parents on Long Island, or been missing and now coming home in the symbolic remains of the Soldier in his silver coffin.

II

In 1984 in Rochester, New York, a woman's peace group asked to join the 115-year-old Memorial Day Parade, as was their legal right. They felt that the best way to honor the dead from all wars (the dead on all sides, they said) was to fight for peace now, to struggle against the nuclear arms build-up, to help America understand that another war could mean the end of life on this planet. Local veterans' groups met, decided not to march in the parade with the women. Their sole purpose, they said, was to honor their fallen comrades, to remember. Some said that to associate themselves with these women would be to distract from and even dishonor their dead friends. "The ball is sure as hell in our court," a local V.F.W. commander said, and they were not going to parade with these women. Even when the veterans' responses were not redneck and sexist—the women were sometimes called peace dikes, bitches, and whores—most veterans wanted the parade for themselves, the way they'd always had it, simple in its veneration of their fallen comrades, unclouded by other issues. Only one group of veterans, after intense debate, decided to march with the women. These were the veterans of Viet Nam. They were part of the 1000 or so marchers in Rochester's Memorial Day parade. There were no bands. There were few spectators. This was not the martial spectacle to which the city had become accustomed. The women marchers had their peace banners, the Nam vets marched silent unto themselves, each man no doubt a complex of emotions.

When I saw them, though I could not understand all the reasons for my own feelings—as I cannot fully understand them now—I felt such joy and hope that I cried. The Viet Nam veterans' participation in that parade, their willingness, so to speak, to allow the women voice and presence on this most meaningful of days, was a sign to me of their recognition *not* that they necessarily supported the myriad causes and means of the women, but that nothing in the world, after Viet Nam, could ever be simple again. Their own presence in the parade no doubt alienated them from the traditional veterans' groups of the "good" wars, but this would be nothing new to them. These battered and courageous men—if not before, I felt, God blessed them now. My heart went out to them and I truly, perhaps for the first time, welcomed them, and myself in their spirits, during this terrible ongoing war, home.

III

Several times during his Arlington speech President Reagan used the word "noble." Viet Nam had been a noble cause, he said. I saw a vet wearing a T-shirt reading "Viet Nam/A Noble Cause."

I don't think that Viet Nam was a noble cause. I will never be able to feel otherwise. I think the war was the outcome of a failure of vision and leadership.

We were not fighting a monolithic Communism that threatened our own security, but some amorphous fear. Unless Viet Nam's lessons keep us from inflicting another such war on a generation of Americans and on the peasant population of underdeveloped countries we do not understand, those whose names are incised on the Viet Nam memorial will have died in vain. For all those who loved/love them, we must not allow this to happen.

The young soldiers themselves went to war for many reasons. Most believed that they would help free the people of Viet Nam. While there, involved in chaotic jungle combat that nothing in their lives had prepared them for, many did things, as General James Gavin (one of the first American military men to turn publicly against the war) said, for which they might perhaps never be able to forgive themselves. We have seen the burning huts, reported as "structures" destroyed, and the maimed or dead children of napalm. These things happened. Lieutenant William Calley who slaughtered a ditchful of innocents at Mi Lai was not a dream. Our men captured ground at great cost and then had to give it up, and then had to capture it at great cost again, and give it up again. In the seemingly endless siege at Khe San—just one of the aburdist positions brought home to us in this televised war—they suffered the isolation and mind- and body-breaking pressures that our men at Anzio and Cassino had suffered. More than 50,000 would never reach America alive again.

How to find the language for this? Except for chance, I would have been with those men, done what they did, lived or died. As an American, as a human being, I am who they are. But many more, twenty or fifty times more than 50,000 Americans died in that war, and many of the dead were innocent peasants, families burned and executed and otherwise subjected to horrible deaths because a failure of American vision and leadership placed me with my comrades in that war. Bring home the coonskin, said one of our presidents. Bomb and bomb and bomb and bomb them back into the stone ages, said another. I can never pass over what I did there, forget it, bless myself and be done with it. I can never, now, completely excuse myself (the self I was here at home) for paying taxes all during the war. And my other selves, those who out of bravery or fear, convenience or moral courage or whatever, went to prison or Canada or elsewhere?—in their circumstances I am also who they are, and must not deny myself by denying them. As long as you and I live, we live with what we did during Viet Nam. When we narrow our response to ourselves, to our Nam veterans, to our conscientious objectors, we diminish ourselves as a nation and learn nothing. Each of us is the well-meaning soldier who came home, at best, to embarrassed silence; each of us is the protestor who knew that Thoreau told us to serve our country first with our spirits, not our bodies. Each of us is partly in the grave at Arlington with the Unknown Soldier. As *one* nation, under god, indivisible, we must now accept ourselves, welcome and love those who would not participate, welcome and love those who did. But there must be knowledge and resolution within this welcoming and loving of ourselves. Looking into the suffering eyes of a veteran or conscientious objector—and in my poetry workshops and other classes I have seen many—I must see myself, or live hateful and divided.

If Viet Nam had been the noble cause some tell us it was, we would not now be as haunted as we are. But, surely, in our efforts at reconciliation and acceptance, our chances for nobility double and redouble every day. If we can only, somehow, temper our passionate divisions with wisdom and compassion for ourselves, our America will not lose its belief in itself.

I heard a veteran at the Viet Nam Memorial say, "We didn't lose—spread the word." Indeed, Viet Nam will have been at least as great a victory as we won over the Axis if, in the end, it brings us together. On Memorial Day President Reagan said "Let us, if we must, debate the lessons learned, at some other time . . . ." If only, I felt, he had said *as* we must and not *if* we must. We must never have a day of mindless reverence. As patriots, we must not fall into what the poet Robinson Jeffers called patriotism's "blood lakes."

IV

February 19, 1985 (Honolulu, Hawaii)

I'm teaching for a semester at the University of Hawaii. I have with me a draft of the first three sections of my essay, begun last June and then put aside to gain some distance, and the sheaf of newspaper clippings from the weeks before and after Rochester's 1984 Memorial Day parade. I'd never seen any issue generate as much controversy as this one, or as many letters appear over so long a time in the city papers. Cutting them out last summer, reading them carefully and now coming back to them, I've tried to hear them and to get a fix on the Rochester and American communities of which I'm part.

One writer characterized the occasion as an "outrageous demonstration by the female undisciplined bunch out there desecrating the Memorial Day parade. The American people will not take kindly to this outrageous demonstration of our efforts to honor our sacred dead." Another connected the umbrellas the marchers used that rainy day with Neville Chamberlain and his umbrella from when Chamberlain returned to Britain after making an agreement with Hitler: "As the world so tragically learned, surely such an approach only leads to war . . . . The women's peace groups desecrated the day . . . ." Another didn't want women in the parade, period, ever: "There were women in the wars of this century. They were not in the front lines and most of them came out without a scratch and ask for no glory. It should have been the men's day." One writer began his letter saying "Please mom, let us have our Memorial Day back," and ended with this plea: "Mom, there are 364 other days to display your feelings. Let us have our day to ourselves." The daughter of a military man marched in the parade and said that she was "sorry the veterans can't understand the relationship between mourning our dead soldiers and working for peace." Another woman wrote, "Wars are not necessary and should be condemned in honor of the innocent young men they killed. It is not contradictory for peace activists to march on Memorial Day." Another wrote, "As an American, a wife, and a mother, I watched the ceremonies at Arlington as I have watched all the beautiful ceremonies throughout our land over Memorial Day weekend. But I also watched the ugly and despicable and disgusting events that were nationalized on the news that showed the women that insisted on sticking themselves where they didn't belong . . . . If men turn against women, this is one example why. I have always enjoyed being a woman. I taught psychology at the college level and I earned my job and I didn't feel discrimination, and this was pre-women's lib. So, women, please at least make sure you represent only yourselves because personally I think you're all a bunch of jerks."

In a photograph taken during the parade, a mother and daughter hold a sign reading "Peace is Patriotic," and in another letter to the editor a man argued that Memorial Day is set aside for us "to remember those who served their country in time of peril, and particularly those who gave their lives . . . . But, in a larger sense we should also remember why they served and died: to bring peace to the world for their children, and all generations to come . . . . We can, if we choose, claim the honor of being the generation that started in earnest to turn from war to peace. We can, if we choose, join the small courageous band of women who have taken a public stand for peace. Or, like generations before us we can stand against the vanguards of tomorrow, the Susan Anthonys and Florence Nightingales of our time." Responding to the woman who called the marchers jerks, another marcher wrote: "I have also enjoyed being a Christian and a woman. And as such, refuse to be apathetic and complacent about my children's future. The next war will not be with soldiers but with nuclear bombs that will destroy our earth and our children. So if my involvement has offended you, perhaps you should rethink your criteria in defining a normal hard-working American woman." Another writer said that "The veterans' groups were justified in canceling the Memorial Day parade. These women and men who marched are American in name only. They represent the surrogate army of the Russian government. They are ready to do battle with the American government to achieve their Marxist aims." Another writer worried that next year "it would be the Communists and the Nazis who would want to march."

"If it is childish to refuse to march with people who advocate fence-jumping, trespassing, gate-blocking and other forms of what they term to be civil disobedience, then I will be among the children and pick up my ball and go home." Another: "Perhaps the Rochester Women's Action for Peace could join with their Romulus sisters and take their balloons and banner to Red Square in the Kremlin for their next May Day celebration. Jane Fonda would be happy to serve as their parade marshal!!" Another: "The veterans' groups should have looked beyond what they perceived as a bunch of ladies trying to rain on their parade. They should have tackled the question of peace head-on. If they cannot march with knowledge and conviction in that cause, then it's just as well they canceled their parade."

My paragraphs are divided against themselves. As I've quoted my neighbors, I've been in sympathy with some, have felt others to be callous and stupid, and have heard depths in others that I didn't at first hear. Chaotic as it sometimes seems to be (the debate is a metaphor for the war itself, as were the divided administrations, as was the whole libel suit brought against C.B.S. by General William Westmoreland, e.g.), the conflict continues, seething toward resolution in its own way within each of us. We cannot at this time ask for more, I think. Probably, not one opinion in the whole of Monroe County is changed in a month's time. What we must begin to hear is what is being said underneath what is being said. There is much shared pain finding expression in these letters. There is fear and hope in the passionate rhythms of the voices. There is the central desire to make a secure world for our children. We are in this together, this weather in our lungs, this Viet Nam. We must take part together, but each of us in his or her own way, in the next Memorial Day parade, and as we do we must see one another as suffering and well-meaning human beings, hear one another, in all our divisions. As a poet tells us, "We must love one another or die." If I cannot love your ideas, if I think you uninformed or prejudiced or dumb, I must allow your presence here with me in our America. It must be possible for me to bow my head with you on Memorial Day in reverence for the dead and in fierce desire for a future free from holocaust. We must realize that as a community we are working out, slowly but surely, both the past and the future within ourselves now. Let us temper our hate with patience, and give our spirits time to heal together.

V

Today, as I write, is the 40th anniversary of the American invasion of Iwo Jima. The Honolulu papers carry stories of the return to that blood-soaked battleground by Japanese and American veterans, and of veterans' reunions in both countries. I've visited, here on Oahu, the Punchbowl National Memorial Cemetery of the Pacific. Ernie Pyle is buried here next to the men he wrote about, but the missing-in-action are here in spirit, too, their names incised on marble walls. And so many of our dead from Viet Nam lie here in the crater of this extinct volcano. At the cemetery, overwhelmed by time-sense, feeling the full irony of history, I mingled with hundreds of Japanese-American tourists. For I've been to Pearl Harbor, too, launched out to stand on the memorial above the *U.S.S. Arizona*, over 1000 American men—average age 19—entombed below. After more than forty years, droplets of oil still rise from the ship and rainbow across the surface here where WWII began for America. Those young men, all the young men—they are with God, and they are in the air we breathe, wherever we are, as

Walt Whitman said of the Civil War dead. The three bronze soldiers at the Viet Nam Memorial in our capital can see all the way to here.

Honolulu teems with voices. My heart is filled with voices. I try to hear what's being said underneath the words, the language so often so chaotic, unintelligible, imprecise, illogical, contradictory, irrational. Under everything is the idea of America, as yet unrealized, but there in the dead and living voices. This is the music that most matters when, over the rim of the vast gravesite here thousands of miles from my home "Falls the light/and afar/goeth day,/cometh night/and a star,/leadeth all,/speedeth all,/to their rest." We need to rest, now, somehow, within our sorrow and hate and confusion. I pray, then, that despite all our divisions, we will walk together next Memorial Day.

Iwo Dahlia

Thad J. Mularz, USMC
Iwo Jima, 1945/1995

Richard L. Turner, USMC
Iwo Jima, 1945

My high school coach of the mid-Fifties—
he brought us a dahlia, a single purple bloom
my wife and I have floating in a glass bowl on our kitchen table.
Add a couple ice cubes a couple times a day, he said,
and it should keep, as it has, except for corolla petals
now curling blackly downward.

A few years back he gave us a babyfood jar of sand from Iwo Jima.
With six hundred other veterans, he'd returned a half-century after
hitting the beach there, burying his face in this volcanic grit.
At Marine reunions, he can't find anyone from his old outfit.
Dahlia, that widower grandfather now trusts his memories to you.
May you distill color from even blackpurples, and remember.

Autumn means digging up their tubers, wrapping them in burlap,
carrying them to his rural cellar where the mysterious
dormant life in them will overwinter. They need cold,
but he'll check them several times to make sure the ice
or insects or mice haven't found them out.
There's no sump pump, and usually his hard-packed dirt floor—

I've been down there—retains an inch or two of rain,
but he's constructed a path of raised flagstones,
can make his way, he tells me, even without a flashlight,
through the dark to the cabinet where his dahlias sleep.
The promise of them again is always in his mind,
and has been, and will be, one way or another....

D-Night at Iwo Jima was cold, the wounded shuddering,
medics brushing black sand from stumps and bandages.
Six hundred Marines were dead already—the Japanese
had sited their artillery onto the beaches months before,
were hidden behind revetments in mountain caves
and deep tunnels, were seldom seen that day.

Safe civilian litter-bearer, I'll haul Coach's dahlia
to our compost back of the garden, and spade it in, but not yet.
It will lose its colors, its seared purples going to sepia and black
as it edges in on itself, collapses, and begins to smell,
but not yet. For now, whole, it concentrates October light,
seems to sense the silver maple leaffall outside our window....

Inland that first day, a medic plunged into a shellhole,
then looked around. Next to him, the detached arm
of a dead Marine, its wristwatch keeping time, gold band
shining in Iwo sun, 4,000 miles from Pearl Harbor. Dahlia,
transform to gold, keep memorial time. I'm standing again
above the *Arizona*: 1,000 dead, average age nineteen....

Rear Admiral Toshinosuke Ichimaru, commander
of this island named for its springs of sulfur,
to venerate His Majesty the Emperor wrote poetry.
He prayed Hirohito live as long as sacred Mount Fuji.
Grateful to be placed where he could die
against the American assault, he wrote:

> *In the twilight the waters of Lake Hamana cool,*
> *Sending breezes to fill my garden,*
> *Fragrant with sweet oleanders in full bloom.*
> *Let me fall like the flower petals scatter.*
> *May enemy bombs aim at me, and enemy shells*
> *Mark me as their target....*

Tonight, those petals scattered, rain seeps
into my teacher's cellar,
but he is there again, walking on flagstones.
He unwraps burlap and fingers the dirt-crusted tubers.
May he be able, long as he lives, to bear these dahlias
whose names are myriad, whose target is his heart,

but who can?—there is too much in him, all night
white and amber and green-suffused flares
color Suribachi, lives leak through gauze into black sand,
flamethrowers wait on the color-coded beaches in dreamfumes
of burning Japanese meat and the suffocation to be visited
on these unbelievers with revengeful biblical fury....

In the jungle battles at Bougainville and Guam,
men died out of sight, sank into foliage and swamp quietly.
On Iwo Jima, men died in full view, torn apart,
their bones and viscera spraying and splattering,
shrapnel slashing into them as their last thoughts
flew toward the silence of the past, and home.

On Wednesday, the last day of February, 1945,
their tenth day ashore, the Marines held less than half the island.
Hand-to-hand combat in the central hills—
no survivor will describe this terror.
Where is the old man when he is in his cellar
and shuts his eyes and touches the cemetery of dahlia?

In spring, when all chance of frost is past,
Coach plants them in staggered rows, six inches deep,
one tuber per cedar stake, stakes two feet apart,
rows six feet apart so he'll have room to groom and tend.
You lay each tuber down, he says,
with its eye-end toward the stake, pointing up....

The single dahlia head in its bowl sometimes
seems to weigh more than its table can support,
evening light fused with sepals and petaltips,
notes of taps lost in its empurpled and disfigured inwardness,
Time's harvest now, waking and sleep equal,
as though its presence were a cave being sealed from us.

The night sky lit with dead stars, a jugular vein pierced,
but a medic kneels to the panic, slits the bullet hole,
lays the vein bare and clamps it, stuffs the hole with gauze,
holds it tight. Lips pressed closed, he prays
that this day's battle be god's will. Enfold this tableau,
dahlia, succor the striken soldier and his savior....

Wrapped in tissue in a small oblong box under shirts
in a drawer in a chest in a bedroom in a house
off a road in a town in a county in a state
of our country, under a ribbon and stars, George Washington
faces left in profile on a Purple Heart. He's thinking
of his wife and Mount Vernon. He seldom sees the light....

I dreamed countless *sennimbari*,
cotton bands of a thousand stitches
worn around their waists by Japanese soldiers,
each stitch a prayer for their return.
I coughed a belt, a clot of *sennimbari*,
woke from a vomit of blood and magma....

Can the dead remember, Iwo dahlia?
Where were you, what garden preserved you
when their ravines received the flaming oil?
From even this distance, from the safety of our grief,
you still smolder, your tuberous nature wrapped in burlap,
your eyes inured to that incendiary sun,

and sweet water, and the essence of the living who were there.
You depose the sacramental rose, do you, and the dooryard lilac
smug with pastoral remembrance, and the Japanese oleander
whose commander rhapsodized his suicidal honor.
Dahlia, you've lost your heavy heads to mortars,
your petals shrapnel the neck of our hourglass....

Near the end, the fight in the northeast, a Marine lay over
a sulfur fissure, the hot mephitic stench
seeming to help stanch his fatal wound;
here, dahlia, bleed in your bowl,
enemies slash the ears from your helmeted head,
pull your teeth with pliers for souvenirs....

Two months after D-Day a journalist visited Iwo, noticed
big blue flies clinging to broken limbs, "so numerous
and so close they almost touch. They don't hover or buzz.
They just cling. Brushing a limb barely starts them.
They just cling, surfeited." E.B. Hadfield deployed that word,
surfeited, as though the flies were fat and drowsy with gore,

the blue flies and dead limbs a grotesque parody, he said,
Iwo Japanese flower arrangement. Here, then,
the ceremony of dahlia: viscous lacquer pacific pour
of surfeited flies into a cup of porcelain hemlock
as Coach, asleep, or kneeling in his floating cellar,
breathes deep, and resists, but remembers....

When the U.S. returned the island to Japan—1968—
Coach's dahlias surrendered in ironic gloom,
downcellar, in burlap, in his cabinet,
but fought above ground in full gear, but didn't.
He was with them when he was not with them,
living what had once been theirs, life in light.

Back on Iwo, lagged and blitzed, he rode a shuttle
up from crosses to the summit of Suribachi's cone
where bushes and grass camouflaged pillbox rubble.
He'd carried with him a dozen miniature Old Glories
and now pushed them into the mountain, stood at attention,
then packed them for disabled vets at home....

In the battle between oleander and dahlia
in this way in the perfection of Time
Coach has asked me to darken his ashes
with Iwo Jima's volcanic sand
and scatter the mixture, half over his wife's grave—
she who wept with his fear—half in the sea....

Today, Coach walks in elegy above his cellar.
In the synaptic concussions of his daydream, we hear ...
but no one can listen there except dead friends from photos
of fifty years before. Rocket trucks liquid as plasma,
it may be, weeping solid as bullets, time's divisions unraveling to Time's seamless and deathless will;

meanwhile, below ground, in case, cold keeps his ammo.
Which of us would question him, or them,
given the simple faith of dahlia in full beauty and attack?
Spring spirals, never-arriving until, by way of a soldier's valor,
it will. His seasons return, commodious black,
perpetual witness with this flower.

Piety and Home in Whitman and Milosz

In his essay "Religion and Space," Czeslaw Milosz seems almost to lament when he says, "Today I cannot deny that in the background of all my thinking there is the image of the 'chain of development'—gaseous nebulae condensing into liquids and solid bodies, a molecule of life-begetting acid, species, civilizations succeeding each other in turn, segment added to segment, on a scale which reduces me to a particle." He "cannot deny," though it seems that something in him would like to return to his childhood faith, to Mary and Jesus, to the triune God, and to the firmament set solidly under his feet, heaven above and hell far below him.

But I must not overstate his loss. Despite the new knowledge, the Movement (a key word in Milosz) of the ages, he has realized that, for him, no matter what, "the sacred exists." He says he can *intuit*, in bread on the table or in a rough tree trunk or in a letter opener, depths of being. Relativity has subverted hierarchies, he argues, so that

> In his romantic frock coat, standing on a mountaintop, the solitary admirer of his own ego succumbed to panic when faced with his own insignificance beneath the stars. But would that reaction be appropriate now? Movement caused dematerialization and infamous matter, burden of burdens to the faithful, thins into light and whirls into the original "*Fiat lux*" as in the works of those medieval philosophers who interpreted the creation of the world as the transmutation (*transmutatio*) of non-physical, divine light into light which today we would call physical.

Still, if Milosz has been "freed from an image of space as a solid body and container," if Movement has revealed a new dimension in which "all events and actions from all times" persist simultaneously, this does not seem to make him

Mickle Street Review 8 (1986). Revised for inclusion in *Walt Whitman of Mickle Street: A Centennial Collection*, ed. Geoffrey M. Sill (Knoxville: U of Tennessee P, 1994).

any less lonely. His awe is tinged with melancholy, it seems to me. He is that "particle," and for all his intuitions of the sacred, he lives in the existential well, not knowing how he got there, or what he is supposed to be doing there, or whether or not he can ever get out. He does not want to construct religious hierarchies that would leave him feeling superior to anyone else, but, as he tries to take comfort in the fact that "mine, however, is a piety without a home" and therefore not subject to the deteriorations of our physical home, I feel him painted into his own corner. He has defined poetry as "the passionate pursuit of the real." He has agreed with Simone Weil that poets can be forgiven everything except proclaiming an inhuman thing, and in his poem "To Robinson Jeffers," fairly or unfairly to the American poet—Hyatt H. Waggoner says that Jeffers' "single real theme" is his "desperate effort to teach the heart not to love"—Milosz concludes:

> Better to carve suns and moons on the joints of crosses
> as was done in my district. To birches and firs
> give feminine names. To implore protection
>
> against the mute and treacherous might
> than to proclaim, as you did, an inhuman thing.

But is he not himself proclaiming an inhuman thing, an unearthly piety the logical outgrowth of which would be for us to shrug our shoulders as we lose the earth to pollution or nuclear holocaust? Milosz is a noble and enlightened man, one of the luminous spirits of our time. But he has lost his home. Hard as he fought for it, he has been driven from it by the new science, intellectual cellar by cellar and intellectual alley by alley, just as the ghetto fighters of Warsaw he sees so clearly were driven from their city.

And how could he not have been? After the gas vans and *Einsatzgruppen* and crematoria of our century, it is as though we could not, even if we wanted to, make ourselves believe in an earth and human species that matter to any divine power. How is anything but a homeless piety possible?

I don't know the answer to that question, but I do know (and almost blush to say it) that my own piety is not homeless. I suppose that I have not yet been tested. My world has never been torn apart as has Milosz's Poland; but even if it had been, I suspect that my childhood experiences of Long Island's ponds, woods, and waters, those hours of wonder and glory, imprinted me so indelibly that the earth, nature, will always be my home, for better or worse. Reading Milosz, what rises to my memory again and again as contrast is the *intellectually* almost unbelievably faithful section 44 of Walt Whitman's "Song of Myself." Never before or since, perhaps, has piety had, made, realized such a home:

Rise after rise bow the phantoms behind me,
Afar down I see the huge first Nothing, I know I was even there,
I waited unseen and always, and slept through the lethargic mist,
And took my time, and took no hurt from the fetid carbon.

Long I was hugg'd close—long and long.

Cycles ferried my cradle, rowing and rowing like cheerful boatmen,
For room to me stars kept aside in their own rings,
They sent influences to look after what was to hold me.

Immense have been the preparations for me,
Faithful and friendly the arms that have help'd me.

Cycles ferried my cradle, rowing and rowing like cheerful boatmen,
For room to me stars kept aside in their own rings,
They sent influences to look after what was to hold me.

Before I was born out of my mother generations guided me,
My embryo has never been torpid, nothing could overlay it.

For it the nebula cohered to an orb,
The long slow strata piled to rest it on,
Vast vegetables gave it sustenance,
Monstrous sauroids transported it in their mouths and deposited it
        with care.

All forces have been steadily employ'd to complete and delight me,
Now on this spot I stand with my robust soul

All nature has made his passage a safe one, has conspired to place Walt in his here and now. He is no accident or accidental particle. He is himself the end of evolution. He is matter that matters, and will always matter. He wrote this before his experiences during the Civil War, but this was his essential faith, and he held to it for the rest of his life. The cradle of creation endlessly rocks us, whatever our transient aberrations as individuals or as a race.

In his late poem of mystical process, "The Abyss," Theodore Roethke cries out, "Be with me, Whitman, maker of catalogues." The poet complains that his "inward witness is dismayed" and that his is a "terrible hunger for objects." What he feels he needs is some assurance that our world is our home and that, as our home, the world is itself, with all its beauty and death, and at the same time vibrates with otherness, with transcendence. As Walt says in the 1855 "Preface," "The land and sea, the animals fishes and birds, the sky of heaven and the orbs, the forests mountains and rivers, are not small themes, . . . but folks expect of the poet to indicate more than the beauty and dignity which always attach to dumb real objects . . . . they expect him to indicate the path between reality and their souls." He argues, in fact, that "the poetic quality . . . is the life of these and much else and is in the soul." When Roethke calls on Whitman, he calls for a return to poetry itself, for our realization of our earthly home as spiritual body. At the end of "The Abyss," he reaches illumination: "I hear the flowers drinking in their light, I have taken counsel of the crab and the sea-urchin." He sees "great logs piled like matchsticks" ready to burst into flame. He has been visited by, infused by, the great poet of the catalog of our universal human home.

Czeslaw Milosz, contemporary of Roethke but perhaps "displaced" from birth, is in this central regard, however, no son of the ecstatic, celebratory poet who claimed the world as fitting residence for his soul. In his "Supplication," Milosz prays, "From galactic silence protect us"; and in an interview he says, "What do we have to build a world of our own from—the flutter and twitter of language, lipstick, gauze, and muslin, which are to protect us from the galactic silence. As always, it is civilization versus the deadness of the universe." His tone becomes one of ironic musing: "To tell the truth, anyone subject to the laws of earth—meaning the laws of transience, aging, sickness, and death—should curse fate. What else can he do? What is fate—you live a little while, and then suddenly it's goodbye? Why is it like that? This is the anger of earth. I try to find some other, higher law—in religion, in art. An opposing sphere. Because, after all, I should live forever and always be happy." Milosz says that utopia for the poet would be to spend his life in his native city with the woman he loves, to walk to the corner cafe, and to meditate on the word "is"; but something is always in the way: " Either the city burns down or it's taken by the enemy." And he is of course right. We die by pogrom, cancer, decrepit old age, perhaps heartbroken and disillusioned. We die of ennui and bad bowels, and we die . . . alone, it may be. And he is of course at the same time wrong, and has misapprehended, mis-intuited, misread the book of the world that God seems to have placed in the library of nature for Walt. Walt's inner city did not burn down, even as he suffered during the Civil War, even as his bodily health deteriorated. The enemy, despair, never achieved an impregnable position in him. Was this his nature? Did he earn his cosmic optimism? Did this construct of light and eventual glory exist in him *a priori*, or did his writing again and again, even after the initial outpouring of what became the 1855 *Leaves*, help him toward faith? Often, the old Walt tells Horace Traubel in confidence that he has a personal secret. I believe I know what it is—it has to do with the terror of love—but I will not speak it here.

Milosz says, "You live a little while, and then suddenly it's goodbye." He says he spends much time in trance, but somehow we do not sense in him transcendental time, the infinity of the grain of sand or leaf of grass, as we invite our soul to observe. Always in Walt there is the promise of, the *realization* of, ongoingness within what unendowed eyes may see as the temporal. Or almost always. In two late poems in *Good-Bye My Fancy*, we may see, first, a slight slippage to a place where, to my mind, he could fall into Milosz's ravaged city, followed by the reaffirmation of mystical faith, true to himself. In "Grand Is the Seen," he calls the soul "More evolutionary, vast, puzzling . . . / More multiform far—more lasting" than "the sky and stars . . . the earth . . . the sea." This orthodox faith at first seems viable, but it has lost its home, its source; and its abstract piety is subject, it seems to me, to rapid dismemberment. But in the book's very next breath, in the poem "Unseen Buds," Walt returns to that central upwelling intuition of indivisibility, returns to other "dumb, beautiful ministers" acknowledged so long before. This time, infinite buds create our present-without-end:

> Unseen buds, infinite, hidden well,
> Under the snow and ice, under the darkness, in every square or cubic
>   inch,
> Germinal, exquisite, in delicate lace, microscopic, uniform,
> Like babes in wombs, latent, folded, compact, sleeping;
> Billions of billions, and trillions of trillions of them waiting,
> (On earth and in the sea—the universe—the stars there in the heavens.)
> Urging slowly, surely forward, forming endless,
> And waiting ever more, forever more behind.

In his essay "On the Effects of the Natural Sciences," Milosz discovers in himself "a deep-rooted conviction of aloneness, mine and man's, in the face of limitless space, in motion yet empty, from which no voice reaches down speaking a language I can feel and understand."

The doctor who was to weigh it dropped Walt's brain on the floor. I imagine it, now, made of glass, and radiating outward from its burst center in a billion billion particles of material light. Our earth is one. Home for me, for now, is that center.

Unwilled "Chaos": In Poem We Trust

Every time I've thought of how to begin this talk, I've thought of something that comes before, something that needs to be said first. I'll try to begin with a poem I often use at readings to suggest how it was I came to the writing of poetry. This is called "The Crane at Gibbs Pond." I wrote it about twenty years ago:

> The boy stood by the darkening pond
> watching the other shore.
> Against pines,
> a ghostly crane floated
> from side to side,
> crooning. Maybe
> its mate had drowned. Maybe
> its song lamented
> the failing sun. Maybe
> its plaint was joy,
> heart-stricken praise
> for its place of perfect loneliness. Maybe,
> hearing its own echoing,
> taking its own phantom
> gliding the sky mirror of the pond
> for its lost mother in her other world,
> it tried to reach her
> in the only way it could. Maybe,
> as night diminished
> all but the pond's black radiance,
> the boy standing there
> knew he would some day sing

Delivered at a Holocaust conference in Albany, NY, on April 6, 1987. Published in *Writing and the Holocaust*, ed. Berel Lang (New York and London: Holmes and Meier, 1988).

of the crane, the crane's song,
and the soulful water.

That poem came out of my idyllic Long Island childhood. As a boy, I did sense something in the waters of the ponds I waded and fished. I felt they were "soulful," in some way full of souls. And now I think that my own movement from innocence to experience has to do with the realization that people of my own blood flushed the ashes of millions of people into the pond at Auschwitz.

Another little poem occurs to me. It's called "The Eye," and because it seems to suggest so many of the things I think I've been up to in my poetry, I'll probably someday use it as the prefatory poem to a book of selected poems:

As I begin, not knowing what, to write,
the sun, from the clip on my pen,
turns on this page, such a streaked,

burst gold eye,

all I have, all I have ever wanted,
you to see this, to see *with* this,
in case it is dark where you live.

"The Eye" carries my sense of the process by which poems come to me, and carries my desire that the poem be a means of perception and a help. The purpose of poetry, I believe, is to help us live our lives. But how could a book of poems—this was my worry when I first began, after about ten years of writing them, to think of gathering my Holocaust poems together—how could a book of poems about the Holocaust help anyone in any way?

I'll begin, now, where I first thought to begin. I'll trust a poem to be what I need it to be now, a vessel to hold within its form, at least for a little while, my whirling thoughts and feelings about writing about the Holocaust.

This poem is called "Poem Touching the Gestapo." It has two epigraphs. One is from Edward Crankshaw, an English historian of the *SS*. His phrase "willed chaos" is important to my poem, and to what I would like to edge in on, if I can. The second epigraph is from Olga Lengyel, a survivor. You'll hear the echo of "willed chaos" again. At Auschwitz, for example, tall women would be issued very short dresses, short women would be issued very long dresses—all for the sake of gratuitous confusion and humiliation.

*Behind the apparently iron front of Teutonic
organization, there was a sort of willed chaos.*

Edward Crankshaw

*The system of administration (at Auschwitz)
was completely without logic. It was
stupefying to see how little the orders which
followed one another had in common. This
was only partly due to negligence.*

Olga Lengyel

You now, you in the next century, and the next,
hear what you'll almost remember,
see into photos where he still stands, Himmler,
whose round and puffy face concealed visions,

cortege of the condemned winding toward Birkenau,

and how to preserve Jews' heads in hermetically sealed tins,
der Ritter, knight, *treuer Heinrich*,

visions of death's head returning in Reich's light,
the Aryan skull ascending the misformed skull of the beast,
the Jew, Gypsy, lunatic, Slav, syphilitic, homosexual,

ravens and wolves, the Blood Flag, composer Wagner
whose heart went out to frogs, who, like Martin Luther,
wanted to drive Jews "like mad dogs out of the land,"
Heydrich dead but given Lidice,
Mengele injecting dye into Jewish eyes—
Ist das die deutsche Kultur?—
this vomit at last this last
cleansing and an end to it,
if it is possible, if I will it now,

Lebensborn stud farms, *Rassenschande, Protocols
of the Elders of Zion, SS* dancing in nuns' clothes,
Otto Ohlendorf, who left his Berlin Desk to command
Einsatzgruppe D and roam the East killing
one million undesirables in less than two years' time,

lamenting the mental strain on his men,
the stench of inadequate graves,
corpses that fouled themselves in the gas vans,

the graves rupturing, backs, backs of heads, limbs
above ground as they are here, if I will it now,

the day-in, day-out shootings of Jews, some attractive
brave, even intelligent, but to be dealt with
in strict military order, not like at Treblinka where
gas chambers were too small, and converted gas vans' engines
sometimes wouldn't start, the thousands already
packed into the showers for history,

their hands up so more would fit, and smaller children
thrown in at the space left at the top,
and we knew they were all dead, said Hoess of Auschwitz,
when the screaming stopped,

Endlösung, Edelweiss, Lebensraum, Mussulmen, Cyklon B,

"and his large blue eyes like stars," as Goebbels wrote,
and the Fuehrer's films of conspirators on meathooks,

we cannot keep it all, an end to it,
visions of loyal Heinrich, what engineer Grabe saw at Dubno,
he and two postmen allowed to watch, the vans arriving,
a father holding his boy and pointing to that sky,
explaining something, when the *SS* shouted and counted off
twenty more or less and pushed them behind the earth mound,

Stahlhelm, Horst Wessel, Goering in a toga at *Karinhalle,*
redbeard Barbarossa rising,

that father and son, and the sister remembered by Grabe
as pointing to herself, slim girl with black hair,
and saying, "twenty-three years old,"
as Grabe behind the mound saw a tremendous grave,

the holy orders of the *SS,* Lorelei, the Reichstag fire,
Befehl ist Befehl, Anne Frank in Belsen, jackboots, Krupp,
bodies wedged together tightly on top of one another,

some still moving, lifting arms to show life,
the pit two-thirds full, maybe a thousand dead,
the German who did the shooting sitting at the edge,
his gun on his knees, and he's smoking a cigarette,
as more naked victims descend steps cut in the pit's clay,
clamber over the heads of those already dead there,
and lay themselves down. Grabe heard some speak
in low voice, . . . listen . . .
before the shooting, the twitching, the spurting blood,

competition for the highest extermination counts,
flesh sometimes splashed on field reports,
seldom time even to save skulls with perfect teeth
for perfect paperweights,

his will be done, and kill them, something deeper dying,
but kill them, cognac and nightmares but kill them,
Eichmann's "units," the visions, the trenches
angled with ditches to drain off the human fat,

the twins and dwarfs, the dissidents *aus Nacht und Nebel,*

Professor Dr. Hans Kramer of the University of Munster
who stood on a platform to channel new arrivals—
gas chamber, forced labor, gas chamber—and later,
in special action, saw live women and children thrown into pits
and soaked with gasoline and set on fire—
Kramer, a doctor, who kept a diary filled with
"excellent lunch: tomato soup, half a hen with
potatoes and red cabbage, sweets and marvelous vanilla ice"—
while trains kept coming, families with
photograph albums falling out of the cars, the books
of the camps and prisons, the albums imprinting the air,
as here, we close our eyes, and the rain falling from photos
onto the earth, dried in the sun and raining again,
no way to them now but this way, willed chaos,

visions deeper in time than even the graves of the murdered
daughter who tells us her age,
in the round face of the man with glasses and weak chin,
Himmler, *Geheime Staats Polizei,* twisting his snake ring,
as now the millions approach, these trucks arriving with more,
these trains arriving with more, from *Prinz Albrecht Strasse,*

from the mental strain on Ohlendorf's men,
from the ravine at Babi Yar, from the future,
from the pond at Auschwitz and the clouds of ash,
from numberless mass graves where Xian prayer and Kaddish

now slow into undersong, O Deutchland, my soul, this soil
resettled forever here, remembered, poem touching the Gestapo,

the families, the children, the visions,
the visions . . .

I do not know, clearly, what it is that I've done in this poem or in my book, *Erika*, which came together over about twenty years. Many of my Holocaust poems, it seems to me—these are probably either the best ones or the worst ones (though I am probably wrong to separate them)—begin simply, logically, as though toward some traditional poetic coherence, but then the speaking voice begins to lose grasp, begins to rave or hallucinate or become hysterical or speak in tongues. For better or worse, I've come to trust such poems in a deeper way than I trust my more definite and controlled ones, the ones that I understand.

It may be that traditionally most poems have managed, at least momentarily, to compose self and world. Bless such poems that manage to do this, but my heart goes out to those that remain behind the barbed wire of their saying—are they themselves metaphoric concentration camps?—poems that I cannot quite free by means of rational paraphrase. But they shimmer with meanings, with witness, if I could just hear.

Perhaps my root assumption is that the Holocaust is "opaque," as Susan Sontag says it is. We may be able to quantify it, to find out its shape and weight in time and space, but its sources and meanings and losses glimmer in black light into which we try to see, into which we *must* keep trying to see, instance by instance. Some poems enable me to keep trying to feel my way into that which remains beyond my imagining. I think of what is perhaps the best-known of all Holocaust poems, Paul Celan's "*Todesfuge*," in this regard.

I remember that I'd begun working on something else when "Poem Touching the Gestapo" came quickly, almost of a piece. It seemed to choose me and, writing it, I did not consciously adopt discursive strategies or aim for chaos and ambiguity. But I do believe, and this seems to have come through, that our best poems and stories are written with a kind of intellectual passion, with what Emerson called the "flower of the intellect." When they are, they can be read over and over. They hold to their mysteries even as they keep giving of themselves. They create in us the feeling that if we read them once more, once more, we will surely know them. But we won't. But something in them makes us want to keep trying.

It may be that an assumption of mine even deeper than that of the Holocaust's opacity is that it is morally best for me not to be sure of myself. If I think I know how it was that a so-called civilized German engineer could design and build crematoriums to precise human specifications, how a so-called civilized German soldier could execute innocent people all day long, then I might find myself becoming lax about my own potential for evil. I am tall, I was a blond youth, an athlete—if I had been born in Germany in 1920 instead of Brooklyn in 1940, wouldn't I have aspired to membership in the *SS*? My father-in-law, a Nazi who died after Stalingrad in a prisoner-of-war camp in the Urals, had worked for Goebbels in Berlin. When I was with my wife and family in Germany in 1971-1972, a relative gave us a cache of the dead man's belongings that had been packed away since the war, including many smoldering obscenely anti-Semitic books sent to the Propaganda Ministry. I've stared at them, from their color frontispieces of Hitler to their long bibliographies of similar publications—how could I have escaped such poisoning of mind and soul? My point is that if I do not know, finally, how it was that a man such as myself could act demonically, I can fearfully guard against this in me. Maybe. Perhaps I am swimming in waters too deep for me here. But I noticed that many were against Gerald Green's television miniseries on the Holocaust because, for one thing, they felt that viewers coming away from such a melodrama could say forever after, "Oh, yes, we know all about the Holocaust now. We know what it was and what caused it. We do not need to know more or think about it any longer. We are bored." Such an attitude is very dangerous, of course. On the other hand, the series, seen by millions, acquainted many for the first time with the basic reality of what happened to the Jewish people during the Third Reich.

I sent a poet-friend "Poem Touching the Gestapo" in manuscript. He told me not to publish it. He asked me, "Who would want to touch the Gestapo?" I have been afraid of my poem, but have trusted it, in part, because I have not understood it. It is not simple enough for me to put in simple terms just what position its voice has achieved in its single-sentence cry/wail/lament/moan/madsong/curse. I'm not even sure about the implications of its title. *Concerning* them? *Moving* them? *Laying hands* on them? Making them "*touched*," that is, pushing them vengefully toward insanity? Every time I've written one of these ungoverned Holocaust poems I've had to resist, for better or worse—and this is something only a reader can decide—working on it to the point where I would know, consciously, just what it is saying. At the end, my speaker says that his soul is "resettled forever here." Where? In the poem, I suppose, in the rhyme of "ash" and "Kaddish," in the black bed of this history, in the rush and breakdown of the rendering. After the Holocaust, we are all refugees from the human dream. My speaker's attempt at resettlement seems to me to be—and I have not thought about my poem in these terms before I began writing this paragraph—pathetic, heartbreaking. Whoever he is, he has taken Gestapo visions inside himself and broken down with them.

I try to make rational sense of my poem, but it knows more than I do. It goes on speaking itself, turning and turning darkly on itself even while I try to spade its soil up to air and sunlight.

In contrast, here is a poem more willing to reveal itself. I feel I know what is inside this one:

The Numinous

Our language has no term that can isolate distinctly and gather into one word the total numinous impression a thing may make on the mind.

Rudolf Otto

We are walking a sidewalk
in a German city.
We are watching gray smoke
gutter along the roofs
just as it must have
from other terrible chimneys.
We are walking our way
almost into a trance.
We are walking our way
almost into a dream
only those with blue
numbers along their wrists
can truly imagine.

Now, just in front of us, something
bursts into the air.
For a few moments
our bodies echo fear.
Pigeons, we say,
only an explosion
of beautiful blue-gray pigeons.
Only pigeons that gather
over the buildings
and begin to circle.

We are walking again, counting
all the red poinsettias
between the windowpanes
and lace curtains.
It was only

a flock of pigeons:
we can still see them
circling over the block buildings,
a hundred hearts
beating in the air.
Beautiful blue-gray pigeons.
We will always remember.

The word "numinous" concerns spirit of place, and my poem, though suggestive, is never quite irrational as it walks its way almost into a trance. But here is a poem called "Darkness." It begins with the speaker's lament that he will forget the camps:

Thirty, fifty, eighty years later,
it's getting darker.
The books read, the testimonies all taken,
the films seen through the eye's black lens,
darker. The words
remember: Treblinka green,
Nordhausen red,
Auschwitz blue, Mauthausen
orange, Belsen white—
colors considered
before those places named themselves. Thirty,
fifty, eighty years later. Now
the camps—I lose them—
where are they? Darker.
If it is true
that I've always loved him,
darker. If it is true
that I would kill again,
darker. If it is true
that nothing matters,
darker. If it is true
that I am jealous of them,
the Nazis' hooked crosses, the Jews' stripes . . .
He speaks inside me. Darker.
I lie on a table
in the Fuehrer's bunker,
outside his chamber,
in the hall. I am waiting.
They do not see me,
dogs nor people. This

dream begins again, the film
circles and burns. Eighty, fifty,
thirty years. Darker. He
touched my forehead. He speaks now, says, somehow,
lower, tells me to speak to the lower power,
for once, to say,
come back, enter, I was once alive.
Darker. The air
swims with words, hair
twines the words, numbers
along a wrist, along
a red brick shower. Darker.
To forgive them,
killer and victim: darker.
Doctor, help me kill
the Goebbels children. Darker.
Across the street, now,
a cattlecar, stalled.
The skin lampshades darken under varnish.
Fragments. Can I call
him back? Millions still
call him back in deepest prayer,
but the light diffused
as spray, past
Andromeda, in spiral
shadows. Darker, always
darker. *SS*, death's head,
oval hollow deadface hole for boot—
fragments. The heroes
all dead in the first five minutes.
Darker. To enter
this darkness, to dig
this chancellery garden to my own
remains, to watch
as the black face and scrotum
lacking one egg stare up
at the sun, to speak
with that charred jaw,
carrying this with me. Darker.
Under the answer, under
the darkness, this love I have,
this lust to press these words.
He tells me *lower*,

and the black breastbone aches with it,
the last black liquid
cupped in the eyesockets smells of it,
odor of cyanide's bitter almond,
the viscera smeared to the backbone
shines with it, for me
to say it all, my
hands around his neck,
mouth to mouth, my lips
to kiss his eyes to sleep. We
will taste this history together,
my friend: take a deep breath.
Take it. Smell
almond in the air.
The leader lives.

One evening some years ago I saw the film *The Man in the Glass Booth*. There were such strange psychological leaps. I walked home in a moonless darkness, swirling, and I wrote that poem. Writing it, I was not like a man in a train on a track, but like a man being dragged by a horse galloping wildly across a landscape that it knows better than he does. The rider wants to give the horse its head, but wants to feel somewhat in control of the situation at the same time. When he manages, somehow, to bring the horse to a standstill, when he manages to dismount, he is too shaken to know for sure where he has been.

My metaphor, maybe, is too fanciful. My poem's voice has tried to say it all, has made some terrible admissions. I, as a writer finished with his poem, decided not to censor it. It plunges into psychic and sexual depths I do not completely fathom. That is its power. I must not (must I?) break its power with my conscious mind.

Am I using the Nazis' own method, willed chaos, to write about their victims? I don't think so. My "chaos" in certain obsessive poems such as "Poem Touching the Gestapo" and "Darkness" is *un*willed, I think. And I hope—here is my transition to the second point I wish to make—I fervently hope, unfashionable as it may be in our time for a poet to cherish such hope, that in the end my poetry is a moral poetry, is restorative, redemptive.

Although the sources and strategies of poetry must necessarily be oblique, on a slant, somewhat mysterious, indirect, I have always believed, simply, what Walt Whitman said—that literature is a "means of morally influencing the world." If I did not think it was more than a time-killing, whimsical entertainment, I'd pick up my props and playthings and go home. In her essay in *Art and Ardor*, "Innovation and Redemption: What Literature Means," Cynthia Ozick explains very patiently, gritting her teeth, what a writer she overheard meant when he said, "For me, the Holocaust and a corncob are the same." For that writer, a phrase such as "a morally responsible literature" is an oxymoron, since writing is pure imagination, dream, and language responsible only to itself. *But*, Ozick says clearly, "I want to stand against this view." "For me," she says, "with certain rapturous exceptions, literature *is* the moral life." In a beautiful and charged simile she says that "the exceptions occur in lyric poetry, which bursts shadowless like flowers at noon."

But in most literature, she continues, "one expects a certain corona of moral purpose: not outright in the grain . . . itself, but in the form of a faintly incandescent envelope around it." And I wonder if she has not described what I have sensed as sometimes occurring in me as I wrote some of these poems (this is not a value judgment, but a prayer that, as I wrote and as vile things suggested themselves to me in my "lust to press" sometimes sensationalistic images, something deeper gusted into the poems, validating them as human painsongs): "The corona flickers, brightens, flares, clouds, grows faint . . . The Evil Impulse fills its cheeks with a black wind, hoping to blow out the redemptive corona; but at the last moment steeples of light spurt up from the corona, and the world with its meaning is laid open to our astonished sight."

All things are not the same. A poem about the Holocaust needs to be responsible not only to its own language unfolding in the present, but to its particular subject. It must live in the dual world of the deepest racial being of its speaker, and in history. It must mean, and be meaningful.

I'll conclude with two other poems from *Erika*. The first comes from a dream I had after reading about programs for killing children the Nazis believed were mentally retarded or physically handicapped and therefore unfit to live. I need to say one thing about this poem. Often in *Erika*, I, my speaking voice, does not know whether he is victim or murderer, whether he is wearing jackboots or whether he is dying in a gas shower. But here, for *once*, he does know who he is, what he did, and what he would do again. "The Children" may be my most affirmative poem:

> I do not think we can save them.
> I remember, within my dream, repeating
> I do not think we can save them.
> But our cars follow one another
> over the cobblestones. Our dim
> headlamps, yellow in fog, brush past,
> at the center of a market square,
> its cathedral's great arched doors.
> I know, now, this is a city
> in Germany, two years
> after the Crystal Night. I think ahead
> to the hospital, the children.
> I do not think we can save them.

Inside this dream,
in a crystal dashboard vase,
one long-stemmed rose unfolds
strata of soft red light.
Its petals fall, tears, small
flames. I cup my palm to hold them,
and my palm fills to its brim,
will overflow.

Is this the secret, then? . . .
Now I must spill the petal light, and drive.

We are here, in front of the hospital,
our engines murmuring. Inside,
I carry a child under each arm,
down stairs, out to my car.
One's right eyeball hangs on its cheek
on threads of nerve and tendon,
but he still smiles, and I love him.
The other has lost her chin—
I can see straight down her throat
to where her heart beats
black-red, black-red.
I do not think we can save them

I am the last driver in this procession.
Many children huddle in my car.
We have left the city. Our lights
tunnel the fog beneath arches of linden,
toward Bremerhaven, toward
the western shore.
I do not think we can save them.
This time, at the thought, lights
whirl in my mirror, intense
fear, and the screams of sirens.
I begin to cry, for myself, for the children.
A voice in my dream says
this was the midnight you were born . . . .

Later, something brutal happened, of course,
but as to this life I had to, I woke,
and cannot, or will not, remember.
But the children, of course, were murdered,

their graves lost, their names lost,
even those two faces lost to me. Still,
this morning, inside the engine of my body,
for once, as I wept and breathed deep,
relief, waves of relief, as though the dreamed rose
would spill its petals forever.
I prayed thanks. For one night, at least,
I tried to save the children,
to keep them safe in my own body,
and knew I would again. Amen.

Finally, a two-paragraph prose poem called "The Tree":

Not everyone can see the tree, its summer cloud of green leaves or its bare radiance under winter sunlight. Not everyone can see the tree, but it is still there, standing just outside the area that was once a name and a village: Lidice. Not everyone can see the tree, but most people, all those who can follow the forked stick, the divining rod of their heart to the tree's place, can hear it. The tree needs no wind to sound as though wind blows through its leaves. The listener hears voices of children, and of their mothers and fathers. There are moments of great joy, music, dancing, but all the sounds of the life of Lidice: drunks raving their systems, a woman moaning the old song of the toothache, strain of harness on plowhorse, whistle of flail in the golden fields. But under all these sounds is the hum of lamentation, the voices' future.

The tree is still there, but when its body fell, it was cut up and dragged away for the shredder. The tree's limbs and trunk were pulped at the papermill. And now there is a book made of this paper. When you find the book, when you turn its leaves, you will hear the villagers' voices. When you hold the leaves of this book to light, you will see the watermarks of their faces.

I'd like to think that all of us, our whole lives, are reading and writing that book made from the leaves of that tree. When we hold the leaves of our book to light, we can almost see watermarks of all the lost faces.

Home

The most meaningful word in the language for me is "home." I want to feel at home here in Brockport, New York, where I've lived for most of my life, where, probably, I will live until I die.

Maybe, I've thought, I don't quite feel at home because this is not Brooklyn, where I was born, or Suffolk County further out on Long Island, where I was raised. Maybe, just as birds return south when a precise angle of light triggers something in their brains that tells them it is time, I yearn for a particular Long Island slant of light as the sun appears and disappears over those horizons three hundred miles a second away from where it was when I was born on the first of November, 1940, and I desire those gravities, those particular glimmery calibrations—after all, a seismograph is not a thousandth as sensitive as a human body-soul. We are as sensitive as Thoreau's Walden: "Study the dimpling circles which are incessantly inscribed on its otherwise invisible surface amid the reflected skies and trees. . . . Not a fish can leap or an insect fall on the pond but it is thus reported in circling dimples, in lines of beauty. . . . It is remarkable that we can look down on its surface." Following this observation, as though from wherever he is now, Thoreau muses: "We shall, perhaps, look down thus on the surface of air at length, and mark where a still subtler spirit sweeps over it."

Wenzel was a childhood farmer-neighbor who has appeared often in my writing. You'll notice in this poem, "Sheep This Evening," my desire to be home again:

> I live on a star
> moving at great speed,
> directionless, toward Virgo,
>
> but Wenzel's sheep this evening,
> themselves their own cosmos,
> poised in dumbness,
> graze, nip

Contemporary Authors: Autobiography Series, vol. 9, ed. Mark Zadrozny (Detroit: Gale Research Co., 1989).

the growing grass short,
while I gaze Virgo,
its bright star Spica, space
I pray to curve from,

as the animals' world persists,
their bleat-musics,
green-black grass
within the light's years.

Lord, preserve
such fields, and I would be
among them when all matter
disappears, the bodiless

sheep one evening not surprised,
their eyes revolving, light recording
that I've returned.

Maybe, the simple truth is that human beings do not feel and are not meant to feel completely at home, wherever they are in the world, no matter how long they live in a particular place. Home, maybe, is with God, to whom/into which we shall return, and pangs of discontent, restlessness, displacement are reminders of this. Maybe.

(I realize that my word "maybe" is the act of poetry itself, the spider-soul flinging out filament, filament until, if it ever does, Walt Whitman's ductile anchor holds.)

Yesterday, again, bicycling on a perfect July morning through Brockport's side streets on the way to the college gym where I'd play basketball with friends as I have for twenty years, I felt anxiety building in me, that hollow space expanding beneath breastbone, and for no reason that I could locate. My wife and children are safe and happy, I have no money problems, I enjoy my job, I've been managing to write new poems, I have a month of vacation left. But I found myself again, as I bicycled the maple-shaded streets of this western New York Erie Canal village, wanting to hide, as though I didn't belong here, as though I were an interloper. I find myself, often, skulking about, ducking around corners, avoiding even friends on purpose. Part of this has to do with my shyness, certainly, which might or might not have its own reasons. (I've read just recently that shyness might actually be genetic.) But there must be more to it than this.

Maybe, I've told myself, home is not a place, but is a person, and for me home is Han, my wife of twenty-six years, my dear friend, and the woman I love and need in all ways. And it is true that when I am with her I feel "centered"—a word I've taken from May Sarton—grounded, at home. Sometimes, "home" alone, I find myself acting strangely, closing curtains, jumping when the phone rings and then not answering it. When Han is home, I feel much more at ease, let the light in, unlock the doors, even answer the phone cheerfully.

In his poem "Temporary Facts" William Stafford rhymes the words "elm" and "home." For me, from the perspective of my own Brockport acre on which elms are still dying from blight, this is the deepest, most poignant rhyme I know, the "m" sound of blissful satisfaction, the knowledge of loss at the same time implicit, all coming together as Stafford's speaker remembers an Agnes from his boyhood: "On spellbound evenings you call your brother home, / coming toward the streetlight, through shadows of the elm." And in one of my own poems from *Long Island Light* (1979) called "The Elm's Home," written, maybe, before I knew Stafford's, I look up

> into the elm and hear each leaf
> whisper in my own breath, *welcome*
> *home, this is your home,*
> *welcome home.*

Well, come home. Well come, home. Welcome home. So be it, I pray, in the end.

Maybe I am too lucky, too fortunate, make too much money for simply reading and writing and studying with young people, and feel guilty about this, so slant in and out of my life and do not feel at home. Or maybe my equilibrium is uncertain and doom builds in me because our planet loses its ability to sustain life as we rain poisons on our food crops and oceans, as the air we breathe darkens, as the world's population increases by eighty million a year while in the United States alone each year one million acres of farmland go the way of asphalt and mall. Maybe the inevitable catastrophes to come keep me ducking into corners, not wanting to go on witnessing, not wanting to go on deluding myself that all is well because Brockport itself seems on the surface so healthy. When I see the ignorance and stupidity around me—neighbors still spraying chemicals on their lawns as though chicory were criminal—when I see that some nations will not stop slaughtering whales, that we seem bound and determined not to develop solar energy until our last greedy impulse makes the last dime on the last drop of oil (and my internal litany goes on and on, day and dream), then what else can sanity do to protect itself but hide out, live obliquely, consolidate consoling intuitions of the transcendental while closing the curtains?

In "The Snapper," first collected in *Noise in the Trees* (1974), I say of the title creature that he is "the pond's old father, its brain / and dark, permanent presence." At the end of my poem, "He rises: mud swirls / and blooms, lilies bob, / water washes / his moss-humped back where, buried / deep in his sweet flesh, the pond ebbs / and flows its sure, slow heart." Water and snapper seem to be one body in that early poem. In this more recent one from *The City Parables* (1980), the old romantic dream of natural harmony gives way to fear and prophecy.

The Host

In the dying pond,
under an oilspilled rainbow where
cement clumped, cans rusted, and slick tires
glinted their whitewall irises,
at the edge where liquid congealed,
a lump of mud shifted.
I knew what it was,
and knelt to poke it with a wire
from the saddest mattress in the world.

Maybe a month out of its rubbery egg,
the young snapper hid,
or tried to, drew back its head,
but algae-scum outlined its oval shell,
its ridged chine diminished
toward its tail,
and I lifted the turtle
into the air, its jaws open,
its crooked neck unfolding upward.

It twisted, could not reach me.
I found out its soft, small undershell where,
already, a leech lodged
beneath its left hindleg, sucking
some of whatever blood
its host could filter from the pond.
They would grow together, if the snapper lived.
Its yellow eyes insisted it would.
I gave it back to the oil sludge

where it was born, and watched it
bury itself, in time, and disappear . . . .
I'd like to leave it living there,
but churned slime above it blurs, burns,
bursts into black glare, every atom
of chemical water, rust residue, human vomit
shining in deathlight. The snapper's

> bleached shell ascends the 21st century,
> empty, beyond illusion.

Maybe, though, something else is part of my frequent feeling of incompletion and anxiety, of being on the edge of homelessness. Just this week I read a strong and moving book by Helen Epstein, *Children of the Holocaust: Conversations with Sons and Daughters of Survivors*. She quotes an Israeli psychiatrist who sums up much of what she herself came to discover: "The trauma of the Nazi concentration camps is reexperienced in the lives of the children and even the grandchildren of camp survivors." I am not Jewish, my parents did not experience cattle cars or concentration camps ("only those with blue / numbers along their wrists / can truly imagine," I say in "The Numinous"), but Epstein's book has made me realize that I, too, the son of German immigrants who settled in America before World War II, who in their own ways had to diminish themselves within the increasingly hostile community around them—they'll never forget the swastikas painted on their house in Woodhaven (they'd sailed to this country from another "haven," Bremerhaven)—I, too, bear their fears into the future. They know that what happened in Europe could happen in America— runaway inflation and unemployment, hunger, madness, war, and holocaust beyond our imaginations. Within my mother, especially, there has always been an undersong of almost debilitating anticipation and nervousness, and I seem, by family osmosis, to have inherited this.

Many of the children of survivors in Epstein's book heard their parents' stories, when their parents did speak, again and again, but for a complex of reasons could not/would not remember. This has been true of me, and was one reason I decided to interview my mother and father. In 1982 I recorded them for several hours, and have just this summer, six years later, finished transcribing these interviews. I've been dwelling on them, looking up between sentences and trying to feel my way into them.

My father, Henry Jurgen Heyen, was born on May 20, 1910, in his grandmother's house at Walle, a small town northeast of Aurich, which is north of Bremerhaven on Germany's North Sea coast. His father drowned at twenty-six at the port of Emden in 1915, not as a fisherman as I say in my poem "Stories" in *Erika: Poems of the Holocaust* (1984)—was it fortunate for me and my poem that I didn't know better at the time?—but as a sailor in the German navy.

My father served his apprenticeship as cabinet-maker, but there were no jobs, and his stepfather, who worked for North German Lloyd, helped connect him with someone in America who would vouch for him. He arrived on the *Stuttgart*, after a two-week voyage, on March 26, 1929, at the Christopher Street pier in New York, where a man by the name of August Hermann was supposed to meet him. After a time, all others left the pier. My father, eighteen years old with no English and only a few bucks in his pocket in this new world, waited and waited, but August Hermann did not show up. My heart still goes out to that boy sitting alone on that pier thousands of miles from home. And to the young man who, in 1929 when the Depression hit and he lost his job, "took," as he says, "a little satchel with tools and I walked along Third Avenue, downtown New York, where you had a series of antique-furniture stores, and I knocked on the doors, and I asked if they had any work to do, and I landed a few little jobs that way, just repairing some furniture, or changing some furniture, maybe making a chest of drawers out of a cabinet. . . ."

My mother, Wilhelmine Auguste Else Wörmke, was born August 1, 1914—all Bremerhaven assembled in the city square to hear news of the war that began that day. Her father, a streetcar conductor, would later escape from a Russian prisoner-of-war camp, a story "he loved to talk about," my mother says. (My father had no father to hear stories from. I have been both fathers to my children, sometimes there to tell stories, sometimes distanced within the writing always going on in my mind.)

My mother followed her two older sisters to America when she was twenty, though her father did not want her to leave home: "same houses as here, same streets, what do you think America is, a gold mine?" About two years later, after working as live-in maid and baby-sitter, she met my father, and about six months after that, they waited at the city hall in Brooklyn to be married. Guess what? The same man who was to meet my father at the pier, who was this day in 1937 to serve as witness to the marriage, again didn't show up.

By 1941 my father was a foreman at Bethlehem Steel, overlooking crews that refitted liberty ships into hospital ships. When I listen to his proud voice as he tells of how he put together melting-pot work crews to wage war against the "home" countries, I hear America singing: "the old-timers in Bethlehem Steel in that yard had been there during the First World War and this was the Second World War. They were all seniors, senior citizens, all old guys, very old guys, I think the youngest guy was the foreman himself and he was over sixty. And there I came in and all the young guys and I picked them off the boats as they came in because they hired everybody. The boss told me go on the ships, he says, we're getting in seven-eight hundred carpenters this week, go on the various ships and look around. I said okay. He gave me a free hand to hire whoever I felt, and I saw a Dutchman here with a nice cabinetmaker's toolbox and another one there with a toolbox that was dovetailed, so I got Little Joe and John Burgess and Ernst Berg and a few of these Dutchmen, and I got Lisjack, the one who lives in Buffalo, who came to your wedding, and that's how I got them, one after the other until I had— a few Italians of course and other nationalities—but I got a bunch together, boy . . . ."

My mother was at home in Woodhaven, raising my older brother, Werner, and me; keeping my father in some sort of line when he drank and gambled too much; preparing hot meals of kale, spaghetti, beef, sauerkraut three times a day even in one hundred degree weather. She remembers the oak bedroom set my father made in his spare time at Bethlehem Steel and brought home. And she especially remembers, "He worked Sundays, too. Ach, he worked all the time. I was always alone."

There are stories inside all these family stories, of course. My father's two brothers were killed during World War II on the German side, one a hapless apolitical foot soldier who died in Holland the year I was born and for whom I was named; the other a rabid Nazi ("brainwashed," to use my father's word for him) who was shot down over Russia, whose name appears nowhere further down the family tree. "Stories" ends:

> Wilhelm was killed in Holland,
> Hermann over Russia. The North Sea's spawn
> did not miss a rhythm when Berlin
> burned to the ground.
>
> What if the world is filled with stories?—
> we hear only a few, live fewer,
> and most that we live or hear
> solve nothing, lead nowhere; but the spruce
>
> appears again, rooted in dreamed tears,
> yes, each branch, each needle
> its own true story, yours,
> mine, ours to tell.

The spruce of that poem is one I remember from our property in Nesconset, Suffolk County. After the war my parents owned a bar in Jamaica, then one in Hauppauge, and then my father went back to his trade, built a woodworking shop behind the several acres they bought in undeveloped Nesconset, fifty miles east of New York City. I have shards of memories from Woodhaven (a street, a green fence and gate) and Jamaica (the ski-ball machine in the bar, the flight of dark stairs up to the apartment where we lived, a vacant lot across the street), more substantial memories from Hauppauge (riding my first two-wheeler on Route 111, gathering buckets of box turtles at a pond, finding a litter of kittens in a hayloft, seeing my father conked out at midday from the night before, sitting in a first- or second-grade schoolroom and waiting in a parking lot for the bus that would take me home—on one of these bus trips, we passed a dark and swampy area of which I still dream), but when I see myself as a child it's in Nesconset, where I came to consciousness, to personality.

My best friend was Ronny Patac. I was a grade ahead of him later on when I skipped the fifth, but we were the same age. He lived on Lake Avenue, which was across Gibbs Pond Road and across the Terliks' field. He had a playhouse under oaks and within the rows of azaleas and rhododendrons and Easter flowers his folks raised for Mrs. Patac's brother who was a florist in nearby

Saint James, and for the estate—somewhere in Nissequoque, I think—for which Mr. Patac worked on weekends when he didn't work for Grummanns. The Patacs treated me like a second son. They had been born in this country, but often spoke Polish, and I heard that language almost as often as I heard my parents' German. Over the years, I went on dozens of day-long picnics with them to various Island parks, did my first clamming with Mr. Patac and Ronny, and sometimes when I biked or ran across the field to their house and Ronny and his father were away, I'd talk with Mrs. Patac. Glad to have company, she'd come out and sit on their back cement steps. A short woman, she must have weighed two hundred pounds. She always kept her straight brown hair under a babushka, and usually wore tent dresses that she herself made, sometimes out of flour sacks. As time went by, I cared for her more and more, her laughing gap-toothed face. She became beautiful to me. She told me stories that I've since forgotten, but I can still hear her voice.

I remember when the Patacs had their first indoor toilet installed in their one-bedroom home. This was maybe just after mid-century. I'm sure that my generation will be the last one in this country to remember outhouses. Or seeing television for the first time. I remember the late winter afternoon when our first set was delivered, a ten-inch black-and-white Philco. The service man focussed in on the test pattern of crosses over circles, then switched channels and, magically, Howdy Doody appeared. The first film our family watched was a Charlie Chan mystery. I can still see us in our darkened living room. My mother was very happy to be at home that evening. She brought us carrot sticks and ice cream.

There was no art or music or high "culture" in our home. I never saw either one of my parents read a book. For them, life was a serious affair of getting and spending, of consolidating what we had, and of gaining security in the booming Long Island economy. My father built another shop, this one on the Jericho Turnpike. Years later, he moved Nesconset Woodworking right to the center of Smithtown, where walk-in business helped him once and for all get out of debt and set himself up for retirement. But even though my father's business prospered there, people carrying out chairs and tables and cabinets as fast as his crew could make them or as fast as he could order them from mills down in Virginia and the Carolinas, not one of his four sons showed any interest in taking over the business from him.

Because of Mr. Patac, I thought that someday I'd be a nurseryman. I planted flower beds at home along our garage. I kept my eyes and ears open at our place and at the Wenzels' and got to know the living things, their colors and edges and textures and names, called carnation, phlox, marigold, pansy, nasturtium, petunia, peony, black-eyed Susan, rose, rose of Sharon, pine, goldenrod, tiger lily, calla lily, lily of the valley, sweet William, tulip, crocus, hyacinth, daffodil, dandelion, dogwood, clover, hollyhock, grape, pear, apple, maple, catalpa, willow, moss, honeysuckle, oak, cherry, huckleberry, raspberry, blackberry, strawberry, gooseberry, daisy, iris, fern, and forsythia, by the time I was nine or ten. I got to know vegetables, moles and mice and the rats that fought Wenzel's terrier, insects, birds, the fish and newts and leeches and turtles and snakes (at one time I had a half-dozen different kinds of snakes, for which my father built me wire-screened cages) and other residents of the freshwater ponds and Lake Ronkonkoma just a few miles away and the saltwater Sound just six or seven miles away. I had a subscription to *Nature* magazine, read books on nature, my mother called me "Nature Boy." Werner raised rabbits and pigeons. I had a microscope and spent hours alone in my room fathoming drops of pond water—it was amazing that I could look until I thought I'd seen everything, but then a monster would appear from another dimension from under a miniscule fragment of leaf or cells of algae. I got to know the sheep and chickens that Wenzel raised and slaughtered for market, the spectacular—at least the males were spectacular—golden ring-necked pheasants he raised mainly for the iridescence that flashed from them between coops and behind the crossbeams from which he hung bouquets of chickens upside down to cut their throats. Later, beginning high school at thirteen, I'd get caught up in sports, in my first infatuations, in rock and roll, but during those first years in Nesconset my mind ramified with such Island profusion that even now I can't begin to surround it all. During the winters, I fingered my shell and rock collections and stared into my several tanks of tropical fish. I raised coleus plants and small cacti in my room: it amazed me how, when I pinched them back, they would grow new shoots and limbs, just like starfish. Now, in my late forties, I try to stay as wide-eyed as I was then, try to *see* so that I do not injure the world by forgetting the myraid miracle it is. William Wordsworth in the meditative blank verse of "The Prelude," Whitman in the conversational free verse of "There Was a Child Went Forth" and "Song of Myself" and "This Compost," and Theodore Roethke in his beautifully modulated "North American Sequence" are the three poets—Rilke, also a poet of things, is too artificial for my sensibility—who give me the most pleasure, who best capture for me the vibrations of nature within the poet's brain and heart and the occasional soulful conjunctioning of both that is the moment of poetry itself, the poetry of poetry.

But I was not all sweeetness and delight. I was a murderer, too, killed hundreds of birds with my BB gun, shot squirrels with my .22, killed stray cats, gathered thousands of baby toads and frogs and catfish and turtles that ended up dying in my leaky backyard makeshift pools when I turned off the hose and left to play baseball or to play pinball at Bertino's Sugar Bowl a quarter-mile up the road. As most young boys are, I was stupid and selfish, a marauder, took things for granted. Now, I hesitate to fish, or even to kill insects, though I do: couldn't, I keep wondering, God's creation survive without mosquitoes? (A Greek friend told me, as I keep telling myself, spiders in the house are lucky, but I still squash them.) Wendell Berry discusses "kindly use" of the land, of our whole cosmos, as our salvation, and I try to make this Brockport acre (or at least leave it alone so that it can become) a place that balances the scales of my life. All winter now I feed the same black-capped chickadees that I used to shoot. They were so easy to kill: I could drop one out of the row of pines between the Wenzels' property and ours, and its companions would remain nearby until I ended their singing, too. Even when I felt sick at heart when several corpses lay under the pines, I'd be back the next day and kill more of them. I liked them, but shot them anyway. Now, many chickadees have been born on this acre. Each spring, I hear the young ones in their annual nest just fifteen feet away from where I write in this eight-by-twelve-foot cabin at the back of our property. They mean, I tell myself, that I'm forgiven. There's a line in the seventh section of my book-length poem *The Chestnut Rain* (1986) which mentions "the black-capped chickadee's ministry." It's a playful line, as the black-cap is a playful and trusting creature. Now, I try to justify that trust, and in turn hope to trust you as reader not to end my life as I run my tongue along this sentimental razor of memory and poetry, as I often try to do.

I suppose I know more about sports than I know about anything else. Maybe, knowing so much, I haven't had to write on this theme to try to understand. I've a few sports poems—"The Stadium" and "Mantle" have been reprinted often—including this recent one which was published in *America*, an ecumenical newsletter distributed to some sixty congregations in Alaska and four other states. I like to think that a few bored kids yawning in their pews picked it up and passed time with it during the sermon.

Until the Next Time

If Jesus played football,
he'd be an end.
He'd lope out under the long, impossible passes,
cradle them in his arms,
or, if he had to, dive for them, his fingers
owning that space
between ball and ground.
On short routes, his sprints, feints
and precise cuts
would fake the defense out of their cleats;
on his feet, still running,
in a moment of communion
he'd knock off their helmets
with a stiff arm.

Once in for six,
he'd spike the old pigskin.
In that spot would sprout a rose,
or a sunflower.
By the time time ran out,
both end zones would bloom with roses and sunflowers

where we would wait for him.
After his shower, he'd appear to us
to pose with us for pictures by his side.
He'd ask us home for supper.
We'd glide from the stadium together,
until the next time—
happy, undefeated, unafraid—
if Jesus played football.

And I've written, just over the past few years, about twenty short stories that have sports themes. But, for now, only the remaining arc of this paragraph to note something I would someday like to flesh out in a book, but probably won't. "Coming or going / always at home"—this little Zen poem of enlightenment apprehends that centeredness I spoke of, and I've realized these past several years that I feel always at home in a gym. Basketball, especially, which I've played since five or six (long hours by myself in the Nesconset schoolyard, practicing, and then years of pickup games, and years of organized ball) and which I still play three times a week over the noon-hour, connects me with my childhood, with my childhood body, with my fearful years of high school when my only identity and sense of self-worth came from sports, with the thousand practices and hundred games in college, the years of town-team ball. When, now, I dress to play, tighten my knee brace, walk into the gym, I close my eyes, inhale, and feel at one with the person I am, have always been. Eternity is *now* say the mystics. Playing basketball, thoughtlessly thinking, I sometimes know and feel what this means. It is as though that boy I was forty years ago always knew the man he would become, and vice versa. Playing basketball I know, too, that I am the father of that child, and that I have always been all ages at once. . . . I walk into the gym. I walk to where my friends are warming up. We begin to talk, to bullshit, to shoot baskets. We divide up into shirts and skins and begin to play. Rhythms of muscle memory. Sweat and pleasurable strain and the basketball equivalent of what Richard Hugo described as the "ghost bearing of old sluggers." I try to play fast and slow at the same time, the way Sam Fathers in William Faulkner's "The Old People" tells Ike McCaslin to shoot, the way Eugen Herrigel in *Zen in the Art of Archery* tries to release his arrows, the way Sadaharu Oh in *Zen in the Art of Baseball* tries to hit—he needed an eye in his hip, he was told. The way language-images well up in the mind, and the way good sentences are released. I know, when writing or when playing basketball, I need to see with my whole body. For the next hour, running, paying no attention to anything and yet concentrating at the same time, coming and going within the astral plane of the court, I'll be at home.

A few years ago Han and I drove through Springville, south of Buffalo, where I'd taught a year of junior high school after graduating from SUNY

Brockport in 1961. I wanted to see my old school, maybe sit in my classroom—second story? third?— beside the huge maples. But I couldn't find the school, even though I'd thought I knew its street, its exact place. Finally, we walked across a patch of lawn to a plaque to learn that the venerable Griffith Institute had been torn down years before. It may be that the emotions I felt at that moment are often the emotions of my poems.

Hannelore Irene Greiner and I were married in 1962. She was born in Berlin a few years before her father was captured at Stalingrad and died in a war camp in the Urals. Her mother fled Berlin just before the Russian army broke in. A few years later she married an American soldier mainly, I believe, to reach the States with Han and her two brothers. They arrived when Han was eight. They found an apartment in Dunkirk, in western New York, and then managed to buy a farmhouse in nearby Nashville. Han's mother and stepfather worked as unregistered nurses in mental institutions. Han's mother died in 1982 after being in a coma for months. A few years ago Drachowski married a much-younger Yugoslavian woman he'd met only two weeks before, whose language he couldn't speak, a woman who again mainly wanted citizenship from him. Han and her brothers were suddenly completely disinherited, even from such things as their mother's papers and their childhood toys. The woman told us that since she was going to bed with Drachowski, she deserved and wanted everything. Drachowski and his stepchildren were never close. In fact, it grew much worse than that. Han has sometimes had a hard time breaking emotionally with the only father she ever knew, as insensitive and even brutal as he often was. From the dead German soldier she at least has a Meissen brooch he gave to her when she was an infant, imagining her, with love, as a young woman. There is too much to tell in all this, too much that I find myself not wanting to call up, so won't, at least now. For twenty years I've kept a diary-journal. Let my journal remember family misery, the stories that never seem to resolve themselves or to end.

Depth of Field, my first book of poems, most of which I wrote while teaching for two years at SUNY College at Cortland between graduate degrees or while in graduate school at Ohio University in Athens—I finished the Ph.D., dissertation on Roethke, in 1967—was published in 1970. Since I'm a book collector and one of the writers I collect, as though I didn't know him, is William Heyen, I still have several copies pristine in their original shrink-wrap. These copies remind me of the best poems in the book, ones that seem to preserve their words as petrified wood preserves its grain. I can respect them, but can't quite befriend them. They came into their crafted beings as objects almost apart from me. The title poem is representative:

> The dew's weight is imperceptible
> that gathers like haze on the dark grass
> and darkens imperceptibly the whorl
> of threads in which the widow curls to pass

her night. Now the first shaft of sunlight
steers among the blades, touches and drums
taut by drying the edge of her vapor-white
web, now free to the low wind that strums

it alive. Unraveling her legs, hearing
her net sing the music of a dying fly
or violin of a gnat's feeble wing,
she rises to focus her hundreds of cells of eye

upon her field. And yet, within her sharp
geometry of sight, she is not angling
deep enough, or high. It is the harp
of the curved sun that orchestrates the morning.

To write such poems, and others even tighter, more literary, and more pyrotechnical, I often stood up all night drinking coffee, smoking, trying to become a writer. A poem such as "Depth of Field" might have taken a hundred drafts. I have no regrets. I learned how slippery language is, how even a slightly different rhythm or line break creates different thoughts, how I wanted simultaneously to dominate the poem and to give it its own say so that it would be able to go on suffusing meanings within itself or to a listener forever. I wanted a cut-glass perfection, a master engraver's control. I wanted my poem, as my life was not, to be invulnerable. I was anxious about school, marriage, our two children born in Athens, getting a job, the Vietnam draft, finding home, but I wanted my poems to be assured, to speak a speech that couldn't be interrupted or laughed at: I wanted my poems to be Poetry. During those years, I learned—much of my learning, of course, was not conscious, and I understand better now what I was up to then—that the writing itself, the semitrance, the long-staring, the mantralike repetitions I went through as I wrote the same phrases over and over in different contexts, the *process,* helped me find my balance, helped me to compose myself (in the several senses of this phrase). The act of writing was as strenuous as running, the concentration required sometimes made me feel as though a smoky flame-thrower had been touched off in my skull. With luck and perseverance, the poem, in the end, burned clean.

It was in Athens that I first came into contact with people who wrote and published poetry, stories, novels, criticism. My first summer there—this was in 1961, the year before Han and I were married—a Brockport professor who happened to be teaching at Ohio University invited me to meet a friend of his, Jesse Stuart, the first writer I ever heard read. I'd bought *The Thread That Runs So True,* a touching autobiographical book that should be required reading for prospective teachers, and the Kentucky author inscribed it to me. (I now have thousands of inscribed books, but that was the first.) Later on, in 1966 or 1967,

James Dickey read in Athens. I didn't meet him, sat far in the back of the auditorium, reminded myself no doubt that I had long-range plans to become a poet, that this would take me at least as much hard work as it had taken me at Brockport to become a first-team all-American center halfback in soccer. The way to poetry, however, was much more uncertain and mysterious to me.

I'd pass Daniel Keyes, author of *Flowers for Algernon,* and Walter Tevis, author of *The Hustler,* in Ellis Hall. David Madden swept in and out. I had classes from Hollis Summers, Jack Matthews, and Richard Purdum, a quiet and deeply thoughtful teacher about whom I've written in my memoir *Noise in the Trees.* He killed himself the year after I left graduate school. Here's a recent poem, written quickly but twenty years in the making:

Waterhook

My dead teacher, a suicide, as a boy in Michigan:
the trees so green they seemed created instant by instant
by his own wonder, river so near to the real.

Here, now, as he taught me to know, somehow,
he's there again, if there is a there, there.
He hooks a bullhead, whiskered lunker so black

I create it now, imploded star—
the exact location of his soul—
to hook this to to fathom the baffling waters.

(for Richard Purdum)

Among fellow students, Mark McCloskey was publishing, as was Stephen Parker. Benjamin Franklin IV was a lively spirit. Barry Leeds would go on to publish books on Norman Mailer and Ken Kesey. He and the poets Stanley Plumly and Anthony Piccione are still friends from those Athens years, as is Patricia Goedicke, who with a friend edited a small magazine called *Page.* Each issue was just a page or two, and you could buy it for a nickel or dime at the local bookstores. They accepted two of my poems, and I've never been more excited to see something of mine in print, unless it was to see a poem from *Prairie Schooner* not only appear in *Best Poems of 1965,* but win the Borestone Mountain Poetry Award first prize of three hundred dollars, better poems by Dickey and Richard Wilbur being ranked second and third. I lost sleep over my luck. Summers and Matthews also had poems in that volume, so they saw my poem and were proud of me. From that point on, I felt as though the English faculty knew me. It was a good feeling. While still in graduate school, I had other acceptances from *Poetry, The Southern Review, Western Humanities Review, Wormwood Review, Poetry*

Northwest, The American Scholar, and other little magazines. (I even co-authored, with my friend Bill McTaggart, *What Happens in Fort Lauderdale,* a soft-porn pseudonymous piece of trash excerpted in *Evergreen Review* and published by Grove Press/Zebra Books that is now so rare I don't have to worry that you'll find a copy.) I wanted to belong, wanted to be at home among those lights in Athens who were all far ahead of me. Writing and publishing helped. The day he received a boxful, Jack Matthews inscribed and gave to me a copy of his novel *Hangar Stout, Awake!:* "For Bill Heyen, with great esteem & high good hopes for his continued success with the word." That rare man is still inscribing his books to me, and I'm thankful I've had some of my own to send to him.

I should point out that this community was there at Ohio University before the twentyfold proliferation of creative-writing programs across the country. I was studying literature, took only one creative writing course. But this was a place where many of us, faculty and students, had it in our minds to make our own poems and fictions, if we could.

During the 1966 Christmas break, I drove the hundred miles from Nashville, New York, where we were staying with Han's mother—I've always thought of it as *her* place, not her husband's—to Brockport to interview for a job. There were several openings, and my snowy drive back to Han and the children was a happy one. We'd be moving to Brockport the following fall. Han and I would be returning to the place where we'd met, the place about which, as I'd say in a poem years later, "We know so much we never have to think of." All I had to do first was to finish my dissertation by the end of the summer. I did. (Its often heavy-handed three sections were later published in *Texas Studies in Literature and Language, John Berryman Studies,* and the *Minnesota Review.*) At graduation in August, I bent my head and received the Ph.D. hood. Have I felt like an imposter ever since, never to be at home among scholars? In any case, Han and I took out a loan, loaded all our possessions and our son and daughter into our old red Dodge station wagon, and headed back to our home state and school.

In Brockport, we rented a house for two years, and then (thanks to a loan from my parents, a couple good poker wins, and a summer writing grant) managed to put a down payment on our home at 142 Frazier Street where I have placed myself on this .95 of an acre as few of my poet friends have placed themselves. I've had opportunities for more prestigious jobs at more prestigious universities, but I know that in this floating world this small property of house, trees, lawns, cabin within this village, this woof and warp of generations of Brockport friends, is crucial to me. More and more, I'm reluctant to leave this acre for any length of time. Whenever I find myself at an airport, I think I must be crazy.

Those first years back in Brockport, my anger and disgust with the undeclared war in Vietnam deepened. I took part in local protest marches, wrote antiwar poems including, I remember, one about our increasing troop commitment, "Good Money after Bad," that appeared in the *Nation.* I remember leaving a party one evening with the late John Logan—a party thrown, in fact, by Michael Waters, a Brockport student at the time—and with John speaking and reading to students on the college mall. I told them they would be victims if they submitted to the draft. But I did not translate my feelings into proper action, did not stop paying my taxes, as I probably should have (though now I am cynical enough to know that I'd spend my life in jail if I did not pay taxes each time I felt betrayed by our government's policies). I was building my academic career, writing and publishing poems, essays, reviews, applying for grants, finishing *Depth of Field.* And I was beginning to think about and write about Long Island, which would be the subject of my second book, *Noise in the Trees: Poems and a Memoir* (1974), five years later expanded to *Long Island Light,* a book I hope to revise and expand again.

For several years, too, I'd been working on poems about World War II, the Holocaust, the Third Reich. By 1971, when I began a Fulbright year in Germany with Han and the children, I'd written about half the poems that were to appear in *The Swastika Poems* (1977), but hadn't thought consciously about making a book of that work. The purpose of poetry was to praise, I thought, to give hope, to affirm. What possible good would a book of these other poems do anyone? These poems seemed filled with unrelieved, insoluble darkness. But, after a dream, or after a walk in the German woods, or after reading another book on Hitler or by a survivor, I'd write another poem, sometimes in one rush, sometimes after many drafts. Back at Brockport, I sporadically continued reworking these poems and writing others. I began to see that they were stronger than my Vietnam poems. I remember that I was very worried about some of them, wondered if I should have written them, wondered what they were, wondered if demonic impulses of mine were down inside them despite my conscious effort to control them and know them—and I knew/know that the *poetry* of a poem cannot lie, however much the conscious mind and will attempt to manipulate. I began to shuffle the poems into various orders and to see various possibilities. And then I discovered an essay by Susan Sontag that I felt allowed me to publish a book of these materials. In her essay on Rolf Hochhuth's controversial play *The Deputy,* Sontag mentions "the moral function of remembering." Such remembering, she says, "cuts across the different worlds of knowledge, action, and art." Whatever my many motives, I was trying to remember. And at the same time that I was straining to be responsible, I suppose I sensed that I had to let my poems breathe, had to allow them their own psychic life (Emerson says that he does not believe that he has the devil within him, but would have to speak from the devil, then, if that be the case, rather than censor himself), or they would themselves be victims of an order and a reason that would leave them as dead as the innocent slaughtered by the *Einsatzgruppen.*

As *The Swastika Poems* was about to appear, and when I thought I was done writing such poems, I had a dream and wrote "The Children"[see pp. 101-103 above] I realized that maybe this was the most optimistic poem I'd ever written. It does not veer from the reality of Nazi programs that exterminated children considered subhuman and worthless—"Later, something brutal happened, of course"—but its speaker *still* says he tried, and would try again, to rescue the dead. Otherwise in my Holocaust poems my speaker is confused ("Did I close those doors / or did I die?"). Here, for once, at last—and true to at least this dream—a flicker of light. Other poems flickered ("The Halo," "The Vapor"). I was anxious to add them to my book. I revised and expanded *The Swastika Poems,* changed the book's title to *Erika: Poems of the Holocaust.* Since 1984 when *Erika* appeared, I've written other such poems, and I hope to revise and expand this book, too, one of these years. Now, for better or worse, I'm not as afraid of such poems when they come to me as I once was, even when they rave and get away from me, as does the long "Poem Touching the Gestapo." But I want to remember how uncertain I was about what I'd done, how afraid I was that I'd done something gauche, unconscionable, self-serving, evil. As Elie Wiesel has said in so many ways, the subject of the Holocaust is sacred, and must be approached fearfully. And I want to remember how it was that *poets* understood, how they helped me. I first read any of these poems at the Allendale Poetry Festival in Michigan in July of 1975. I remember a full auditorium, almost pitch black. I was listening hard to myself, trying to stay within the poems, but I could hear sighs and weeping from in front of me. Then someone yelled, "He's a Nazi," and clattered out, willfully misunderstanding even "Erika," a prose piece about a visit to Belsen. Shaken, I read more poems. When I was done, silence. Then, a silhouette rose from a seat on the aisle against the back wall. I knew that it was James Wright. He clapped, slowly, solemnly. He allowed the poems to exist. It seemed that everyone else stood to do the same. And when, two years later, I received from Vanguard Press statements they'd gotten from poets to whom they'd sent proofs of *The Swastika Poems*—Archibald MacLeish, Richard Wilbur, David Ignatow, William Meredith—I read them and wept. Gratitude and relief.

Later, there were many reviews. A few were negative, but only one of these seemed to me gratuitously nasty, a *Chicago Review* reviewer quoting lines from "Two Relations" for example and saying they were badly written, ignoring the fact that these lines were taken directly from a source identified in a note. I'm glad I didn't see this review until ten years after it appeared, by which time other writers (Anthony Hecht, Hayden Carruth, Vince Clemente, Sandra McPherson, Cynthia Ozick, Norbert Krapf, Harry James Cargas, Karl Shapiro, and others) had spoken up for the poems, allowing them their precarious existence. Years later (by the luck of the draw, was it?) that same reviewer attacked *The Chestnut Rain* in the *New York Times Book Review*. Again, he did not once suspect his own ability to hear, or question his own assumptions, his own sense of what a poem must be and do, but bayonetted his way in. Only one other review of my work ever drew blood, a review in *Poetry* of *Noise in the Trees* by someone who had apparently never written any poetry, or anything else for that matter, himself.

By inspiration, luck, hard work, necessity, accident, you write a poem. You've spread your arms wide. You've said to a reader, hit me, take your best shot. You can work ten years on a book of poems, knowing full well in the end how some arrogant fool (I have myself been that fool) might try to take your work from you so that you will never be at home with it. Even though he has not been through the process, even though he cannot imagine how a poem might just already far in advance have laid up its stores, how a poem might just already have considered and dealt with and resolved within itself what will be his objections, he will not blink or stop for a thoughtful moment to question himself. But you will persist. You will read your own work over and over a hundred or a thousand times—no exaggeration here—until you feel and know it as best as you'll ever be able, until you know it is what you are, in its images, echoes, rhythms, yearnings, hesitancies, tides, contradictions, declarations, idiosyncrasies, balances, asymmetries. You dasn't (Mrs. Patac's word) be intimidated by those who are not among the roughs (Walt's word), who probably (not maybe), as I say in my poem "The New American Poetry," were "born in the Ivy League, and inbred there," who "wait by their coffins in the parlor, applying rouge to Poe and Beau Brummell," who do "not hear the cheap and natural music of the cow" (Thoreau's point and image), who "wash their hands of subject matter," who do "not harvest thought, or associate with farmers," whose "city is not the city of pavement or taxis, business or bums," whose "emotions do not arise from sensible objects," who dwell "on absence and illusion, mirror refulgent flames," who do "not define, catalog, testify, or witness," who hold "models before the young of a skillful evasion, withering heartlessness" (MacLeish's argument). You will have done what you can do. You will release the work to do its own talking when you are not around, or even, should you plant your feet solidly enough in an increasingly psychotic world, when you are. Then, you'll start over again, in essential ways always a beginner.

September now, and classes have begun again. As always, I've finished only two or three of the six or eight summer writing projects I'd set up for myself. It's easy for me to read and daydream whole weeks away, I guess, but whether I'm lying to myself or have hold of something true to myself, I think I do get to the writing I should do. I mean that if I spent eight hours a day in my writing chair rather than an hour or three, the resulting poem or story wouldn't get done any sooner, wouldn't be any longer, or better. In general, I write in bursts after a matrix of language and feeling has been both firming up and agitating the swamp of the unconscious. When the time comes, I will find footing. The best description of poetic inspiration I know is by Max Rieser in his *Analysis of Poetic Thinking* (1969):

> In the instant of creation the realistic efficiency of the consciousness of the poet is toned down. Musical images, symbolic sounds, flow in a rhythmical narcosis . . . . There is a

world of subjectively determined associations (similes and symbols), a pointedly sensuous, colorful psyche, . . . and a certain blunting of thought-activity.

In language that I could elaborate on into a book of my own experience with writing poetry over the past twenty-five years, Rieser continues:

A twilight-world evolves, a world of dim lights, a rhythmically moving world of visions, plastic images, similes, symbols, onomatopoetic effects. It is a world whose mode of association diverges from the customary one, a world in which the need for casual comprehension aimed at in the realistic-scientific exigency for the unveiling of the world recedes in face of the more primitive need for expression.

I have a section of American Literature II this semester with fifty students. About half of them are English majors, and about half of these will go on to be teachers. I see myself sitting out there in front of me. I began at Brockport as a sixteen-year-old physical education major. (Because of my mediocre grades, I'd been turned down by the only other two colleges I'd applied to, but Brockport's soccer coach interviewed me in New York City—my high-school coach, Thad Mularz, had played for him—and that did it.) Two years later, for several reasons—I was afraid of an upcoming apparatus course, I realized I wanted to coach high-powered teams but not run gym classes the rest of my life, I knew there were few if any available teaching jobs in physical education, and maybe, just maybe, I sensed a different life cresting in me, a life of reading and writing—I switched to English education. As sappy and suspect as I sometimes seem to myself, I've never been sorry.

When I taught at Cortland, I supervised student teachers, drove out to a dozen rural high schools, and I can now picture my Brockport students teaching in those and in city schools, teaching in part by way of things that they have learned from me. But what, beyond information, do I have to give my students? What do I *profess?* What *is* the true subject matter? What have I given Bill, my son, who graduated from Cornell and is now an engineer at Kodak in Rochester? What have I given Kristen, my daughter, who graduated from Ithaca College and is herself an elementary-school music teacher in nearby Webster?

We begin the semester by reading and discussing two of the greatest poets who ever lived. What a blessing that we have them. Without Whitman and Dickinson, the nineteenth century in American poetry would seem like what Ezra Pound called a "blurry, messy" period. And beyond the things I've learned over twenty years to do so that a class develops and intensifies, beyond assigning my students a demanding full-semester writing project that will help them feel and think their way inside our texts, I try to keep in mind what my friend Walt declares and exemplifies, that "folks expect of the poet to indicate more than the beauty and dignity which always attach to dumb real objects . . . . they expect him to indicate the path between reality and their souls." I try to keep in mind Allen Ginsberg's rock-bottom assumption: "There is a universal consciousness, folks." Great poetry has always been a ship, an icebreaker, keeping the channels open to the spirit-ocean. I try to keep in mind, studying literature with my students, living the quotidian in all ways, Stephen Spender's "those who were truly great / . . . remembered the soul's mysteries." In "The Poet" Emerson quotes Spenser—"For of the soul the body form doth take / And soul is form and doth the body make"— and then exclaims, "Here we find ourselves, suddenly, not in the pleasant walks of critical speculation, but in a holy place, and should go warily and reverently. We stand before the secret of the world—there where Being passes into Appearance, and Unity into Variety." I believe that I believe that "there is a there, there," and that our way to it is through the things of this world, the "dumb, beautiful ministers who wait, who always wait" as we break toward awareness.

But even our weather changes, the Environmental Protection Agency estimates that temperatures will rise three to ten degrees over the next hundred years, that ocean levels will rise up to ten feet (they're probably underestimating), and I know we are losing the earth, that in a century or two, or sooner, there might be no human life on this planet. The oceans will be as dead as the Baltic Sea is revealed to be in the current *Greenpeace.* I trust myself in this bone-white realization because, in part, I know what I saw and felt, and what saw and felt *me,* as I waded those Island ponds when I was a boy, what sees and feels me now as I sit in this chair in this autumn cabin as leaves fall and as birds migrate through this acre. What I must give "all my sons," what I must myself *become,* is imagination itself. We suffer from some lack of perspective, some lack of balance that almost makes it seem as though we do not want to survive. The greatest poems and fictions tell all these truths, even if they tell them slant, and we need to learn, past the dulling habitual mindlessness of our works and days, to hear.

November. I've read over, again, what I've written. I like what I've done, despite all that is left out, and I seem to have said some things central to me. But I still have the feeling that the voice of this autobiographical piece is not quite mine. Maybe the problem is that I spend most of each day within a kind of dishevelment of language, daydreaming or thinking in fragments and tangles of thread, and that whenever I write in sentences and even semicoherent paragraphs I seem too clearly to be someone else invented for the occasion. I like to wear dungarees, flannel shirts, like to watch junk television in my old bathrobe with holes at the elbows, not in a satin smoking jacket.

This past week, a new book of my poems arrived in the mail. It's called *Brockport, New York: Beginning with "And,"* and since once a book is past the proof stage I almost forget about it until it is published, it seemed to have appeared from nowhere. And since I try to distance myself from my poems, keeping them in my mind in the third person even if their speaker is an "I"—I do this in order to ask if they are complete within themselves and satisfy or if they or I have more to say about what they have to say—as I've been reading the book over, several times, I've managed to get inside and actually hear this Brockport resident who speaks these poems of his home. At one point, he imagines a visit to his village by

Brockport Sunflowers

If they could walk, they would walk slowly.
They would shuffle onto our roads from their fields,
lally-gag into our village, sway on sidewalks,
dangle their silly and beautiful heads.
Sexless, they would not bow to women,
or shake men's hands with their leaves.
Desiring nothing but sunshine and water,
they'd peer into our shops with amazement.
Seeing themselves in windows, they'd know themselves holy.
They would love the children, and listen to them,
all day long, until the children were ready for bed.
As the evening star rose in the heavens,
they would nod goodbye to us, not having said a word,
and return, like walking haloes, to their fields.

This is an easygoing poem. In no hurry, unambitious, it proceeds at sunflower pace. The resident knows what is wrong, and here imagines, in effect, soul embodied in sunflowers. There seems to me to be much yearning in this poem, a yearning for a timeless and spiritual home.

I've another Brockport poem, one done since I put together the new collection. My resident, this time, enters more nearly the language-stream that I usually feel within me, the language of rhythm and place that keeps helping me know where I am, and where I am not, yet.

Parabola

I kneel at auction to a box of the woman's things who is
buried in Brockport's High Street cemetery I
walk there once a month or so summer winter they
rest in merged lilac- and maple-shadow snowlight these
whisperers villagers home to the place born from I
pick through spools of thread thumb address book then—she
must have been almost blind—silver-framed pair of her

half-mooned bifocals so thick I
close my eyes try them open up to her
fields woods beyond and all is the gray blur of her
nine decades' parabola here from which we
see too clearly for maybe five or fifty more years all
wanderers for now until we return to the same place with her.

Aspiraling

I've never been able to sleep in the same bed with anybody else, not even with my wife. We sleep in beds about ten feet apart, old brass beds higher off the floor than modern beds.

Two days ago she reached over quickly to turn off her alarm because she gets up earlier than I do and wanted to give me a chance to sleep an extra half hour in case my semi-insomnia condescended to indulge me. She fell out of bed. Her feet had become twisted in blankets and this had caused her to fall straight down and hit the oak floor hard with her jaw, which she dislocated.

So there I was at mid-morning at the hospital with her, scared and waiting to find out about the x-rays, instead of being at home in my easy chair and being smug and cozy because I could spend the morning answering letters and/or reading and/or writing while it was snowing outside and the great American work force was fighting traffic. I wouldn't have had to drive to work until afternoon— my first class on Thursdays meets at 2:00—by which time the roads would be plowed and, with luck, if the day warmed a little as my first cup of coffee of the morning would have been warming me, my car would start and get me to that class, which was only two miles away and which I could jog to if my car wouldn't start and my heart wouldn't stop, as I didn't think it would, because I'm only forty-seven and in pretty good condition. But there I was in the hospital waiting for x-ray results instead of being in my easy chair, just as now I'm at home nursing my wife—she's a good patient but there's so much to do and there have been so many visitors to giggle at her in her neck-brace and try to get her to laugh and cry at the same time—instead of beginning some writing I've wanted to begin. I've wanted to enter a spiral—this is hard to say because I only sense this, do not understand it though I've experienced it a few times—a necessary spiral of thought (this sounds pompous, I know), during which everything gets said. You can't know it when you're inside it—conscious knowledge disrupts it. If you become a good reader, you can sometimes know it later, days later or years later.

Come to think of it, did you ever see that partners' move in figure skating called "the death spiral?" When she's out there descending in her circle on one leg, her head thrown backward and her hair sweeping the ice, she's almost lost,

The Ohio Review 41 (1988).

almost diffused into the cosmos of eddying speed and entropy and music as they lose momentum, but he draws her back again into his power and she is saved.

My wife's accident has made me remember a book I read back in graduate school, read and in fact reviewed for *Southern Humanities Review*. In most graduate-school ways I was backward, though in some I was precocious. This was back in Athens, Ohio, where I attended Ohio University by way of a few accidents, in fact, though these are not my subject here.

The book I read and reviewed was by a humanist philosopher. He defined accident, I still recall, as "the casual intersection of two or more previously unrelated causal series." I especially liked the accidental way the words "casual" and "causal" collided in his definition the way the *Titanic*, in his illustration of his definition, collided with its iceberg. Dig this: we can discover a or many causal series behind why the iceberg was where it was (a glacier advances, etc., and breaks off, etc., and certain currents carry it such and such a distance in a day, etc.), and we can discover a (or many) causal series behind why the *Titanic* was where it was (begin anywhere: a cave man finds a way to ride a log on water, etc., and the hull of the great ship is laid in Southampton on such and such a day, etc., and a schedule for crossing the Atlantic is agreed upon, and the boss who makes the decision decides this way and not that way because of something he ate for breakfast that affected his brain chemically this way or that way, or because he had an argument with his wife, etc.), but the *intersection* of boat and berg was casual, was an accident. This makes living sense to me now in ways that it didn't then. I understood it then, you understand, but I didn't *appreciate* it. Now that I've lived a while, I appreciate this idea of accident.

My wife tosses around in her sleep. She dreams a lot, as I do. I suppose there's a causal way I could research the exact configurations of the bedsheets twisted around her feet by the nature of her dreams. I mean there were reasons the blankets were wrapped around her legs just the way they were. Her leg positions and the blanket-twistings around her legs were the direct result of her dream or dreams, and her dream or dreams were the direct result of her life, of course, and this can all be logically followed (what were her anxieties that day? what colors did she see at work that affected her mood? etc.) and explained, if we're wise enough and patient enough and if we care enough to know, which maybe we don't, which maybe we shouldn't. And, too, her alarm went off when it did because of a few dozen causal series that began with the history of metallurgy and the building of the clock factory and back when my wife's father met her mother (or a thousand generations before that) and back in the government bureaucracy—she works in a politician's office—where things like working hours are decided on. I don't know how many causal series were involved—the high brass bed has to figure in, too, and the oak trees and sawmill in the history of the floor, e.g. — but when my wife's jaw struck the unyielding fact of the hardwood (heed this well, ye pantheists, as Ishmael says when he thinks of falling from the crow's nest to the deck of the *Pequod*, another ship, as you know, that went down subsequent to a collision with white) in what we call accident, the collusion (I'll let this typo stand with all its baffling and spooky possibilities) of these causal series was casual, to say the least. You get my drift.

I was thinking today about the American poet Richard Hugo, a man I was privileged to call my friend. I was thinking about him because I'd heard from another writer, another friend, who had just had most of a lung cut out, and I was remembering a phone call from Dick Hugo a couple months after he had had a lung removed. And just last week an ex-student of Dick's sent me a poem he'd written about two trout he's kept in his freezer for years now because he went fishing with Dick once and had caught these fish, so now, though he'd at one time certainly meant to, he wouldn't eat such memorial trout, or throw them away. So I've been thinking about Dick, a man who loved fishing and loved many flavors of ice cream (in one of his letters Wallace Stevens says that ice cream is an "absolute good") and loved smoking, and tonight, tired from nursing my wife and thinking about these things, going through one of my semi-insomnias out of the haze of which I am writing this and trying to be clear about accident at three in the morning, I was looking for something to read and picked up a book I'd bought a few days before my wife's dive. I'd bought this book and others because I'd had a big win at poker, more than a grand, the night before, and though when I play poker, which is not gambling but concentration, intuition, and the law of averages, I combat my psychological problems (tendencies to feel guilty for taking money from friends, to throw money away the hand after winning a big pot, to play macho instead of folding pathetic random combinations of cards, etc.), otherwise during the day I indulge my psychological problems, so I was guiltily spending my illegally-come-by lucre to at least support the American publishing industry, and this book I'd bought among others is called *Captain Maximus* by Barry Hannah. I'd read the first story in it right after buying it, and a little while ago, at two in the morning, read the second, which is called "Idaho" but turns out to be about Montana and about Hannah's acquaintance with Dick Hugo. I don't know about you, but I get interested and depressed when all these causal series keep intersecting in so casual a way. The word "casual" just knifed me again. I'd prefer "inexplicable" with its shadows. "Mysterious" would be okay, too. Even "enigmatic." Even "whimsical," which would give us some room to breathe. But the fulcrum word was "casual" in that book I reviewed back when I was a graduate school nerd and smartass.

I remember a particular letter from Dick Hugo. My wife and I had seen him and hugged him at the White House during a reception for American poets thrown by Rosalynn and Jimmy Carter in maybe 1982 or so. *Poetry* magazine had something to do with this, I think. Thanks to John Frederick Nims who actually took the time to read my books and find out what I was building, I was publishing often in *Poetry* in those days, but now there's an editor whose idea of a rejection note to me after I'd published in *Poetry* about fifteen times over the years under three other editors, was to tell me not to send so many poems at once—out of respect I'd sent six or eight new poems to him instead of the three or four some magazines I suppose call for—so *Poetry* can kiss my royal American forever or until they get an editor who worries more about serious things like what a man or woman might be building during a life's work than about how many poems he or she submits. Come to think of it, wasn't *Poetry* founded the same year the *Titanic* went down? (What do you think of those silver spittoons and *soi-disant* soggy banknote and unintelligible language-machine poems they've been bringing up from those wrecks?)

Anyway, my wife and I met Dick in the Blue Room and we hugged, and then we met others, and after the honor-guard United States Marines in dress-blues secured, as they said, the house for the President for the evening, Dick went back to poetry Montana and James Dickey went back to poetry South Carolina and Karl Shapiro went back to poetry California and Donald Hall went back to poetry New Hampshire, and Dave Smith spiraled back to wherever he was teaching at the time, etc. and soon afterward I got a letter from Dick. He said he loved being at the White House, but was glad as hell to get out of there, too, because there were too many angels there. I wish I had his letter on hand to quote, but I don't, but I still have it, but don't have it on hand because of a few other causal series which are not my subjects here. I am just not able to direct this essay to intersect directly with Dick's letter, right now. But he used that word "angels," which rhymes with "casual" and "causal." And he was probably thinking that one of the angels was Jim Wright who, by the time of the White House reception, had throat cancer. And I remember that years ago Annie and Jim Wright spent an overnight here with my wife and me. They slept down in this room where I am close to spiraling (though the thought of it diffuses it, defuses it) with anglers and angels. . . .

I keep thinking of those freezer trout. Maybe, come to think of it, it was Dick himself who landed them, and not my other friend. Yes, I think it was Dick Hugo who caught those fish that my friend Walt Pavlich took home to freeze. Walt will never throw out those fish, never, even if he throws them out, you understand. The currents of Walt's poems will always be shadowed with Hugo-trout.

In Walt's poem about those particular fish, you can see tinges of blood in the ice crystals around their gills. This makes me think of lung cancer and my other friend, who is also a fisherman. I'm talking about Ray Carver, who has had most of one of his lungs removed. He's going to recover completely, and won't mind that I mention his name and say so. "We're going to be all right," he wrote me—I think this echoes something in his old friend John Gardner (maybe in "Redemption," though I can't lay my hands on that story now either) who was suffering from cancer when he died in an accident about fifteen miles from poetry Brockport. I attended the memorial service at what had been John's boyhood church in Batavia. I remember one hymn, "Be Still My Soul," set to Sibelius—for a week I heard the whales that were singing in that music.

A few years ago Ray invited me to Port Angeles, Washington, to hit some trout with him. I haven't made it there, yet. Someday, maybe, to echo Bill Stafford, who was probably Dick Hugo's closest friend. And now I remember that I saw a Hugo drawing of a steelhead in a letter he sent to another friend, Jerry Mazzaro, back when Dick was working for Boeing, in Seattle in the olden days when he was young and things seemed clearer, things as abstract and terrible as WWII or as objective and beautiful as a steelhead, which, as I understand it, is a rainbow trout that can grow monstrous in marine waters or lakes. Jerry gave me that letter, so I can show you Dick's drawing which, now that I've gotten it out of my file-freezer, looks like it might not be a steelhead but an angel fish.

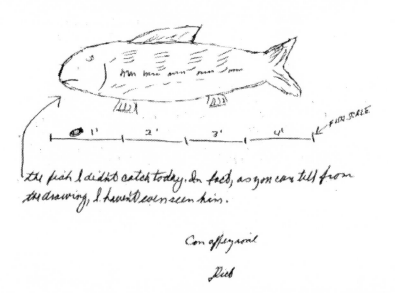

the fish I didn't catch today. In fact, as you can tell from the drawing, I haven't even seen him.

Con affezione

Dick

I wonder if Ray ever met Dick. I'll have to ask him. They would have loved one another. I draw them together forever here—it is useless to try to resist me, as Walt Whitman wrote. Dick once wrote me that he'd like to gather all his friends together in our own university of creative writing. That would be okay, I guess, though, in paradise, I'd rather have us all spaced along a trout stream running into deep pools. After a day's fishing we could gather for poker and whiskey and talk. Then, at night in the great long house or mead hall (as in a dream I had after reading John Gardner's *Grendel*) where we lived, unless we needed to sleep we could each write with one of those excellent pens—my wife got me one for Christmas—whose tip lights up so that you can write in the dark. In the great long house or mead hall, you'd just be able to see the tips of those pens writing just the right words, the right number of words in their right order. You'd look up once in a while and wonder which of those pens was Walt

Whitman's and which was Emily's and which was Dick Hugo's and which was John Gardner's, but it wouldn't matter too much because this activity was one you all did together, like fishing for those lunkers in those deep pools.   •

I have a copy of Dick's first book, *A Run of Jacks*. On a front flyleaf, he wrote out for me and my wife the book's first poem. The poem is called "Trout." "I envy dreams that see his curving / silver in the weeds," he says. Maybe my wife dreamed she was oscillating in weeds like a trout before she fell out of bed and struck her jaw on the floor because her legs were twisted in blankets like the oozy weeds that about me twist in *Billy Budd*. Later in his poem Dick writes, "And I have stared at steelhead teeth / to know him, savage in his sea-run growth." Maybe my wife saw some steelhead teeth just before she took her plunge. Or maybe she was dreaming about Ray Carver's poem "The River," a broadside of which Ray inscribed to us. Ray's poem is about being watched "by the furious eyes of king salmon," but then being touched by something we can't describe or see. "And this river . . . had suddenly / grown black and swift. / I drew breath and cast anyway. / Prayed nothing would strike." Yeah, I've made semi-light of it, but my wife was only an inch away from paralysis, her doctor said.

There's a good chance I can intersect with some sleep now. Yes, I'm going to try to get some sleep. I'll read this tomorrow and either leave it in this aspiring spiral notebook or type it up. Maybe I'll send it to Ray Carver and Walt Pavlich. Maybe I'll fold copies into Dick Hugo's *A Run of Jacks* and Ray Carver's *Ultramarine* and Walt Pavlich's *Of Things Odd and Therefore Beautiful*.

No doubt my wife is already dreaming again. Probably, her neck brace will affect her dreams and thus affect the configurations of her legs and blankets. But she'll be home from work for at least a week and won't have to turn off the alarm these next mornings, so she won't fall out of bed and almost break her neck. There are still some things I casually count on.

Open Letter to Oates

Joyce so help me today with you always half on my mind and this that might come to be I stopped at a Brockport garage sale and found a gold ring with a red gemstone late afternoon and all had left it for me, 10k, a sign, something I have to do you'll understand I can trust you of all people who knows this necessity most intensely. I'm not now with this letter where you were you said—said at Southampton 7/24/87—when you wanted desperately, after trying and trying, to write and finish your boxing book. You said you hated to think where you'd be if you hadn't managed to finish it. I wrote down your phrases you were answering questions you said "I was finished" you needed "a life-line," "life-raft." You were "sinking and drowning." "I don't even want to think what my life would be like if I hadn't finished it," "I don't feel you can ever give up on anything you've got to finish it." I felt for moments chilled and terrified—didn't anyone else there hear what you were saying?—an esthetic, a *life* that invests *everything* each time in each piece of writing no I didn't want to hear this, told you at lunch the next day wanting why (I almost know) to act like priest or father or older brother told you *no,* told you put the thing away even lie to yourself a little tell yourself you'll pick it up in five-ten years and finish it (what the hell the boxing book is fine, yes, as it did get written—got written when you took the pressure for excellence off yourself by beginning with a poor first fight between lugs, and this is how you saved yourself, metaphorically lowering the wick of the excellence-competition candle giving yourself to maybe a "sweaty despairing clinch into the ropes that provokes a fresh wave of derision"), told you not to be afraid to put things aside get out of the ring sometimes but who am I to say the way you choose to die, to live? The boxing book mosaic—so what if it didn't come to be at all?—but everything is in everything and I felt of course dense and insensitive in saying this but stand by it now because I want you near all the way in my own life need you to keep doing what you're doing and fear turmoil and explosion in you if there isn't in you some kind of compromise with that bone-white beautiful frightening commitment to each piece as though your whole creative life imagination sexual life the unfoldingness of language and story depended on whatever was at hand at the moment. Stop it goddamnit I wanted to say you don't know what you're saying or these smilers around you I need to save you from this so please promise to walk with me long walks in Brockport along the Canal before desperation sets in when a story-novel-play-essay will not come and will not *come* as could be the case next time who knows maybe even today.

No, I'm not in this letter there at that point where everything is at stake, but of course I would like this to be something to send you to say something to you to send love to you and Ray and to have my say or have a sense of having had my say at least for now as Walt said at the end of his life that he had *had his say* O paradise! and of course in the way that Dickinson as you say in your new essay was seizing Higginson "a character in a drama not of his devising" I seize you in this way, too, as Picasso you quote says "I have less and less time, and yet I have more and more to say, and what I have to say is, increasingly, something about what goes on in the movement of my thought." But we are real, too, material, aching for the "drama in the flesh" that boxing is, though even the stuff of stones is cloudy, and Hannah Stevick in *You Must Remember This* is right she reprimands her husband Lyle *of course* the tree in the forest still is a tree and still falls though there is no human witness. Do I follow me? What a writer you are in these 1987 books I am wavering, faltering, falling back, I've been struck, rocking with your punches I was smitten wanted to protect you who sat there on edge of chair leaning forward rt. leg crossed over and wrapped from shinbone down behind left, rt. instep hooked behind left Achilles tendon arms on table up to elbows hands praying then unfolding with speech hooking toward breast and heart or either hand up toward audience or fingers touching nondescript silver necklace or rhythmic click of watchband on table with speech, black sandals with straps above insteps and behind and just above heels, pink and white shorts pink/orange shirt frizzy permed hair owlglasses little sister vulnerable and fragile but the power how long would it last it must last as long as I'm alive genius by definition you said *sui generis* Faulkner and Lawrence quintessential writers writing out of their "blood and guts" you said and this is my Oates you skinny little thing how can you stay so strong you must here please eat this.

But I *am* again and again where Enid Stevick is when you write "and the thought of it like the ache in her loins gradually lightened, faded like an exercise at the piano she'd practiced so long that at a certain point merely to strike the critical note was to strike all the successive notes with no further conscious thought, only her fingers and nerve endings engaged." Enid's "it" different from my "it," but for years I've struck the "critical note" a thought of you and then the stream of unconscious thought and feeling flow but now I want to interrupt myself for once with speech. Thus this.

Let's posit then as you did as poles a novel as a twenty-year project, the planning maybe and the drafting and then the reading over and writing over the emery board and the polishing wheel and the nail clippers the pleasure and pain of going over and over something, so delicious—revision conscious, not, as you sometimes seem to say, just as tranced or semi-tranced and intuitive as the first writing that "flower of the intellect" Emerson wanted from us the poetry the wildness of the American writer he called for not I think going over and over something moving it toward we delude ourselves perfection. And the other pole writing the novel in a month or a year and soon after writing it sending it in to the publisher as you did with *You Must Remember This* you said but then within days sending in corrections and thinking of scenes to insert and wanting to do more with the book and not able to let go of it quite until the Dutton people maybe wished you said that this would be your last even a posthumous novel (heartskip from your joke) and I thought fast for a second then ferchrissakes you impatient bitch why not wait six months or a year or five and get the thing the way you want it so it stops talking to you before you send it in and make your publisher and yourself nuts (and who can blame me for thinking this I'm the twin brother from under your sternum dissolved to hair and teeth for your fiery life), but you know this but know that *the thing itself is in this* the trust in this way and this is why I know you are the most important writer we have, sometimes the best but abidingly the most important, and this is just to say this I was stricken as you spoke this blade you keep tempering, beating and shaping, sharpening, defining, designing and etching, holding against your throat.

So, between the poles of a novel as automatic writing let's say and as twenty years' maybe deepening genuine work muse-encounter or maybe delusional constipated upper-mind superficial emulate-the-anthology pieces work you keep faith (and how many tricky intricate corridors of doubt you have to blast your way through to find air to keep this faith I think of the *NYTBR* review of *You Must Remember This* so grudging and vapid no center or spirit or poetry its pedestrian assumptions blah what the fuck is going on how boring) you keep faith in that which insists itself the process whereby (your central theme maybe) the saying is said the story stories bless you. That other way is much easier—cautious, think twice before you think, make sure all criticisms that could be lodged against a piece are answered within it so the dumb bastards can hang themselves you can insert unities and convoluted slides and make sure there are no extra parts words in the machinery. And what a poise of personality it takes to work your way and not pull punches and not shadowbox with those who will shadow you with their own assumptions about what you must do. But you know the passage *what you must do* in Walt's weird (in the root sense in Melville's "weird John Brown") 1855 *Leaves* preface that stands up for the holy mad as you go on not writing a book a book at a time but writing a life making the life that can make the great book you are writing you point-woman on this mission and there like that in the fifties of *Remember* beyond the anti-art-spirit inside us I described in an essay who wants pause and triplethink his twin who tells us everything perfect let be but you in another mastership yes shoeshine and smile out there lonely but always listening to Sam Fathers whisper to Ike you shooting fast *and* slow you the swift and cunning dolphin entwined with the Aldine anchor Aldus's motto "hasten slowly" and this is the Oates story come into being and *this* to which I must pay attention as in the great Foreigner pop-gospel song "I Want to Know What Love

Is" where I need to read between the lines because (not just in case) I *will* need it when I'm older to stay alive. I don't *know* but know this is only my own periscope up from Lyle Stevick's bomb shelter seeing fast and ocean-slow seeing your landscape by my own lights my own brain within its sane grooves while you write splinter-swerves and still come back to us letting them talk, you said, letting the students talk because they need to so you can get on with your own work.

I look up at my shelves of Oates their teeming thousands of people yearning to be free in their blood lives the frenzy and automobiles and neon danger gleaming cities and lamplit gothic villages dreaming America and I say yes, yes, despite my own doubts at the same time stay with it for me, please, don't do anything differently—"Is there any mystery like who you finally turn out to *be?*"—and the creative "process" as you describe Lyle's stiffened penis "precarious as a lighted candle in a breeze" as I descend steps in *Light* holding a candle and moving as fast as the candle will allow me without blowing out, so you slipped immediately onto your finger the silver Himmler-inscribed *SS* death's-head-oval-hollow-hole-for-boot ring (Enid's "eyeballs rolling in their sockets and her lips drawn back in a death's head grimace from her teeth") that I showed you that someone had given me saying I'd know what to do with it the ring I didn't try on my own finger for a few days not because I was afraid to try it on or was superstitiously or morally somehow spooked but because I was playing at a role I thought I was supposed to play the role I condemned in Berryman I mean he had a *role* he thought the writer should play as his friend Saul Bellow said of him— while you slipped the swastika silver ring light right on right away so normal and human a person you are this action is what your best fiction is as you've always trusting yourself known, and there's a new Oates sound in the sentences in *Remember* the way you've used or not used commas like never before I mean that MacLeish said that when Keats's brother died in his arms John was not watching himself from outside seeing a poet at work holding a dying brother as though that would be a good subject, poetical, no, Keats was not split, differentiated, he grieved truly, and this is my essential Oates, you with your "spatial sense of where you're going" but that sense never locked in I think of fluid walls words making a music that means as MacLeish says and as your Lesnovitch says in *Remember* "music is only itself, you see"—watch my sentences, Frost says—using words to get at the meanings beyond words Stevens says, calculating some effects I suppose who can help it but in a wordless metacritical way in the main staring into the rooms in the red gemstone of the ring Enid stares into and saying what is felt-seen, but keeping to the blade, "Half the mantis still prays / on my scythe blade" in one of my poems and you said at Southampton "all novelists feel a sense of mortality, almost morbid—you feel you're going to die before you finish it"— and the thing is Joyce you *are* going to die of course before you finish *it* the it being the one book Oates is writing so I hear myself saying again please O.K. go on put your life on razor's edge with your next novel boxing book story biography of Tyson sequel to *Solstice* I once asked you to write whatever but know at the same time where you are centered where Buddha and Christ dwell in that center everywhere circumference nowhere you love, that you are going to die before finishing "it" before finishing a tenth of it so what the hell paradise be well even if maybe this next time God forbid the thing won't come won't come to be won't no matter how hard you try then let it go and walk with me here (you and Ray get yourselves a big goddamned Caddy like our 1980 white whale I won at poker to tool the American highways not your dangerous little piss-ant Toyota you're millionaires what are you waiting for an accident to kill you that in a bigger car would just maybe bruise you?) walk with me and Han here away from the city for breath for now we'll hold you up the three of us sister you should know by now when you put that ring on your finger you broke my heart I understand the psyche of the mobile the infinite possibilities of movement within limits the planes or birds or cars taking infinitely different courses and relations to themselves as in the image you love of those globes shaken into snow-storms while I dwell sometimes too frozen inside paperweights where there is no movement I try to stop time but you are healthy Zennist mobile-spatial.

You boxed the shit out of this new novel (it is there now knocked out of time where we can enter its scary unconsciousnesses and you are the boxer in the neutral corner now in time again until the next time) "it was all good, it was all goddamned fucking good, nothing like it," and it Oates's one book will rise to its feet again like Felix Stevick after he gets the near-to-death beating he is looking for desires it will land on its feet be careful he's in trouble so much death here so much death-in-life I was so scared when I was ten-eleven after I read a paperback book blue cover I can still see it about the Scottsboro Boys read it under blankets flashlight saw the words for blood and semen and sexually rolling eyes hard breathing gangrape for the first time so scared in my Nesconset room I couldn't sleep for days trembling praying and it's a wonder I could even years later get an erection more wonder love after that as now I love my wife and children so much, and when I read of Enid at the first fight she sees I was feeling what she did but she will land on her feet too and I'm so glad, I want to be where love is, that this time at least I wanted you to I kept saying Joyce please this time let Lyle manage to do it while Felix the basically selfish good-for-nothing can't get it up can't please let Lyle that well-meaning and suffering and thoughtfully clumsy citizen of this century despite complications and fantasy necessities and the death let him manage somehow to keep his pecker stiff and come in his wife Hannah and he does and you got there in that bomb-shelter because of your courage "the quiet nearly inaudible reply, 'I love you too.'"

The Boulder: A Journal

April 6, 1981

For about three years I'd seen the boulder a few times every summer in a hollow at the back of our acre. For a year or two I'd thought about moving it over to my cabin, rolling it to near the door where people would notice it when they came back here. This is part, again, of my odious will to impress, but as I've begun writing this now, stiffly, too aware of what I would like to make, I have resolved, past these few stiff beginning sentences, to consider what it means to consider the boulder.

I decided to locate this object outside my picture window on the side of the cabin where I write. Billy and I got it up out of its hollow yesterday morning, pushed it over briers and grasses foot by foot and got it to where I want it, in the space in front of me. . . . I just now looked up: bright sunlight falls on it for the first time in my sight, the overcast sky breaking, as though to allow me to begin this. I'm still lurching toward the present.

Overnight, a dust of snow. This morning, the snow that fell on the boulder has melted, and dark streaks of wetness run down its face.

It is a solid entity in front of me. Around it, a few feet from it, red-twig dogwood, honeysuckle bushes, and ash trees. It will not reach up into much sunlight this summer, and there will be times next winter when I'll be unable to see it at all.

I see now that its right side, which is rougher than the face toward me (a necessary correction already past my idea of its simple and singular face) is in shadow.

Somehow, my son and I have placed it perfectly. It is already a pleasing shape. The wind lifts red-twig dogwood and honeysuckle branches up and down, but the boulder stays, though sometimes it too suggests to me that we are all moving through space.

I am not happy with this beginning, but think that it is a good thing that I am unable to speak in crystals. If I were, I might try to drop the crystals in water to see if they would bloom into a poem, or would dissolve. But I have at least begun something here.

The Ohio Review 59 (1999).

April 8, 1981

This morning I've stared mindlessly at the boulder, but my eyes have drifted over to the waving bushes, and up to a passing seagull or cloud. But now I may be noticing some arced lines, rays, from the boulder's top right to bottom center, rays maybe made in its forming, as though I should have the boulder turned so that what is now its right side is its bottom. The lines now, though, when I sometimes see them because they are there, or when my eyes make these rays from accidental shadings, give a moving force to the boulder, a torque, as though it were throwing itself into the ground, or arcing away past its right shoulder. As I will now arc away from it.

April 11, 1981

The boulder is wet from rain. How far into it does water seep?

Yesterday I was back here in front of the cabin straightening the cedar sapling next to the door. I was thinking of nothing when I looked over and there was the boulder, a presence, as though an old man were sitting in a chair in that clearing and I'd suddenly come upon him. . . .

Between paragraphs, I've had to go back to the house to the toilet. The boulder does not have a rumbling stomach.

Today is scattered. I don't feel I have the time to center myself within the boulder. . . . I see so many faces in it, as I used to find faces in the grain of my childhood bed's oak headboard. Is this, then, the act of poetry itself, or just the opposite, the reduction of the itness of a thing to my own limitations, my haphazard fancy? Destructive imposition of human will upon the world, or natural and necessary analogizing? The moral lesson that everything is in everything, or the egotistical resistance to even a boulder's silence and solidity?

Eventually the boulder will crumble into gravel, and then sand, and then dust. But now I've brought the boulder into my own condition, and this time tainted it with my own death-worry. For this reason, too, I tend to keep contrasting it with the blowing bushes and flying birds and insects. If this is my genius, I will let it be. If not, I hope to know, and know the boulder.

April 16, 1981

This morning at this moment the top half of the boulder is in sunlight, the bottom half in shadow. I realize that when I stare at it I stare into the center of its shadowed half. When away from it these past several days, I pictured it darkly as the brooding presence and spirit of my acre. Is darkness any more soothing than brightness? Is there something inside me unjust to the other experience? Both light and dark are present at once, and the division is our illusion, all holy texts teach. If my first impulse here today was to call the divided boulder a brain, the movement of my pen has become one with a new thought almost ready to be known, and language is the thing itself, this boulder music . . . .

I've looked up at it again. Already the sun has taken most of the boulder, but the boulder's inner self is the balance. There are suns inside the stone, and the whole night sky, and a world where boulders bigger than itself turn toward and away from the central mind, the central light.

May 28, 1981

Since my last writing here in this Brockport cabin, I have been to South Carolina and back, to New York City and back, and then to England and back. I've often thought of the boulder.

The further I go, the closer to home . . . . I've brought back from England the kinds of remembrancers I collect: a stone shaped by neolithic human hands, a stone from the churchyard of Saint Margaret's in Knotting—I stood in its chancel where people have prayed for almost a thousand years—a bit of brick from the ruined "Palace Beautiful" of Bunyan's *Pilgrim's Progress*. I had these things in my jacket pockets when I was on the train from Kensington to Heathrow, and I had the boulder in my mind, superimposed it on the landscape. It was transparent, and the English city rushed through it, horse chestnut trees in bloom in parks, and backyards with laundry flapping from corner to corner. Now, here, the boulder is heavier, has those things inside it, keeps them until, if ever, I'll want to call them forth again.

The day before yesterday I was back here but did not write anything. I'd missed weeks of wild grasses and weeds growing toward it. Dandelion puffs were already standing tall in front of it. Already, today, after rain, those same puffs are beaten and bedraggled, one bent on its stem in front of the boulder's front face, as though mocking a mustache. The boulder is a caricature of Hitler! . . .

I'm sorry I saw and said that. Now it will be like trying not to think of a pink elephant. But there are white bird-droppings on top of the boulder, and ants, and a few flies spinning around it, and Adolf is disappearing into the boulder's history.

It's not raining now, but it's a wet day, wet as the day I visited the church at Little Gidding. A service was beginning on that Sunday morning. I stood outside in that small valley, between church and pond, in the wet heaviness of gravestones and time where, as Eliot wrote, "prayer has been valid." This England/Adolf/Eliot-boulder in front of me now—but I want an uneven balance: history drying away as I and the boulder live our own lives.

June 3, 1981

I have been reading John McPhee's *Giving Good Weight*. Just now, in his piece "The Keel of Lake Dickey," I found him talking about a run of river filled with rapids. He uses the word "bouldering," and I have come to stare at the boulder again on this bouldering day, overcast, becoming heavy toward rain.

The dandelion puff-stems have wilted around it now. Buttercups have taken their place, and a small red-twig dogwood bush, climbed by bindweed which mixes its arrow-headed leaves with the ovate leaves of the bush. The boulder sinks further into the lush undergrowth. The leaf-tongue of a weed I can't name is stretched out along a few inches of its top surface.

Today, my mind just bounces off the boulder, ricochets. Yes, it's a bouldering day, and I am ricocheting down river, waiting for rain.

June 6, 1981

I have a headache, and sunlight is flashing into my eyes from the window in front of me. Out there, today, the boulder is distinctly an Other. It is of course good health that makes us feel reciprocity and oneness, illness that separates us. My headache: too much coffee. Caffeine unnatural to my body.

(But the headache is now stopping me from tracing this thought to its end, but it has something to do, therefore, with the idea that nature never lies, and the body never lies, but becomes unhappy—displeased, of course, but also distanced from the whole cosmos when it is made to ingest anything other than what has become natural to it.)

I cannot now walk into the cool corridors of the boulder, cannot remember ever having done so, cannot imagine doing so. And won't, until I flush my body free of caffeine and other distractions. Rimbaud's "derangement of the senses": if I had my druthers, I wouldn't, except naturally, during the music of the lyric poem.

December 31, 1981

More than six months since I've picked up *The Boulder*. I didn't think I'd write here again, thought I'd scratch out or rip the used pages out of this handsome red hand-bound blank book, and save it for something else. But this was year's end, and I came back to the cabin to finish the 3rd volume of my other journal, and did, and to finish the 3rd volume of Traubel's *Whitman in Camden*, and did. I was about to go back inside, when I saw this red book, and picked it up, and began reading it. It has *something*, a kind of deliberation, a mind that even when circling or just launching out in straight thrusts has a central dark heaviness, an anchoring, a boulder under its waves.

Today, almost the whole boulder is covered with snow. Only part of its right side shows, a dark place like the opening of a cave in a mountainside of snow. If I could close my eyes and walk into that cave . . .

I don't know what, if anything, will happen to *The Boulder*. I have seen its main character in many moods over the missing months. I won't plan. I may or may not pick up this boulder over the next several months, or ever.

What is the temperature of the stone at its center, I wonder—colder or warmer than the stone at the surface, or the same? This cabin is obviously frail and tentative, as are this paper and thread of ink and the hand-and-finger-flesh that moves the pen, and the mind that moves the hand. The boulder has all time. But for now everything is coeval. Since, in fact, the boulder can't think, I'm tempted to say that in various senses it may not even *be*. I am. I am also, now, drinking the visible world's water, boulder-water, while saying the boulder is dryer than desert.

It has no story, no sword is sunk to its hilt in its stone. Except, a man and his son one day rolled it in front of the biggest window in the man's cabin, and the man began to stare at it, and then began to write of it, following himself, his brain waves into the world of the boulder. This journal, *The Boulder*, begins, now, with that story, to become itself, not personal but whole within itself. It has its frame. Never mind *me*. A man and his son rolled the boulder to its place alongside the man's cabin. Weather and mind flow against the boulder. It is there as you read. The writer has no face, was not born any particular year. The boulder stayed here within its story even when the writer traveled to Europe and saw London through the boulder. That has to be understood. *The* writer of *The Boulder* has created by now a writer who lives within the boulder's story. The writer is now satisfied, and thinks he has created his frame, his setting, that frame and setting have found themselves naturally, that should you go on from here you'll go on in the right knowledge and spirit. You now know, or should, who the "I" is, who will begin the next entry, and what the boulder is to him. This is no autobiography. Who are you, anyway?

February 16, 1982

I am back here in a melting world, but the boulder is not visible. A mound of snow covers it, but of course it's there: I believe in the continuousness of our reality, and in the reality of objects; also, who would want to steal this boulder? And in another day or two of this temperature, it will appear again. For now, rabbit tracks travel over it. I've just made the connection with the story of the princess and the pea. Rabbit, did you know? . . . Now I see bird tracks, too, which I didn't at first notice.

I seem to have forgotten the boulder's shape and color. This may mean that I never saw it, never was interested in it, or it may mean that I saw it from so many different angles and in so many different lights that I cannot now isolate it in a single image. A man can be married to a woman for fifty years, in love all this time, and when she dies he may not be able to see her vividly, and this may cause him sorrow, but shouldn't—he knew her so deeply that she was much more than body-in-time to him.

Very wet snow over the boulder. The rabbit and bird tracks enlarging— soon it will seem as though an abominable snowman walked by here and stepped on it.

The boulder, then, disappears from view in summer and in winter, the world too full for it of foliage and snow. A night's sound sleep is like a boulder. A remembered dream is like spring and fall when the boulder is most vivid and visible. . . . Yes, I could keep talking forever about something I can't see, but don't want to.

March 15, 1982

About half the boulder is visible today. I've stared at it for ten or fifteen minutes, trying not to think, but I keep seeing in it a seal's head rising out of a blow-hole, its nose to the right, its flat forehead and the top of its head on the left, its body down under the ice where I can't see it. . . . I have a small, alabaster polar bear on my desk, my favorite souvenir of a trip to Oslo many years ago. Now there is this other stone mammal outside my window, rising into a world it never knew of redbird twitter and spruce-reflected sunlight. The earth's animals seem to be dying, slowly, almost unnoticed as they disappear without protest, but surely. In a thousand years boulders will not rise up out of the ice like seals. What will the mind, then, do with the boulder? When Stein said "a rose is a rose is a rose," she made the rose red again, she said, for the first time in three hundred years of English poetry. Maybe she did. But the boulder as boulder is too heavy. It is not enough. It does not move. It does not eat fish. It does not know I am here, to be afraid of me or to menace me or to be my companion. But when I close my eyes, my seal rises to an Eskimo's spear, is dragged over the ice, is eaten, swims in his dream that night, appears in its generations to his generations, for now.

April 3, 1982

A sodden day. All the snow gone. The whole boulder visible again, washed clean by rain. Grasses at its base beaten flat.

It seems to stand taller than I ever remember it. There is more green in its stone, too, than I recall, shadings and streaks. It is as though the boulder has risen up out of the winter, as though, too, this is its season, the one time before spring flowers and running sap and chlorophyll relegate it to drabness again. On this raining and overcast day, the boulder could be looking for a mate—my mind is part of the mush the boulder is lucky not to sink completely under. . . .

April 10, 1982

A junco is hopping around the base of the boulder, disappears behind it, reappears, disappears, reappears. . . . At one moment, when it is completely behind the boulder, sunlight angles just so from behind it off to the side, and I see the junco's shadow thrown past the boulder although I cannot see the bird itself. The junco exists, blocks out light, casts an outline of itself, even when I cannot see it. Thus the junco refutes the Bishop.

I keep picturing a plant growing upward into the boulder, readying to split it into several slabs. Wishful thinking. This has been a brutal winter—it will, at last, reach 40 degrees today, and I'm waiting for a flower to break open the tomb. One forlorn weed leans weakly across its stone door.

April 16, 1982

White splotches of birdshit on the boulder, no doubt from the robins seeming to shout one another in and out of the clearing as they establish their territories. The boulder knows nothing about dignity. It has no sense of humor and can't even laugh at me as I talk about it in my language. I'm a little tired of it right now, its dumbness, smugness, solidity, impenetrability. I stare at it and impose a smiling mouth on it. The mouth mocks me doubly and then disappears into the stone.

April 23, 1982

I don't know why, can't quite see why, but the boulder appears distinctly vertical today, "tall and of a port in air." And just now a swallow glided through the boulder's clearing—the bird has a sharp silhouette, sharper than those of other birds. The weatherbeaten grasses around the boulder are standing straighter. Today, everything is reaching and ascent, not the boulder, of course, but the boulder the living world has made me see. Living things give motion to everything. Animal-shaped clouds make mountains move. Sun and wind and moving water, and the boulder, in constant motion.

June 10, 1982

Just what kind of stillness does the boulder possess? Israel has invaded Lebanon, the British are readying for their final bloody assault on Port Stanley in the Falklands, huge anti-nuclear crowds will protest Reagan's visit to West Germany today. The boulder is low in shade and half-hidden behind green weeds growing up into the light. It seems close to the earth today, not so much invulnerable as unnoticeable and stolid in its permanence. Three or four bits of sunlight reach its surface. Weed-leaves touch it, flatten against it. It deflects my gaze and itself disappears while I think of sea turtles off the Falklands and tanks treading dust in Lebanon. Eggs inside the female turtles, missiles inside the tanks. Come back, boulder, be as human as I am.

June 13, 1982

My relationship with the boulder has something to do with the essential unity of my experience. I am often amazed from day to day that I am the same person, know the same people, live in the same house, see the same kinds of foliage, amazed that I do not awaken into other worlds as different beings. The boulder is emblem of coherence, evidence that I am not flying apart, diffracted, exploded, differentiated, myriad. It exists as I do, as presence now, as memory (past), as anticipation. For me not to have the boulder would be amnesia, schizophrenia, would be for me to be hopeless and without future. If the world consisted only of snow or flowers . . . O thingness, boulder, ark, solid altar, I am whole.

July 7, 1982

A woman close to me, a woman I loved has died. I saw her in her casket a few days ago. She had been in a coma for four months, had lost half her weight, was already dead, only her eyes opening and closing reflexively. In her casket, eyes closed peacefully under her eyeglasses, her hair done in a way she would have liked it, she was one image of what she would now be for us for the rest of our lives.

Twenty-five years ago I saw a friend in his casket. His face was over-rouged, stiff and grotesque. I can see it still, am still bothered by it, but this woman's face will not decay in the grave for me. Her eyes are closed. She is resting. She is changeless now, serene and beautiful as, for all I know, she may be again. She may be with that lost soldier, that Stalingrader of hers. The seasons can no longer touch her. Snow or leaves will not obscure her face. When my children are eighty they will see their grandmother as I see her now, as we saw her a few days ago.

August 3, 1982

Today, the boulder is boring. I keep looking at it to see if anything about it is at all interesting, but in its shaded stolidity and stupidity it makes me yawn. When I yawn, air fills my lung sacs—the boulder should shatter as witness to this miracle. Last evening a firefly winked on and off a few times where the boulder was, and caught me up in its rhythm. Today, a few red honeysuckle berries shine through from among leaves above it. But the boulder does nothing, sees nothing, *is* apparently nothing but insensate matter. I should test it, should kick it to find out if it is even real, to find out if it even exists. What is its claim on this planet of lungs and fireflies and berries?

August 8, 1982

Is it possible, as I stare at it, that what I sense in the boulder is truly within it?

No, it must just be my reading, a moment in an essay by Wendell Berry in which he describes watching a great blue heron descend from the top of a hill into a valley. He sees the heron, for no apparent reason, depart from its usually dignified and stately passage to do "a backward turn in the air, a loop-the-loop." Berry concludes that this could only have been a gesture of joy, the heron's happiness with the day's beauty and fulfillment. The heron's loop-the-loop "seemed so perfectly to confirm the presence of a free nonhuman joy in the world," says Berry. Yes, I want to ascribe these feelings to animals and plants, even to insects, but to the boulder?

Is it possible, as I stare at it today, plants waving around it in the sun and wind, that it itself redefines knowledge and knows joy?

August 30, 1982

Restless this morning. I said to myself, "take a piss, and then stare at the boulder." I did. I stood outside the cabin and watered the poison ivy patch to the right of my door. Then I came inside, sat down in front of the window, and stared at the boulder, or tried to. Once in a while I've met someone hard to look at, and haven't known which eye to look into as we spoke. The boulder is today something like this. It has no central feature, one to focus my staring, so my eyes bounce off it and around its whole visible surface. Most of the foliage has thinned around it in this autumnal August weather lately, and I can see most of the boulder, but this doesn't help. Today, it is featureless, without character. . . .

I stare. I go into a daze, my gaze holding still on the boulder. A face appears to me. I did not know that I wanted a face to appear, but it does, the reddish spots of eyes apparent even if I look away and then look back again. A definite skull shape in the stone, and an open O of a mouth. No hair, but the forehead swept back. The eyes seem half-closed. I did not know that I wanted these Buddha eyes to look past me this way—they look past my left shoulder. In my daze, nowhere, my subconscious did not find for me eyes to look squarely at me, but somehow combined with the boulder to find eyes that would look past me.

Now I see another face, or the face I saw has turned to its right. I see the profile of a lion, its nose blunted, its one eye still half-closed. No, it is more like a buffalo's head. Yes. I can see it so clearly now. It is the head of a dead buffalo, foliage its shaggy mane. It is the petrified head of a buffalo.

May 20, 1983

This has been the hardest spring in coming I can ever remember. The ground still clay-cold, the boulder barely beginning to give up its winter heart.

When we are away from anything for what seems to us but isn't a long time . . .

Expeditions head out into the snow- and ice-fields of the Poles to find meteorites where they are most easily identified. One in a thousand is found to be a piece of the moon, long ago struck by a meteor and flinging this out of itself to the earth.

Moon in the night sky, pockmarked gray face, brain of the boulder . . .

Flinging this bit of itself . . .

> Had the herds roamed the moon,
> we could have seen them
> in the clear night sky,
> rivers of black light flowing
> and emptying into the sea.

May 23, 1983

I've had a good morning of writing. I've looked up to the outside once in a while—to a bumblebee against my window or to a yellow warbler in an ash branch—but haven't looked at the boulder, or even, I think, thought of it.

A thin weed in front of it, the stock cartoon joke: the boulder is a moose or elephant trying to hide behind a sapling.

Patches of sunlight on its crown on this cool June day. Honeysuckle shadows moving the sunlight around. The shadows of the leaves, I see now, resemble fish schooling somewhere on or in the boulder. Weightless fish on the surface of the boulder. Wind scatters them, but they reassemble into their school again.

The boulder as water for the shadow-fish. My mind has passed through something then, a slight (for this is play) but necessary extension of the senses. As a hand can pass through a board, a pine needle through a hand, I look up and for a moment the fish are still. Their bodies, the leaves, look nothing like them. The boulder looks nothing like whatever its essence may be.

June 8, 1983

Movement in front of me. I look up, and an orange cat is perched on the boulder. I smack my window glass. The cat looks up at me but does not leave. I get up and slam out the cabin door, hoping to spot a stone to throw at it. The cat is gone.

It used the boulder as a weapon, an elevation from which to see mice or young birds. The boulder's solidity under its feet— the ground otherwise wet around it—must have been welcome. The boulder must have seemed to the cat to be placed there in the world of earth and foliage for just those moments it smirked and waited there until that other creature banged out of its cave, angry, murderous.

That other creature wanted the cat dead, wanted, at least, to maim it so that it would drag itself back to its owner and spend the rest of its life on a rug in the corner of a kitchen or in front of a fireplace, dreaming of moments it looked down on a world that would soon give up to it something warm and filled with blood and filled with something else that would disappear when the cat crushed it in its mouth, as I crush the cat in my mouth here.

Now that other creature laughs at himself for thinking of pulverizing the boulder.

June 16, 1983

I was reading over something that I'd written a few days before, written closely, lines consisting mostly of accented syllables. What had been clear and simple to me at the time, was now strange, seemed to lose itself within itself as I read; i.e., I was not outside it, applying thoughts to it, but was absorbed in it without an outside structure with which to tame it.

This is the language of the boulder, its own words so nonhuman and imploded and self-defining that when I stare at it for a long time from that center of myself that has outgrown or at least put aside all I have "learned" of reality, when I listen to its contours, when I feel its patience and weight, I sense it not as dreaming of meaning, as I am, but as a single note or dust-bit of that natural mindlessness there in the beginning. I think of it now as talking to itself, but in a bookless language without syntactical pattern or consistency, with melody but without concept, with engagement but without past. There was never a time when it wasn't, somewhere. It is now my moon, singing to itself in that language which will survive all life on earth, the language of pure intelligence sometimes reached by the most unintelligible poetry, if ever, when we listen as though from inside the boulder.

July 29, 1983

I'm sitting at my cabin table. A dictionary stands between my eyes and the boulder. I push it into the stone, give the boulder all its words, begin to hear some of the words the boulder has fashioned from all the raw materials of English: *pressquat, peskaditch, berrytypen, cuprabloom, medrashit, scumlas, eyedict, bracktone* . . . . The words seem to be nouns. The boulder's first sounds, near as I can hear, are nouns.

July 31, 1983

Now in the evening dark if I did not know the boulder was there I would not notice it. After rain, its surfaces are the color of the air, and even when I locate it I cannot make out its edges. How can I see the boulder and yet not see its outline?

I remember once that my mother was crying. I went into her dark bedroom to ask her what was wrong. As children are when adults cry, I was confused and afraid. She lay there somewhere under covers, sobbing. I could not see her, exactly, and she didn't know that I was there until I spoke: "Mom, Mom, what's the matter?" When she turned toward me, I could see her, her shoulder and neck, her face and hair. I was of the human world. She hugged me, and I began crying with her.

If I ran through the dark unable to see the boulder, it could strike and kill me.

If I walked through the dark to the boulder, would my weeping mother be there to open its door for me?

August 18, 1983

I hadn't remembered how at mid-August the foliage would lift away from the boulder, leaving it almost free again in its clearing. At this moment it exists—to use a word that avoids the pathetic fallacy—in the double-dark of an overcast day and foliage shade. Only four or five low weeds around it.

It has a greenish tinge, maybe of microscopic moss chlorophyll-healthy after recent rains. Maybe sunlight usually bleaches the air of this tinge. Whitman thought of the cosmic color as yellow, yellow suffused with brown. The boulder, today, exists in a greenish tinge, but that other color is underneath any organic color on its surface.

The boulder seems very squat and heavy today, nothing to lift it even an inch out of its boulderness. Today, it *is*. I think for a moment of pushing it over to see if it has a face or function underneath today's heaviness, but no. I think for a moment of my brain and the boulder, but no. The world is flat for all it knows or what I may know of it.

November 4, 1983

First snow overnight. Wet, heavy, dripping this morning. The boulder has a completely new look: a honeysuckle branch has bent down on top of it, leaves and wet snow obscuring half its surfaces. I don't know whether the branch will lift away from it this winter, or whether the plant is bent permanently onto it. When the leaves drop away, the branch will . . . but that is the future. Now, the boulder seems to me to be a bush half-covered with snow and leaves but only because I am busy with it, and I am busy with it because I have not seen it clumped with leaves and snow this way before, and because I am thinking of what I did not do to get ready for this winter.

First snowfall in a village in eastern Europe. It is the nineteenth century, I think. A pine forest broods around the village, branches of green blackness between the village and the moon, trees flowing into the village streets and bending them into lanes where the houses with their small gardens get ready for winter: wood stoves warm the kitchens, sounds of latches, muffled animal sounds as the snow and pine branches bend down onto thatched roofs. I boil water in a tin cup swung over a pine fire at the hearth. My cup blackens. The coffee I will drink is bitter, strong, delicious. The boulder rolls into a field below a hill below my house.

I have so much to do, but the snow thickens. The boulder rolls to a stop, and will remain where it is, all winter, under the village snow.

February 12, 1984

Warm weather for two days after three days of snow. Walking across the snowfield just now, I noticed depressions where bits of windblown bark or leaf had warmed their ways down. In the same way, the boulder this morning has melted a two- to three-inch band of snow from around it. In the same way, ash saplings and honeysuckle bushes nearby have melted the snow from around their trunks and branches. Matter, by way of sun, melting snow. The boulder is still green-tinged, sensitive as a mayfly's egg to the warmer air and the sun around it which it circles, as I do, as spring returns.

April 14, 1984

We have had terrible weather, including one of the worst ice storms in the area's history. But now the snow is gone, the rains drained away.

I'm back from two trips. I feel scattered, but am winding down. But I am not ready for the boulder. Staring at it for maybe a half-hour, I've felt mainly a sense of its openness, now, to the light, to the inevitable season. Green-tinged birds on the honeysuckle branches above it, and now its own green is that green, not the wintergreen I noticed a month ago but a first green again, a hint of the color that will be darkening with the season. Its countenance, too, I see, is the texture of tree bark, the bark of the nearby ash trees and of the thickest honeysuckle branches. And now I see that I have been staring at a precise spot on its surface, and now I realize that this is the spot where, if it could point to itself to say where it is, it would point, as I once saw a child point to her heart when asked where she herself truly was. And now I see that the spot on the boulder I am staring at is a bit left of center, so that if I were standing inside it looking at me as I write this, and if the boulder and I were to touch our hearts, we would both be touching that same place. The boulder's heartbeat is slow and steady, very slow and very steady.

May 21, 1984

A bit of garbage has blown from somewhere to in front of the boulder. It seems to be the top of a cereal carton. It's only a few square inches of distraction, and already seems to be molding away in this wet weather.

One thin honeysuckle branch is now bending over my companion. The branch seems to curve parallel to the hard surface below it as though a force field were keeping it in place. But it, too, has power: when it lifts in a slight breeze, the boulder's upper edge seems to lift with it. I would like to allow the branch to lift the whole boulder right up out of the earth, but my mind won't let it. This reality-pull is no doubt necessary, and is something I share with the boulder itself, though not to its own degree: I can alter my state of consciousness with drugs, derange my senses, but the boulder's dense membranes are impenetrable. It would require real force to lift it. It is not fluid or malleable. It does not swim or waver. Seasickness will never distort its weight or give it visions. As long as it is there, I can't travel away from it, but nothing can be real for me without the center of gravity I share with the boulder.

The honeysuckle branch lifts away from its surface. The bit of garbage is not a lost book of a lost bible. I am here, and real.

May 28, 1984

Sometimes my eye is distracted upward from my writing desk by something, some bit of blackness, buzzing outside my window. Usually it is a bumblebee, or, at evening, a moth. Sometimes it is a leaf, and sometimes nothing. But just now, it was a hummingbird that stayed in full view maybe four feet away for about fifteen seconds. It thrust its beak into a half-dozen honeysuckle blossoms, rested for a few seconds on an ash branch, sipped another blossom, and was gone. As I looked out through the foliage to where it had buzzed away, a big black spot jerked my eye downward. The boulder.

July 2, 1987

In the years since I last picked up this journal, something has happened to the ground around the boulder. There is no longer a low growth of weeds and grasses; instead, bare earth, a few small patches of moss. Could I have done something to have caused this or has this happened naturally because of the thickening shade? All around the boulder's clearing, honeysuckle bushes push upward, ash trees push up above them. Is my soil washing away from the few heavy rains and from ice- and snowmelt each spring so that now even poison ivy does not take the ground, or is something more complex going on? Should I cart some topsoil to the area and try to plant grass or other ground cover, or should I let it be, wait and watch? Laziness, if nothing else, tells me to wait. Or, I could terrace some earth beside the cabin, slope it toward the boulder against the slope of the land.

Leaf-fall and thick leaf-fall and no raking back here, and the loss of ground cover as the trees grew—yes, natural to a new wood, I think. . . . Still . . .

Three years by three years, what is becoming of me?

I am forty-six. My eyesight has dimmed. I will soon need reading glasses. But never mind that. Never mind my left knee that sings like a cricket or my ankles that resist fluid bending. I want, I demand mind-focus, brain- and soul-singing and -bending. Or I may as well be dead.

What is this, anyway? Am I speaking to you? Will you ever be born?

Gloom and rain this July morning, leaves trembling around me, rain-sounds like shadow-weights on my cabin room. July morning darkness, and rain.

A moss- and rain-patterned monkey-face in the boulder. Now a dog's face, as clear, almost the caricature of a dog. When I look up again, a wink, a prolonged wink. . . . But now, again, the mutt dissolves into an owl-beaked Ur-face, now into a figure worn and robed and headless, inviting me into its fat belly. . . . Welcome home, please, to a few moments of namelessness. . . .

But now, startling me, as though I should always have known, the whole boulder in profile as a massive primitive head, its forehead and right eye, its nose and bearded lips and chin, its right ear protruding—all so definite that no light or weather or seasonal change could alter him again. Welcome, my brother. I was lonely, and you have risen up into my clearing, up to the base of your neck. Was it always you? You've got a contusion on the back of your head, but no son-of-a-bitch can harm you, not even erosion. Even poison ivy has run from you, or you have eaten him as you have eaten my east-west questions, and the past three years.

June 1, 1988

I have taken the table out of my cabin. It was when I sat at the table that I stared at the boulder. Now, when I sit in either of the easy chairs, my head is about even with the windowsill, and I cannot see that heavy head under the honeysuckle and ash. But I see it by thinking of it. Today, it anchors my acre as I imagine its neck, shoulders, torso, legs, beneath it, its body in the ground, stone, as is its head, but with a heart, a diamond from a billion years of pressed ferns, beating under its breastbone. Old man of Brockport, are you chained there? If you were able to pull yourself out of the ground, would you slam your fist into my temple until I knew?

I lift up on my easy chair's arms to see the boulder. Birdlime streaks his chin.

Time was when my stone man's pet was a pterodactyl. The world has evolved to black-capped chickadees and robins, and fools, some of them holy, as you or I may be.

July 11, 1988

No rain for six to eight weeks. The heat had begun to sap the boulder's color and strength. But today, a thunder shower is bursting down through the leaves to that parched stonehead. I want to hear him sigh in relief, but his warrior's heart won't allow him. I wink at him for confirmation, but he will give me no satisfaction. He is all helmet and breastplate. But the siege has lifted, and he knows it. His every internal particle dances like a victorious drunk around a campfire after the fall of Troy, or Masada.

June 14, 1989

Today, I don't care about the boulder, and it doesn't care about me. One of those two declarations is true, but maybe it's not the one I think it is. I have made four—this is the fifth—statements already, and have just begun. That last statement was the sixth, and this is the eighth. I'm right in this. This statement is the tenth.

So go our days, avowals and launched filaments, while the boulder abides. In this wettest of all springs since at least 1909, it is prepared for anything. Miniature lagoons have formed in what only appears to be its smooth surface, and microscopic creatures swim from shore to shore. Surf's up!

Overcast today, gray as the boulder, but ultraviolet light is still strong, and it's a good day to burn.

June 28, 1989

This morning, after weeks—maybe even a year—of worry, the boulder is off my back. It weighed as much as forty poets as I tried to carry it to 2000. Now I have decided to drop it, to let it sink away behind me into the earth. Boulder of faith and unfaith, of mixed motives, of details and problems and smug ownership, sink away in all that mud of the past behind my back. Boulder, I wanted to carry you into the future, but human news appalls. I'm straightening up. I need to do some serious thinking. You're to become part of the literary compost. . . .

July 23, 1989

I'm back from two weeks away under the Southampton windmill of people and words and laughs and muck and a grungy motel room. I walked back here to the cabin this morning carrying a boulder of mail and loose ends. I sit in this easy chair. Quiet begins quieting me. The boulder outside my window hasn't moved. One sunspot on its face. An eye. If I dive into that eye I would come to where I want to be again. This paragraph is a beginning. I'm home. The boulder of things to do was just an illusion. This other boulder winks with shade, and knows everything worth knowing until that other time to come. . . .

April 26, 1990

First cabin-morning after the long winter. But what's up? My slippers are missing, and the small electric heater I bought last fall. And the heavy red flannel shirt I keep back here. And the Porky Pig glass filled with cheap pens. And a couple shelves of paper and envelopes. I'm pissed. Who has been messing around here in the dark? This is no kid's prank—useful things were taken. No busted windows or other damage. The thief could have been here yesterday, or months ago. I've walked by the cabin, and have glanced in, but haven't stepped inside for months until this warm and green-bursting morning.

So, there is someone in this village who needed slippers, a flannel shirt, a heater—and paper and envelopes. I do not lock the door, thinking someone who wanted in would break a window, and maybe I'm right. The thief gave me these emotions this morning, and I need to experience them with an effect of Zen delight, go with them, live them as part of the parabola of the eternal present, and I do, almost. No one can steal from me what I don't own. The boulder hasn't budged. Some watchdog. I could pick it up and play it between my ears as though it were a videotape to see the thief at work, but I won't.

Maybe some books are missing, too, but not this blank book which has been here in this 8' x 12' cabin for ten springs now. Sorry as it is, I wouldn't have wanted to lose it, it's true. This place would have lost part of its placeness for as long as there will be a Brockport. Slowly but surely, I'd better push this book into the boulder's forehead so it can stay hidden there while time out of time I keep writing in it.

June 27, 1990

A dead branch has fallen into the small clearing in front of the boulder. The ash trees around this cabin have to grow tall fast to get their share of sunlight, and they shut off their lower branches as they do, the way we turn off the heat and close the doors of unused rooms during the winter. No, the figure breaks down, but never mind.

Once in a while I walk this acre and pick up such deadwood. Before falling from the tree, such a branch served as bird-perch and insect haven for several years. Now, barkless, it will become part of a pile at property's edge— making life a little more secure for rabbits and mice—before it rots and crumbles away. After a few years, I poke at these piles with my rake and they disintegrate into garden mulch.

I share my time on earth with these piles of branches. They disintegrate into shapelessness, into soil, as I grow old. They are a slowed-down version of the annual appearance and disappearance of the leaves. Most of the trees around me will outlast me, but their growth rings will record the sunlight and rain that I knew. There's a Jack Matthews essay called "The Bracketing of Time" about "chronologies," books whose columns list synchronous events—and some of these concurrences are surprising and edifying—and I am bracketed in time with these living things on this acre, the trees and rabbits, the mice in my garden shed, the toads that are plentiful this year, even the insects, ephemerae whose lives are like eye-blinks. But the boulder . . .

The boulder came into being in a bracket of time unimaginably distant, so remote that nothing in my mind—human minds did not exist, nothing organic existed—connects with it, vibrates with it the way a willow twig in the fingers of a dowser will dip toward an underground spring. By the time the boulder disintegrates to dust, there may be only a rumor among the stars that this civilization of which I'm part ever was, or there may not be even the slightest whisper. Brockport will be a shadow, maybe, rippling across a far galaxy, or nothing at all. Unless . . . unless in fact a sensible chronology would bracket the boulder with god whose bracket is the whole book of the universe, myself and the ash branch included, all othernesses of persons and events subsumed like the illusions they so far only sometimes, during my most illumined moments, seem to be. Eternity is now.

March 29, 1991

Three weeks after a tremendous ice storm, the worst natural disaster, it is said, in the history of New York State, the boulder's aspect is unchanged. It is high and dry this morning in spring sunlight, oblivious, of course, of course not, to the several chainsaws grinding away from different directions. In pre-history, it sensed/recorded more extreme weather many times. Did the great glacier, as it advanced, push the boulder here, or pull it here as it receded? Was there desolation out in front or behind the timeless inexorable glacier, or were lizards and larks and dragonflies living along its edge? The boulder has almost all time not to answer me, and will be here for the next ice age which might begin within a mere few thousand years, or might already have begun—there being no contraries in the mind of god—with global warming.

June 20, 1991

In one of the vignettes in his *Moments of Reprieve* Primo Levi, who committed suicide some time after this book was published, remembers taking refuge in a pipe from an Auschwitz rainstorm. In the pipe with a man named Tischler—& my own father was a *Tischler*, a carpenter—he enjoyed conversation about God & Evil & Lilith—and then was the recipient of a wonderful gift, a slice of apple, the one time in a year of imprisonment that he tasted fruit. In another vignette, he is down in a cistern reading a forbidden & miraculous letter from his mother by the dull gleam from the one bulb of that subterranean world, when the young friend with him pulls a radish from his pocket and gives it to him. Gifts of a slice of apple, of a radish. But, in the end, Levi's inheritance from the Nazis, & the inheritance of those Jewish writers I'm reading in David Rosenberg's *Testimony* collection, and even mine when I am most human & inside history with my heart and soul, is a boulder in the chest, another in the brain.

Today, this perfect day on the cusp of summer, my irony boulder squats smug & malevolent in its shadowy clearing under honeysuckle. Primo, you were a chemist, weren't you? But even you couldn't concoct, in the end, an antidote for Holocaust stone.

August 23, 1991

How foolish of me it is to look up once in a while from my easy chair to see if the boulder is still there. Of course it's there, and is going to be, until the next owner of this acre decides it's in the way & rolls it somewhere else. Then air will close in where the boulder was, and the book of the boulder will turn another vellum page.

Of course it's there, but sometimes when I stare at it for a long time it disappears, or becomes a smudge in the shadowy landscape. It's as much there behind my closed eyes, too, when my eyes close after long-staring. And that's the place I want to enter when I die from this planet. And if I'm able to do that, I'll be able to walk into and through the boulder to where the universe begins without beginning and ends without ending.

June 9, 1993

Now, after a dozen years, the boulder is part of its place as though it had never been anywhere else. Successive winters and then spring thaws have lowered its jawline, moss cups it, today it is part of the world's wet and blowing blackgreen shadows as it has not been for me before. Yes, I've been afraid of time passing, of dying, so have wanted to resist the boulder, to make it something that it isn't. But now, here, there is nothing permanent about it, nothing to fear. It has its own tenacious but evanescent being in its place, my place, as does any insect, though it lacks fear, lungs, love, a beating heart. To live out of time where living is best lived, is to let go of it. During its transformation, it can keep *me* in *its* bouldery thoughts. . . .

With Me Far Away: A Memoir

I

I sit in my Brockport cabin this August morning shuffling a sheaf of my poems and sections of memoir, writing in this notebook and drinking coffee from a mug marked "Chu Lai RVN." The mug was a gift from my brother-in-law who was a Marine pilot in Viet Nam.

Birdsong floats in through the screen door—a cardinal declaring its territory, the twitter of sparrows. The mug's gold rim gleams. Now I see my frequent visitor, a catbird, cocking its head to look in on me. Of all birds, it seems always the most curious, and seems to enjoy my presence here. I like its black head, blacker eye, gray-black body, and the twirling way it moves in the branches, moving from window to window to see me from all angles.

Over my right shoulder a pair of binoculars hangs from a nail. Foliage is thick and close around the cabin right now, and I haven't used the binoculars in a long time. I lift them down. They are marked "*Dienstglas*," duty glasses, and were probably issued to a German officer in WWII. I bought them at a country auction for $5. They were probably a souvenir brought back from somewhere along the Rhine. I imagine the American soldier, now back to being a farmer, plowing, thinking about those other days. At the auction, forty years later, he sits on a milking stool in the door of his barn, lost in thought and pipe-smoke, as the rest of us rummage among and buy the things by which he has remembered.

I sip coffee. The catbird is out of sight now, mewing somewhere behind the cabin. I focus the binoculars on a spot in the foliage where sunlight bursts in on a red twig dogwood bush. Its branches, this time of year, tend toward a yellowish green, but in autumn will turn an amberish red and hold that color all winter. The bush is being overtaken by bindweed, which climbs and pulls down

---

Published as a limited edition illustrated by John DePol (Roslyn, NY: The Stone House P, 1994). Previously, sections appeared in *Prose, Strivers' Row, Our Original Sins*, and *The Southwestern Review*, and/or in *Noise in the Trees* (New York: Vanguard P, 1974), and/or *Long Island Light* (New York: Vanguard P, 1979). Section LI appeared as a holiday card in 1985, and the poem "Americans" as a Memorial Day broadside in 1989 (Concord, NH: William B. Ewert).

milkweed and other small plants here, and forces the ash trees upward, choking off lower branches. Bindweed, with its arrow-shaped leaves, climbs no higher, though, than about ten feet by season's end, and begins to climb again each spring all the way from the ground, does not renew itself along its old vines as do wild grapevine and memory.

The bush I've singled out does not know, of course, according to any human concept we have of knowledge, that it is being observed. It is there in the August foliage in a happenstance of sunlight. It makes a million slight moves in soft wind. It supports the bindweed, whose morning glory-like blossoms are already closed, and bears clusters of its own waxy-white berries. There are dozens of such bushes around my cabin.

This is all a fragmented music for me this morning—Viet Nam, WWII, arrow-headed leaves. I have lived a life of luck, have not spent one night in a bomb shelter. I hang the binoculars back on their nail. I hear the catbird. I laugh inside myself, now knowing what this is all about, and what has happened to me—as though I didn't know all along what was at the center of the morning through which I've been moving.

> Slate-gray in an ash branch,
>   a catbird sings the black top of his head off.
>   He warbles a disconnected song.
>   It has no past. It never returns.
>
> It searches for melody, almost finding it,
>   but going on, for the flow of it.
>   Is this enough, then,
>
> song empty of obsession,
>   this warbling not knowing where it's going?
>   Between infrequent mews,
>   the catbird is busy singing.
>
> He is slim, agile, the color of a mouse
>   in the ash branch. This morning,
>   my own warbling is broken,
>
> ending without repeating its beginning,
>   its almost-remembered meaning.

II

I have not walked this way for a long time, but I am not surprised to find myself walking here.

I have not, I consider, walked this way for ten years. The shops in Saint James have not changed, and the elms, at this time just before evening sets in, still throw a weak shade on the sidewalk.

The air is cool. It is spring. I am wearing baggy black pants, and I have the feeling that my shoelaces are untied or not tied tightly enough. My walk is awkward.

There are no cars on the street or people on the sidewalks. I tighten my belt a notch and hitch up my pants. My undershirt keeps pulling up, pulling my shirt out of my pants.

In front of her father's shop on the corner, his barber pole, already dimly lit against the evening, spirals its red and white stripes. Moths batter its glass cylinder. We must receive the light, I say to myself, we must not attack.

I see myself in one of the shop's windows, and see myself again in the mirror behind the cash register between the chairs. He would say I needed a haircut.

His register gleams softly, silver and black. I wonder if what she told me is true: that each day Gregersen descends with his proceeds to his cellar to hide the money in a tin can behind a loose cement block.

I have lost my shoes. I am obsessed with the idea that I have lost my shoes, that they must be somewhere in the Gregersens' apartment behind the shop. They have no right to my shoes. I must get them back. I move around the corner and enter their garage. They still have the green Oldsmobile. I open the door of their car that leads to their kitchen. Remembering that there are three steps up, I am careful.

Night has fallen. I stand in their kitchen and can hear crickets singing from under the stones of the neat flowerbeds outside. I remember passing a florist's shop down the street. Only calendars gathered dust on the display shelves in its window, their monthly flowers flat and dirty in the dull light.

I make my way to her room. She is asleep on a dark blue bedspread that drapes to the floor. Her face is turned to the wall. Somewhere in the house water trickles in the plumbing.

I can just see the heels of my shoes jutting out from under her bed. As I reach for them she turns over, her hair yellow in the soft light. Pretending I do not know that she sees me, wondering if she will give me away, I pick up my shoes and leave.

I am outside, cutting across their lawn, my shoes still in my hands. The grass is wet. I am almost to the row of poplars that lines the sidewalk when the screen door opens and Gregersen shouts:

...I told you never, you, never to bring my daughter home this late. I warned you. I've called the police. Who do you think you are?

The door slams. Shutters on an upstairs window open and Karen leans out. She is wearing a white blouse. I am glad it is dark. My hair is too long and my pants are baggy. She slams the shutters.

...Karen, don't, I say.

She opens the screen door. She points a finger and shouts at me.

...I told you it was all over I told you. What did you think? Leave me alone stay away....

My son is with me. It is too damp here for him. I slip my shoes over my wet socks and, without bothering to tie them, lift him up. We brush through poplars into the deep shade of elms over the sidewalk. I walk toward home as fast as I can.

III

To the right, in a clear area with a sandy bottom, I saw a pair of green swordtails, the male following the female very closely, skimming above her, folding himself to her sides, nosing beneath her. These were tropical fish, and I was surprised to find them here. I'd never thought that green swordtails were particularly beautiful, but these were lucent, their squiggled trail glimmering ghost-green behind them. I wanted them for my aquarium. But there was some kind of problem. Maybe the pail I wanted to place them in was filled with cement. I can't quite remember. The dream goes dark.

When I ask myself if I was really the child of ponds that I've thought of myself as being, I realize that, in truth, I was. I played baseball and went swimming, but always with others. But at the ponds I was alone, intent on ripples from a frog's throat-pulse; the shadow of a sunfish crossing its circular sand nest; the brightening pink of a patch of mud as tube worms extended themselves; a water snake's furrow a hundred feet away, its sign as certain as the V of migrating geese. I knelt to stare at pin-point snails on the stems of lily pads, watched dragonflies dive to dip their abdomens into the water (each time, as I know now, releasing a single invisible egg).

The last part of my senior year in high school and the following summer, because he was in the service, I had use of my older brother's car. After dates, Karen and I parked at the ponds. In the darkness and the night sounds, we lay on the front seat, my head on the elbow-rest of the right door, my legs bent at the knees and angled up against the back of the driver's seat. We kissed and rubbed against one another for hours. And one evening, when the perfume of the night air was perfect, as we lay pressed together on the seat, I trembled and came while kissing her, and she knew, and kept kissing me, and a few minutes later I came again.

That night, before driving home, we got out of the car so that I could tuck in my shirt and she could smooth her rumpled skirt. We didn't, of course, mention what had happened. She leaned against me, and I leaned back against the car as the pond's moonlit scents mixed in for me with what I thought was love for this girl, this Island, soon lost.

IV

The histories do not agree, but this is true enough to serve: in the seventeenth century Richard Smith, a farmer, was given by the Indians, in return for some guns and cattle and trinkets, as much land as he could encircle, riding bareback on a bull, in one day. Today Smith's bull stands, cast in bronze, glinting maple shade from its horns, just off the Jericho Turnpike on the western edge of Smithtown, where Smith began and ended his ride. One summer, working for the town's highway department, I cut brush along Bread-and-Cheese Hollow Road—where Smith stopped for lunch.

Nesconset, where I grew up, and Saint James are two of the villages included in Smithtown Township. At Saint James, a windmill, a Long Island landmark that made its way across the country on postcards, cast its shadow on the harbor's water. The last hundred yards to the mill was a dirt road.

A door swung open on rusty hinges. I'd stand inside, letting my eyes adjust to the dark, until a well took shape in front of me. Then the stairs, about twenty sets bolted to the walls and curving upward at angles. All the way up, cobwebs and spiderwebs, ropes and, somehow, branches swayed from a thatch of beams that blocked most of the light that made its way down from the door that opened to the mill's platform. The windmill was alive. Its steps and banisters creaked like bones. Small windows on the landings were its eyes. The wind whistled through broken wooden shingles.

Most of the Island's ponds, once accessible only by paths through scrub-oak woods, have been bulldozed in. Children ride their bicycles on sidewalks in front of homes built directly above what was once Shenandoah Pond in Nesconset. Also in Nesconset, Grove is gone, and most of Spectacle, and most of Gibbs Pond.

In Smithtown, Miller's is almost gone, the pond behind which a girl was murdered in 1953. She was seen leaving school with a tall, blond boy on her last afternoon. We were lined up in the halls of our schools for inspection by the teacher who had last seen the girl and her probable killer. But the case was never solved. I pictured her as having fallen asleep in the woods. I imagined a turtle, big as a house, rising from the mud of Miller's and slashing the girl's throat with its claws before lumbering back to its ooze. With red eyes it looked up through the dark water at its roof of lily pads.

My father had built his woodworking shop behind our house, but my three brothers and I were not as interested in his lathes and ripsaws or the stairs, windows, cabinets he built as we were in everything that went on at Wenzel's farm, adjacent to our property. Wenzel raised sheep, chickens, pheasants, rabbits. The earth in his pheasant pens was scattered with purple and gold feathers; the earth under the elm's limb from which he hung his slaughtered sheep, and the earth under his chicken gallows, was a deep red, almost black; the earth on Wenzel's farm smelled like manure and crushed apples and newly mown grass and the sweet, acrid body of a snake in your hands.

And of these things, Walt Whitman's Island wove the song of myself: the blue shadows of jays streaking across the shades of my bedroom at first light; a black ball of newly hatched catfish at Gibbs Pond; a lamb, a red and blue translucence, swaying from a branch, its nose dripping blood; a spider, with a scarlet gash on its body, hanging from a single strand of web behind my father's shop; the three dogwoods on our front lawn covered with pink blossoms and as many bees; initials cut in the tar roads, in the shingles of the mill, on the backs of box turtles, in the bark of trees; a cardinal that hurtled its body through the screen of a window beside my bed; a cow-bell, high up in an oak, clanking wildly in a hurricane wind; a cherry tree that rained its fruit on our roof; the gulls and V's of geese that passed overhead, washed in the yellow light; the long-fingered catalpas that lined our driveway.

V

My stomach seems to empty and fill again as I drive over the humps and into the valleys of Gibbs Pond Road. It is dusk. The sky is shredded pink in the direction of Lake Ronkonkoma, which I plan to circle before driving home. I turn on the low beams, which make only vague impressions on the tar road. Just past the pond I cross Nichols Road and enter the aura of the six huge elms that shadow the corner.

I am driving very slowly. The car's windows are open and I can hear frogs serenading their log king, and small animals rustling the brush.

Three people are walking toward me on the other side of the road. I pass them under the elms. She is in the middle, and waves. Her father is with her, and another man. I do not think it strange that they would be walking along Gibbs Pond Road. It seems inevitable.

I do not wave, but pass them; then, regretting that I did not wave, I tap my horn ring, which emits a sound as of one more frog. I can hear everything. The hairs at the nape of my neck are bristling, and my ears seem to draw back and grow larger.

I am glad she saw the left side of my face, the side of my head where I comb my hair straight back, the side of myself I like best. I can still hear the three of them. They are laughing.

I look into my rearview mirror. She has not turned. She is wearing a white blouse, and, if my eyes see correctly into the pools of darkness out of which the elms seem to be growing, she is holding hands with the other man.

A car is approaching from the direction of the lake. For a moment I concentrate on its headlights to make sure we will not collide, and once it has passed I slow down. My car is halfway up the rise of a small hump, and I slow down to a crawl.

I can see the other car's tail lights in my rearview mirror. It stops under the elms. I brake. I hear shouting, and then hear her scream. Looking back, I can see that the driver's door is open and that a dim light is on in the car. Its headlights are off.

I lift the automatic shift into reverse and, looking over my right shoulder at the whitish sand edge of the road, begin to back my car toward the shadows of the elms. I am aware of the noise of the woods above the hum of my car, and of an increasing hysteria of crickets.

...Watch it, someone yells, watch...

The rear wheels of my car whine in mud and then slip backward into the pond. In a moment I am completely under water, holding my breath and trying to force the door open against the dark water and air. My strength seems useless. You fool, you fool, I say to myself. The door is jammed against the thick roots of lily pads and against elm branches.

VI

My wife and I had spent our honeymoon in the Smokies and were driving north to Athens, Ohio, where we were to attend graduate school together.

The Tennessee and Kentucky roads we traveled were twisted and slow. More than once we'd pass over railroad tracks and a hundred feet further have to pass over the same tracks again. I thought of the spiral ascent to a tower in the mountains not far from Gatlinburg that overlooked several states.

Gatlinburg: we walked through candle shops and knickknack shops, ate fine meals topped off with our first pecan pie, played miniature golf a few feet from main street, jumped on trampolines, dropped paint on a piece of cardboard that spun on a wheel. Our cabin at the motel was called Mountain Laurel.

We had met at Brockport four years before. I taught a year of high school English while Han finished college. Our marriage date, 7/7/62, is engraved inside our rings.

The road back from Gatlinburg was torturous. And my wife was afraid of the mountains. She'd talk to herself aloud and plan the perfect crime: we'd be shot, robbed, and buried, and our car hidden forever in one of the thousands of earth-colored barns behind rows of tall trees far off the roads.... When dark came on she sat quietly and watched the gas gauge.

Less than a year later, just before my Master's comprehensives, our son was born. We moved to Cortland, New York, where I taught at the college for two years, and then returned to Athens. Our daughter was born just before my Ph.D. examinations. We left for the good life once and for all in August of 1967. I'd waited as long as I could to hear about a job at Bennington (Theodore Roethke's old job, I fancied), but then decided to return to Brockport where we knew some people and where Mary Jane Holmes had written her thirty-nine or however many romances.

In Athens, I'd been closest to Richard Purdum, who directed my dissertation. Often, when we sat in his office without talking, silence would hum. We would both look at the floor and wait for a feeling to find its words. He would tell me of his insomnias, and of how he was progressing with the game he played: lying awake at night he'd organize the chaos of retinal imagery that danced against his eyelids. He'd gotten to the point where he could make the geometric shape he concentrated on appear, and in the desired color.

His poet was the Wallace Stevens of the deliberately believed-in fiction. He would read Stevens's *Collected Poems* through and then begin again. He'd been doing this for years.

He was a small, thin, gentle man, and wonderfully sad. I could recognize his head-down shuffle across campus. When, in the halls or on the brick walks of the university, we approached each other, we would slow down, stop, and sometimes talk or sometimes just exchange helloes and move on. He might say, "Hey, I think I know what 'A Rabbit as King of the Ghosts' means," and tell me, finishing his explication with a series of "buts" that served to leave him where he began. Whenever I left him I was dizzy and he was entangled in speculations that would result in another sleepless night. What carried him through his depressions and always would, I thought, was his sense of humor. When our eyes met, the expression on his face would seem to say that we were taking ourselves too seriously.

Two months after leaving graduate school I received a letter from him; six months later he was dead. He'd been on sabbatical, visiting relatives in Michigan. He'd bought a gun, and at break of spring, in a wooded area as wild as the old Island must have been and so remote his body was not found for weeks, had shot himself.

In a way I am guilty for not hearing the despair of the only letter I received from him. But now I also realize that his voice was the same as I'd known it over the years. In the letter, dated October 27, 1967, he wrote: "The weather has definitely changed this morning. It has been colder, there has been wind, I've been as blue, but the sound of the wind in today's trees is different, and I don't want to make out the words; so this letter will no doubt say nothing .... "

VII

And I am back again, this time walking along the south shore at Shinnecock Inlet. I am with Werner, my older brother. The tide is out. Skate eggs shine in the sand; sandfleas hum inside upside-down horseshoe crabs. I pick up a small piece of driftwood so soft I can press my fingerprints into it, can see the whorls of my fingerprints against the grain of the wood.

We climb up on a jetty. Somehow, I've seen it before, from above, reaching out into the ocean like a spidercrab claw. Its rocks are fitted together like a jigsaw puzzle, like the continents pushed together on a map, becoming again the original land mass. We walk along the top, moving from one boulder to another. Shells and kelp and wine bottles dropped by fishermen are wedged among the rocks.

Straddling two rocks, I see something white in the shadows and crevices below me, maybe the belly of a fish, maybe a shell or a piece of paper or plastic or a lure snagged at high tide. But then I bend my neck and can't see it. But there are wide steps leading down among the rocks. I take off my shoes and descend, step after step, past walls of rock and sand, past the jawbone arches of whales scrawled with a nineteenth-century script I cannot read, past a wall of water, past a wall of mist I walk through like a ghost. My feet find the steps by themselves. My brother is calling:

...Bill, Bill, where are you going? What are you doing?

Then I am below his voice. The mist rolls away. I have reached bottom. I am in a cave floored with white sand, its ceiling supported by fluted columns of bone. I have not moved, but I have lost the stairs. I am alone in the cave, now wandering the floor of the Island, calling out, crying for someone to tell me where I am.

VIII

Toward the end of the summer of 1957 after my last year of high school, I developed a strain of encephalitis. At first, my parents thought I'd contracted polio, then were relieved that I hadn't, and then, when they found out what encephalitis could do, they became frightened again. In the beginning I couldn't move my legs, and I lost hope quickly. But my legs came back to life.

My recovery began, or at least my spirits revived, when I learned that the neurosurgeon who came around to stick pins into my legs was the doctor who worked with Roy Campanella after the Dodger catcher's automobile accident. Maybe the pros were still interested, I thought. Maybe they hadn't signed me at their tryouts that spring because I was only sixteen. I remember asking the doctor if I'd ever be able to play ball again. He said we'd see.

She visited me often, though I'm sure now that her affection for me had already grown thin and her visits to the hospital served to satisfy only her senses of martyrdom and duty. I was six feet four inches tall and down, at one point, to a hundred and twenty pounds. I was too listless to comb my hair and lay for hours listening to my records, especially the plaintive wail of a song by the Tune Weavers.

Before I left the Port Jefferson hospital I'd grown close to several of the nuns, one especially. Sister Mary Joseph, her neck rucked as a turtle's or the skin on your elbow, made an effort to combat my loss of weight with several orders of toast and jelly a day. Her old age and implacability helped me keep my own problems in perspective. It is in their eyes that old people seem to hold the difficult knowledge absorbed during their long lives. Her irises were gray and bottomless as an animal's.

When I drive along the Hudson River, or on the Skyway into Buffalo, or along the Jericho through Smithtown Branch where great locusts shade the traffic, I think of how wild and beautiful the Island must have been. Is it inhuman to say there is no such thing as an improvement of nature? Just as cold is simply the absence of heat, and there is, so far as we know, no such thing as absolute cold, we ought to measure our architecture, our rearrangement of the landscape, in terms of how little it offends nature, which is right, perfect, unfathomable, rhythm within rhythm. Were we all to disappear, lily of the valley and wild roses would break through the pavement of Times Square. Our bridges would fall into the rivers and be buried like the skeletons of beasts. Smith's bull, if there is spirit in metal, would stamp its hoofs as the old Island again broke into being.

Deep in the woods behind our Nesconset house a foundation was sinking, ferns were growing up through the two-by-fours and shingles spread about, and gnarled apple trees were merging with the underbrush; and when I left the hospital that summer and walked through the woods again I thought on these things. I fancied myself as powerful as Gulliver among the little people, and force-fed every human being on earth a capsule of poison. To allow the world to live, I was ready to die, if only everyone else would die at the same time.

IX

The movie house in which I am sitting is cavernous. Bats hang from its ceiling like black gourds. The air is cool and smells slightly of lilac and fern.

The screen is a square of white in the dark. A shaft of white light appears over my head and then takes color. The screen's white curtains part. She is walking on the sidewalk in front of her father's barbershop. Music begins, a sad ballad by The Platters. She walks across the street and waits at the curb. The music stops.

She is wearing her graduation robe. The robe's sleeves fill out in a wind that also blows her hair back from her forehead. The only sound is the sound of leaves in the maples behind her. The film stands still for a long time as she waits by the curb. The film jumps and her sleeves again fill with wind. She waves. I pretend she is not waving to me.

In this melodrama without end, a hearse stops in front of her and blocks her from my sight. As the hearse pulls away I can just make out her profile past the flowers and through the glare of the back window. I don't know if she is inside or is still standing by the curb.

The camera shifts across the street to the window of her father's shop. I do not see myself, but see a reflection of myself in the glass. My hands are in my pockets. The camera moves left and I see myself, from the back, standing with my hands in my pockets. I turn around and see myself sitting in the dark. We are both crying.

X

I lived an archetypal American boyhood, but my Island, at first Huckleberry Finn's territory, is now, certainly, Willy Loman's territory, land of the big sale and the big kill. Oaks over the Smithtown Bypass have hollows in their trunks where the gunshots of a gangland rub-out still reverberate. All over the Island, softballs hit foul drop through trees around lighted diamonds behind which knives flash and muggers proliferate.

June 1971. Suffolk has changed more rapidly and violently than anywhere else in the country. It would take generations to see these changes somewhere else.

Maybe because this is a land that brings in topsoil by trucks rather than time, Wenzel grows strange. I cut back some weeds along his fence this morning. He watched me work and then walked over. Wenzel had lived here ten years before we moved here. He once had thirty acres of woods, thousands of chickens and pheasants, dozens of sheep, but ended up as a salesman in J. C. Penney's. He had whistled as he worked his farm, the hair on his shoulders glistening. He would rub manure on his chest and tell my brothers and me that the earth cured everything from warts to Weltschmerz. Wenzel, who was the happiest, most self-sufficient man I had ever known, who years ago had made an egg run to New York City every Friday night, is now afraid of the traffic, the new neighbors, the spotlights in the sky announcing new shopping centers. And he is now a foxhole convert.

Wenzel has gotten old and, as an old German saying goes, "*Wenn Leute alt werden, werden sie wunderlich*" (when people grow old, they get odd). This morning he lectured me on the impending return of Christ. He told me that I had nothing unless I had Christ. He shouted hallelujahs so loud that my mother's cat ran off. Wenzel has gotten himself some religion in a hurry. He spends his time rocking in his back yard and laughing out loud: They are all fools rushing by in the streets out there past his hedges. Heaven is Wenzel's personal pastoral. Heaven shall restore the things that once were.

It takes the fingers of both hands to count the old neighbors who walk their yards talking very loudly to themselves. At Kings Park Hospital the Old Professor, as we used to call him, sweeps a section of lawn under the trees with an imaginary broom and guides down a flying saucer. Here in Nesconset, spaceships land every day. But not birds. For picture Wenzel down in his basement workshop, among old candlers and egg washers. Chuckling to himself, he hinges together an elaborate construction of boards, shows his invention to his wife. And when he hears jays in his pines or crows at the top of his oaks, he rushes outside and sets up a racket and clatter and consternation with this prayer wheel, his heart raging faster and louder than his boards.

XI

A Model A rusted on the shore of Gibbs Pond. One door was locked shut and one swung on one busted hinge. We fished from its hood. It spread a circle of rust into the pond. We did not think of the rust as poison, but thought it drew the fish toward our bobbers.... The history of one small shop along the Jericho: Guarini's Pet Shop became Helen's Drapes became Midas Muffler became Greg's Lawn Mower Service became Uncle's Florist became Garage Door Alarms became Ed's Automotive.... The Japanese beetle, its back a myriad of metallic sheens, when it feasts on a grape leaf seems to uncover the leaf's hidden form, its white tracery of veins. Our grape arbor after one onslaught of beetles fifteen years ago was white, unearthly, ghostly. From a distance it seemed the whorl of a great spider.... In "The Open Boat" one of Stephen Crane's characters says that gulls seem to have been carved with a jackknife. The clumsy artisan, of course, is the god of fate, or chance, or irony, who drowns the strongest crewman. The gulls that passed over Nesconset were sleek, silent; they glided over our property without a single wing beat. They flew lower than the V's of geese or the circling hawks, but higher than the starlings or Werner's pigeons. The gulls, every day of the year, headed to the Sound on a straight line. They seemed white as bone, clean as icicles. When I saw them up close at the Sound or at St. James Harbor they were jagged and dirty and raucous. I remember thinking that these had to be different gulls, these scavengers. These could not be the same ones that reflected white sunlight over Nesconset.... He was the most popular and promising of us all, began to drink heavily and became an alcoholic by twenty. He was involved in a freak accident: One night he ran his sports car into a highway department truck that had rolled down from its parking place and waited for him on the Bypass. Scarred and crippled, he won a large settlement from the Town of Smithtown, threw away thousands in two months over one bar. Became an addict. Is now institutionalized.... Terlik, another neighbor, cooked a half bushel of blue claws at a time. The colors: the crabs' blue luster, their shades of blue enamel; sprigs of parsley added; then a cup of salt and sliced lemons. Tonged out of the boiling water, the crabs were bright orange.... Wenzel's terrier up on its hind legs fighting a rat almost as big as itself; his chicken gallows, the cutting of throats, white chickens running headless, splashing blood on themselves; a black cat with a Baltimore oriole in its jaws; bludgeoning the sandsharks drawn up from the deep waters past Crane's Neck in the Sound.... Mrs. Patac's memories of Lake Avenue, once a dirt path under oaks, neighbors visiting one another on Sundays in horse-drawn carts, gifts of cakes, baskets of squash and wildflowers plucked along the way.... I dream I am barefoot, walking the edges of Gibbs Pond. I sink to my knees in mud. Trees grow out of the water, their roots raised—cypress, a thousand years old, dark and alien to the Island. It is evening. The pond becomes a swamp. But I still wade among the roots of the trees. I'm trying to catch tropical fish, swordtails and tetras that glow orange and green and dull yellow in the dark water.... When I turned over a rock in the woods, I'd lean close and my skull's shadow would seem to fill, even blossom with small things: slugs and worms, glazed in mucus, would contract like bits of muscle; beetles, spiders, ants balancing blue eggs ran for the security of the leaves; fire-red centipedes, thin tongues of flame, licked in and out of tunnels.... I was clamming in the harbor's soft swells. It was a beautiful evening. Something touched the back of my knee. It felt like a hand of feathers. It was a dead gull. In a rat's nest, in a sprinkling of bones, under one corner of the garage, I found a robin, eyeless as the gull but otherwise still whole.... I once dreamed that I tangled in the branches of the great tree at the center of the lake and drowned, but breathed water like a fish, and sang in its blue branches like a bird.... 1796: Long Island's first lighthouse erected at Montauk Point; described by Gabriel Furman (1874) as "a very massive and durable tower of stone"; but September 21, 1815: gale winds shatter its lantern: the lighthouse stands dark as a tree over the jagged rocks: ships search for its light over the whitecaps, search for the lantern, search for its star above the duned glacier of the sea: too long ago not to remember: before the glacier receded from the Island: before it left a fish with two flukes, melted to lakes: Panamoka, bottomless Ronkonkoma: before it left the Island under the stars, under the hot sun to leaf to beauty: white and black oak, hickory, dogwood, locust, fragrant cedar: before the shorebirds: too long ago not to remember: before the changeless crab that now drags its ridged dagger through the sands and mud flats: before the bluefish, bass, buffalo whose hoofs still thunder in shells: in the beginning: before the Indians, before the colonists, before Smith, before Washington rode through Smithtown Branch and stopped at the Widow Blydenburgh's and wrote in his diary: "The herds and woods are died red with berries": too long ago not to remember: before the farmers of the salt meadows of marsh grass: before the Southampton and Sag Harbor whalers: before even the dream of it: before the glacier descended, heaved, split, receded: before the lighthouse at Montauk lost its lantern to gale winds, waves swept the edges of an island, wind sang in the dark branches of a shore....

William Bradford (1630): "And though it was very dark and rained sore, yet in the end they got under the lee of a small island and remained there all that night in safety...." " Seon Manley (1966): "On Long Island, time, tide, and the wind have moved with frightening splendor. Add to the picture the increase of tropical storms and one can grasp some shadow of our future. Each century is marked by a rise of two more feet of ocean level." Ralph Henry Gabriel (1921): "Long Island lies offshore like a giant tree, uprooted and fallen in the water, its trunk and branches half submerged."

XII

We are lying down somewhere in the woods, covered only by a thin blanket of leaves. It is nearly dark. I am worried that she will awaken and not want to spend the night here with me. I touch her hair. I do not know whether I am talking to her or whether the words I hear are only in my mind. I do not understand all of the words, but I know this is the first time, perhaps because she is asleep, that I have been able to use words this way, words I did not even know I knew. But I also know I am not the self, here at this time, that I should be. I am older, or I have somehow learned the words that tell what I feel, or the words are in the leaves that cover us.

...I want to tell you. There are forgotten meanings in the Noh, in the arrangements of tea leaves; there are lines in the psalms of fathoms; there are words in the blue irises of shadows; there is something we cannot ruin. I mean the sun is a power rooted in darkness, whose roots are darkness.

It is too cold for us here, but the wind increases and more and more leaves fall to cover us and keep us warm. My hands rake leaves over her. The wind seems high above us, seems to hack stars from their nests in the trees.

The words stop. Now oak leaves cover me completely. I would be able to sleep if I knew for certain she still slept beside me under the leaves.

XIII

In 1643, local Indian tribes were preoccupied with defending themselves against Mohawk marauders from the west. One William Kreft of the West India Company, who claimed he had purchased Long Island from the Indians, chose this time to perpetrate atrocities against Island tribes. David De Vries, the first owner of Staten Island, knew Kreft. These paragraphs, which describe events that took place on the night of February 25, 1643, are from De Vries's diary:

"The Wannekens, as they call the Dutch, had done it…. When it was day the soldiers returned to the fort, having massacred or murdered eighty Indians, and considering they had done a deed of Roman valor, in murdering so many in their sleep, where infants were torn from their mothers' breasts, and hacked to pieces in the presence of the parents, and the pieces thrown into the water, and other sucklings, being bound to small boards, were cut, stuck, and pierced, and miserably massacred in a manner to move a heart of stone….

"Some came to our people in the country with their entrails in their arms, and others had such horrible cuts and gashes, that worse than they could never happen. And these poor simple people, as also many of our own people, did not know any better than they had been attacked by a party of other Indians…. After this exploit, the soldiers were rewarded for their services, and Director Kreft thanked them by taking them by the hand and congratulating them."

As the frontier moved west and as the white man consolidated his gains on the Island, corpse was piled on corpse….

Washington Irving describes Sleepy Hollow: "A drowsy, dreamy influence seems to hang over the land, and to pervade the very atmosphere." Today, on the Island, people have triple-locked their doors, and for good reason. Who knows what madmen prowl the streets? Half-wit cowboys pound their fists on the bars, shout that "if guns are outlawed only outlaws will have guns," and drink until their beer joints close. The insane are let out on probation from the overcrowded hospitals that dot the Island. Kids gun their rods and blast out streetlamps with shotguns and deer rifles. Deranged veterans haunt the dark carrying bayonets in their back pockets….

Using a rifle as a cane, I am walking Lake Avenue to Saint James. I remember Hawthorne's sentence in "Young Goodman Brown," maybe the darkest sentence in all of American literature: "The road grew wilder and drearier and more faintly traced, and vanished at length, leaving him in the heart of the dark wilderness, still rushing onward with the instinct that guides mortal man to evil." I begin to feel my own power. I am capable of any crime. A patrol car slows down as it passes, and I shout at it, dare it to stop. I have not walked at night for years and experience, now, an intense satisfaction in the knowledge that the people who pass me in their cars are afraid of me, a furtive figure in a dark jacket. In the black and fragrant shade of the dogwoods that line the road, time and space expand to timelessness, morality to amorality, until a thought that has always been on my mind, the thought that it would be of no consequence were I to enter a home and kill its inhabitants, that this act would in no way matter, becomes a truism, becomes an emotional and intellectual fact. But not for long. I am not afraid of them. They have not harmed me or threatened my sense of myself, and they have nothing I want.

XIV

Hurricane Nancy arrived at mid-century....

Our tree, maybe the biggest in Nesconset, was a wild cherry. It descended intact, uprooting the earth, baring a half acre of grass to the storm. We worked for days in dying tailwinds, chopping the tree up and carting it away. Those nights the tree hovered its ghost, continued its reawakening to another April, refused to fall, still supported its nests of songbirds, still swung the bulb of a pair of orioles that returned each year, still shook with dark red fruit, still dripped prisms of rain.

Years later when only the tree's burnt stump remained, in our cellar to look for something, I kneeled on the cement and noticed that the cherry's roots had broken through our foundation. Maybe roots strengthened the house, as they sometimes strengthen the walls of a cistern; maybe the tree would have brought our house down.

XV

The seats in this small plane are numbered from one to thirty. Number thirty is in the left front and Billy, my son, who is seven now and with me, holds to edges of seats until he gets to seat thirty, where I'm sitting, but it's too high for him there, the plane is swaying and lurching like a bus, and there are gaps in the floor and the floor is shifting as the metal floor between railroad cars seems to shift, and we're high above the earth, so he makes his way across the aisle to seat seven.

...What can we do? he asks.

...It's all right, I shout above the racket of the plane's engine, we'll make it.

I tell him that he couldn't fit through one of those holes in the floor if he wanted to. He laughs happily, hysterically.

Our pilotless plane is hurtling downward now, and now, somehow, I am lying down on my stomach, controlling the plane with my weight as though it were a bobsled. We must land. We must land somewhere. I can make out the Sound below, then St. James Harbor, then Lake Avenue where it crosses the Jericho.

We are down now, scraping pavement crazily in this plane without wheels, whipping along, past Brown's Road and the hardware store, past the telephone company warehouse. We veer onto Gibbs Pond Road where it forks away from Lake, the fire department whizzes past us on our left, then the school, and our luck is still holding out because even one car would do us in. We are still going fast, our wings are just making it between telephone poles on both sides of the road. Billy is screaming somewhere behind me. We're past Zauzin's farm now, half flying and half scraping toward the Bypass intersection swarming with cars and will never, I know, stop in time, and suddenly night has fallen, we're whipping over the slight hump of blacktop past Zauzin's, and I decide quickly to lift and shift my weight right, and do, and the plane lifts slightly, we just make it over Terlik's hedge, between his hedge and the telephone wires scrawled against the darkness, we just make it onto his field, the only open area around. We settle down, still moving fast, but slowing now, grass underneath us now like lily pads under a rowboat, and I tell Billy to keep his head down and his hands inside and I tell him something about biting down on his sleeve, and I am wondering whether we will stop before we crack into the grape arbors or the barn beyond the open field when I realize we have stopped. We've stopped. I roll out of the plane onto the grass. Billy is with me. We both yell that we've made it, we've made it. We roll in the grass. We have never, I know, been so happy. The grass is wet with the night's dew and thick as clover and a dark, dark green, and smells so sweet.

XVI

Someone is reaching out his arms toward Long Island Sound and is weeping. I approach his silhouette across a dark lawn. I am only vaguely interested in his problem, whatever it is; in fact, I am intensely happy about my own life at this moment as I approach this poor fellow holding his arms out toward the waters I used to crab and clam. I have no idea what is wrong with him or why he is carrying on this way. Is he an actor in the heat of a soliloquy? Is he about to commit suicide?

He steps into the water. At that moment there is a blare of lights in the trees past an acre of lawn behind him. I can see outlined there what must be his house, huge and incoherent, lit up like a birthday cake. He must be very rich to have a house like that, I think.

I walk over to where he is standing in the water. He is still holding his arms out to the Sound's blank face.

I tap him on the shoulder. He turns to me. He is not surprised to see me there, but I am surprised to see how much he resembles me. Still, I am relieved that I am not him. I know who he is. He is Joe McCloy. I would know Joe even though I have seen him only three times before. Even though I know that he lost Karen as I did, I wonder if she is in his house. For a moment I think I can make her out coming across the lawn to where Joe and I are standing ankle-deep in the water. No, she isn't there. It is only a deer that turns around and moves away from us again.

...Why the hell are you continuing to cry this way? I ask him. What are you doing?

...I am eating my bitter heart, he answers. Tears are streaming down his cheeks in the moonlight in this incessant foolish lamentation of a soap opera I seem doomed to live through to some whimper of a conclusion. He says: I am eating my bitter heart out. His face is a farcical caricature of the weeping Christ.

He says: I am eating my own bitter heart out, but I like it because it is bitter, and because it is my heart.

XVII

There's a poem by Gary Snyder called "Hay for the Horses" in which an old man says he'll be damned if he didn't go ahead and spend fifty years of his life bucking hay. But Snyder, I think, likes this fellow. And the old man is not angry, really, or discontented. He's wistful, and he's amazed that life could have gone by so quickly. The poem is about the old man's love for his life as he has lived it. He is just beginning to understand his commitment to a quotidian of haydust and grasshoppers and shingle-cracks of barnlight. He says:

> I first bucked hay when I was seventeen.
> I thought, that day I started
> I sure would hate to do this all my life.
> And dammit, that's just what I've gone and done.

But it has been a good life for him, and he knows it. The life is the work, and he has chosen perfectly. He knows that he could have done differently, but never knew where he was likely to go better.

There's a character in one of the sketches of *Winesburg, Ohio* so upset with what he in his own life has come to be that "Every time he raised his eyes and saw the beauty of the country in the failing light he wanted to do something he had never done before, shout or scream or hit his wife with his fists or something equally unexpected and terrifying."

Ray Pearson is the character's name. He feels that his own years have been mean, that his marriage has been only a burden, his thin-legged children only millstones. So many of Anderson's characters are caught up in feelings of yearning so vague and obscure that we complement their pain with our own. The difference between Snyder's old man and Ray Pearson is that Pearson never feels complete. He is angry and frustrated. He feels that he had it inside himself to become so much more. He feels that he has wasted his life.

A man, says Anderson, becomes a grotesque when he fastens upon and commits himself to the reality of one of his fictions. Of the book's dozens of characters, Doctor Reefy seems the most balanced and speaks best for his creator. We think of Anderson when the good Doctor writes his momentary truths and systems on bits of paper, rolls the papers into little balls, and, when he has too many, throws them in the face of a "blithering old sentimentalist."

It may be that the man who believes in anything at all is a sentimentalist. But it may be, as Wallace Stevens says in "The World as Meditation," that the planet sometimes encourages us toward meaning. And the sort of character who moves past even Doctor Reefy's balanced cynicism to a life blessed by being at ease with its own imperfections is nowhere to be found in *Winesburg*. We are left to think of Anderson, the man himself, writing, writing, writing all those memories and dreams in all those lonely rooms in all those slums.

•

XVIII

Carbone's place was across Gibbs Pond Road and about a hundred yards past our house. The Wenzels had a house, the Zauzins had a house, we had a house, but Carbone's place was just a tarpaper shack, square and dirty, its low flat roof sagging and streaked by residues of leaves and pine needles. This was, I think, 1950, but I can see Carbone's place still, shadowy and squatting back off the road among oaks and pines like a spirit toad. And I've only now realized what was so different about Carbone's yard: he didn't have one. We and the Wenzels and the Zanzins had a lawn and hedges and even rows of trees. Carbone's yard was scrub oak, scrub pine, thistles, goldenrod and ragweed and piles of sand left over from some old cement project. Along one side of his property garbage rattled and blew down a slight ravine, a rat and snake heaven.

I would see him only every few weeks or so. Winter or summer, he'd be wearing an overcoat that reached to his ankles and a floppy hat that reached to his ears. He'd be pulling a rusty child's wagon or pushing a rusty wheelbarrow filled with empty bottles that had lost their labels. Where he was going or what he was doing with all those bottles or where he got them I don't remember, if I ever knew. I do know that I never heard him say a single word, never heard him shout or laugh or even mutter.

Carbone was only a moment's curiosity for us when, on the way to swimming or to a ball game or to a hill on Southern Boulevard for some sledding, we passed him. Something seemed to be wrong with his eyes, as though there were too much white in them and too little iris. But there were two meetings with him that I do remember.

The first time, I was selling seeds. I must have been in about the fourth grade. Something possessed me to try Carbone. The side door to his shack was half open. I knocked on its tarpaper shingles and saw at the same time some movement inside. I stepped inside and saw Carbone sitting at a table, facing me, his hat on, fumbling at an egg, trying to peel it. I backed away. I didn't know if he had seen me.

And then there was the autumn day I was walking back from school along the side of the road that brought me directly past Carbone's shanty and I saw him stretched out flat on his back, almost hidden by patches of thistles and weeds. I stepped across his property only half way to where he lay, only close enough to see his eyes staring straight up through the fall trees that were blowing leaves down around him. I think he was breathing, and I remember thinking that old men were crazy and maybe Carbone had just fallen asleep outside and did not have a hammock. But something scared me. I ran home and told my mother. Then I forgot about Carbone. It was months later before I realized that that afternoon I saw him staring his white eyes toward the autumn skies was the last time I'd seen him.

Maybe ten years later some of his relatives knocked his shack down and built a new house, one with a yard, on the property. The garbage ravine is filled in now, and the name on a new mailbox says *Carbone* in gold letters, and some of the kids who play there now must be grandchildren or great-grandchildren of the man I didn't know.

XIX

There was a stretch of shore at Short Beach that was all stones, millions of stones, and not just a single layer, but deep. The largest stones were as big as maybe your hand. You could walk the water's edge, trusting the summer's calluses on your feet or the smoothness of most of the stones, and could let your mind wander over the kingdom of stones at your feet, until a different color or striation or glitter of mica stopped your eye and you bent down and reached into the cold clear water for that particular stone.

This is where we were, the four of us, but I was not really part of what was happening. I was watching. I couldn't see myself, but I was watching, standing at the edge of the water, looking at the other three men, one to the left side on a dune of stones, two kneeling in the stones. The one on the left wore a serape, and was back-lit, the sun falling behind him and outlining his profile in red-gold. His arms were raised; he was facing the other two, and his shadow fell across to them. But it was somehow a white shadow, gray white, only slightly darker than the day. He stood there, I thought, like the statue of Jesus overlooking Rio de Janeiro. And he was silent, holding up his arms, his serape falling gracefully around him. No, it was a gown, it was as long as a gown, and its bottom folds grew to marble. He was that statue, but he was not. It was a serape, and he was a man I knew. I knew his gossamer hair, his glasses. I knew how his voice would sound were he to talk or laugh. But he was silent, and still. But the two men kneeling in the sand were moving and talking. And I knew them too, and could name them. And they knew one another, I knew, and had for a long time. There was a pile of stones between them, stones through which the light shone, stones that glowed. And the one man—I felt that I didn't like him, didn't understand him—was passing the stones to the man I loved, was asking him to name them. And then I knew I was right for what I felt about them. And behind them the dying sun shone through the man in the serape onto the two men kneeling in the stones. And the man I didn't like picked up one stone. And that stone was beautiful to me. It was as beautiful as the bloom of an iris, and was somehow translucent, and I wanted to hold it, and my eyes filled with tears. The man I didn't like handed that stone to the man I loved and asked, impatiently, "What should we call this one, what should we call this one, what should we call this one, what should we call this one?" And the man I loved weighed the stone tenderly in his hands and held it close to his eyes and then at arms' length and said, "We will call this blue. We will call this steep blue." His voice tightened my throat. He spoke again. He said, "We will call this stone a steep, steep blue."

XX

From *Webster's Geographical Dictionary* (1949): Island, SE of New York and S of Connecticut, lying bet. Long Island Sound on N and Atlantic Ocean on S; 118 m. long, 23 m. at greatest width; 1401 sq.m. (including water, 1723 sq. m.); pop. 4,600,022; comprises Suffolk, Nassau, Queens, and Kings cos. of New York state; borough of Brooklyn (Kings co.) at its SW extremity. At W end separated from the Bronx and Manhattan by East river and from Staten I. by the Narrows. Has 280 m. of coast line indented by numerous inlets and bays, esp. Peconic and Gardiners Bays at E end and Great South and Jamaica Bays on S shore. Hilly along N shore; has many fine beaches along the S (Rockaway, Jones, Fire Island, Coney Island). At its E end is Montauk Point with several large islands in adjacent waters (Shelter, Gardiners, Plum, etc.). Has grown to be great residential district for New York City.... Included in grant to Plymouth Co. by James I, 1620; conveyed to William Alexander, Earl of Stirling, 1635; became part of British colony of New York by treaty, 1674; earliest settlement by Dutch 1623, and by English, ab. 1640; scene of battle of Long Island (at Brooklyn Heights) in Revolutionary War, Aug. 27, 1776, in which Lord Howe defeated Americans under Washington, who, however, successfully withdrew his forces across the river.

XXI

I am walking down steps again. This time the steps are narrow blocks of hewn stone, and curve as though I am walking down the steeple of a great cathedral embedded in the earth. The fingers of my right hand trace the line of my descent on the wet stones of the wall, my feet move easily into the depressions of the stone steps. I am holding a candle in my left hand, its flame gusting toward me and then away. I am descending the stairs as fast as the candle will allow me. But it goes out anyway. I stop. But the stone steps and the stone walls are not as black as the black air, and I can still move down the stairs. I feel curiously at ease, as though some part of me knows where I am going and is unafraid. I feel it is right that I am walking down these stairs. I descend the stairs for a long, long time, thinking of nothing that could serve to fill the dark.

Now one of the wallstones seems to glow with blue lines, but no image appears. Now I can make out the profile of a snout, coyote or wolf, glowing with a dull pearl light from another wallstone. Now the flank of a horse glowing a beautiful rose-red from the stone ceiling. And now I am entering a chamber so overwhelming that I have to close my eyes to its walls and ceiling. For this is the chamber of reverence. Eyes and horns adorn the stones, buffalo and bear and pheasant, each animal standing out from the stones in the color of blood or pearl or pale sunlight or grass. I have so much to learn here. Buffalo and bear and pheasant, otter and owl, boar and fox and wolf and horse. When I see them it is as though I hear their names for the first time. And now I know that at a moment like this I must hold my breath. I must allow the animals to find me in the air of the dark chamber. If I clear my mind, if I believe for once in my life in silence, if I disavow declaration...

I sit down on grass under the sky of this cave back where the land began. There is plenty of time. I will wait here for everything and for nothing. I will, at last, be still.

XXII

One morning a long time ago my mother came running into the house. She finally gasped out that she'd been picking strawberries in the patch way in back of our property against the woods when she'd stepped right into the coil of a snake. If she really did step into a circle of snake, it was probably just a harmless garter sunning itself or taking advantage of the worked loam and strawberry shade.

But another time, while outside hanging laundry to dry, my mother screamed and did have something to scream about. She said that a cat had run out of the woods straight at her and attacked her. We could see that her left calf had been punctured by at least four teeth.

Cats were a problem for us back then. The Suffolk woods were home to the offspring of domestic cats that had littered in the wild. The generations flourished there, and grew wild again. We could hear the cats' screams as they fought. One of my most vivid memories is the night sound of teeth against bone outside my bedroom window, not a grinding sound but almost a cluck, a liquid tear as though of knuckles and joints popping apart, or the sound of your jaw if you momentarily dislocate it. One morning I found two dead toms under a rhododendron. Both were torn apart, shreds of fur, ripped eyes and nostrils.

We had three rifles in the family, three 22's. I had a single shot, my father and older brother Werner had clip models. We killed dozens of cats over the years. Cats would scream outside at night and we would go out in slippers, shine a flashlight into the dark, and fire bullets between their slashes of yellow and green eyes.

There was another summer morning I can still see clearly. My brother and I had fired at a cat during the night. For some reason, we'd both fired birdshot; we were sure we'd hit that cat, that some pellets had found it in the dark, but were pretty sure we hadn't killed it. It took 22-longs to kill cats. When we walked outside that morning we heard snarling at the edge of our property and approached what was apparently the cat we'd shot. It raged at us, rocked on three legs, one eye flashing in the morning shine, one closed and weeping blood. It was the biggest cat we had ever seen, a red, but its coat almost one solid rust, not quite like other reds we'd seen. It crossed my mind that this was a real wildcat.

We ran inside for our guns, ran back to the cat, and fired, almost together. The cat seemed to rear up and throw itself back over its own shoulder. It didn't drop. It took to the woods, dragging one useless leg. We followed, certain it would die. I knew that my bullet had hit it full in the chest.

We waded through lily of the valley, its millions of small white bells, that bordered that edge of our property. We walked through ferns that blanketed the wood's floor under the oaks, and followed the snarling cat. We were both afraid of this cat but never considered not following it and making sure it was dead. I already felt, also, sick at heart, felt that this cat was more than the other cats, more important, that I was in another dimension, another world, desecrating that world, that this was somehow personal, that this cat knew me, that something outside ourselves was bearing witness to this whole episode to which I was somehow committed. These were the woods of the old Island; this was center Island, the awful power of its perfumes.

About a hundred yards deep in the woods we caught up to the cat. I remember ducking under some brush into a small clearing, the cat only about twenty feet away, at the base of a tree, its back arched, its rust fur matted with blood. Werner and I knelt there and fired. My hands managed to fumble four or five bullets into the chamber of my rifle. I fired directly into the cat's face and could see the bullets strike, could see round spots of blood appear as the bullets entered its twisted face. Werner must have fired the eight shots of his clip. But the cat wouldn't fall, wouldn't fall, but didn't attack us as I was afraid it would, until it finally did fall, its front paws still jerking, still clutching for something it could tear apart. It did fall, did stop snarling. I dropped my rifle, sat down, breathed deep, tried to get hold of myself. It was only another cat, I told myself.

XXIII

I have not had a memorable dream for months. But last night I dreamed and woke up and remembered, then fell back asleep and dreamed again and woke up and remembered again, then fell asleep and dreamed a third dream. I don't know why, unless: in three weeks, after ten months here in Germany, we'll be flying back to America. And when we fly back to America we will be flying back to Long Island for ten days before we drive back to Brockport.

First, I am far away from home. I am to give a poetry reading at a college. Yes, I am in California, where she still lives. No, I am at William Smith in Geneva walking across rolling lawns shaded by groves of great elms under which there are marble benches and chairs. I remember phoning her when I arrived, picturing her as we spoke on the phone: She is older, has lines on her forehead and around her mouth, and she is sad, but smiles as we talk. But I am walking the lawns now looking for her. Didn't we make an appointment? And where was it to be? Just what did we say on the phone? I am sweating and my feet are beginning to hurt. I have slung my suit jacket over my shoulder and rolled up the sleeves of my white shirt. I am lost in a grove of trees and will never find her, at least not here. Anger and humiliation. I shout something obscene. I sit down in a marble chair. It is as though I am in a cemetery. The afternoon grows hotter and hotter. I tell myself I must be crazy to be here. I would leave if I only knew the way home....

Another dream: This time she is in my arms. We are sitting on stairs. The stairs are carpeted and comfortable. They may be the same stairs on which I sat so often with Han before she was my wife, but I'm not sure.

She is sitting on my lap, her back to me. She moves her hips counterclockwise, slowly, keeps moving them as we talk and keeps me in a state of excitement and knows she is keeping me hard. My hands are cupped over her breasts under her blouse as we talk, and as we talk I am thinking to myself it is pleasant to have an erection but that I will not be able to have an orgasm, that somehow there will not be time. She turns her face around toward me. She is very pretty, streaks of blond hair falling over the left side of her face as she rides and swivels on my lap. I lean back, uncup my hands from her in a gesture of, perhaps, disdain. Why didn't you do this when we had time? I ask her. I didn't know how, she says. She smiles, and closes her eyes, and bites her lower lip, and leans back into me until I awake....

I am walking with my son, who is half my son and half Henry, my youngest brother, who is the same age in this dream and in my life now as Henry was when I used to watch over him, play with him, take care of him. There are many photos of Henry and me playing ball one summer under the pear trees of our back lawn in Nesconset under the Long Island sky, the same sky under which we are now, my half-son half-brother and I, walking across Terlik's field, but at evening, dusk, too dark for faces, walking toward the house and barns. Harmonica music from a distance, maybe an accordion playing, sweet rasping sounds, low chords, and laughter rising above the music, shouts. Then I notice strings of colored bulbs in the trees behind the house, crepe ribbons twined in the branches, people's shadows. Billy, who is just Billy now, and I stop in the center of the field in the darkness in the damp grass and listen to the noises coming out of the trees and watch the colored lights and shadows behind Terlik's house. Then we are standing inside somewhere, inside a barn, what used to be a barn but is now polished and shined. It is, in fact, almost elegant inside, the timbers rough, but silks hung all over, and I should not be there because I haven't shaved and I am wearing baggy pants and my old ski hat pulled down over my ears, and we are standing at a street corner in the barn in a crowd, the sound of chimes and small bells coming toward us from the left. I realize we are at a wedding.

Four horses come into view, round the corner where we are standing. Chimes and small bells, a throaty humming as though the chimes and bells were accompanied by a harmonica or an accordion. Or maybe it's the background of one of the Shirelles' records. Four horses, a magnificent carriage, cheers from the faceless crowd for the driver. The driver of the carriage is the groom. He is wearing a silk hat and tails and is reining the horses around that corner perfectly, the left front horse just grazing its left ear on the barn wall. Cheers, applause, the sound of bells. They are very rich, I am thinking. I strain to see the bride. Yes, I am thinking, she must be very rich. The groom is reining the horses, guiding them around that corner perfectly. My only thought about the bride is that she must be very rich. If, inside that dream last night, I saw her and recognized her, I cannot recall even a glimpse of her now. Nor am I sure whether or not I was the groom. A split second after the profile of the driver of that carriage passed us, Billy and I were walking back home, our backs to the colored lights strung out like eyes in Terlik's trees.

XXIV

From John Woolman's *Journal* (1774): "Then returned to the island, where I spent the remainder of the week May, 1756 in visiting meetings. The Lord, I believe, hath a people in those parts who are honestly inclined to serve Him; but many I fear, are too much clogged with the things of this life, and do not come forward bearing the cross in such faithfulness as He calls for."

William Oliver Stevens (1939): "The little white church at Smithtown Branch is not much more than one hundred years old, but, like that other church in Huntington, its predecessor on this site had a hard experience during the Revolutionary War. The preacher, Joshua Hart, was so fearless in the way he denounced the behavior of the British troops that one soldier took a shot at him from the pews, but fortunately missed. It is one of those rare cases in history when some member of a congregation has dared to answer back the man in the pulpit, but he might have done it more decorously than with a musket."

From Wallace Stevens's *Journal* (Jan. 4, 1907): "There is so little in reality. My office is dingy, and I go to and from it, underground.— But sometimes I get glimpses of Washington Bridge and its neighborhood, and I think it all very impressive and Roman and wonderful, in its way.—And on Sundays I take walks here and there: one, lately, through Yonkers Park, Scarsdale, along Weaver-Street to New Rochelle, and then down Pelham Road to Bartow. Twilight clings to the shores of the Sound like mist to a wood. There is no country here: That's one trouble."

Lois J. Watt (1963): "The Indian hunters' footprints disappeared and the wood from their arrows deteriorated through the hundreds of years since they lived here. At least we have their 'arrowhead footprints,' positive evidence that they once walked and hunted on the shores of Lake Ronkonkoma." Martha B. Flint (1896): "The Indians had a most superstitious reverence for Ronkonkoma. They even refused to catch the fish thronging its clear waters, believing them under the special protection of the Great Spirit, while on its beaches were held the most solemn of their ceremonies." F. W. Hodge (1885): "Offerings were made to beings in lakes, rivers, springs, except that in such cases poles were placed at the edge of the water. Dogs were hung on trees or tall poles."

From a letter to Lord Howe, Commander of the British forces in North America, published in *Pennsylvania Evening Post* (Sept. 7, 1776): "Let your lordship select ten thousand of your best troops and officers, with your lordship at their head; draw them up on the extensive plains of Long Island, where you will have every opportunity of displaying your great abilities. Arrange them in whatever manner you please; then let an equal number of Americans form themselves in battalia, and let each army be provided in all respects equal, with trains of artillery, and all other offensive weapons; then, on a given signal, begin the attack, and leave the issue to the God of armies. This is what the Americans propose to Lord Howe; and the sooner he agrees to the proposal the better."

Walt Whitman (1882): "As I write, the whole experience comes back to me after the lapse of forty and more years—the soothing rustle of the waves, and the saline smell—boyhood's times, the clam digging, barefoot, and with trousers roll'd up—hauling down the creek—the perfume of the sedge meadows—the hay boat, and the chowder fishing excursions."

XXV

This is Gibbs Pond. I know this from the rise of the woods behind it. But it is very different. It is perfectly round now, and I can see through clear water to a sand bottom. The whole pond is only three or four feet deep, its whole bottom is sand. Not a single weed, no mud, not a branch or a log, just the clear water and yellow sand. I am wearing my bathing suit. I wade into the pond up to my waist. I have a snorkel and flippers. I submerge into what seems to be bright yellow water and swim languidly to the center of the pond. I touch the sand. It seems pasty. The water is very warm. It occurs to me that the water is unhealthy, and I am careful not to swallow any of it. At that moment I know that it is a terrible thing that has happened to Gibbs Pond. The water is much too warm. But I have no historical sense of what has happened to it.

At the center of the pond is a big round metal swimming pool. I reach it and stand up beside it and look inside. The water inside the swimming pool is brackish, and most of the water's surface is a tangle of lily pads and weeds. It is all that is left of the old pond. I touch the water inside. It is cool. A perch rises to my fingers as though to bits of bread. It is only about six inches long. It is banded gray and black, and I can just make out the red-orange tinge of its gills.

I can see, a few feet away, a painted turtle rising from far down. The turtle hovers just under a pad, its nostrils break the surface of the water at the notch where a stem is joined to its pad. As always before, the turtle's set of inner, cloudy lids is down over its eyes, but not the outer lids as it drinks air. The milky lids, I've always thought, give turtles an expression of obliviousness. The turtle drawing in the air above its small pond has the expression that my daughter had as my wife nursed her. My daughter's eyes would seem to be covered by a film. She often seemed to be dreaming. She often fell asleep while nursing. Without a ripple, the turtle descends again from where it had surfaced for air. I love that turtle. I picture its long claws curving into the bottom mud as it rakes for worms. It must be a female, I tell myself.

I am in the warm water of the outer pond up to my waist. The water is very uncomfortable. It smells, too. But the water does not carry the rich fragrance of mud or dead fish or lilies. The water smells of chemicals, peroxide and ammonia. I am very hot now, and I am getting dizzy. I am under the water swimming for shore again. Why is it always noon here? I ask myself this question again and again.

XXVI

(A letter to Vince Clemente)

May 28, 1973. Vince, I'm back on the Island for a week for a last look at the home and grounds and town where I grew up. My folks have sold out and are moving to a small house in a retirement community further east, about twenty-five miles from here. The property just got to be too much for them to take care of. The new owner and his wife dropped over yesterday evening. He grew up in Franklin Square when it was country. I took him around the property and pointed out the stump of that magnificent cherry tree, and told him what the woods were like and where my father's shop used to be. He's a tile contractor, but I had him touch the bark of one of the last of the old apple trees. I took him under the grape arbor that is now completely undergrown with maples and weeds and black-eyed Susans and the spike stems of tiger lily that will bloom in late summer. I showed him the hundreds of dogwoods crowding the edge of the property. (I read somewhere that the English soaked the bark of these trees in water and used the mixture to wash down stinking dogs.) Some of the ones under the edges of the pine trees have been cut by the power mower so often that they now come up like bonsai—thick and small and old. Those pines behind the hedges along Gibbs Pond Road are at least seventy feet high now. Show trees, and still healthy and growing. The catalpa trees along one side of the driveway are all dead or dying— "like walking wounded," as Richard Wilbur says about those lilacs.

But between them other trees are young and flourishing. There are more birds here now than I ever remember. Even crows, which were never around when I was a kid.

Tonight I walked up the road past Zauzin's to Nesconset School. I stood foolishly in the moonlight and thought about the cornerstone and the day in 1949 when a newspaper was sealed into it, and my brother Ed's ball, and my brother Henry's rattle. I read a speech that day—I think the speech is in the cornerstone, too—about all the improvements over the old school. I must have already learned to exaggerate by then, because I distinctly recall someone coming up to me later to say that I'd been wrong in saying that the windows of the old school had been dirty. Anyway, I began the sixth grade in that building. The teacher was a Mr. John White. It's odd, but I remember so much about that year. I remember things Mr. White said in class, and what we studied, and where I sat. Mr. White had been on the boxing team at Yale, and he cuffed us around often, but we knew he cared for us. I suppose he became another kind of father for me.

I walked over to the Nesconset firehouse, too. There's a commemorative slab of cement on the lawn that honors the veterans of this volunteer department who are dead. I remember so many of them—Abe Cohen, Tony and Louis Vion, old man McManus, Henry Dorfer—I remember their faces and manners. They always seemed to be over there at the department, shining the trucks or manning the booths at the annual carnival or running their clambakes and bingo parties. They were all *characters*. I spent a lot of time over there because I was a bugler with their drum and bugle outfit. I was a good one, too. Lots of wind. We practiced on the school field. The majorette was Claudette Cohen, Abe's daughter. She was an absolutely beautiful girl, blond as buttercups, friendly, a terrific figure, tall, leggy. A guy one class ahead of Werner's married her later on. His name was Buddy Fisher, and he must have been the envy of dozens of his friends. I mean she was a sweet girl, too. I heard about ten years ago that she was dying of cancer. And she did die. Then I heard that her father committed suicide. It all came back in a rush tonight. All those men whose names are on the slab are their own stories. I wish I could tell them. Is there nothing in our lives that can slow things down, can stop things for even a little while? I want to be able to turn the faces of those men in my mind and cherish them. Vince, have you seen the new James Wright poem in which he realizes that he has become one of those old men? This is serious business, as Berryman would say. It will seem like ten minutes from now when you and I will be among the old guys. The older I get, the more amazing and astounding and astonishing and miraculous this life is. How is this consciousness of ours possible? How can we possibly exist as we do? And just what is this blur and depth that we call time? Lord, Lord, it all comes back to You.

So I am seeing this house for a last time and helping my parents move out—a twenty-six-year accumulation of *things*. Box after box after box. The wealth of America pouring out of every closet, drawer, cabinet. I'm taking back to Brockport with me a bowl and a creamer that belonged to my father's grandmother, a couple of pieces of crystal my mother got from an old woman when we lived in Woodhaven, and a few other nice things. I don't want to give the wrong impression. My folks are not rich and the house is not filled with antiques and crystal. But it is filled up. Leslie Fiedler says in an essay that there's only one thing for sale in America, and that's the Dream of many guises. The Dream comes disguised as Things. But what can we expect, he asks tenderly, of the culturally deprived and the dispossessed who came to America from all those tired lands? Things. Oh, and my folks have actually bought all these awful things that I've been helping to pack and move! The whole house is one knickknack shelf of glass and false gold and gaudy jeweled sequined shelled grotesque ornaments, tall plastic plants with exotic plastic birds. Immigrants. I've seen this phantasmagoric display so often with immigrants, the tractor tires painted white on the lawns of Italians in Lake Ronkonkoma and Kings Park, pink flamingos in the sand inside the tires and false brick tar paper on the porches and colored cement blocks along the walks.

I packed up all the stuff on the shelves over my father's bar. The liquor and wine went yesterday. Today was left the incredible variety of gimcrackery and gimmicks that surrounds the essential loneliness of alcohol. I packed boxes of cheap steins with false pewter lids. I packed my father's dodo-bird that dips its beak into water forever. I packed statuettes of drunks with red bulb noses, and glasses with false bottoms, and lucite ice cubes in which flies are embedded, and glasses with real rocks glued to their bottoms and "You asked for one on the rocks" printed on their sides. There were spouts of peeing boys and swizzle sticks with peephole girlie shows and coasters to cradle your drink between rubber tits. God knows what to make of all that stuff. My parents owned a bar in Hollis and then one in Hauppauge before they moved to Nesconset and my father went back to carpentry, his trade from the Old Country. He now knows five hundred jokes about drunks and treasures his collection of alcoholiana. God knows what to make of it. Anything for a conversation. Maybe this is what he learned after ten years of tending bar.

I am finding out about things here, Vince. How is it that this acre or two of ground can mean so much to me? I'm a happy man! Then why does my mind skip back to the two maples, the three dogwoods, the pines along the road here, the single blue spruce hidden in deep shade? I'll be driving or walking along or talking over the phone and suddenly one or two of those particular trees flash into my mind. Vince, there's a perfect sentence, and a lead, in Allan Seager's biography of Roethke. Listen to this: "The first definitions, the fruits of the primary glances, can never be supplanted, for the trees of one's childhood are the touchstones of all later trees, the grass of the back yard the measure of all greenness, and other lights fail because they are not the true sun that brightens those trees, that grass." And think of that line in Roethke's "The Far Field": "The pure serene of memory in one man."

I'll leave here tomorrow, then, for the last time. I will probably never return to Nesconset, or even to Smithtown. How can this be? Brockport *must* become my home now. I must allow it to become my home completely. Partial denouement: Mrs. Terlik, surviving her husband by twenty years now, plans to sell out and move to the city to live with her son and family. Wenzel is in the hospital and seems to be dying of stomach cancer. My father said he dreamed last night that he found Mrs. Wenzel dead in the front hedges. The wood my father sold next door is now a development of dozens of houses, and as Mrs. Terlik and Mrs. Wenzel and the Zauzins sell out, the development will spread. I've not gotten to St. James, and don't plan to. I suppose that her old man's barberpole, like styles of hair these days, goes around and around.

XXVII

Our son is only a month or two old as I see the three of us, now, in the center of a scene the edges of which are smoke. The scene moves closer now, or I, the eye with which I see this, move closer. In this dream my wife and I are bending over our baby boy. He is on his back, on a blue bath towel, the towel tucked warmly around him, wisps of steam rising from his body into the air of this room: the back shed of a farmhouse I have somehow known. Old cupboards and a head-high cast-iron stove are presences in the background.

It is after his bath, and we are drying him, and I am burying my nose in the sweet-scented flesh of his neck. The three of us are happy. His little fingers swim the air like minnows, his legs are drawn up like a frog's as they were when he was this young. The corners of his mouth bubble. I can circle the whole girth of his chest with my two hands. I touch his nipples tenderly, run my hands smoothly over his belly. I notice his penis is straight and hard now, important twig of boyflesh, bud waiting to bloom. I touch him softly, the sacks of his testicles, his penis. I notice he is still now, his blue eyes gazing dreamily into the clouds of white haze at the edges of the room. He exhales a hum, as when he is nursing, from deep in his throat, contented.

A bubble of his mother's milk appears on his lips, and now, as she and I look down, one pearl drop of his semen glistens, a drop of dew, a single frog's egg. His eyes close, but blue glows through his lids and lashes. He is asleep now, our boy. We are still bent over him, wrapping him in his blue towel. Though I see us from somewhere else, I know how I feel in this dream. These are our bodies, I say to myself. This is the peace that is possible in our lives. This is our love. Our son's eyes glow blue through his lids as he sleeps.

XXVIII

I am with Billy, my son. We are clamming at St. James Harbor. I am crippled, but doing the best I can in the low water. I have used a board to scrape away layers of sand, and I am down now like a crab, feeling for clams with my hands. I hope to help my son fill two or three bushels before the tide is too high, but I am crippled. In this dream Billy is strong, muscles rippling his back as he bears down on his rake. He seems to be about fifteen, and is filling his basket, but I want to help, but I am crippled, but I strike a pocket, begin pulling as many clams out of the sand as my hands can stretch to hold.

...Look at this, I shout to my son.

He wades over, the blue water lapping his knees. I am still pulling clams by the half-dozen from the pocket. Then one clamshell splits open. There is a mother-of-pearl box inside. Inside the box is an unsigned letter. The letter says, *We left these here for you.*

XXIX

It was a May afternoon in 1957, my senior year in high school. I was at home, shooting baskets by myself up against the old woodshed where a rim was mounted, when my mother called me to the phone. It was Karen. She said that there had been a terrible accident on the Smithtown Bypass. She was crying. She said that Ellen Wagner and Bob Lahahn had been driving around after school and that there had been an accident, that Ellen was actually dead. I went outside again and began shooting baskets again, but dizzily and in a kind of frenzy. My mother called me to the phone again. Karen sobbed, Oh God, that Bob was dead, too. I couldn't believe it, and thought there was a chance I was dreaming.

I went to Bob's funeral, saw his cosmeticized face and hands in the casket, my first such experience. I made it through that. But Ellen was a Catholic, and our whole class attended a mass for her. I'd never been inside a Catholic church before. The crucifix, incense, the Latin and dark strangeness, frightened me and broke me down completely. I wept, right there in the presence of my friends, who also wept.

It is four in the morning now. Just a little while ago, seventeen years later, I dreamed I boarded a bus and walked down its aisle, its tunnel, to the back. Outside its windows, a starry blackness streamed by.

I first tried to squeeze into a seat in front, but it was too close, there were too many people. I was uncomfortable and moved to the back. Then there was an argument behind me—a friend of mine was involved with a tall man dressed in a black suit, a man handsome as Valentino. He was with a woman. She was wearing a beige veil. I looked back at her and then away and then back at her. She saw me.

...Is it you, Bill? she asked.

...Is it you, Ellen?

She has gotten older, is my age now, but is still beautiful, wearing her auburn hair short as she always wore it, her teeth perfect as always.

I lifted her shadowy veil. We embraced, and because we both now realized the truth about so much that had once frightened us, cried. The altercation between her escort and my friend turned into a handshake. Ellen and I held one another for a long time...

XXX

We'd moved from Woodhaven (which was anything but wooded) to the wilds of Hauppauge when I was four or five, and then to Nesconset where I began third grade. "O world so far away! O my lost world!" says Roethke. (A dictionary of American place names says that "Nesconset" is from the Algonquian, meant "second-crossing-at," and was also the name of the tribe living there.) Later, by school bus, or riding with my parents, or hitchhiking to high school on New York Avenue, I would pass through Smithtown Branch, under the great locusts, beside the Blydenburgh house. The one-room Smithtown schoolhouse where Whitman taught is just off the Jericho in the area across from the old Presbyterian Church where 25A begins its winding to St. James and Stony Brook, and Route 111 right angles left to Hauppauge. You can see it from the Jericho. Last I knew, it housed a lawyer's office. When I think of Smithtown, I first think of that place, that confluence. I understand that our word "nostalgia" comes from two Greek words for pain and for a return home.

I didn't know anything about Whitman. When I remember myself as I was, I picture a boy wading Gibbs Pond in Nesconset or the nearby salt waters, the natural world bending in. I spent so much time in the water that this is the most enduring image I have of myself, and now I know that Whitman saw me, and now I know that the presence I felt when I was otherwise alone at a pond or walking through woods or, later, clamming at St. James Harbor, was his, as he is abiding spirit, as he is the miraculous confluence of space and time within a human voice.

XXXI

This is Brockport, New York. The college's Hartwell Hall is much the same shape, and is built into the same air, as was the Baptist College constructed here in 1834, and the larger State Normal and Training School, which opened in

1867. (For just a moment, I float into the inner-rings of a maple in front of the building: I hear what it heard when it was a sapling—voices, another century's wind, the brooks and small creeks that drained this village, cartwheels, the wing beats of millions of pigeons in a viridescent cloud shadowing the six-acre campus.) Now I know it is almost morning, and I am close to awakening, but, yes, this is Hartwell Hall, and I am staring at its facade, which is dirty and cob-webbed as I have never before seen it, the legend *State Teachers College* above its center doors incised in stone as always, but now lined with grime.

I am passing through the basement of this building, walking to a class. Two or three women are clearing out an alcove in the east wing, and in the back of my mind is the knowledge that the building is being shut down and its contents sold off the way an old church that has lost its congregation will sell off its pews and silver and hymnals.

The women have uncovered some things there in the dust of the alcove under papers and behind a pair of unhinged doors. They've brought out candle molds, a pleater, two circular stained-glass windows, a posthole digger, Normal School textbooks, old amber bottles, and a wicker planter with copper lining that needs only a spray of white paint to be worth fifty bucks. And they have placed on a window ledge another small object. I pick it up and skim the dust from it with my right thumb.

It is a trapezoid of glass. It is a small cowbell, not metal as is every other cowbell I have ever seen, but blown from blue glass, the pontil on its crown. Its small clapper hangs inside its dome like a single perfect grape. It is, as I weigh it in my hands, the most beautiful piece of glass I have ever seen, and it is marked 1914. The date stands out clearly. I hold the bell up to my eyes, and look through it, and the building's long lower hall is bathed in blue light.

It is urgent that I talk to one of the women and ask the price of the cowbell. Fifteen dollars, she says, and says that all these things will be brought over to another building to be sold. If only I had that much money. I begin to leave, but think of my wife, who would want to have the glass bell for our china cabinet, and then I check my left pocket and see that I have more than enough money, a whole fistful of fives and tens and singles. I return to the woman and ask her if I can buy the bell now, please. No, she says, you can never buy it, but you can be the first one on the list. All right, I say, and ask her, please, to be sure.

XXXII

During my grammar school years I had seven or eight aquariums filled with tropical fish. I remember a list I once made of fifty-six different kinds I had collected, bicycling back and forth to Guarini's Pet Shop on the Jericho Turnpike, exchanging weeks of my allowance for a pair of pencil fish (though it was almost impossible with any egglaying fish to tell male from female) or blind caves or gouramis. All these tanks were in an alcove behind the living-room couch where I would spend my evenings, especially in winter when I missed the Nesconset ponds, maybe glancing over at the twelve-inch black-and white television set we had, but usually staring into an aquarium.

I didn't like ornaments, the bridges, galleons, divers my friends had in their tanks—a few weeks and these things looked algae-sick. And I knew that the lime in sea-shells dissolved to kill fresh water fish. I liked only gravel, enough plants for the live bearers' fry to hide in, and the fish themselves. But there was still a lot of color and glitter in those tanks, shine of neon tetras and rosy barbs, the mica-flecked hatchets, the bright orange swordtails.

This morning, in this other life, twenty-five years and the width of New York State away from that one, I was downstairs looking out a window at birds scratching in the snow a few feet away. Low drifts had covered the sunflower seeds I'd thrown there, and juncos and sparrows were getting down to them. I was daydreaming, remembering hundreds of chicks warming themselves around a stove in one of Wenzel's sheds, remembering that they scratched instinctively, even if the grain was spread on a sheet of tin.

A pair of cardinals has stayed close this winter. I see them about once a week, along the wood line in back. They appeared there this morning, and then, as I hoped they would, flew into the midst of the other birds in front of me.

The male is a jolt of red, brilliant and striking. It is amazing that nature can distill and hold this color within a world of snow and brown sparrows and gray-white juncos and brown woods. The male is a phenomenon, but the female is a more subtle gift, her body a luminous silver-gray, only her tail, wingtips, and crest touched red.

I watched her this morning, remembered, and received with another eye the fish I most loved. I had only one. Guarini had received it as a stray in a batch of guppies, and had given it to me. We didn't know what kind of fish it was, but I realize now that it must have been a female. Her body was a luminous silver-gray, and only the edges of her fins were touched red.

XXXIII

Jack and his wife Gail live a few houses down the street. He is self-employed, an electrician, and works hard. Gail is not well, usually stays inside, and when in company talks incessantly and loudly as though a moment's silence would wound. Their only son, Chuck, was nineteen when he was killed in Viet Nam in the Mekong Delta in 1969. They were the first ones on the block, as the song from *Woodstock* went, to have their son come home in a box. Jack has been in a daze ever since, rushing from job to job in his green pickup, but always distracted. I have seen him have to force himself to attention three times to change a light-switch. All of us along this street sense great pain and unhappiness emanating from their home. We pray that Jack and Gail will be all right, in the end, after a time, somehow.

Jack has kept up everything at his place, paints at least one side of the house every summer, mows his lawn, washes his pickup. But there's an in-ground swimming pool in their back yard they haven't used or taken care of for five years. One of its cement sides caved in a couple of winters ago because he didn't drain the pool or throw some logs in, and the water has been black-green with mud and algae.

Last summer my son and the other neighborhood boys who fish for bass, carp, suckers, catfish, and perch up at the Erie Canal, got the idea of bringing their catch home and dumping it into the unused pool. Jack told them he didn't mind. Every couple of days the boys dumped in a bucket of fish. I walked over there once to watch the fish-shadows sail up into the shallow end and disappear again into the depths of what had once been this suburban swimming pool. In the evenings, from our back porch, I could see across our yards to Jack sitting beside his pool. He'd throw bread to the fish and stare down into the murky water. The neighborhood boys didn't bother Jack on summer evenings. Even at night, I'd see his silhouette over there, leaning over the pool. Sometimes, by moonlight, he must have seen his own face in the water. Sometimes, the black water must have seemed to be his body.

We all wondered, of course, if any fish could survive the winter in a pool only eight feet deep at the deep end. I didn't know why not, I told my son, but didn't know about a food supply or about how much mud they might need at the bottom.

Now it is January and the pool is frozen. This morning I walked across the snow to Jack's yard where my son and his friends had cut holes in the pool's ice and were fishing with worms one of the boys had frozen in his parents' freezer for just this occasion. The water was very dark under its sky of ice.

And the fish were biting! I could see the poles snap down. In those seconds I remembered ice-fishing at Gibbs Pond from the hood of a Model-A rusting in the water when I was a boy.

I saw Jack watching the fishing from a back window. I waved to him, but he seemed not to see me. I waited around for a while to see if one of the boys could land a fish, but it seems that Jack had told them to file the barbs from their hooks.

At dinner this evening my son said that one of the boys had managed to bring up a perch. Jack was outside then as the fish flapped on the ice. He grabbed it quickly and slipped it back into a hole and looked down through that hole, my son said, for a long time. Then Jack said, "That's right, Chuck. Make sure you throw them all back. That's the way. You got to make sure you throw them all back."

XXXIV

Mid-November after three days of rain, sleet, winds that took a couple of shingles from the roof. Today the sun came out for the afternoon and I rushed to clean out the garage for winter, backed the car, moved the bicycles, lawnmower, wheelbarrow, got things onto shelves and into the garbage cans, and swept the cement. An apple had rolled into a corner and scented it to ripe sweetness. Are apples the only flesh that rots with such a constant delicious smell?

I gathered some flower bulbs that hadn't been planted, and wrapped them into newspapers for the spring. I was about done when I found a coffee can on a ladder-rung. It was half-filled with dirt, something we never waste here in suburbia. I thought I'd empty it onto the front lawn, maybe under our flowering mountain ash, now leafless, its bunches of orange berries ready for the grackles, the only birds that seem to want them.

When I emptied the can a ball of worms rolled out onto the lawn, a glistening fist of mucus, night-crawlers with their darkly swollen sex segments, and smaller, very pink worms, and a few worms white and apparently dead, the whole mass not unlike a brain dripping ganglia, or intestines suddenly shocked to find themselves in the sunlight and chill November air. They lay sodden for a few moments, but then began to move, the outer worms already sliding quickly away under the grass, earth instinct, gravity, some dim and simple cellular pleasure and necessity drawing them into the ground again. A half-hour later, they were gone, every one, even those I thought were dead, and every idea about them.

XXXV

Sunrise. The Island is a cradle below me, and I am falling, without fear, slowing as I near the earth. Then I am there, a hundred yards from the sacred tree, walking toward it, but this time not along a tar road, but on a path, as it must have been, the tree's body a wall at the end of the path.

This is your Island, Island tree. This is your Island. What is the music in the air? I know it is made of leaves and the sun rising, of crickets and small animals, but this does not explain this world's melodic hum. In music, I walk the path descending toward the tree, as I have before, and will again, knowing even as I dream that my dream is dying. But what is the music in the air?...

My dream took me to a slight valley in Setauket, to Lubbers Oak, probably the Island's oldest living thing. A guidebook says that it dates back to the 1400's. Now, reaching into the 1980's, it is almost dead, its one living limb the only one not cut back fifteen or twenty feet above the ground.

It is a white oak. Its bark is smoky gray, and its remaining leaves have rounded lobes. I have never seen a tree as vulnerable, as darkly beautiful.

Much of its great base is rotted out now. When I last knelt there, I found inside it on the ground a smooth white stone as big as your skull. Maybe it came from the Sound, toward which its one living limb points.

I'll tell you a secret: I placed the white stone inside the tree. So that you'll always know me.

XXXVI

I am walking across Main Street in Brockport, the plant shop behind me, its windows filled with vines and wild beach roses that I can see with eyes at the back of my head. I am walking across to the movies. I know I am supposed to meet my wife and children when they come out.

A girl is standing at the curb where I am crossing. She is wearing a black rubber diving suit, and goggles. She is still dripping, having just surfaced. She holds out toward me in her right hand the shell of a chambered nautilus. For an instant, I am lost in its swirl.

I got this down there, she says, pointing at the pavement with her left hand.

I am crossing the street. Under the traffic light, the blacktop has worn away. I can see the red bricks of the old street, and hundred-year old rails embedded in the bricks. I close my eyes: I can see flatcars of America's first reapers, built in Brockport, traveling these rails toward the vanishing point of the prairies.

I am almost across the street. Water laps the exposed rails now, and almost reaches the top of the far curb. The water is pure, pale green and black-green, and restless, the ocean water I knew as a child. I can taste its salt on my lips.

Have I ever been this happy? I am glad about the plants filling the windows behind me. I am glad about the ocean water rising onto the Brockport sidewalks....

XXXVII

Time is not a line in space, already existing. Time becomes itself, gathers and circles. Time is a memoir, but I did not think that mine could continue after its thirty-sixth section. It had made its way from the old Island to Brockport, and then, in several pieces, in a cowbell and in a pair of cardinals and in a swimming pool/pond and in a dream of Ellen, those places and times had come together. At last, too, a girl had risen from the sea to stand on the Brockport sidewalk. I knew who she was. I was at home.

Beside the plant shop that I saw in the dream described, is Brockport's First Methodist Church, built in 1840. One day, walking home from work, staring down as I always do, thinking about nothing, I came to that corner where in my dream that girl in a diving suit had stood and ocean water had risen to the curb. Now, awake, reminding myself that I was awake, I was standing in sand, white sand. Sand covered the sidewalk and street.

It was just that the old brick church had been sand-blasted, but for a few seconds I knew everything in the Upanishads, the Koran, the Christian Bible. All my life and in lives to come I'd been and would be walking through beach roses across that sandy corner again.

XXXVIII

(Sept. 2, 1971)

I am in my bunk, writing under the nightlight, curtains drawn. The wall on my left is against the ocean. The family is asleep, and this floating city is alone out here under the starlight and above the water. Wood seems to be rubbing against wood around us, creaking, almost like the sound of straining ropes. These are old sounds of hammocks in holds and of masts bending against the wind, the sounds my father's father, a fisherman who drowned at twenty-eight in the North Sea, must have known. I think I would have liked going out on a trader or whaler for two or three years as in the old days. The retired captains of Sag Harbor and Southampton, rocking in front of their fires, must have had a wonderful sense of having been there, having known, having seen. And their own mortality, after experiencing such depth and space, must have been especially poignant to them, as mine is to me even now.

(Dec. 25, 1971)

Last week we visited Han's aunt in Hildesheim. It was eerie. We came back to our small apartment here in Hannover with boxes of Hansjörg Greiner's belongings, left behind when Han's mother fled Berlin, kept by Tante Liesel all these years. Now we will send some things back, and carry other things with us. We have a diary that Han's father kept during all of 1940. It's written in a very tiny, crabbed script, and I can't read it, much less translate it, but Klaus will help me with it. So many boxes of papers and books. One volume, Leni Riefenstahl's *Schönheit Im Olympischen Kampf* is inscribed: "Froliche Weinachten 1935—Dr. Goebbels." Greiner worked in the Propaganda Ministry before volunteering for or being ordered to the eastern front. To see that signature, to know that Goebbels touched that page ... Other books are obscenely anti-Semitic. Two volumes are no doubt products of that false racist science that turned the non-Aryan into inferior animal, so filled with diagrams of noses and skulls are they. I have gone through one book of pure propagandistic filth several times. It is dedicated to Hitler, and a colored photograph of the Fuehrer is used as a frontispiece. It was published in 1939, is filled with pictures juxtaposing bedraggled Jews with handsome Germans: a golden-tressed maiden with a flap-eared "Jüdischer Student" whose photograph looks doctored—the caption reads, "Wie es unmöglich ist, aus einem deutsch geboren Menschen einen Juden zu machen, so unmöglich ist es, aus einem Juden einen Deutschen zu machen"; a group of blond athletes marching in shorts in the sun contrasted with a group of old bearded Jews dressed in black and walking with canes. I can now see, from the bibliography at the back of this book, the tremendous flood of similar publications, all of them black, hysterical, vicious, written by what some postwar Germans might call "idealists," men who were true believers in Aryan supremacy. The death camps are their legacy. And these books were not written by uneducated rednecks and published by fly-by-night outfits. The author of this one was (or is) a Dr. Robert Körber. And the Vienna publisher: Universitäts-Verlag Wilhelm Braumüller whose motto was (or is) *per noctem ad lucem*. The title of the book is *Rassensieg in Wien: Der Grenzfeste des Reiches*. Damn them all to hell. Damn them all to hell, but that poison would so surely have taken my own mind during that time. How could I have escaped? It came down with such *authority*! No doubt hundreds of such books were sent, as this one was, to the Propaganda Ministry in Berlin. We can be sure that authors received commendations for their contributions to the Reich. Medals are hidden in the backs of wardrobes and only taken out on special occasions. Damn them all.

Other of Greiner's things now cluttering our apartment are less dramatic, are the stuff of nostalgia and melodrama: his fraternity cap, his set of monogrammed beer mugs, photographs (including many of bloody fraternity duels—Han's mother once mentioned that Greiner had dueling scars on his left cheek), love letters, a Rosenthal platter part of the wedding service, a model ship that was his father's. So much more. We'll be weeks sorting it all and deciding what to save. And what to make of it, God knows.

(Jan. 14, 1972)

I had delivered a lecture and directed a workshop at a retreat in the region called Weserbergland. I had spent three days there, each one ending late at night over drinks in deep and serious conversations with German gymnasium teachers who were the participants in the conference. We spoke about the German character, the war, the destruction of European Jewry. I can see some faces now. Two of the young men had lost their fathers, German soldiers, in the war. One disavowed what he said had been his father's fanatic nationalism. The other seemed ready to go through another such war, and for the same reasons: *Lebensraum*, he said; pride, he said.

We spoke below ground in a sort of wine cellar that had been built into this ex-monastery. There was a sense in which, though other Americans were there, I felt alone with Germans as I had felt nowhere else. I wasn't comfortable. My head buzzed with German history and with thoughts of these people, its inheritors. I slept in a room that Chancellor Bruning had often used. I wondered if, years before, he had lain in my same bed, wondering what to do about those damned Nazis. I thought, too, about that famous rose bush that has been growing beside one church in Hildesheim for a thousand years.

When it was time for me to leave, a German who worked for the American Consulate in Düsseldorf, which had sponsored the conference, drove me to the Paderborn railroad station. I just missed one train to Hannover, and sat on my suitcase at the station for two hours waiting for another. It was dusk when my train pulled out.

A few minutes later, for no reason I could see, the train pulled to a stop in the middle of nowhere. I was alone in my compartment. Evening had fallen almost to full dark, and it had begun to rain. Outside was a meadow edged with pines. I pressed my face against the glass and stared. The meadow was desolate in its green darkness. Then I saw what was probably an owl glide out of the pines and across the meadow and begin to circle. Yes, it was an owl. It swept by only a few meters above ground. I don't know how this could have been, but I thought I heard it cut the air as it leveled off and disappeared into the pines, swift and mysterious. This landscape, this meadow and owl and raining sky and pines going about their business—imagine, I said to myself, imagine that during all those nights of that war, during all the centuries of this frenzied country, there were moments like this, oblivious, perfect, and eternal.

(Feb. 13, 1972)

My desk here is in our living room behind the couch. I am leaning back on the back legs of my chair with my feet up on the back of the couch. The sun is setting on what may be the warmest February day I've ever known. There is a streak of gold in our curtains, and the poinsettias in our window are edged with flame. It's five o'clock, late afternoon, and the room shines, now a redgold as the sun falls lower, now falling behind houses opposite our apartment building. This is a world made beautiful because I will not always be thirty-one and be hearing Han and the kids play a game in another room, made beautiful because the sun is falling.

(March 18, 1972)

Our three days in Leipzig in East Germany: it was all really there, was no film or novel. The watch-towers at the border manned by silhouettes with rifles strapped to their backs; the proliferation of police between the border and Leipzig and in Leipzig itself; the starkness of the lives we glimpsed in some of the small towns all boarded up, the old businesses all boarded up; the children coming up to us on the streets asking for a western coin to use in the "Intershop"; Leipzig striving for a monumental effect, striving to be a city of marbled heights while apartment houses are falling apart and building materials and paint and labor are as scarce as unrestricted travel for most of the population; the constant propaganda of the separateness of this country from the Federal Republic; a woman working in a ceramics shop whispering to me that she and all the other easterners were Germans, too; the four-hour lines at a store because a shipment of bananas is available; the fact that one of those women working in the freezing cold at parking cars makes maybe 150 marks a month; the musical director of a church, Werner's friend, crying when I gave him four West German marks for good razor blades from the Intershop; Han leaving her sweaters behind after finding out the need; the slight traffic, and that western, in a major city, and the frightening vision of what it must be like to live there when all foreigners are gone after the industrial fair that was the excuse for our visit; the surprise and irony of finding downstairs in a bookshop, among only a dozen or so books written in English, a study of Benjamin Franklin in the old American Men of Letters Series; Thomaskirche, where Luther preached (probably from the pulpit I touched) and Bach is buried; the watery cola and orange juice, the weak and bitter Bulgarian wine; the massive Battle of the Nations Monument, and the beautiful Orthodox church where the commander of the Russian forces against Napoleon is buried; the feeling I had that we were being followed; the despair that would not leave the eyes of all the people Pastor Merten visited with gifts of clothes and fruit we smuggled in; being inside Nickolaikirche at night, within its enduring columns; eating breakfast at the Mertens' friends on a service of very old Meissen, a reminder of another time; the differences in the eyes of Imke Merten and her dear friend—they were schoolgirls together, but now can see one another only during the time of the fair. The eyes of the people. The people know, whatever the other facts of life are, that they cannot get out. They cannot get out.

(April 2, 1972)

Easter today. Rain this morning, and I led the family to church, holding an umbrella in my right hand, holding a paper-wrapped bouquet of flowers in my left, looking down at the splashing cobblestones as the church bells began echoing down the streets. The shine and beauty of the rainy air. I'd close my eyes for a few steps at a time, and smell the flowers, and feel the wet air, and hear the bells. Now those moments are already past. Still this life is a miracle, and nothing less.

(April 16, 1972)

Some rain, some fine weather in Berlin. A pleasure just to walk up and down Kurfurstendammstrasse—so much going on.... In East Berlin I actually *saw* the great dark ruins of Speer's buildings, *saw* the square where Goebbels watched the burning of the books. At the Soviet Cemetery at Treptow I touched the marble of Hitler's Chancellery.... An emotion, or a series of emotions, a cluster, very close together, a meaning felt months ago in Bremerhaven, that I can't express: there my body actually passed through the same airspace on this planet that my ancestors' bodies had passed through; then, in Berlin, the same eerie sense of my own body moving through precisely the same space on this planet that Hitler passed through, spaces on earth where history and the future were generated, air that held up blood and bone so close to mine. *Here, here, and only thirty years ago*, I kept saying to myself, as I said to myself at Belsen.

(May 15, 1972)

Each apartment in our building has assigned to it a small room, a storage space in the cellar. Tenants who have been here for a long time have furnished and carpeted theirs, or have workbenches and shelves for groceries. Ours is just empty and dusty. We do have our steerage trunks and suitcases down there, and our bicycle, which I carry up and down the stairs maybe three or four or five times a day, in and out, locking and unlocking doors. It is somehow down in that small room that I mark time here. I close the door and close my eyes, listen to the hum of my blood and of this building, place this building within this suburb of this city of this country. Five minutes is a very long time in that cement-walled and -floored room. Suddenly, it is another day, and I am down in that room again, as though I have never left it.

(May 17, 1972)

There are many bike paths through the woods in and around Stöcken. I bicycle every day, sometimes, I suppose, for twenty or thirty miles, and have been to several neighboring towns. At Celle I found and walked through a British military cemetery. In another town, one that doesn't seem to have a name, I found one antique and junk shop that caught my eye because of an eighteenth-century English silver candlestick in its window, cherubim holding up a delicate rose that would hold the candle. But it's 300 marks, and sort of a cornball piece anyway, said the fox.... I know no one in these small towns, and don't speak to anyone, and never run into anyone who recognizes me from anywhere. I pedal past dozens or hundreds of people, find my way back home, put the bike away downstairs, and then walk up to our apartment, to a wife and children who know me, people I need. I seem to live in a series of miracles, and can't shake off the pleasant but somehow uncomfortable sensations of strangeness that sometimes last all day.

Every Saturday morning the four of us take the bike to the fresh-air market just a few blocks down Weizenfeldstrasse. It's been open all winter, but now it's really a pleasure to stroll the aisles of flowers and vegetables and fruit. There are barrels of fish from North Sea catches, mackerel with blue iridescent backs, tangles of brown-black eels, flounders and doormat fluke—these are the fish that my father's father must have known. There are cheese trucks and wagons of nuts and stands of chickens and pheasants and counters of chocolates and cakes. I hear that the oranges, grapefruit, and lemons are imported from Israel.

(May 19, 1972)

About halfway to the University is the baroque Great Herrenhausen Garden, second in Europe, if second at all it is said, only to Versaille. I've been there maybe twenty times, have watched winter take fall and now spring take winter there, have spent much time under the famous rows of ancient but now failing lime trees. There is no experience quite like strolling the Garden's symmetries, your line of sight to the left, each hedge or statue or row of trees, matched by your line of sight to the right, each row of trees or statue or hedge. I've spent much time here—the gardens within gardens, the fountains, the rows inside of rows inside of rows of color-schemed and height-schemed flowers (during displays at night even the fireworks seem to trace baroque patterns in the sky)—but not as much as at the Berggarten across the street. Here a path takes you beneath trees from all over the world. You end up back under great beeches and elms in front of the mausoleum of George I, the only English king buried in a foreign country. A guide book says that more than 100 bombs hit the Berggarten during the war, but there's no sign, of course, now, though some of the ponds are probably bomb craters.

Near the entrance, inside a simple building, you can turn left and enter a lush rain forest, the tropical trees dripping orchids; or, you can turn right into a room with hundreds of species of cacti. The emotions of wetness, lushness, shadow and extravagance to your left. The emotions of strong sunlight and bare intellect and the desert on your right. Images of soul and brain, but allegory is boring and false next to these living things.

XXXIX

I am forty....

In my dream last night I was at Lake Ronkonkoma. It was dusk, but a tunnel of rose- and yellow-streaked light shone from across the lake. I was there at the shore, under trees, with my wife, but I walked some distance from her to where a man and boy were fishing. While I was standing near them, the man reeled in a fish, a pike bigger than any I thought lived in the lake. I wanted to help by taking the fish off the hook and stringing it. With my left hand I held the fish behind its gills, and with my right forefinger and thumb grasped the hook's shank. But the fish had very dangerous teeth, and I was worried—its lower jaw seemed double-jointed and able to stretch up toward my fingers. I let the pike swing loose on the line toward the fisherman.

Then he reeled in another fish, one I thought I could handle. It was mud-colored and bass-shaped, and lay almost still at the end of the line. As I held the fish, I saw that it had been snagged, no, not even snagged, but that the line was actually wrapped around it. I held the hook, which lay loose, and began untying the fish, but found that the line was embedded in its flesh. I kept pulling the line out of the fish's body, going around it and around it with my hand. I saw that the fish could see me, was watching me. As the line pulled free, the fish's flesh closed over its wounds....

At the back of our Brockport acre, when we bought this land which was once part of a farm, was a beech tree wrapped with barbed wire that had sliced into the trunk as the tree grew. I grasped the end of the wire with pliers, and walked around the tree, pulling the wire out. The tree's smooth smoky-gray skin closed over its wounds. Did this have anything to do with my dream, or did the beech just appear here as I was remembering freeing the dreamed fish?

This memoir is sometimes a matter of following the lines of a dream, unwinding them and the life in which they are embedded. This living memoir accepts a shifting map and/or momentary wounding, but closes over my dream, and keeps it, mysterious, in dusklight, in time, within its body.

XL

The five paragraphs of the preceding section are dated January 10, 1981, in my notebook, and I've just found them again, January 2, 1982. I'd forgotten that I'd written them. In the copy of *Long Island Light* that I keep back here in my Brockport cabin to read from once in a while, I found a note to myself: "maybe add prose piece beginning 'I am forty.'" A later note is set in brackets beside it: "[did I write this?]." So, I went looking through notebooks and found that I did write that piece, the five paragraphs above, and had forgotten it, until today. And today I see what I did.

The fact is that it wasn't a beech tree wrapped with barbed wire at the back of our property, but an ash wrapped with steel cable. The fact is that I wasn't able to pull the cable out of the tree, or even chop it out. The cable is wrapped in such a complex configuration that I can't tell whether or not it encircles the trunk completely, and if so, whether or not the tree is growing over the cable and will be able to continue to feed itself, or whether the cable will kill it. The ash's foliage this past summer seemed sometimes thicker and sometimes thinner than it did the year before. In any case, in writing the previous section I followed someone else who was telling a story. That story paralleled my own life to a point—in the images of the dream—but changed things for the sake of its own teller and telling. This section, and the previous one, are part of the same tree, the same memoir. The tree is a fish. No, the tree is a beech. No, the tree is an ash. Whatever, I hope the steel cable doesn't kill it.

XLI

I am running again, this time through tiled corridors, across cement walks of the college's campus. I am trying to get to my next class. I am crying and running, books under my left arm. I am almost mad. Now, somehow, to get to class I have to hang onto girders way up in the back of a building in the half dark somewhere. I am swaying in the dark, sweating and cursing. I could fall, I know. Maybe I should, I think, just to show the bastards who built this crazy obstacle course entrance to my classroom how negligent they were....

No, I think, I cannot survive this heartbreak, thirty years after that other one. I cannot survive it. Then I am running again, crying, worried about being a spectacle, books under my arm. There will be no reconciliation, I know. The conversation we had, her assured smile, the face of that damned kid she is going to leave me for—the back of my throat aches.

I am walking into my classroom when I see a friend, a colleague. I tell him what is happening to me, how I can't believe it. The marriage was such a good one, I tell him.

The black weight of another conversation is on my mind: she tells me it has not been right with us since I did something to her at Christmas two years after we were married. What? I don't know. It was then, she thinks, that she made up her mind it would come to this.

I am suicidal, I am wrenched back into my old world of regret and pain. I love her but now have lost her and this time won't be able to make it through the years. I call up images of the most attractive young women in my classes but know immediately that I am being ridiculous....

I awaken. Relief floods. I breathe deeply. It is the morning of our twenty-third anniversary. I won't wake her. I know that she still loves me.

XLII

My mother-in-law had a series of strokes and lay in a coma for four months before she died. No one knows what goes on in the minds of the comatose, whether or not they have a language, whether or not their lives are films inside them. Sometimes my wife and I thought Mom knew we were with her; sometimes, her breathing quickened, but when we lifted an eyelid, there was only dead light in the dilated pupil.

I was back at the farm—this was Nashville, New York, dairy and grape country west of Buffalo—but later on that day would drive to the hospital to join Han. I was walking inside and around a granary that had been unused for decades. June wasps were busy under rafters, mice under floor joists. Swallows sliced through broken windows into the black air to their nests cupped in the rafters. I'd visited this place for twenty years, and didn't seem to be any wiser about anything as I stood there that day. Maybe swallows know something about the comatose, but that day they weren't talking.

Grasses sprawled up to the sagging walls, honeysuckle and forsythia bushes poked through gaps in the boards. The sweet smells of must and grainrot had me closing my eyes again, knowing nothing except that my own life was timebound and timeless, beautiful and sad in its passing.

I haven't been back inside that granary for years. It may have become its own grave, but I ask you to close your eyes with me for a moment, now, and breathe the black air of that place on this planet where swallows will always glide from the outer world to the inner and out again. We can close our eyes and see them.... Now.

Beside a rain barrel behind the granary, wild roses were in bloom. That day I broke off one as big as my fist, and drove through the countryside with it. At the hospital, I held it close to Mom's face. She became agitated, her eyes rolling under her lids. Then she became calm and began to breathe deeply. She seemed to want to inhale more and more of the flower.

I believe that the rose colored her dreams that day, that every rose she'd ever experienced was with her, is with her, wherever she was, wherever she is now.

XLIII

I want to tell you about something that happened last evening, at Adam's Basin, along the Canal. There had been an outing. About ten couples, Han and I among them, had rented a boat and sailed from Adam's Basin west to past Brockport and back again. It had been a cool but perfect evening filled with birds and wildflowers, honeysuckle, the smells of freshwater, oil, minnows in the air.

Back where we began, we debarked. I walked hand-in-hand in darkness with my wife along what I thought was the dock back to where our car was parked. We stumbled a little, but there was no problem, and we just walked straight ahead. The moonlight made black-on-black shadows in front of us. I stepped into one, fell straight down, and found myself wide-eyed under the water, looking up to the pale surface. I came up, and thrashed around, heard screaming above me, dogpaddled in the pitch dark to the side of the Canal. I was heavy—pants, sneakers, T-shirt, shirt, sweater, jacket with pockets filled with keys, a corkscrew. The side of the Canal was smooth. I scraped my fingernails along it, trying to hold on, couldn't. I paddled beside it, tired now. I didn't think I could stay above the water for long. I then thought of swimming across the Canal, but I was blocked in on my left, too, by a solid wall. I was confused, disoriented.

There was only a crack of light above me. Ten or fifteen feet along, I saw what I thought was a rope dangling. I grabbed for it and missed it. Then I gathered myself, lunged for it again, and had it with my right hand. It saved me. A friend, a big man by the name of Bill Rose, straddled the shore and the flatboat from which I'd fallen, reached down as I climbed the rope, and hauled me out. I weigh about 200 pounds, and was of course clothed and wet, but he lifted me straight up and out. My wife was safe. She had somehow seen what that shadow was, a space between two flatboats, and had jumped over it the same moment I stepped into it.

I was at no time afraid. I believe that if I hadn't been tall and an athlete, I'd have drowned, but I was calm. Just before I reached that cable, I wondered whether if I were to drown some part of me, a voice, a seeing voice would survive, or whether everything would go black, whether I'd be extinguished. I believe that I felt that if I were to die, some part of me, some part located in the brain but beyond the brain would have gone on. What is the exact location of the soul?

That's that. One second I was walking along, and in the next I was under the water. For a few moments, and this was what I mainly wanted to tell you about, I had only one thing in my mind, a connection that flashed to me. I was at Seaford on Long Island. I was six or eight. I'd been out night-eeling with Artie. I'd tried to step from Artie's boat to the dock, and had fallen in. I went straight down, but kicked and groped upward. Artie somehow hauled me in. There, in the Canal last evening, the decades disappeared. Time was sensibly apprehensible. I experienced time from somewhere else. Thirty years had been only a moment or two, or less. Time revealed itself to me as a wordless illusion for which I now have the word.

XLIV

I've awakened from a dream in which I saw myself walking in shadows through Island woods....

I knew I was going fishing, or would wade Gibbs Pond's edges to see if there had been a new hatch of painted turtles, but when I got close to the pond I heard the noise of machines, maybe chainsaws. Then I was on a hill and saw the pond in bright light below me. The noise came from two motor boats, the first I'd ever seen there. They were racing back and forth across the pond's human face.

I saw myself turn back toward home again. As I did, the two boats raced from the far side of the pond to the side nearest me. All the time I walked home, the noise got louder, became almost deafening. I held my hands over my ears. Then I was running back to the pond with a rifle. Then I was firing bullets down at a distance into the silhouettes of boats on the pond, which was now my own face. There were swirls of water under my eyes, tears. The boats were now gone, and when my bullets struck my face, they made black holes which widened, and into which the pond emptied.

XLV

Morning. I'm at east Quogue at a friend's house. I'm sitting out back on his pool deck. His tool shed is off to my left, under white oaks that have come back after being stripped two years running by gypsy moths.

My friend leaves the door of the tool shed open all day and all night to allow a pair of swallows to build and fulfill their nest, built inside above a light switch. They've come back to this place for several years. One of them is gliding over the pool, fast. I can just catch glimpses of its off-white and -yellow underbelly.

An insect trap hangs from the eaves of the tool shed. All night its oval of light drew in mosquitoes and moths and anything else in the air too curious or sexy for its own good. A blade inside the trap chops them up. They fall into a bag that my friend empties every few days under a juniper bush. This morning, a bluejay is enjoying its lazy luck there.

There's a little poem by Doc Williams called "Nantucket." I remember it now, its austerity and cleanliness, the lace curtains in its window, the linen on its bed, the glass on its table next to a key with which we feel, as we read, that we can unlock the lyric of that world.

I am imagining a poem called "East Quogue," sharp mentionings of this treated-lumber deck and the too-blue pool and the metal weatherstrip blazing along the shed door, the delineations of the swallows' wings, the edges of oak leaves that we can never be sure we'll ever see again.

XLVI

A friend of mine keeps a small piece of polished wood, the product of his first assignment in graduate art school, on the desk in his study. His teacher had told him, simply, to shape a piece of wood so that, when held, it would give pleasure. It does. The small object of rounded walnut fits in my palm, somehow, in every way. I don't know why, but sometimes when I hold it I close my eyes. And when I touch it, moisture forms fingerprint blossoms on its surfaces for a few seconds, and then the shape of wood is all itself again.

In a dream last night I was at a Long Island pond, Brown's Pond in Hauppauge—I doubt that it still exists. In the dream, just as I did when I was a child and awake, I was prying box turtles from the fragrant lily-mud and -muck at pond's edge. I'd often fill a whole pail with them and carry them home, pen them up and feed them grasshoppers for a few days before letting them go.

The yellow-to-orange and brown-to-black box turtles congregated at the ponds, but were Island wanderers. I'd sometimes find one in the woods, or crossing our lawns. They were able to survive, I read, on just the few insects a year they were able to catch. I remember once being very still as I watched one under our grape arbor eating a cricket, almost distractedly, as though it were chewing its cud.

Did you ever hear the sound of a bullet as it punctured a turtle's shell? I did, just once. There was something so final and sickening in the sound, so imploded, that I never wanted to hear it again.

Why was it, though, I still wonder, that I saw hundreds of those turtles over the years but only once saw a very small one? The ones I found were inevitably almost full-grown, the size of maybe your kneecap. Every year at the ponds I caught many painted turtle babies, but the box turtle babies were nowhere to be found, though I often looked for them. It was Mrs. Wenzel, in fact, who gave to me the one I once had. She'd plucked it out of her strawberry patch. It must have weighed about half an ounce. Its undershell enclosed it very tightly, the trapdoor under its head drawing up at an angle I liked to hold against my cheek.

I kept that baby turtle with me for whole days in school. I'd peek inside my desk and see that my turtle had begun to open. When it saw the light, it closed up tight again.

The baby turtle within its shell within the shell of that desk within my skull within the shells of memory and time … While writing—I'm right-handed—I still like to think that for balance I hold that little pale yellow turtle in my left palm.

XLVII

This was Woodhaven, before we moved to Hauppauge and Nesconset. I must have been only four or five. I was in our cement driveway.

I was back against our garage with my father. A man I didn't know was sitting on the running board of a black car. He had just come back from Forest Pond—I remember the name. He had a pail between his feet. What happened next happened quickly and unexpectedly.

The pail was filled with black water. The man reached in with both hands, felt around, and pulled up a large, dark fish, its black scales lightening in shades of bronze down its sides. Its belly was white. It flapped, jumped out of the man's hands, and landed on the cement. He picked it up again and slipped it back into the black water.

The man said something in magic, winked at me, and felt around in the water again. This time, when he brought the fish back up, it had changed into the most beautiful thing I'd seen up to that time in my life. My whole head seemed to buzz. I couldn't quite focus on it. It lay still in the man's hands, but sucked and puffed. It had no distinct edges; its form was a blur of soft orange-gold light. In the lower corners of its eyes were spots of red.

How had it lived under tree trunks in the black water of Forest Pond? How could the man possibly have caught it? Was that its shadow I had first seen? That fish still swims upward into my eyes in its own undiminished light.

XLVIII

In his autobiography *Of Men and Plants*, healer Maurice Mességué says that when he was about four in 1925 in the remote French village of his childhood he was sleeping badly, tossing and turning all night. "We'll give him a linden-blossom bath," his father said.

His mother set out a copper basin and poured into it a golden liquid she'd been warming. Father and mother plunged Maurice into the bath. At first he yelled, he remembers, but then began to feel very sleepy. His father carried him to bed. "My father often put me to sleep in this way," Maurice says, "and I have done the same for my own sons."

Linden blossoms would be picked warm in sunlight and buzzing with bees, then spread to dry on canvas sheets in the shade. Later, the blossoms would be soaked in huge copper basins full of water, "and the resulting infusion was then stored and could be used five or six times for bathing a highly strung child." Linden-blossom osmosis. Copper basins: "Look, my boy, that's copper, it's finer than gold. It's red like that because it has been a mirror to the sun and the fire, and you are going to have a bath in it."

In Nesconset when I was a boy we had a huge linden outside our kitchen window. Each spring it hummed eighty-feet high with bumblebees and honeybees and blossoms. But I was often, as I am now, unable to sleep. And I remember in the late '40s and early '50s the gatherings of Germans, the *Volksfests* at Franklin Square that my parents took me to: picnic tables in deep mid-summer shade under the lindens. The drinking and forced laughter. Oom-pah.

It is as though we are unable to rest, to sleep. And it is as though God has placed with us the means by which we can restore ourselves to the natural morning. But we've forgotten, and will probably never remember again.

XLIX

1.

Climbing inside Diamond Head again, I saw a cave behind brush up near the rim where an ancient king of Oahu had been buried. I saw dripping honeycombs hanging down across the cave's mouth. Bees glistened for split seconds in sunlight as they flew from the cave. Those returning disappeared in shadows as had every word the royal one had ever spoken.

From the summit, west past the coral curve of Waikiki hotels, I could see Pearl Harbor. A squadron of warplanes was lifting off. Their wings flashed before they disappeared into the Pacific....

2.

Americans

We launched out to the *Arizona* at Pearl Harbor,
stood above a thousand sailors where they died.
Some of us dropped flowers, bits of color
to float the length of battleship shadow,
their grave that dug to its depth in eight minutes.
December 7, 1941. Dawn. Average age: nineteen.

If people and places appear in joy
before us as we die, then high school sweethearts,
family, village trees, city street lamps
lit ocean in instants of cellular thankfulness,
but we call them "black tears," the droplets of oil
still rising to rainbow the surface here.

L

Because I fell in love with bullets—those 22-caliber beauties: how their gently-rounded lead tips seemed like cherry buds to bite into or like tiny rocket ships, how their brass casings gleamed—I decided to steal some from Wenzel.

I was ten. I couldn't sleep. I twisted in my sheets, wanting bullets. Wenzel had let me touch them, had let me insert one into the chamber of his single-shot, had let me squeeze the trigger on a squirrel. I hit back under my target, but didn't care. The gun fit my shoulder, its slight kick made me happy, I could picture the invisible power streaking in a direct line to the tree and burying itself, could smell the sweet gunsmoke. I felt as though I'd released a death ray with my fingertip. I experienced my first remembered erection. For days I could feel that smooth and rounded gunstock in my hands, the cool metal barrel against my cheek, but what I most wanted were some of the bullets. I wanted to wet them in my mouth. I wanted to roll them in my fingers in my pocket. I wanted to keep some under my pillow and from time to time warm them with my body.

This was 1950. I followed Wenzel around as he mixed feed for, fed, slaughtered by slitting the throats of, gutted, soaked, plucked his leghorns, gathered eggs, opened cartons of newly-arrived chicks in their heated shed, swept and shoveled and carted manure, shot rats, shot a groundhog, shot a stray cat, shot squirrels, buried them, cleaned his rifle with an oily rag, put any bullets he hadn't used back into their box in a cabinet above his workbench in one of his sheds.

For lunch, I always walked the half-mile home from school. I planned to watch for a day when Wenzel's Willys jeep wouldn't be in his driveway, and to hide from my mother for the few minutes it would take me to pass through the gate between our properties, make my way between coops to that shed, and steal some bullets. How many would I take? How many would he miss? How many, exactly, would I need to be satisfied? If I took the whole box would he think he'd misplaced it? It would be safest to take only a few, but I wanted as many as I could get away with.

I'd not stolen anything before. When I did fall asleep, it was for only a short time, those weeks, before I jerked awake and could almost see through my bedroom wall across the dark to where Wenzel's luminous bullets waited in their cabinet. I wanted to tongue that crimped line between their lead and brass, wanted to press their bases, that circle where the firing pin would strike, into my forehead until I bled.

As I walked home for lunch on the day of the bullets, afraid that Wenzel's jeep would be there and afraid that it wouldn't, he beeped and passed me, waved at me from behind his windshield. I saw him only as a bearded blur in the glare, but was sure it was him, and Mrs. Wenzel was with him, so I wouldn't have to worry about her, either. I turned and waved to their backs. My heart beat so hard that I held my hands against it and pressed....

I got up on the workbench with both knees. I opened the cabinet, found the box of bullets. I took many, about a third of the box. Every chicken on Wenzel's acre squawked as I ran home, ducked behind bushes, ran back behind pines around to the road and then, whistling breathlessly, walked back up our long driveway so my mother wouldn't see me running from the direction of my crime.

At lunch, the pocketful of bullets made me sweat and blush—do I remember that my mother took my temperature?—but at last I was running back to school.

My friends were still at recess—Butch Babinski, Richie Paland, Bob Stekete, Johnny Vion, Ernie Olsen, Billy McLaren—and playing where they shouldn't have been, where new classrooms were being built, where there was a drum of trash burning, no construction workers or teachers in sight. The boys were throwing wood and insulation into the fire, circling and whooping, the girls—Pam Muller, Gertrude Zoller, Gertrude Abel, Diane Munch, Faith Baldasara—watching and yelling and pointing. And there I was, running with them, running into them, my secret bullets in my pockets. This was fourth grade, and I was the leader.

It could be that what happened was that one of my friends impressed the girls by doing something impressive. Maybe he put a board across the top of the drum and got up on it and stood above the fire and above me. Whatever. I ran to the drum and flung my precious bullets, every one of them, down into the fire.

Soon, one by one, the bullets began to crack off, blasted and puffed holes into the drum. My classmates backed away, but I screamed, I danced, I circled that fire, I whirled and stood still sidewise and stood still broadside and dared it to stop me from screaming and dancing, but it didn't. That will come in time, but it didn't then. Today is my 50th birthday. I am still throwing Wenzel's bullets into the fire.

LI

When in 1982 in his 88th year Archibald MacLeish fell and broke an elbow, two friends and I wired him flowers. He was at home in Conway, Massachusetts, with Ada, his wife of more than six decades. He wrote his Brockport friends what may have been his last letter. "Neither Ada nor I will ever forget that evening," he said. He described the delivery of the flowers: "Feet through the crust on four-foot snow and a knock on the door and that luminous whiteness: whiteness everywhere—whiteness of snow, of flowers, of love."

It is evening and snowing as I write, the spaces among trees around my Brockport home filling with white silence, that whiteness he described, that snow and those flowers. Near me, I have the photographs of two poets: Walt Whitman, in his full beard of snow, faces the other poet, one born the year he died. Camden and Conway, they are in the ground now, but no matter what happens to the surfaces of things, from where they are, "Luminous whiteness—whiteness everywhere."

LII

The national news carries a story about a murder in Northport. During the five-second clip of the murderer being led to his arraignment in handcuffs, the wild-eyed boy glares at the camera and sneers/hisses/growls as though possessed. He is wearing a Satan T-shirt, and is apparently a member of what the newspapers and television describe as a "satanic cult." There are shots of a local park smeared with graffiti: "Satan is King."

The victim had stolen some bags of angel dust from the murderer, and had been dragged into the woods. The murderer, and maybe others, tied, stabbed, tortured the victim, but the murderer did not deliver the death blow until he saw a crow, a sign to him that his Master was ready to receive the victim, or maybe he thought the crow was the Son of Morning himself. He then cut out his victim's eyes.

I was on the Island when I heard and read this story. The same day, I walked a wood path in Roslyn when I heard a crow in the top of a dead tree not far away. At first, I didn't break my stride, and the crow stayed where it was, but when I backtracked and placed myself where I could glimpse it through the leaves of an oak and where it could see that I could see it, it flapped away....

The words "numen" and "numinous" have always seemed elusive to me, but have something to do with the spirit of a place. In my poem "The Numinous" in *Erika*, I use as epigraph a sentence from Rudolf Otto's *The Idea of the Holy*, a study of mysticism: "Our language has no term that can isolate distinctly and gather into one word the total numinous impression a thing may make on the mind." I have seen a hundred dead crows tied to a "killing tree" at the back of a farmer's field in Knotting in Bedfordshire, England. I have seen crows flying above the mass graves at Bergen-Belsen in northern Germany. I have dreamed of walking through crow-shadows in a medieval forest, each crow becoming, somehow, a beat of my heart. Now I have seen that crow in Roslyn, and in my mind have seen that Northport crow. The natural world in its repetitions sometimes seems to force me toward definite ideas about it, but I must not delude myself or damn the crow. I am glad the crow will not quite let me see it, will always flap away, only and always itself.

LIII

In old Nesconset we had two driveways, about ten feet apart, divided by grass and trees and a wire fence. The first belonged to the house, was there when we moved from Hauppauge. It was maybe a hundred feet long from Gibbs Pond Road to garage. I remember the huge white pines to the left as I walked or drove in, and the catalpas and smaller pines to the right between the driveways.

We dug the second driveway ourselves. I helped strip and roll up the sod, though I was very young and probably did very little. This driveway went past the right side of our garage and curved left into a clearing and my father's wood-working shop, Nesconset Woodworking. Wenzel's hen houses were only a little ways away, across the clearing. Only now can I imagine how upset the Wenzels must have been when Long Island progress meant that a bar-owner from Hauppauge decided to move with his wife and four sons to sparsely-settled Nesconset right next to him, build a woodworking shop, and cut a second driveway up and down which lumber trucks and pickups and cars of salesmen and customers would rumble from eight to five Monday through Saturday. The Wenzel hens probably needed tranquilizers, probably laid some hollow eggs.

Mainly, my father built the shop by himself, and it was no shanty. At one time he employed twenty men, each with an area of floor, each with his own band saw or rip-saw or lathe or bench for gluing Formica or building a set of stairs. Attached in back to the new shop was a low, tarpaper-roofed chicken coop converted now to a lumber shed. The trucks would back up to this shed, and I'd sometimes help unload, sliding the long 2 x 4's or pine boards or oak planks into place from truck across shed window sills to cement floor. I don't know how many board feet of lumber would come in, but sometimes it would take an hour or two to unload one of those trucks, three or four men working. And all that lumber made its way across the Island transformed by men and machines into tables, chairs, beds, kitchen cabinets, vanities, stairs, picture frames, pigeon cages, window sashes, work benches, cribs, cupolas, wardrobes, dressers, doors.

A customer would come in with an idea for some piece of furniture. My father would sketch it—I saw him do this hundreds of times—and the customer would see his idea take shape in front of him. Some customers had careful measurements (some of which later proved wrong) and others would ask my father to visit and take measurements. Everyone seemed to be in a hurry. Half the phone calls at Nesconset Woodworking were from customers wondering when their orders would be ready. It was not unusual for my father to promise that something would be finished in 6-8 weeks, and then finally get it done a month or two after that, so busy was the shop, so many orders were there, even with my father often extending the shop's hours, working alone some evenings but usually early mornings after his 4:30 or 5:00 breakfast of rye bread, herring, and coffee.

Many of the workers had served apprenticeships at their crafts in the old countries. They knew what they were doing. They were almost all on different salary schedules, according to how good they were and how long they'd been working for my father, who did all the books himself. They did the best work in Suffolk County, probably—orders came in to Nesconset Woodworking from many other shops, even from Nassau County, when those places had a problem or couldn't handle a certain item. My father—I think my memory is fair to the truth when I say this—was the most skilled of all. Again and again workers would come to him, and he'd show them a way to machine or assemble something. Henry was not only the boss, but the most respected worker in the shop.

As a 19-year-old immigrant who couldn't speak English, years of apprentice-work behind him in Germany when he would travel from master to master and have to build something and be graded on it, my father's first job was in a basement workshop in Brooklyn. I'd sometimes prompt him to tell the story of how he built a secretary-desk to his boss's specifications that first week, and was proud of what he'd done, but stood there in shock when the boss came in on Friday afternoon and smeared ashes on the secretary and beat it with chains. "That's what we make here, Henry, antiques," the boss said to him. O America.

The time came when he wanted a bigger and better shop. He had one built on the Jericho Turnpike between Nesconset and Smithtown. He began to do less custom work, and to sell more of the ready-made unfinished furniture that trucks from the big mills in Virginia and the Carolinas dropped off. He hired an accountant to take care of the books, but needed fewer and fewer workers. Some of these branched off to set up their own shops, but these didn't last for long, not because their own skills were not sufficient, but because by then the Island economy had no time to appreciate those skills.

Soon, my father sold his second shop and moved Nesconset Woodworking, name and all, directly to Main Street in Smithtown. By that time, only three or four workers were still with him. He never made as much money as he did during those last several years when all those trucks dropped off all those loads of hastily-built furniture and people would come in off the street and cart it away. That third shop still had a few machines out back, but was nothing like the first shop in Nesconset. The furniture built in that first shop will stand sturdy centuries after the last piece of that rickety stapled stuff from the Carolina mills is fed to fireplaces for kindling.

I remember my parents arguing about money, money—no matter how busy that first shop was, money was always tight. Later, in the second and third shops, my father and the craftsmen who worked for him would of course have been happier taking the time to build, say, a bookcase right, but the necessary money flowed to those jimmy-built cheap bookcases that anticipated the case-bound, unsewn, cheap paper, false-cloth books that would soon fill them.

LIV

Nesconset

Werner raised tumblers
that could enfold themselves
to fall, so couldn't be struck
from the Island sky....

Later that year, in their loft,
one puffed her soft breast
and cooed into the grain
of my palm.... My brother did

not say, *This may someday
create the past.* Still,
I remember her one black
and one wall eye. Tumbling

keeps me closest to her
in that then, and will.

The Child at the Bus Stop: On Abortion

Nine or ten years ago, a friend whose youngest of three children was fifteen was surprised and afraid when she found herself pregnant again. She strained to decide whether or not to have an abortion. Questions of her age, of her new job, of her husband's ability to cope with a baby at this time in her life—he was almost sixty—and moral questions, of course, made her lose sleep, lose weight. In the end, she decided she could not have an abortion.

Now, mornings when I drive to work, I often see this child waiting for her school bus. She is there, a person in the world. If her mother had had an abortion, this child would not be here on my Brockport street waiting at the bus stop. If her mother had decided to have an abortion, her decision would have been about this particular girl. Logically, is there any other way to look at it? This child was born into the cosmos at the moment of her conception. If her mother had aborted her at two minutes or two weeks or whenever, it is the *child* at the bus stop who would have been aborted. What difference does *time* make? The girl at the bus stop began growing toward me and our village at the moment of her conception. It would have taken an *act* to remove her from our presence. Any argument against this plain fact seems to me to me to be casuistry.

This girl was moving toward my life as surely as, say, a friend driving from New York City to see me in Brockport, or, rather say, a friend being driven by his mother. Let's say he's sleeping a warm, comfortable, dreamless, defenseless sleep all the way. If his mother pushes him out the door and he dies, it doesn't matter whether she does this in Syracuse or in Rochester. She has terminated his life before he has reached me. Whatever his age, he was wholly dependent upon her for his life. It doesn't matter that he was sleeping and that I couldn't see him as he moved closer to me. I would have seen him, if his mother had not caused his absence, as surely as I now see the girl at the bus stop.

Having said this, I've said only the one thing about the abortion issue that seems clearest to me: we are nine months old when we are born. Not to realize this, is to be lacking not only in logic, but in imagination.

But I know, too, that our planet will not for long sustain a population that has tripled in about forty years. I know that sexual ignorance and immaturity and

Rochester Democrat and Chronicle/Times-Union (July 3, 1989).

promiscuity and violence and carelessness and bad luck and accident result in millions of unwanted pregnancies a year. Many girls and women are poor, desperately unhappy, unwilling. They demand free choice. I believe they should have this choice. I believe that when I say this, when I vote to give them this choice, when I vote to provide money for social services so that they will not have to rely on back-alley incompetents with coat-hangers and dirty hands, I myself participate in a kind of necessary evil, for a society should protect even the weakest of its members, including that girl at the bus stop who was on her way to me from the moment of her conception. But I am not myself willing to nurture and raise these millions of children unwanted by their parents, nor would I, even along with millions of other Americans, be able to, for long. It seems to me that abortion is terrible, and necessary. Until we can get to the roots of the problem, the reasons for these unwanted pregnancies in the first place, depending on our degree of sensitivity we may be doomed to share the debilitating guilt and sorrow experienced by some women for the rest of their lives because of their choice to abort. As I condone any woman's legal, immoral right to an abortion, I participate in the killing of children who would some day be waiting for their school bus. God help me.

Note:

Of the essays in *Home*, this piece on the abortion question worries me the most. Its words and arguments and assumptions become more and more slippery and complex for me as I grow older, while, as a piece of writing, it remains sure of itself, filled with liberal practicality and guilt. When I wrote it, I wrote as deeply and truly as I could, of course, but now I consider it as something I say in the always present tense of this book to see what the effect will be of my having said it. History's evolving eye will stare through these five paragraphs, especially the last, in soulful or political ways. Since I published this, I've written a story called "The Babies," and my daughter and her husband have adopted two children.

(February 2001)

The Babies

Mary and me, we always wanted more kids. This was what was on my mind the whole time, there and back.

After the boss got the rush contract, I got to Detroit and got my eighteen-wheeler loaded at the Gerber Foods warehouse. I headed south on coffee and No-Doze. Sometimes I half-slept while I kept to the road. Instead of seeing cards as I sometimes do after a poker all-nighter, I was picturing millions of those little jars of baby food—black-purple beets, pale orange carrots, golden apple sauce—all the stuff I was hauling down to Cairo.

I'd read the stories about what was going on down there, and had heard a couple brief reports on television. It's supposed to be a sleepy town. They've got a river going through the place, and one morning the locals saw patches on the river drifting toward them. The patches—damndest thing—turned out to be babies. I couldn't believe my ears, and couldn't believe my eyes when I saw the pictures. The babies were still alive, just floating in their raggedy blankets or on stick rafts. The Cairo folks pulled them out of the water as fast as they could, but they kept coming, hundreds of them, then more and more. One woman said you could have walked on them to the other side, there were so many. One emergency worker said it got to the point where the babies were clogging the current. President Wharton pledged National Guard help and all the resources of federal disaster-relief agencies. A lot of these agencies sub-contracted. Here's where me and a thousand other truckers came in.

Driving down, I gassed up and got coffee, got coffee and gassed up, and took a couple No-Doze every hour or two. As I said, I was thinking of my own kids when they were born. The pictures of those babies in the river must have spooked me. And I was remembering how me and Mary always wanted more than two, but the doctor said she'd be better off not going through another pregnancy, and Mary sometimes had women's problems and eventually had to have a hysterectomy, and that was that. But we were never unhappy, exactly. Two kids kept us plenty busy, until they were grown and on their own. Then I'd sometimes walk around the house, looking at the trophies still left in Bill's room, looking at the high school cheerleading and prom pictures in Kristen's room, wondering where the years had gone. It was good to be out from under college bills, of course, and we no longer felt we were supporting half the country's farmers. It was a good life. What else can you ask for except more?

But I'll tell you what bothered me. Even though I knew we weren't going to have any other kids, I had to sign a form that said I understood this. This was just before Mary's hysterectomy. They brought a form to me saying I realized that the consequence of this surgery was that the patient would be unable in the future to bear any children. After I signed, I felt a little dizzy, like most of my life was over at that point. I mean, it wasn't as though I thought I would be a father again, anyway. But signing that form made me face the fact. I guess that's what it was. It didn't hit Mary the same way. She was the one under the knife, of course. But, besides that, she's always adjusted to things better than me. "We're in our autumn years now, John," she says once in awhile.

I happened to hit Cairo at evening. I was spaced-out, but hyper at the same time, anxious to get the tons of cases of food I was hauling to where they'd do some good. I got my rig into a line of others converging toward a field of tents down against the river where helicopters were hovering close to one another over the wide water, blasting their spotlights down and making a hellish noise.

Everything was crowded and seemed chaotic, as though there'd been some huge catastrophe here, flares, sirens whining, car horns and red ambulance and police lights blinking and revolving. But I had to give the locals a lot of credit. When I got to where I could unload, a bunch of high-school football players in their matched jackets got right to it—pulled out my ramps, went in with handtrucks, and had my rig emptied in a little over an hour. While they worked, a cheerleader showed me to a picnic bench and brought me a box of sandwiches and coffee. She reminded me of Kristen, when she was this young—long kinky brown hair, glasses, wearing jeans on legs too long for the rest of her body which would take a couple years to catch up. This girl wore the same maroon and white CAIRO jacket that the football players wore. I thanked her for the food and asked her how it was going.

"We figure we've got about a hundred thousand babies to shore."

"How many are there still out there?"

"Nobody knows. They just keep coming."

She giggled, but I'm a father and could tell she was close to crying. "I've been up two days. They called off school and let us come down here. My brother and mom and dad are here, too." She pointed over to her brother, one of the jocks in jackets. "We don't know what to do. We think some of the babies are going under." Then she did cry. I wanted to hug here, like she was Kristen. I got up and went over to her side of the bench and stood behind her and patted her head and put my hands on her shoulders and said, "It'll be all right. Just wait and see. You ought to go home and get some sleep. Everything will work out."

I told her to take care of herself, to let the adults do most of the work, that she ought to go home now and maybe come back when she was rested. "Oh, I can't," she said. She got up and kissed me on the cheek and said thanks and

220

goodbye, and walked into a tent, and that was the last I saw of her. Kristen wouldn't have left this place, either, even if she was sleep-walking. Not as long as one baby needed saving.

When I drove away from the unloading area, it was about a half-mile before I could park. I walked back to where I'd been, walked through the food-distribution area and area of tents where thousands of babies were being tended. I walked up and down three or four rows of them—they were white babies and Indian babies and black babies, Hispanic and Asian babies, all sorts of babies there in the tents lit with neon lights and strobes that must have been the only lights they could scrounge up on such short notice. Some babies were sleeping with pacifiers in their mouths and some were crying and some seemed to be having a hell of a good time. One baby looked just like Bill when he was about a month old. I remember I seemed to have to blink a lot in that light, I don't know why except I was about blitzed out and could have dropped right down next to one of those babies and conked out.

I admit I wondered for a minute if I could just claim one or two of these kids, pick them out and take them home—who did they belong to anyway? Now that Kristen and Bill are on their own, maybe Mary and me are ready to raise a new family, but we're a little old for this, and have waited to do some things, travel and fix up the house, maybe put in a wood stove, one of those efficient units that can run on compressed pellets, so I didn't ask any of the nurses or other volunteers staffing the tents if I could just take a couple of the babies with me. But I wouldn't have had to ask, either, let me tell you. There weren't any strict controls there. No one would have missed a couple or a couple hundred of those kids. Wharton just should have announced that anybody who wanted a baby should just drive down to Cairo for one. Maybe he'd visit the place and that's what he'd say, and maybe to set an example he and the First Lady would take a baby or two back to the White House with them. But if there were such a policy, you'd have to worry about what some nuts these days would do with a baby, of course. You wonder what rock some of these perverts were born under. There would have to be some controls. If you ask me, everything is getting out of control.

When I walked down the riverbank to the water, there I was, right away, right where the incoming babies were. They were pushing right against my ankles. Right away I reached out and pulled a couple in, and for a second I could see light—light from helicopters and neon lights and starlight—reflected in the water where I'd removed the babies, but right away other babies filled the gleaming spots. For the first time, I was just plain scared. I went cold. I was in shell shock. Everybody around me was dazed. Everybody was moving in slow motion. But they kept working, passing the soaked blankets and babies from hands to hands up the bank to the tents. I pulled a few more babies to shore, but there wasn't any room, everybody had their hands full, and I thought maybe the babies were better off in the water, maybe the water was a little warmer than the autumn air. I thought maybe I would get into one of the lines and help pass kids up from the river, but I was just too tired to be of much use, everything was starting to spin, I felt like I was underwater myself, a cop touched my shoulder and asked me if I was okay. Yeah, I said, I'd be okay. The river seemed to swell and then subside, pushing kids against my legs, but then receding. It was like the river was breathing.

Then there was a strong surge against my legs, more and more bundles pressing me. When I looked upriver, all I could see were bundles of babies moving toward us out of the mists over the river. The moon was out there in the mists somewhere. The kids I'd pulled to shore seemed to be wailing, but I couldn't really tell because of the tremendous volume of sounds from the river, the helicopter engines and the whooshing and beating sounds of the blades and people calling out, but above and below all this were the moans and cries and sing-song and babbling and gurgling voices of the countless babies darkening the autumn river. Sometimes I thought I was listening to some kind of crazy organ or maybe a loud church hymn sung out of time, it was all so loud and confused. Smells of diesel smoke and baby formula and river water mixed with wet diapers and the memory of Mary's perfume. There was nothing I could do. I wondered if Mary would ever believe this. I had to get out of there. I started to slip my way up the riverbank, away from all these babies, all these people. Where in God's name were they all coming from?

Something

People ask me, "Do you feel guilty?"

My Christian parents emigrated to this country from Germany in the late 1920s. I was born in Brooklyn in 1940. So far as I know, I've never done anything intentionally or unintentionally to hurt the feelings of or to physically harm a Jew.

I don't feel guilty, exactly, but I feel *something.* It may be that my poems have been an attempt to understand and dramatize this *something* that I feel. It may be that there is no single word for this feeling I have that I am involved in, connected with, responsible for history, a fated participant in that period when the Nazis forced us into an abyss that will from now on color all our thoughts and feelings, even our most hopeful thoughts and feelings, with darkness.

In "When Memory Brings People Together," his November 10, 1987, address in the West German Reichstag, Elie Wiesel said, "As a Jew, I have never believed in collective guilt. Only the guilty were guilty. Children of killers are not killers, but children."

Surely. But what of the parents of killers? When they raise their children to be anti-Semites, do they not share in their children's crimes? And what of the parents of these parents? And so on back to the dim beginnings. But, in any case, the present generations of children, myself included, did not murder Julius Meier at Buchenwald—see Walter Poller's *Medical Block Buchenwald*—or Anne Frank at Bergen Belsen.

And what of all those that my poem "Riddle" snags in its net?

> and some planted the wheat,
> and some poured the steel,
> and some cleared the rails,
> and some raised the cattle.
>
> Some smelled the smoke,
> some just heard the news.
> Were they Germans? Were they Nazis?
> Were they human? Who killed the Jews? . . .

And, in theological terms, what of a deity who allowed the Holocaust, who "watched, and witnessed, and knew" ("Simple Truths")? Is God guilty?

God as reciprocity and presence and circular power must at least feel, must be made to feel, by way of our prayers and poems, the same *something*.

Over twenty-five years I've finished about sixty Holocaust pieces. I've been over them so often—hundreds, thousands of times—have heard many of them over half my lifetime in such entangled and complex contexts of thought and theory that, as a whole, a single unit, a book, they seem now almost opaque to me—Susan Sontag speaks of the "sheer opaqueness" of the murder of the six million European Jews—a Holocaust muse's utterance of

> red streaks of voice across
> an ionized atmosphere,
> gassed Hungarian clawhair & ribnails & tongues, a burst heart
>
> breaking into static as she spoke,
> into cancelling sparks,
> her now never-ending speechlessness, never.
>   ("The Secret")

I am not clear about what I've done, what my poems as a whole do. There seems to be much static, many cancelling sparks as I try to remember, imagine, curse, pray, understand that which for me seems almost beyond memory, imagination, curse, prayer, understanding.

But I meant to mean well, of course, and to be truthful about human nature and the human condition in some fundamental way, of course. This is why what Anthony Hecht wrote of my Holocaust poems raises the question that is with me every day. Hecht wrote that the poems reach "that domain of art in which criminal and victim, caught in the light of a steady vision, are virtually the same."

If this is true—I'm not sure it is—was something operative in me that needed to degrade the innocent who, after all, were not, at least in their earthly incarnations during the Third Reich, themselves murderers? Or, if Hecht is right, would this mean, hopefully, not that I've needed to level all humanity to one and the same determined actor-acted upon-victim-perpetrator, but that my writing sensibility, my conscience over the years has tried to identify with both the victims and the criminals—by way of dreams and ravings and readings—and share pain and suffering and responsibility? "Do I follow me?" as I ask in "The Census." Do you follow me? I am, surely, responsible for the *way* I remember and *what* I choose to remember.

I do not feel guilty about the Holocaust. But I do feel part of it, and always will, I believe, even at the moment of my own death. But I wonder what the *something* is that I feel. I was not there shooting people into the ditches, or within the gas or flames, but was I there? And in what position? Perhaps in both positions, as part of the unitary experience that is in the end my spiritual life? And you? In countless subtle ways are we not part of the human ecology of the Holocaust? The something I feel keeps me, for better or worse, from the silence I both yearn for and resist. It may be that the "domain of art," that place beyond dimension, has its own resolutions. Meanwhile, I do not feel guilty, but something in me, something beyond blame or blamelessness, has its own moral necessity, and I must acknowledge and keep committing myself to this something.

Against Which It Stands

Some years ago I took a bus tour of East Berlin, saw the rubble of the Third Reich, police with machine guns, the infamous wall. When we passed back through "Checkpoint Charlie" (near where Hitler's underground bunker had been), guards rolled mirrors under our bus and questioned each one of us. At last, we were allowed to pass through. We reached western soil where an American soldier saluted us. A flag waved over his post, my flag, our flag. I buried my face in the crook of my elbow and wept.

A high school teacher and dear friend of mine served with the Marines at Iwo Jima. He was there when our men raised the Stars and Stripes above Mount Suribachi. When I am with him, when I am with any veteran of any of our wars, when I even *think* of them (as I often do), I am deeply grateful. At Punch Bowl Cemetery of the Pacific in Honolulu, I visited many graves of our dead from WWII to Viet Nam. These are all our wars, all our dead, all our men and women, and our flag is the flag of memory and promise.

I know that Old Glory is more than bunting and a three-color design. A symbol's meanings can never be exhausted, and each of us is touched by our flag both in shared national and more personal ways beyond our ability even to express our feelings. The flag welcomed my parents to America in the '20s, and protects my children in the '80s.

When someone burns or in any other way desecrates our flag in prank or protest, we may feel hurt, disgusted, outraged. It is not something you or I could do, probably not even if we felt the flag was being disgraced and diminished by a current national policy or a president's speech or by some governmental action that seemed to us fascist. We would struggle and protest in other ways. We might, in fact, protest with the *help* of our flag, hold it high, try to get the perpetrators of injustice to realize that our flag *demands* that they behave better, that they think more clearly and act more justly in the name of millions who have sacrificed for the survival and honor of America.

Our flag is myriad. It cannot be burned, and cannot disappear in flames, even if every single one of its material presences is reduced to ashes. The American flag doesn't need cloth and dye. It lives inside each one of us, in the eye of our heart, as a great poem in which we invest a faith that sustains us. When

Rochester Democrat and Chronicle/Times-Union (March 8, 1990).

someone "burns" a flag, that gesture is of course possible because of what the flag itself stands for.

I believe that our wise founding fathers want us to think more clearly about this than some of us have. We must not ram through a constitutional amendment that compromises and jeopardizes the Bill of Rights. I love the American flag, but I'll be afraid, and ashamed for it, if political bandwagoning and false patriotism insults Old Glory with an amendment against which it has always so courageously stood, against which it stands.

John Berryman: "Off Away Somewhere Once"

This context: during the short years since John Berryman's death in the winter of 1972, what was a vaguely disturbing dream for mankind has assumed body and will never allow us back into a night that balances and restores. Our ecological situation now is grave, is *unprecedented*, and, it seems to me, has not yet struck most contemporary American poets as real (as it must, as perhaps *by way of poetry* it must). We have not realized, made real for ourselves, the chaos and death into which we are drifting. It seems to me that even though we speak the facts and "know" them, we have not imagined. Our life remains a blur and a daze as we lose our hold on the planet.

By general scientific consensus, we now understand that global temperature has risen about one degree Fahrenheit since the Industrial Revolution. By about 2030, we are "committed"—a word the EPA uses in a report to Congress—to a rise of two more degrees because of greenhouse gases already in the atmosphere. Nothing we can do about this. This is in the pipeline for us. Three degrees. This in itself is a frightening increase. Berryman's phrase "irreversible loss" becomes prophecy. Listen to Bill McKibben in *The End of Nature* (1989): "That is to say, if all the liberals and all the conservatives in all the countries of the world had gotten together a decade ago and done all the most dramatic things they could think of, it wouldn't have been enough to prevent terrible, terrible changes."

A likely scenario of these terrible changes is outlined in a chapter entitled "The End" in the extremely important book—"Required reading for responsible citizenship" says Thomas O. Lovejoy—*Dead Heat* (1990) by Michael Oppenheimer and Robert H. Boyle. "Imagine—the year is 2050," the chapter begins. What follows is the breakdown of ecological systems, the virtual end of the world as we know it, place by place. And this is not wild speculation or science fiction. Just the three degree rise in temperature to which we are committed is already, Oppenheimer and Boyle say, "a point which marks the boundary of a climatic no man's land." Says Bill McKibben bluntly, "A few more decades of ungoverned fossil fuel use, and we burn up."

Delivered at a conference on the poet at the University of Minnesota in October 1990. Published online at *Poetrybay* (2001).

We will, you know, continue these next decades with our fossil fuel economies. All gains in engine efficiency or alternative energy are being more than offset by increasing populations of fuel burners—China, Russia, India, the new Germany want cars, cars. Oppenheimer and Boyle say, "Should individual gasoline cars come to dominate the rest of the world as well, the greenhouse problem will become intractable." Another unprecedented way of considering a human problem: "intractable." It is likely that from 2030-2050 on, the temperature will rise one degree a decade. A seven degree rise would probably mean an 18-foot rise in ocean levels—nightmare. Many serious thinkers believe that only a tremendous catastrophe that wakes us up can save us, and the sooner the better.

This catastrophe may be very close. We are losing, according to Lester Brown of Worldwatch, 24 billion tons of topsoil a year—an amount equal to the topsoil of all Australia's wheat fields. We are on the verge of a food emergency— U.S. dollars will likely be competing with Japanese yen for U.S. food. With increasing loss of topsoil, desertification, swelling population, the environmental support systems on which the global fossil-fuel economy depends is deteriorating at an accelerating pace.

I could go on with the likely loops of heat and storm and flood and forest dieback and disease ahead of us on our collision course with the end. I'll strike to the root of this in a hurry. From my intuition, from my experience with ponds and meadows and with fields of asphalt, from my book knowledge, I believe what Kurt Vonnegut has said: "I would say 100 years is a long time for us to last." An October 1990 *National Geographic* article on global warming concludes, "What we are doing to the earth's atmosphere, to the blue planet on which we live is not merely ominous. It may already be beyond correction." Despite my desire for a contrary "supreme fiction," I believe we are going to die out, and die out fast, once we pass certain limits, and we are speeding toward those limits. When I think deeply about this for only the few seconds a month I am able to, when I imagine extinction, I almost extinguish myself. This is central to our plight: we may be physiologically unable to imagine what is happening to us. In the second of his "Eleven Addresses to the Lord" Berryman says, "Man is ruining the pleasant earth & man. / What at last, my Lord, will you allow? / Postpone till after my children's death your doom / if it be thy ineffable, inevitable will." An abject recognition and resignation here.

Given all this, then, in government or industry or education or at conferences devoted to beloved poets, business as usual will become increasingly irrelevant, silly, trivial, suspect. In modern and in post-modern poetry, anything has gone, even the attempt to free art from memory, as John Cage has described his own desire. Wallace Stevens' 1940 lyric "Of Modern Poetry" recognizes that script and theatre have changed, but within its aesthetic of meditative play argues for a poetry which "In the delicatest ear of the mind" speaks those exact words that it and we want to hear. Stevens says that the new poem "must / Be the finding of a satisfaction, and may / Be of a man skating, a woman dancing, a woman /

Combing." Maybe once upon a time, but we no longer have time. Recent poetry especially has flourished on subtlety, evasion, indirection, silence. In his two volumes of essays, *Preoccupations* (1980) and *The Government of the Tongue* (1988), Seamus Heaney has argued in various eloquent ways that poetry operates under a special dispensation to be inefficacious. But this, too, is a traditional argument, and, as Erich Harth says in *Dawn of a Millennium: Beyond Evolution and Culture* (1990), another unsettling deliberation on our chances for survival, "So far, our minds are still tradition bound and barely aware of where we are heading." Now, the stakes being what they are, the facts being what they are, it seems to me logical and urgent to argue that poetry must find ways, direct ways, to help effect a change in consciousness and behavior, or it must cease distracting us from the crucial work at hand.

From being the skinny four-eyed kid "Blears" to being a distinguished Regents' Professor of Humanities here at the University of Minnesota and one of America's most famous poets, John Berryman fought all his life for a sense of self-worth. He found both his defensive and offensive strength not in people or in nature but in books, in literature. In "Friendless," remembering his student days at Cambridge, Berryman says "I don't do a damned thing but read & write"—this could serve as a basic description of his works and days. His style, as it evolved from academic "period style" to his distinctive barbed-wire torque of jittery syntax and excited darting rhythmic phrasings and leaps, forged his focus as he circled from outer political world to his pizzicato self.

In "Matins" of *Delusions Etc.* he writes, "past forty years / . . . I strayed abhorrent, blazing with my Self." If Berryman's self was abhorrent to him, Walt Whitman of course tells us that he felt his self to be luscious and luminous, even if deceitfulness and craftiness and sly words were not lacking in him. This is one reason why Berryman's essay on Whitman's "Song of Myself" is such uncomfortable reading for me. (I was not fortunate enough, as were Philip Levine and others, to hear Berryman in class ecstatic with Whitman.) In this essay, Berryman seems to will himself to try to pin down this elemental force of nature who is, or who has convinced himself that he is, beyond linguists and contenders, at ease with himself and his sure knowledge of the beauty and deliverance of death, of his mentor Emerson's various apprehensions of nature's ministry and circular power. All his writing life Berryman was both amazed and troubled by the aboriginal Walt. How could he not be? In the *Paris Review* interview conducted by Peter Stitt in 1970, Berryman remarks, "Take observation of nature, of which I have absolutely none." Then he says something that Walt would find extremely "curious": "It [the observation of nature] makes possible a world of moral observation for Frost, or Hopkins. So scholarship and teaching are directly useful to my activity as a writer." The observation of nature made possible *any* world at all for Walt. He, Thoreau, Emerson, all begin with the something we have, the only *given*, nature. How could Berryman possibly read "Song of Myself" without being shaken to the bone? He was much more comfortable with Stephen Crane. "Work and grief made up the context," Berryman says of Crane. Throughout Crane, throughout the Naturalists, nature is abstracted, allegorical sign, it may be, rather than symbol.

Berryman often felt abhorrent not only to his God being addressed in the late books, but to his inner-self. When I was young I suffered not just feelings of inferiority, but an inferiority complex, and whenever I read Berryman it is jarring for me to sense, beneath his whine and bluster and compassion, beneath the idiosyncratic music he hears with the ear in his brain, his casting about, his lostness, his recognition that he has not yet found the ground of his being or whatever it is, if anything, that can nurture and sustain him. Especially in the *Dream Songs*, it seems to me, his subject matter *is* his differentiated personality's search for lost meaning, for unity with something that will give him peace. His contemporary Theodore Roethke always, at heart, knew that in the end only one thing could save the individual or the race, the "eye quiet on the growing rose." There is little or no observation of nature in Robert Lowell, either, or in Delmore Schwartz. Even Schwartz's dreams, as recorded in his journals, are usually about conversations with poets about poetry—I think I'd rather go sleepless! At the end of his life in some of the most beautiful and moving writing of the generation, "North American Sequence"—I've seen the manuscripts of these poems, by the way: they came to him quickly, were not tortured into being as so much of his work was—Roethke, because he has won through to a sense of oneness with the natural essence of being, can remind himself "not to fear infinity." In the late poetry, deepening what we sense since the greenhouse poems, Roethke experiences "a steady storm of correspondences! Death of the self in a long, tearless night" ("In a Dark Time"). This is enough for Roethke, the essential Romantic reciprocity which demands that the world of reptiles and of roses rooted in rock *be* there. "By all the things that are, / I've come to be," he says in "The Changeling." He doesn't even *exist* except by way of a long-staring at and an immersion in the natural world. Is *this* what we have to know, is this what we have to worship and preserve to stave off insanity and death?—these are the questions throbbing in Roethke.

In the early "At Chinese Checkers" of *The Dispossessed* Berryman says, "The fox-like child I was or assume I was / I lose, the abstract remember only," and in his first books nature is primarily cipher and tonal decor, a kind of sign language. When a firefly or a dandelion or a whip o' will or a sea-shell or a nest shows up in *The Dispossessed*, or a rose or a gale or a tulip or a wasp or a daisy or a brook or a loon or a sheep in *Sonnets to Chris*, it seems reference by habit. Maybe Berryman will mention "oak" or "sycamore," but it's usually just "tree" or "trees," and in any case the tree never seems to be in a particular place, or to have been stared at intently until it has yielded itself to him in a flow of inward and outward tendings. The most telling and touching and bereft nature image in *The Dispossessed* occurs at the end of the title poem, which concludes the volume:

"The race / is done. Drifts through, between the cold black trunks, / the peachblow glory of the perishing sun // in empty houses where old things take place." We have lost something that was once aura, Berryman feels and dramatizes. The *moon* is his central nature image in the early books—"the moon in the breast of man is cold," he says in "The Moon and the Night and the Moon"—and we notice that he does keep his eye on the skies and on corresponding weather beneath the breastbone throughout his poetry.

I once said to him that I was smitten by *Homage to Mistress Bradstreet*. I said that the 31st stanza especially sang in me:

> —It is Spring's New England. Pussy willows wedge
> up in the wet. Milky crestings, fringed
> Yellow, in heaven, eyed
> by the melting hand-in-hand or mere
> desirers single, heavy-footed, rapt,
> make surge poor human hearts. Venus is trapt—
> the hefty pike shifts, sheer—
> in Orion blazing. Warblings, odours, nudge to an edge—

He replied that this was the best stanza in the poem. Here, I know, he imagined, and his own heart surged with the presence of nature in Anne's New England. Twenty years later the mature poet knew he'd gotten something down there that he'd gotten down almost nowhere else, and there are instances in Berryman of intense yearning for the Source itself. In "Note to Wang Wei" of *His Thought Made Pockets & the Plane Buckt* (1958) he wonders how the poet, "now some thousand years / disheveled," could still be so happy. It teases him to the "verge of tears," he says. "It makes me long for mountains & blue waters." In "Compline" of *Delusions Etc*. he senses

> a rapture, though, of the Kingdom here, here now
> in the heart of a child—not far, not hard to come by,
> but natural as water falling, cupped
> & lapped & slaking the child's dusty thirst!

But maybe the most striking instance in Berryman of his abiding sense of loss and indirection occurs in "Dream Song #265." In this direct introspective song Berryman lays bare his abiding intimations of the wrong-turning of his life. "I don't know one damned butterfly from another," he blurts out to open, but it is too late for him, too late to change, he feels—it seems always too late for so much in Berryman, while in Whitman, of course, it is never too late for anything, all is always the flux of inception—so he mumbles a prayer for reincarnation in two words, "many returns," and swears that "next time it will be nature & Thoreau." This song at this late time is about all that he can allow to surface to acknowledge one undercurrent of irreversible loss that we've heard in bits and snatches: "Once in a sycamore I was glad / all at the top, and I sang" (#1); "The glories of the world struck me, made me aria, once" (#26). In the end, in the last song, he can't sense the middle ground between things and the soul, which is the ground where Walt's child goes forth. As the leaves fly, he wonders whether turkeys ever "greatly flew," or wished to. He says, in that voice that keeps breaking through, "off away somewhere once I knew / such things." Where is that place? we wonder. It is as though he refers to a childhood, or pre-childhood, or pre-incarnation where he was instinct with nature. Questioning his bookish life to the end, he feels he has to scold the present book, his "heavy daughter."

Here in Minneapolis Lea Baechler has reminded us of the 1957 short story "Wash Far Away" in which Berryman's professor-protagonist tells his poetry class, "but if the flowers are nothing more than words for us, we miss a good deal." This understated moment wells up from a life, from beneath critical theory, and is too deep for tears. Kate Berryman mentioned to me that near the end, between episodes, John bought a telescope. I think of him studying the star-glitter of the out-there, balancing himself, readying himself for whatever would come next. For me, the essential Berryman, the necessary Berryman exists in this poignant tension between the life as he and almost all of us have lived it, and that other life that—could it still?—could save us.

Open Letter to the Ad-Hoc Committee Studying the Incinerator, to Mayor Stull and the Village Of Brockport Trustees, the Village of Brockport Planning Board, and to Town of Sweden Supervisor Henion and Board Members

In his 1990 book *Making Peace with the Planet*, Barry Commoner, one of the world's leading scientists—*Time* magazine has called him "a professor with a class of millions"—reports that Wheelabrator Environmental Systems has proposed a "state-of-the-art" incinerator for Falls Township, Pennsylvania, which would burn 2,250 tons of trash per day and would emit 5 tons of lead annually. This would equal the emissions of 2,500 automobiles using leaded gasoline. We all know by now that lead is extremely debilitating and dangerous, especially for children, affecting nervous systems and leading to all the symptoms of mental retardation.

I've heard that the incinerator proposed for Brockport would burn 1,350 tons of trash per day. This (60 percent ratio) would result in the emission of 3 tons of lead annually. The Brockport incinerator would apparently also emit other toxins and carcinogens in these annual amounts: 10 tons of mercury; 348 pounds of cadmium; 348 pounds of nickel; 1348 tons of nitrogen oxides; 510 tons of sulfur dioxide; 466 tons of hydrogen chloride; 52 tons of sulfuric acid; 10 tons of fluorides; and 58 tons of dust particles small enough to lodge permanently in the lungs. These are *emissions*. The metals, including chromium, would remain toxic for thousands of years, while most landfill liners are guaranteed not to leak for only 20 years. Says Commoner, "Coincidentally perhaps, the legal responsibility of the incinerator operator, Wheelabrator Environmental Systems, for the ash also expires after 20 years."

But this is just the tip of this toxic iceberg. Incinerator technology—and it seems generally accepted by all but industry spokesmen now that such technology is *not* "proven technology"—is most seriously called into question by a pollutant and carcinogen of extraordinary virulence, dioxin.

Distributed locally in 1991.

Measurement and evaluation of dioxin emissions are uncertain and complex, involving "the chemistry of combustion; the physics of air movement and dust settling (part of the emitted dioxin is attached to fine dust particles); the biochemistry of the cancer process;" etc. It seems, too, that there are 210 different compounds that are called dioxin, while consultants called in to test might only test for one or more. A well-known feature of environmental impact statements, says Commoner, is "errors and absurdities." And with dioxin, there is no margin for uncertainty or mistake: the EPA says that soil contaminated with 0.0000001 percent of it (*1 part per billion*) is unacceptable.

Nor should we be persuaded that a high enough temperature during incineration will destroy dioxin. A study by the Center for the Biology of Natural Systems at Queens College found "no statistically significant relation between dioxin emissions and either furnace temperature or combustion efficiency." Nor should we listen, if we are told what at least one other prospective host was told, that dioxin would merge with and be diluted by soil: "dioxin will not readily penetrate the soil; it is so firmly bound to soil particles that, according to several studies, dioxin will hardly penetrate more than a few millimeters of soil when deposited on it as dust." The dioxin would be there for Brockport Village and Town of Sweden children to pick up on their bare feet or shoes and bicycle tires and to lick from their fingers. We would be washing it from our cars and hands. *No one* can now assure us otherwise, and this is the reason that between mid-1985 and mid-1989 about 40 incinerators were blocked around our country. No amount of money would be worth turning our Village and Town into a future cancer-cluster.

One of the most terrible and disturbing findings recently has been that not only does dioxin result from the burning of materials containing it, but that incinerators are actually responsible, through a complex chemistry, of *creating* it, that incinerators are themselves, in Commoner's phrase, "dioxin factories."

Add to this the method of monitoring by the State or by EPA as described to us by Professor Ditz of Cornell University's independent Waste Management Institute at an informational meeting a week ago. Typically, the monitoring would take place maybe once a year on a pre-arranged date. The incinerator would be mass-burning for 24 hours a day for 365 days, but we'd have a monitor in place for maybe a day, in anticipation of which the operator could clean up its act, make sure what trucks were coming in with what materials, etc. We the people would already have ingested such mistakes.

Hundreds of trucks would daily be dragging their smells into Brockport and disgorging materials over which we'd have no control at an incinerator over which we'd have no control. (And keep in mind that an incinerator generally burns about 70 percent by weight—this goes up the stacks and into our air—and leaves a 30 percent residue of ash, so 30 percent of all garbage that comes in would have to go out again, compressed but extremely toxic.) On any given day or night, truckload #139, for example, could deliver us an illegal PCB or dioxin blow so severe that we'd never recover from it.

It is public opposition that has led to scientific scrutiny, not the industry itself, which has fostered "specious attempts to downgrade the toxicity of dioxin," which attempts have "seriously eroded the integrity of federal and state environmental programs." Meanwhile, the level of discourse here in the Village of Brockport has in some quarters fallen so low that one resident could suggest to those of us against the Wheelabrator incinerator that we shouldn't drive in the Village or mow our lawns!

I understand that Greenpeace, The Sierra Club, and other environmental organizations have called for a national moratorium on the construction of incinerators.

We'll never have peace of mind should an incinerator come to our Village or Town. Never. The longer this poisonous proposal hovers in our air, the worse off we'll be. Never in the history of Brockport have our leaders had to make a more important decision. I believe that the great majority of our citizens join me in asking you to reject the Wheelabrator proposal and the whole misguided notion of incineration, and the sooner the better.

The Green Gate: Memory, Extinction, and the Artist's Imagination

At the end of his long poem "Audubon," Robert Penn Warren, moving beyond all the sound and fury and obsessive art that was Audubon's life, says, simply,

> Tell me a story.
> In this century, and moment, of mania,
> Tell me a story.
> Make it a story of great distances and starlight.
> The name of the story will be Time,
> But you must not pronounce its name.
> Tell me a story of deep delight.

I'd like to tell a story, one I'd like you to keep in mind all during my talk. It's a story about what seems to me to be the deepest possible human delight, though I would not be able to pronounce its exact name.

False Advertising

The boy was only eight, but knew the difference between egg-layers and live-bearers. In the pockets of his shorts he had only a quarter—all fish were fifty cents a pair in the tank of live-bearers—but he had a plan: he hoped to buy a pregnant female. He had a bowl on his desk at home all ready, thick hairgrass planted in gravel at the bottom and duckweed covering the whole surface. He could picture a batch of tiny fry, eyes half as big as their transparent bodies, waiting for him some morning if now he could only spot the right fish, the right live-bearer—you just couldn't raise egg-layers at home—and if Mr. Guarini would only sell her to him for a quarter.

Delivered to the National Council on Education for the Ceramic Arts in Cincinnati (1989). Published in *NCECA Journal* (1990-91).

They were alone in the small shop. Mr. Guarini was screwing together a hamster-wheel. The boy was staring into one tank in a row of tanks, the one with assorted live-bearers. It was the Saturday morning after the one Friday evening a month when tropical fish were rushed to Guarini's Pet Shop directly from the city airport. The boy was looking intently for the one swordtail, platty, guppy, or black molly that would fulfill his fervent wish to see some morning soon a batch of big-eyed young hiding from their mother. After she dropped them out of her abdomen, tiny balls defenseless for a few seconds before they uncurled and swam for their lives into the plants, he would net her and place her in the ten-gallon aquarium. He would be able to watch the babies grow and breed and grow forever.

But now he saw a fish different from any he'd seen before. It was shaped almost like a hatchet-fish, though its chest was not as distended. It swam in quick flits, an inch or two at a time, before hovering motionless except for a pulse-quiver as it gilled oxygen. But what was more remarkable about it was the fluorescent orange-gold-yellow streak over each eye, the band of fluorescent ruby red where its tail joined its body. When it turned a certain angle, he could see only the three lights, as though the fish were a constellation in the night sky.

"Mr. Guarini, Mr. Guarini, would you come over here, would you look over here please?"

The old man in slippers shuffled over, screwdriver in hand, glasses down on his nose.

"There, Mr. Guarini, that one, what is it, do you know, the one right there, that one?"

Mr. Guarini pushed his glasses up on his forehead, bent down, placed his face beside the boy's against the glass. The boy held his breath, hoping Mr. Guarini would be able to see the fish, hoping the fish would not disappear.

"Oh, that one."

"Yes, Mr. Guarini, what is it, do you know, how much is it?"

"Oh, that one there?" Mr. Guarini pointed at it with his screwdriver.

"Yes, Mr. Guarini, yes."

"Oh, that one there is probably a ten-dollar fish got in there by mistake! I probably got me a ten-dollar fish there."

The boy said nothing. He could hardly breathe. Mr. Guarini shuffled away. Now the fish seemed to remain still in the center of the tank for a long time as though it were fixed at the end of a beam from the boy's eyes. He kept staring. Other fish swam back and forth in front of him, but he saw only the one with the ruby band at the base of its tail and the streak of sunrise over each eye. He felt his throat tighten up as it did on him sometimes, and he closed his eyes hard to squeeze off any tears.

Mr. Guarini was beside him again. "Look at this, Brady," he said. He had a book open to a color picture. There it was, the same fish. The boy touched the picture. He could see the name of the fish above Mr. Guarini's pointer finger.

"It's a head and tail light, Mr. Guarini," the boy managed to say.

"Would you say?"

"It sure is, Mr. Guarini, it's a head and tail light, it sure is, it's right there."

"You're the expert, Brady. I'll tell you one thing. If it's what you say it is, I've got me a fish that comes all the way from the Amazon River!"

The boy had to catch his breath.

Mr. Guarini left him alone again. Brady had seen all kinds of egg-layers, neon tetras and cardinals, angels and silver danios, rosy barbs and blind caves and pencil fish and zebra fish and fighting fish and blue gouramis—he'd even tried to raise gouramis—but he'd never seen a fish like this one. He could close his eyes and still see it.

Maybe he could come back to Mr. Guarini's shop every day to visit it, he was thinking, but what would he do if someone else bought the fish and took it away? What would he do if he ever lost this fish?

Mr. Guarini called him over to the counter. Even as he walked away from it, the boy could see the fish. It swam in the back of his head, behind that surface layer of sight with which he saw the pet shop and Mr. Guarini. It was dark back there in the Amazon River where the fish was the only source of illumination.

Mr. Guarini put down the screwdriver and pushed his glasses up his forehead. He peered out to Main Street and over to the door as he spoke in a low voice. "Brady, I've got me a confidential problem," he said. "I've got me a confidential problem on two counts.... You've heard about false advertising?"

The boy nodded, trying to pay attention.

"You've heard about it, Brady?"

"False advising, Mr. Guarini?"

"Well, it's a serious thing. It's got to do with honest business. Now, I've got me a single ten-dollar egg-layer in a tank where it's marked live-bearers fifty cents a pair. And what can I do about it? I dasn't just net it out—that would be false advertising, don't you know? I could be sued. I'm too old to spend time in court and maybe get thrown in jail for something that wasn't my fault. Sometimes you got to get around things. You got to imagine things a little. You got to adjust. So, I've got me an idea and a favor to ask...."

Bicycling home, holding the bag containing the paper carton to his chest with one hand, the boy could feel his heart beating loud enough, he thought, for the fish to hear.

All evening and for much of that night even after he turned off the light in his room, he stared into the bowl on his desk until the object of his contemplation created its counterpart that for as long as he lived would swim in that other dimension behind his eyes....

My wife and I collect Roseville, a pottery produced in Ohio from about 1900 to mid-century. She especially likes the floral patterns in blue backgrounds—White Rose, Zephyr Lily, Freesia, Iris—from the '40s. They're okay with me, but I've come to care for the older pieces in matte colors. One of these is a green 4" x 8" double bud vase identified simply as "The Gate" in a Roseville catalogue. It was made, the catalogue says, some time before 1916. I now have several of these on a shelf beside my writing chair in my study. With their rhythms of picket and post, they are a refrain for me, a ceramic music of past and future.

I care for and collect this early example of Roseville in part because my earliest memory is of a green picket fence and gate in front of our house in Woodhaven, on Long Island, when I was a boy. I was three, or four, or five, inside that fence. Now I can still sometimes see it in my dreams, a green gate in Woodhaven, which was not wooded, though it was a haven, I now know, for all of us who lived there while the world was at war in Africa, in the Pacific, in Europe.

Later, as a teenager, further out on Long Island, I leaned over a rowboat's side and tonged for clams with long poles in deep water. In one of my poems I say that I "Still feel those tongs scissor / and fall, still claw / that bottom of weed and shell / that yielded bushel / after bushel." The poem ends:

> I warned you:
> now, in my loneliness,
> be with me

as I tong.
Are we the last
to hear it?
That beauty disappears,
but lives,
if this is the pulse
of waves,
if this is the Island's vast
soft wingbeat and heartbeat,
if ours is the only
abiding love.

Are we the last to hear it? Be with me as I claw my way into this subject.
In one of the most passionate sentences in *Walden* Thoreau says,

> Let us settle ourselves, and work, and wedge our feet
> downward through the mud and slush of opinion, and prejudice,
> and tradition, and delusion, and appearance, that alluvion which
> covers the globe, through Paris and London, through New York
> and Boston and Concord, through church and state, through
> poetry and philosophy and religion, till we come to a hard
> bottom and rocks in place, which we can call *reality*, and say,
> This is, and no mistake: and then begin. . . .

I believe that most people do not know what they know, and do not know what they do not know. I believe I do. I have come to this only lately. It took me a while to know, and then to face my knowledge, but now I know what our living world is coming to, all its porcupines and pear trees, all its potters and poets. Because of what I know, I sometimes verge on incoherence, but glossolalia is in part poetry, too. In any case, as I open the gate into our next century, memory is my balancing pole. Here's what I know and refuse to forget.

When I was eight or ten I discovered a pond in the woods past the dead-end of a dirt road. For two or three summers, I spent much time there, always alone. It was only about an acre, as I remember, but it "led forward life" as Walt Whitman, the great world poet of my old Island, says. I refuse to forget that profusion, every cubic inch of that place filled with duckweed and dragonflies, wild grapevines, honeysuckle bushes overhanging the shore, swirls of catfish hatchlings, frogspawn, a buzz of waterlilies, spiders walking on and waterbugs flitting through the clear brackish gradations of color, swallows skimming the surface, a white crane sometimes lifting away—not in fear but in annoyance, it seemed to me—when I pushed through brush toward its resting place. Wading that pond, discovering snapping turtles whose neckfolds grew leeches, noticing pinkish tubeworms that at first seemed mats of hairgrass, I felt myself part of something, though I had no words for this at the time. There was proof there, I now know, that the natural basis of things, of time, of *reality*, is toward more life and the creation of new forms, toward infinite trillions of intricate interchanges and connections so mysterious and complex that banks of computer information will never be able to do more than suggest to us the gift and miracle of this gospel.

And then one spring the dead-end dirt road was bulldozed all the way to the pond, and someone had pushed a doorless wreck of a car into the water. Bags of garbage appeared and rotted down to rusting tin cans. I remember a stained mattress half in and half out of the water. And then someone apparently poured gasoline into the pond to kill the mosquito larvae—housing developments were eating away at the woods, and a polio scare was in the air. And then one day when I was eleven or twelve I realized that this pond was dead. It stank. It was a refuse pit where only a dispirited frog or two still lived in deceptive rainbow oil slicks among surviving reeds. And that was that. I didn't much care, it may be. I went home. I went to high school. I went to basketball and poker. I went to rock and roll. I went to college as a physical education major, and to graduate school as an English major. I went to marriage and children. I picked up some book-learning. I came here to talk to you.

And I believe I've said something akin to your own experience—an American experience of malls and asphalt—but I'm saying I have returned to that pond and refuse to forget, I have returned underneath my own so-called adulthood and maturity to restore to myself my sense of god in nature. And this is what I *know*. And I can talk only from this, can read the news only from this, can write only by way of this, can profess anything at all only by way of this repeated instance, repeated when one of my dozen boyhood aquariums suddenly sickened with red stains and everything alive in it died. Or when a terrarium of coleus and moss for some reason gave up its ecosystemic ghost. I *know* what it is we are coming to. That pond was so beautiful that I will see it with the eye in my heart when I die. It sustains me with a sense of the nature of things even though it is gone. I can open the green gate and walk to it, still, through the woods. By way of this pond, I know what I know, and, when I speak with you or see what you have made, know what you know or do not know, what you remember and do not remember. And I know I must be loyal to this knowledge despite my life's distracting traffic. I cannot speak as I've begun to speak except for that place in me, which is stopped in time but simultaneously alive with dragonflies and lilies. Whitman says he is stuccoed with birds and quadrupeds all over. My brain is bathed in that pondwater. Sunfish fan their nests at the base of my skull. Here, all in a scatter but with a center, is what I know.

First, this reality, one of distances and the light of comets: the fact is that we live on a star. Right now, you and I are traveling, or drifting, four to seven hundred miles a second—I've read two estimates—on our star in the direction of the constellation Virgo, which is also on the move, of course. Either a big bang has flung us, or we are being drawn by gravity toward a star or star cluster beyond the known universe so immense that our minds will shut off when we try to imagine it. The fact is that there are two to three hundred billion stars in the Milky Way, our solar system's home galaxy. If you wanted to count all the planets in just our one galaxy, you'd have to count one a second for twenty-four hours a day for about six thousand years . . . and there are billions of galaxies.

Either the big bang is causing all this drift and change, or gravity from some unknown source—or, for all we know, and maybe we don't even have a clue, something else entirely, something beyond dimension and conception and language. For all we know, all of us now and forever here and everywhere are held in our travel in the mind of Jesus, or a Zen master, or a god-creature who smiles at our attempts to say that any particular way is the way things are.

But I must touch down toward practical reality. I listened to the news, as you did, that our space satellite had made it to the vicinity of Neptune. Our probe sailed twelve years over billions of miles, discovered ice moons and ice volcanoes, helped us see things we have never seen before, and all this was reported to us in the proper tones of awe and reverence as though we were on the threshold of a new world, a new frontier, one with which we could relate as we relate to the pioneers and prairies. We didn't get the most practical and essential news, which is this: after twelve years and billions of dollars and miles, we have found nowhere in the universe except here on earth a single other living cell, not one evidence of algae, not one amoeba or hydra or frog's egg, not one bison or butterfly or buttercup, not one Great Wall of China or green ceramic gate. Nothing alive, no evidence of anything that ever *was* alive, or that was created by anyone or anything alive except god. All the pinks and blues, the gases and fiery rocks, the rings of ice slush and crystals, are dead. And there is no chance of a bodily elsewhere for us. We are here, on mother earth, and it is obvious that in the conceivable future we will not be able to leave. I listened very patiently to a 1989 article in *New York Times Magazine* on the super-collider by an oaf who kept talking about the economic benefits of such research. At last, he let the whole suffocated cat out of his bag and said we need to go on with this megaproject because of "what history books 500 years from now will say about our time," and because it "fulfills a worthy dream—the freeing of humanity from its captivity on our planet...." He needs the implant of a pond in his head. He needs to read and realize just one paragraph from a 1989 article in *Country Journal* by Lester R. Brown, Christopher Flavin, and Sandra Postel: "Indeed, climate change, like no other issue, calls the whole notion of human progress into question. The benefits of newer technologies . . . could be overwhelmed by the catastrophe of uncontrolled global warming. Some warming is inevitable. But unless trends are reversed, tragic change could occur in just the next two decades . . . ." Two decades! To think of departing for someplace else habitable, or to think as some do, of space stations suspended somewhere above the earth where humanity could continue, is nonsense and distraction, even if one Trump Tower or White House or Playboy Club does lift off to try to save itself and its privileged and politically powerful inhabitants. We are here, but doing what we are doing now, we will simply not be here 500 years from now. "The Infinite Voyage," a television documentary, points out that the rhinoceros has been on the earth for 60 million years, but is now, as is the whole living world, "poised on the threshold of extinction." All life "is threatened by a single species." The program concludes, "Is this the beginning of a long goodbye to the only home we know?" We are here, and here carbon dioxide levels are rising. Five or six of the hottest years in recorded history occurred in the '80s. The British journal *Nature* reported that the oceans are warming about twice as fast as we'd previously thought. Destruction of the protective ozone layer in the atmosphere increases, while our cities often experience dangerous concentrations of this and other gases. Ocean levels are rising while, for example, the volume of our Great Lakes, which hold 17% of the world's supply of fresh water will decrease, and while, for example, as a 1989 Worldwatch Institute study shows, global food production diminishes as water is diverted from agricultural lands to urban populations. At the same time, toxicity around the world becomes more and more dangerous. Many East Bloc and Third World countries are environmental disasters, as we are, or are on the verge of being. We've run out of room for our garbage, including our nuclear garbage. The human body is under carcinogenic siege. It is estimated that by the year 2000, 40% of all of us Americans will at one time in our lives suffer from cancer.

The world's population, maybe a billion when the green gate left its Ohio kiln, about two billion when I was born in 1940 (the U.S. population in 1940 was 140,000,000) is over five billion now, and soaring—ten billion estimated for fifty years from now—with no end in sight, except the obvious and inevitable end. Deforestation continues, supported by various political scams, and by our general shortsightedness and stupidity, and because, of course, of immediate and understandable human need. Here's a poem called "The Gift."

> Because, he said, he didn't want,
> because he didn't want them,
> because he didn't want them to live,
> because he didn't want them to live in poverty,
>
> rainforest Governor Amazonino Mendes distributed
> two thousand free chain saws
> to his peasant constituents because
> he didn't want them to live in poverty,
>
> & it's easy, it's easy for me,
> it's easy for me to start this, easy
> for me to fill my own chainsaw with gasoline & oil, easy
> for me to start this chainsaw snarling, to say

that with his gift Mendes cuts off the feet
of the peasants' children, clear cuts
the family trees of his constituents, easy
for me to speak with a chainsaw tongue

as the trees fall, as the air burns & darkens,
as the forest's blanched soils wash into gullies
because I want peasants to live under trees,
because I want them to live in poverty,

because money means that my nearby mall
carries the perfect gift, & I can easily afford it:
a teak desk set, a box inside a box, envelopes,
paper, knife, & and a coil of U.S. stamps.

We understand the excruciating problems of rainforest governors, but, in any case, and wherever the blame for ongoing deforestation around the world lies, humanity cannot survive without trees, and we are progressing toward the scene in the movie *Soylent Green* in which we see maybe the last tree in an atmospheric tent-museum built for it. Our America is becoming a Great Mall, and Russia and China and Europe and South America and the rest of the world apparently want to hook up with this Mall which to live needs to keep selling us things we don't need but with which we hope to fill some of the emptiness in ourselves which comes from we're not sure where but which is the result of our confusion and our being sick-at-heart as we lose the world. Harvard biologist Edward O. Wilson says that deforestation alone is causing the extinction of 6,000 species a year—this is a rate 10,000 times greater than before human beings appeared on the planet, so we cannot argue, except by twisted and cynical and exclusively human logic, that all this is natural. We photograph dead planets a billion miles away while life here on earth vanishes. Because of what I saw happen to that childhood pond (not to mention what I have seen happen to all of Long Island since then), because I refuse to place that knowledge on a shelf of rationalization somewhere, I know, beyond contradictory or cautious scientific models, beyond our general inability to conceive of this, that there is every good chance that no human being will be alive even a century or so from now. Either because we can't, or don't want to, we have been unable to imagine this. Meanwhile, in the arts or in politics, we seem to have no leadership that recognizes this and arranges priorities to reverse our direct course toward our coming extinction. We are busy working or watching television, or going to art openings, or writing, or shopping, or seeing that our children get into college. We are busy living as we have lived, while the aquarium-terrarium of our world becomes diseased, dis-eased, at an accelerating pace. Our world once had enough margins, hedgerows for robins, edges of meadow for milkweed for monarchs, alkaline lakes to balance acid rain and acid snow, oceans for what we thought would be the limitless absorption of carbon dioxide, fat cells in our bodies to assimilate poisons, but we've saturated our planet with all it can take. It is no longer stable, predictable, sustainable. We used to think that our atmosphere, our air supply, reached above our heads all the way to the stars. We still behave as though it does, as though it were not a thin envelope around us.

But we have all, of course, heard what seems to be this endless litany of present problems and impending disasters. But we're dizzy, and our situation seems beyond comprehension. In his powerful and moving *The End of Nature* (1989), Bill McKibben gives us a reality check. In a kind of settling summary of what we can expect in the near future he concludes, "If all the liberals and all the conservatives in all the countries of the world had gotten together a decade ago and done all the most dramatic things they could think of, it wouldn't have been enough to prevent terrible, terrible changes."

Ecology is "the branch of biology dealing with the relation between organisms and their environment." The word's root comes from the Greek "oikos," *house*. At one point in *The Unsettling of America* (1977), Wendell Berry zeroes in on my own dwelling place:

> With its array of gadgets and machines, all powered by energies that are destructive of land or air or water, and connected to work, market, school, recreation, etc., by gasoline engines the modern home is a veritable factory of waste and destruction. It is the mainstay of the economy of money. But within the economies of energy and nature, it is a catastrophe. It takes in the world's goods and converts them into garbage, sewage, and noxious fumes—for none of which we have found a use. And the modern household's direct destructiveness of the world bears a profound relation—as cause or effect or both—to the fundamental moral disconnections for which it also stands. It divorces us from the sources of our bodily life; as a people, we no longer know the earth we come from, have no respect for it, keep no responsibilities to it. And few who are acquainted with the young can doubt that the modern home has also failed as a place of instruction and that the schools are failing under the burden of that deeper failure.

It is not fashionable or easy for us, is it, to speak of, to deal with "fundamental moral disconnections." Politicians, scientists, artists, educators evade the austere thought that coming to grips with our spiral toward chaos would demand. And Berry's phrase "the economy of money" reminds me that recently, just for the hell of it, I watched Louis Rukeyser's television special on stock market expectations and strategies for the next decade. For a whole hour I listened to analysts and wheelers and dealers until I began to talk to my television, "Fools, don't you know what we're coming to?" Rukeyser ended his upbeat program by summarizing expectations in this way: "We're looking forward to the '90s like kids at an Indiana Jones movie—we can't wait to see what happens next." You fool, Rukeyser and Icahn and the rest, what happens next is that we all die out on the way to the bank. For a kind of grim comic relief, I picture the Wall Street inside trader and swindler Ivan Boesky walking with his wife in Paris on a moonlit night. His wife says to him, "Ivan, isn't the moon beautiful?" "Yes, dear, but what good is it if you can't buy or sell it?" Ivan replies. True story.

What's more, the home that Berry describes is becoming larger. In the suburbs of Rochester, New York, and no doubt around the country, traditional floor plans are doubled, kitchens becoming restaurants, bathrooms becoming pleasure palaces, family rooms becoming media rooms for the giant television screens that need space. These new homes commonly have triple garages. In another of his reality-grounded sentences, here is Thoreau on this subject:

> When I consider how our houses are built and paid for, or not paid for, and their internal economy managed and sustained, I wonder that the floor does not give way under the visitor while he is admiring the gewgaws upon the mantle-piece, and let him through into the cellar, to some solid and honest though earthly foundation.

But, of course, I am a participant. I love my television set, and my wife and I keep two cars on the road, and finger-pointing and name-calling are useless except insofar as they can occasionally serve to wake someone up to share this knowledge of our dire predicament. Misery needs company. Just as my home is poisonous, my mind is filled with toxic sludge, my daily life often a blur of habit and fossil-fuel convention. How hard it is to wedge down to the stones in place that Thoreau mentions, how hard it is to think in a serious and realistic way, how difficult to remember what I know. Even when I do remember, I'm not sure what to do with that knowledge-pond in me. I am also selfishly afraid that I could lose my own life in gloom, and depress others around me. It is so profoundly important that I not do this, for even beyond what happens to the whole body of the world, human joy might pool in a spiritual dimension in another evolution infinitely beyond our ability to do other than intuit it, as I do during my best moments when I realize that *of course* there is more to all this than matter, that maybe, in the end past my poor understanding, whatever happens will be the right, and inevitable, and just thing. Listen to Emerson in his ultra-Transcendentalist mode in his essay "Fate."

The whole circle of animal life—tooth against tooth, devouring war, war for food, a yelp of pain and a grunt of triumph, until at last the whole menagerie, the whole chemical mass is mellowed and refined for higher use—pleases at a sufficient perspective.

At a sufficient perspective. What a phrase! Yes, seen from a billion light years away, our infinitesimal earth, what does it matter if it becomes a dead radioactive cauldron of poison.

But even if to lose the world of our senses is to gain another, *still* we cannot forget, can we, how we feel when in the presence of living nature, which shares this mysterious "wholly other" with us—as did "Martha," the last of her species, who died in a zoo in Cincinnati in 1914.

The Pigeons

Audubon watched the flocks beat by for days,
and tried, but could not count them:
their dung fell "like melting flakes of snow,"
the air buzzed until he lost his senses.

He heard, he said, their *coo*
and *kee* when they courted, and saw trees
of hundreds of nests, each cradling two
"broadly elliptical pure white eggs."

Over mast, they swept in "rich deep purple
circles," then roosted so thick that high limbs
cracked, and the pigeons avalanched
down the boughs, and had not room to fly,

and died by thousands. Kentucky farmers
fed their hogs on birds
knocked out of the air with poles. No net, stone,
arrow, or bullet could miss one,

so horses drew wagons of them,
and schooners sailed cargoes of them,
and locomotives pulled freight cars of them
to the cities where they sold for one cent each.

When you touched one, its soft
feathers fell away as easily as a puff
of dandelion seeds, and its delicate breastbone seemed to return the pulse of your thumb.

Years after writing that poem, I saw in a rare book room Audubon's folio of *Birds of America* under glass, open to his painting of the passenger pigeon. For a moment, within colors of branch and vanished bird, I imagined extinction: my mind went black as though I'd been struck with a club. And here's a poem about two other creatures, one long extinct, and one, a tree, on the brink:

Dodo

Large. Flightless. No predators.
Secure in Mauritius for ten million years.
Slow moving. Trusting. Ungainly
and beautiful. Eyes gray, maybe—
no one knows for sure.

 Dutch sailors. Later, colonists'
clubs and dogs. The last
dodo died in 1680. Ungainly
and beautiful. Eyes pink, maybe—
no one knows for sure.

Ate the fruit of *Calvaria major*,
the dodo tree, which could not propa-
gate itself without its dodo, ungainly
and beautiful. Eyes blue, maybe—
no one knows for sure.

By 1970, only thirteen trees, the last
of their species in this world, were left....
The dodo sometimes seemed to smile, ungainly
and beautiful. Eyes black, maybe—
no one knows for sure.

To germinate, the tree's seeds
needed to be crushed
in the dodo's craw. Ungainly
and beautiful. Eyes ochre, maybe—
no one knows for sure.

On other secret intricacies, it's mum,
and will be. In the British Museum,
I saw one stuffed one: ungainly
and beautiful, with one socket
empty, one sewn shut.

Though usually beyond our awareness, nature is our evidence of reciprocity, but we feel simultaneous separateness and connectedness, a tender yearning-toward and frightened yearning-against. We want to appreciate and eat nature at the same time, to preserve but to dominate at the same time. McKibben tells us that we are turning the world into a cloddish science-fair project, that the whole planet, from its bacteria to its weather, has been so penetrated and manhandled that we can no longer experience nature as we once did. (Much of his discussion, in fact, has to do with the awesome implications of genetic engineering—we are on the verge of inserting ourselves into everything else alive, everything once indicative of the mysterious and awe-inspiring oversoul beyond any of our time and spacebound dimensions.) Surely, it is harder for us in 1990 to sense the source, harder for us not to lose that nameless pond in us. If the forests are dying, if the oceans are dying, if the atmosphere is dying, can my thumbnails' half-moons remind me of the thousands of generations of my ancestors as they evolved toward such a creature as I am to be speaking here now? The rotting Halloween pumpkin still reminds of the miraculous compost of the earth. The hundreds-of-millions-of-years-old cockroach that hitched a ride to Brockport in my luggage from Hawaii still stuns me with my own place within such cosmic power. There are still redwood trees and starfields in each cell of a horsefly's eye. Hard as it has been for me to realize this as I've grown away from what I once knew, it will be harder now. Artists may be my only hope.

I would like my poems to be, in their own ways, sculptures, to be perfect and invulnerable, to hold time still as though their subjects were caught in amber. I yearn for what we call a "sacred text." At the same time, I want them to be active. If I make them from the natural rhythms of my thought, from what I truly know and truly do not know, they will be. They will be havens. They will be able to shrug their shoulders when criticism, or acid, rains down on them. While thinking about this talk, I read a newspaper report that anthropologists have concluded that "the Stone Age people who invented ceramic technology about 26,000 years ago created their clay figures . . . in such a way that the objects would explode during firing . . . . Priests or shamans may have then interpreted the breaks in the figurines." I would like my poems to serve in this way, too, as knowledge of where we are and as prophecy or warning of what is next for us. I would like them to fulfill themselves even at the moment they craze or break in the kiln of heart and mind.

A friend said to me that when he thinks of the catastrophes in store for us, when he thinks of extinction, he can't bear waiting for the end. He wants it to happen right now, wants to get it over with. I couldn't get the resolute hysteria of his voice out of my mind, and a few weeks later wrote this poem:

Harpoon

>   Now that blue whales are as few as two hundred,
>   I want the last one dead.
> I need to forget them right away,
>   before the last reports:
>   ships stripping lost codes of flesh,
>
>   the last calf wandering away, &, later,
>   are there any left?
> Before the last eye is cut out, dumped overboard,
>   & floats away,
>   & what it sees. Kill them now, please,
>
>   before politics can't save them—
>   *the fountaining overtures*
> *the biblical jaws the blue tinge fathoms deep*
>   *the evolutionary curves our*
>   *predecessors' pitiful & beautiful last songs.*

Here's another, cracked with irony by the kiln, maybe holding to sanity only by its fingernails:

Birdhouse

For three or four seasons I'd seen
black-caps trust it, and wrens

in their turn, their twittering young ones
emerging, trying their wings,

being fed, learning to feed themselves,
then departing this acre for other remaining margins

of their shrinking world. But,
last week, the living dead visited,

Halloween, and knocked it out of its silver maple.
Next morning, I lifted its busted gable,

removed petals and stems twined with hair,
feathers softened with rabbit fur,

bits of grass, clover and dandelion heads
dried to the scent of ancient autumn,

no vomit or death smells, no dirt
after seasons of tenants, not even

broken shells or traces of shit,
but clean bedding. Imagine,

hundreds of millions of tons of waste
flushed into the sky each day

in our America. No wonder, last night,
I slept in this house

among birds, the shadows of bombers
flying in and out with water and food,

sweet fume of crickets, intermittent
phosphor of fireflies dropping fuel,

all fused, confused,
as I totter here, out of nature

on the dowel below its eye.

I've used the words "know" and "knowledge" a dozen times, but when we merely know something, we do not necessarily become responsible to it. We do not necessarily comprehend it correctly and deeply, do not necessarily make it real to ourselves, do not necessarily *realize* it, or *act* on it. In order to act, we need first to imagine. Imagination is rare, I believe, but occurs to artists during the conception of and the making of art. If our political leaders imagined, truly imagined our predicament, the extinction into which we are plunging, they would act. If you and I truly imagined, we would begin to find direct ways, despite the aesthetics of indirection and subtlety that has been the mainstay of our artistic educations, to deal with this central theme from which all other themes ramify.

Last year during a session of the summer poetry workshop at Southampton College on Long Island where I had come to expect anything from the beautiful Gloria who sometimes wore earrings filled with tiny gyroscopes and sometimes wore stockings with letters slanting up her thighs and always wore little peaked caps the color of her knickers or kilts or feathery breastplates, she suddenly stood up in our circle with what I thought were two rubbery beanbags or whatever, one red and one green, and smacked them together—*whap*, she smacked them together, *whap, whap*, and threw them onto the floor. "See," she said, that's all we're after, that's the whole thing." I threw a poetry anthology into our circle, and someone else threw an umbrella, and then others threw in the whole shebang. We had a happy happening. But it was only that evening in the cafeteria in a crowd of noise that I heard that Gloria's red object had been a rubber heart and her green object a rubber brain. For an instant, all the cafeteria noises went silent. . . . WHAP!

It was hard for me and took me a long time to stop smoking. I had to come to *imagine* what it was I was doing. I had to imagine my body, image it, and had to realize, to make real to myself my responsibility to the long line of family before me and, hopefully, to come. I had to imagine a grandchild, one I'd be able to love and help. Without imagination, there can be no holistic, no ecological action. Imagination occurs when brain and heart fuse to create the image itself, which may be visual and/or olfactory and/or tactile and/or auditory, but which is always thoughtful and passionate, thought suffused with passion, passion suffused with thought, thoughtful passion, passionate thought—I seem to be able to say only half of this at a time. The act of art, the artist's making of it and the audience's experience of it (which is also a kind of making, of course) exists in this realm of imagination wherein a thought is as immediate to us as the feel of clay in our hands, wherein the feel of clay in our hands or words in our mouth is as immediate to us as a thought. When clay = thought and thought = clay, when rhythmic words embody and create feelings that are at the same time thoughts, then I am in the presence of poetry, as I am when I dream the green gate, as I was at the childhood pond, as I am when I know what I feel and feel what I know about gate and pond again. And I believe, now, that my thoughts as I write my figurines and your thoughts as you create your ceramic poems and our thoughts as we teach should be thoughts of blue whales and of our neighbors who are poisoning our lawns and of the lurid secular iconographic arches of McDonald's and of the rainforests that are symphonies of meaning and interconnectedness, that are god's living imagination.

Now, for the first time in our history, esthetics is a matter of life and death. We no longer have all of Time to meander with the muses into pleasant but useless play. Either our art must begin to matter in direct and discernible ways, building a consensus toward recognition of our terrible plight and pointing our way out of it as it moves us to ecological action, or it should find its dunce's corner and shut up and stop distracting us. I believe, in the light of our *unprecedented* situation, that we need to reconceive what it is we're doing. It will not be enough for us to say, "Well, gosh, I don't like so-called people's poetry or proletarian art, and all that stuff's been tried before, art can't teach and you can't beat people over the head, and useful art is a contradiction in terms and anyway, art has its own inviolate nature." This is a matter of our responsibility not only to our future but to our past: if we die out, Michaelangelo and Shakespeare die out, and the victims of the Holocaust are lost to us, and every person or place in all our encyclopedias, *and* . . . .

Today, it seems to me, this responsibility means the realization of the strong possibility of our absolute extinction in the near future. Our minds and hearts will for the first time in history be suffused with this realization, *whap*, or we will be wasting our lives as artists. I don't know what form this art of ours, perhaps the last human art, will take. I want to join with you in something of such power that my mind's atria and ventricles almost burst with it. I want words to be this clay fired to explode again and again into realization for both myself and my audience as we yearn and strain to save ourselves as part of the single infinitely complex ecosystem of earth, our only home.

Maybe what I am asking of myself, of you, is impossible. Maybe true imagination of our approaching extinction is physiologically impossible—we'd just short-circuit ourselves and black out—therefore artistically impossible. If so, it seems to me, extinction will be impossible to stave off. But I must not think so, even if, in this one case, I must compromise my sense of reality. Robert Jay Lifton argues, "Creatively, a survivor has to imagine (the) death encounter in order to create past it, to stay in it and use it, yet move beyond it." This is what we must do, together, during the inevitably tragic years ahead, if we are to come to realization and imagination.

One of our problems, now as we attempt to imagine our situation, is that talking about it has become boring. It is boring to talk in our usual ways about the need to reduce consumption, to recycle, etc. A few weeks ago I caught myself yawning during a television report on the efforts of local groups to preserve open spaces in nearby villages. I'll snap out of my stupid drowse, or I'll deserve what happens to me and all my children. But I will need artists' help to stay alert.

Above all else, Thoreau says, he does not want to practice resignation. We do not want to resign from one another, or be resigned to hopelessness, or fall into feckless habits. We might have to tear ourselves apart, to dismantle ourselves, to crack in the kiln of our knowledge, might sometimes have to humiliate ourselves, might have to risk our stable personalities in order to burrow beneath our habitual delusions and ways of seeing art and the world, in order to begin. But let's begin. If we pay attention to the single thing to which we need to pay attention—it is the hub around which there are a thousand spokes—we might be able to make a difference. At least, when our grandchildren and great-grandchildren ask us what we were doing when salvation was still possible, we will be able to tell them that we were trying to wake ourselves and others up, were trying to make an art, even if sometimes an angry and bitter art, out of our chilling realization.

Fast Food

I sit at McDonald's eating my fragment of forest.
The snail and slug taste good, the leaves,
the hint of termite and bat, the butterfly trans-

substantiated by steer karma, and mine.
Another pleasure: to breathe distillate of foam
scented with coffee and chemical cream.

Another virtue: groups of us all trained
the same way, millions across America
where we flourish, at present, under the golden arches.

As it attempts to remember beauty and to imagine extinction, I don't know what our new art of realization and commitment will come to sound or smell or feel or look like. I might have only a color or a shape or a texture behind my mind's eye. But I'll hazard this: it will know certain environmental facts and statistics; it will know that ecology has to do with sustainable relationships evolved over millions of years: oaks and ozone; it will know why farmers kill themselves in bankers' barns; it will not call attention to itself as artifact, but will be transparent in the sense that it will itself in its own immediacy *be* our predicament; it will be primal, and wounded, and, by the simple fact of its existence, loving; it will see the world with a dodo's eyes; it will be as simple and direct as a withering cactus with a human face; it will know that there is only one story to tell, and it will tell it; it will harbor the black light of the mystics, but will believe in parrots and people; it will be living things inside of and connected with living things inside of and connected with living things inside of and connected with living things; it will be an iron spike in the redwood and human heart; it will insist we change our lives by way of its presence and witness.

I'd like to conclude by swinging the green gate open to one more poem. Maybe it was written by Brady, the boy in the story with which I began, about forty years after he pedaled his bike home with that touchfish, that most beautiful of all things he had every seen. Now, in this poem, it seems to be evening in his mind as he looks out across his neighborhood.

Crickets

Evenings, where lawns are not sprayed with poisons,
you can still hear the crickets,
you can still see lightning bugs signaling,

look, a yellowgreen strobe under the trees,
but gone, but there again, sometimes
in the same spot, and sometimes not,

as the tiny purveyors of phosphor
swim past our houses and the stars looking
for one another, and the crickets,

crickets, crickets, the ones that still
have their legs, keep scraping them together,
listen, maybe for the last time on earth, listen....

The Pipeline

I saw on television yesterday a Viet Nam veteran on the verge of breakdown. He was screaming, "We must support our soldiers this time, we must win this one, we must not go through again what we went through in Nam, we can't let the same thing happen again, we can't let people start saying the wrong things, we can't let support weaken, we must win this time, we must win this war, we could have won last time."

I became afraid for him, and for me. I was thrown back to the '60s. I could feel in my heart the great division of our country again.

For I hate this massive and dangerous American build-up of arms and men in the Middle East, and I want to support the young soldiers again by lifting my voice to bring them home, please, bring them home as soon as possible before the unthinkable happens.

"As soon as possible." Of course, but when will that be? At least, I hope, before *we* start a war with a people that would be willing to fight us all the way into the next century.

We might decide to board, or sink Iraqi ships. Iraqi planes might fly out in defense. Such situations multiply as we pack the Gulf tighter and tighter with lightning and gunpowder.

Robin Wright, a writer for the *Los Angeles Times*, says that "President Bush's original strategy of holding the line militarily while economic sanctions worked their slow will has become untenable." Wright believes, as do many others, that war seems to be inevitable.

Some commentators suggest that American is spoiling for a fight, that our military, which has never recovered from the tragic misadventure that was Viet Nam, may soon have its perceived opportunity to ennoble itself. This may be a cynical, but realistic suspicion. Our posture in the Gulf becomes more offensive every hour, and we are lobbying hard at the United Nations for legal permission to unleash our forces.

I never thought that again during my lifetime I would see American dead brought home by the hundreds, the thousands, from a foreign war. It looks as though this is going to happen.

Rochester Democrat & Chronicle/Times-Union (Aug. 24, 1990).

It seems to me that our policy has been to support monarchies, dictatorships, fossil fuel banana republics in the area for our own advantage, and now what our President calls "our way of life" is threatened. Our petroleum-dependent way of life. I wish "our way of life" had included a realistic look into the future, a national priority to develop solar energy and other environmentally benign sources of power. Maybe, if it had, we would not now be rushing toward bloodshed to defend our right to continue fouling our planet, perhaps beyond redemption, by way of oil spills and toxic emissions.

By general scientific consensus, too—see Michael Oppenheimer and Robert H. Boyle's 1989 *Dead Heat*, which is, according to Thomas E. Lovejoy, "required reading for responsible citizenship"—we are heading into chaotic global disruptions, and maybe worse, because of rising temperature. It is frightening to contemplate what is happening to us while our attention is diverted by other events.

In *The End of Nature* (1988), Bill McKibben says that even "if all the liberals and all the conservatives in all the countries of the world had gotten together a decade ago and done all the most dramatic things they could think of [to stave off global warming], it wouldn't have been enough to prevent terrible, terrible changes." In blunt language he says, "A few more decades of ungoverned fossil-fuel use and we burn up." This is what is in the pipeline for us.

The deployment of our forces in the Persian Gulf is costing us, I've heard, about twenty million dollars a day. Goodbye to the peace dividend from the end of the Cold War. Imagine if this money were put into mass transit, into increased engine efficiency, into development of solar energy, into conversion of engines to propane (as the U. P. S. fleet has done in Los Angeles). Even our President's beloved electric golf cart could be part of the answer to our excruciating dilemma in the Middle East.

Would Saddam Hussein have attacked Saudi Arabia after his invasion of Kuwait and before a balanced multi-national defensive force could have been assembled? Most commentators doubt it. But our President and his advisors apparently felt we couldn't take that chance. And maybe they were right. In any case, let us pray, now, for a stand-off until negotiations by all parties stabilize the situation so that all hostages are released and the faithful and patriotic young men and women of our armed forces return home safely.

And let us now *demand* of our politicians once and for all, as a first priority during the '90s, a concerted and ambitious effort to develop ecologically sound alternative energies. Only this, in the short or long run, can possibly save us.

The Ants

Early in *Treblinka* (1966), one of the greatest books I have ever read, Jean-Francois Steiner introduces us to Pessia Aranovich, a Jewish woman whom the Nazis had shot and left for dead in a forest at Ponar in Lithuania. Rising from the other bodies, including those of her husband and daughter, she somehow makes her way back to the ghetto at Vilna where she finds Dr. Ginsberg.

Because Dr. Ginsberg had known Pessia as a beautiful and happy young woman, he at first does not recognize her. But when he sees that this wretched stranger is indeed her, he asks Pessia to tell him what happened to her.

Her story is that Ponar is not a work camp, as the Jews had hoped. "Suddenly at my feet," she says, "there was a huge ditch full of bodies. I did not hear the shots, but I felt a pain in my arm. I fell forward, thinking: This is it, I am dead. And I lost consciousness." What Pessia tells Ginsberg, in short, is that all the Jews except for herself were slaughtered. "Calm yourself, Pessia," he says, "you are feverish and you have had a nightmare."

The good doctor and his wife believe, as would we in their place, that Pessia is deluded, that she had probably met with an accident and had been wandering Vilna, separated from her family. "What we are going through is too hard for children like her," says the doctor's wife. But when Ginsberg dips a handkerchief into water and begins to clean the wound in Pessia's side, he sees that it indeed looks like a bullet hole. Then he sees something stirring inside the hole. Terrified, he discovers red ants—red ants, he realizes, that could only have come from the forest. Ginsberg becomes a believer.

He decides to warn everybody so that people will not let themselves be taken away, so that they will either resist in the ghetto or will try to escape. He rushes to the ghetto square so that he can begin spreading the news to a group of people at a time, but when a single old man greets him from a chair in front of a doorway, the doctor decides to begin with him. Steiner recreates what occurs between the well-meaning doctor and the old man:

"Listen, I must tell you something, it is very serious," he began.

"Well?" asked the old man in a voice that was deliberately cheerful.

"Ponar is not a work camp."

He stopped. The old man's face was impassive, as if he did not understand what the doctor was telling him. The old man's silence troubled him. He felt that something in his attitude eluded him. Ill at ease, he continued, "No one could have imagined, because it is absurd; only insanity could conceive such a plan. And Germany seemed like such a civilized country. Now that is no doubt. This morning a young woman came to my house; she had escaped from Ponar. It is a miracle that she made it. All the others were massacred."

The doctor had lowered his voice at the end of the sentence as if to soften the meaning of the last word. The old man's eyes had blinked and his face had quivered for a fraction of a second, and then he had recovered his impassivity.

The doctor thought he had spoken too softly and that the old man had not heard him.

"All the others were massacred," he repeated, stressing each syllable. "Massacred!" he shouted.

The old man did not react. Then Dr. Ginsberg was seized by a terrible doubt. But the old man's silence unnerved him, and he stopped trying to spare him.

"Ponar means death! All the people who have been taken there have been exterminated, and so will we! We will all be massacred!" Surprised at his own violence, the doctor stopped.

Then the old man's mouth opened and obstinately, like a child, he said, "That is not true."

Dr. Ginsberg looked at him, stunned. So he had known from the beginning; so he had understood immediately, perhaps even before the transfer to the ghetto. But this truth was too terrible for him, at his age, and he had decided to play the comedy of hope. The doctor was suddenly aware of all that was odious in his own attitude. He looked at the old man and asked his forgiveness.

"It is not true," said the doctor, and he left.

When Ginsberg leaves the old man, he thinks over what has happened. He concludes that many others must also have suspected the truth about Ponar, but for the sake of their emotional and mental well-being they needed to remain uncertain. Uncertainty "protected the weak from despair, and he did not have the right to take it away from them." From this point on, Ginsberg decides, he would speak of the death camp only to those he could trust to absorb and act on the truth.

He next meets a reliable lawyer and tells Pessia Aranovich's story. The lawyer does not believe. When he and Ginsberg go to speak to Pessia herself so that the lawyer may be convinced, they find that she has left the Ginsberg home. Her last words to Mrs. Ginsberg were chilling, and may serve for all of us as an epigraph for our book of the Holocaust. "Nobody returns from Ponar." When we hear this, of course, we realize that she is not only suggesting that even survivors do not survive, but that within us memory itself seems to disavow an experience so brutal, so otherworldly, so *impossible* in this our Twentieth Century. Nobody returns from Ponar, or Auschwitz; nobody returns from that reality, exactly. Pessia herself is dazed into a kind of disbelief even as we hear from those with blue numbers along their wrists that they sometimes cannot believe what they themselves have witnessed.

Ginsberg, Steiner tells us, has learned that people will not believe that they are about to die, whatever the evidence. And die in such circumstances? After all, what human beings would murder the innocent? Did pure evil exist? Steiner is relentless in portraying the national and largely unemotional war by "technicians" to render Jews extinct. But "as long as we have no certainty, we must do nothing," the lawyer had said to Ginsberg. The doctor realizes that hope matters much more than truth.

Pessia's heartbreaking story has the power of parable. In his dénouement, Steiner spirals into blackness. He tells us that Dr. Ginsberg "saw Pessia again a long time afterward. She was working in a dressmaking factory in the ghetto; she seemed to have forgotten everything and was laughing with the other girls. She had never dared tell her adventure again."

In his buoyant and cosmically optimistic "To Think of Time," Walt Whitman sees "Slow moving and black lines [that] go ceaselessly over the earth." Part of the Holocaust's legacy to us is that we cannot now make his transcendental leap to faith ("Whither I walk I cannot define, but I know it is good"). We know that Whitman is talking about the afterlife, whatever our experience here, but we have seen aerial photographs of lines of people on their way into the gas chambers. We remember what Pessia saw and experienced. It seems crazy to us that the afterlife, if there is one, could suddenly reveal itself to be so different from the present life.

Pessia's was a voice crying in the wilderness. *All* the Jews were being killed, she said. But she realized that her story made her unwelcome. It was an anti-social story. As a messenger of extermination, she was an outcast, and perhaps could not even trust her own sanity. The way for her to "survive" was to forget. We hear little else of her or of Dr. Ginsberg in *Treblinka*. They meant well, and they knew what they knew. They *realized*—a truth had been made real within them—but their realized truth was too radical to be believed, at least consciously. We find ways to defend ourselves from imagining such negation, though those red ants from the forest at Ponar have now made their nests in us.

Spring Letter to Geof Hewitt

Geof, for two or three weeks now, after some days of spiralling thought, I've been back to routine—teaching, reading, playing basketball, watching television, spending time with my family, and doing some writing. I've been passing time, living the safe and easy life I've lived since I left graduate school and began teaching at Brockport twenty years ago. But this morning, looking out at mourning doves and squirrels scratching in snow for seed I'd scattered under a spruce, I had one of those moments when I almost blacked out: for a wordless second or two I realized, or imagined, our busy lives on earth coming to an end, our absolute absence.

I don't think it is the thought of my own death that brings on one of these moments that drains me. I've had enough life so that life from here on in—as much as I want more of it and want to feel healthy and of worth as I live it—is "Gravy," as Ray Carver says in one of his last poems. The thing is this: Emerson declares, "To be able to discern that what is true is true, and that what is false is false, this is the mark and character of intelligence," and I at least want to think strenuously and clearly enough to know what I believe even if I believe that we are nearing the end, that human life on this planet will virtually cease to exist within about a hundred years.

I can't change the world (though maybe, deluded as I may be, I think I can affect the direction of American poetry), and I've wanted to forget that we are rapidly choking and poisoning our planet past redemption. Each day, our window of black glass drops a little closer to the sill. Listen to Thomas E. Lovejoy in his 1988 speech to the American Institute of Biological Sciences: "I am utterly convinced that most of the great environmental struggles will be either won or lost in the 1990's, and that by the next century it will be too late." And listen to Lester Brown and Christopher Flavin of the Worldwatch Institute in their foreword to the 1989 *State of the World*: "One of these years, we would like to be able to write an upbeat *State of the World*, one in which we can report that the trends undermining the human prospect have been reversed. It now seems that if we cannot write such a report in the nineties, we may not be able to write it at all." Do we have any sense that we as a nation realize this? Our answers to environmental crises are stop-gap and short-range. We react to symptoms while life closes down on all human history.

We can be only as healthy as our water, which becomes a chemical stew; as our soil, which is blowing away, which is being asphalted over, which is losing its wholesomeness and ability to heal itself because of massive additions of nitrates, clouds of pesticides and herbicides. Thirty thousand new chemicals are introduced to the market each year, loopholing regulations, and we know little about the long-term effects of most of them. As sure as I'm sitting here writing this letter, thinking of you up there in diminishing Vermont, I know that our forests are dying, that in a hundred years there will be no squirrels or mourning doves under spruces in our backyards; I know that our oceans are dying, that in a hundred years there will be no shrimp like the ones I had for dinner last evening. Dangerous concentrations of PCBs and toxic heavy metals are being found in the tissues of penguins and seals in the "unspoiled" Antarctic. Meanwhile, the general psyche of big business (though there are enlightened exceptions) is exemplified by a tobacco industry that won't admit any connection between smoking and the incalculable grief of heart disease and cancer for tens of thousands a year.

Everything is too fast. We cannot adapt to the pace of change, cannot "witness and adjust," as Doc Williams puts it. America is its own pure product, and is going crazy. Walt's "Give me O nature your primal sanities" is like a mosquito-whine in the back of our heads while the Smith Haven Mall on Long Island fills with muzak and begins to connect with Brockport malls 350 miles away. The Mall has situated itself inside us, like the "alien" creature in those Sigourney Weaver movies, but this is not science fiction and we can't/won't kick it out the hatch or blow it to smithereens. And even while I try to think about these things, the landscape changes around me, farmland becoming Frederick's of Hollywood and Fanny Farmer. Our destruction is exponential, our understanding languourous as an oil slick in calm water. Lovejoy wonders whether, maybe, we "evolved in a time of change slower than that we are afflicting upon ourselves." If we did, I think, then maybe we are physiologically *unable* to imagine what is happening, even if the evidence is right in front of us.

So many energetic and well meaning people these days are doing so many decent things—recycling, fighting for consumer protection, trying to save manatees in the mangrove swamps, condors in California, and tortoises in the Tortugas—but it is as though some vast and irresistible force is sweeping us out of existence. We are not getting a hold on things. The planet's population has swollen from two billion to six billion since I was a boy, and continues to swell and fester even while the abortion issue dizzies and confuses us. Our schools prepare students to serve the one great corporation the world seems to be becoming, and this corporation will not be deflected, for long, by spikes driven into redwoods or by evidence of approaching extinction, from what seems to be its one relentless purpose: to make every fast cent from every forced pineapple and potato and pullet, from every drop or carat of fossil fuel, come high water (from the melting ice caps via the greenhouse effect) or hell. (And maybe I play with alliteration to hypnotize myself, somehow, into actual realization of the actual approaching end of all civilization.) Lovejoy's "human prospect," the human vista, is a wall. Meanwhile, poets continue to write as though mankind had margins and could continue to engage in any old aesthetics, as though subtlety and indirection and intricate obliquity—the mainstays of art from its beginnings through 20th-century *avant garde* movements—were still viable.

I *am* that Megacorp, am I? My home and skull are filled with useless things the presence of which has contributed to the obliteration of species. At the same time, I am not that corporation. I scream and drag my feet as it hauls me and my descendents over the edge of what it apparently conceives of as a limitless and eternal world. How can you and I and the others who know what is happening get through to that part of ourselves incorporated, it is obvious, against survival? Distrust, greed, stupidity—throw in some world wars and Chernobyl and we *still* survived—the world once upon a time had tolerance for all we could do to it, to ourselves. It once seemed that we lived within a galaxy whose impalpable presence somehow supported us, and always would. Our earth, our one planetary home, now groans with us as we die off with it here.

It may be of course, that from the deepest perspective none of this matters, our home is elsewhere and non-material. To paraphrase Emerson in *Nature*, we and the world are solutions in hieroglyphics to the questions we put to it, and there is a sense in which whatever is, whatever we become, is somehow right and inevitable. *But* I feel I need this earth for my children's children. It is spirit visible. They need to *be*, to become, to be made incarnate to exist on this plane—that is the cosmic ecosystem come to fruition, or I am the last romantic.

Each of us sailing on the American luxury liner is two hundred times the drain on the world's resources of a Third Worlder. Our attention is frivolous, is focused on sports and entertainments from phony wrestling to dwarf-throwing. In my fantasy benevolent-dictator mode I sometimes reason in this way: if it is obvious that ecosystems are breaking down, that all species are on the brink of extinction; if it is obvious that only a radically new education, one that will somehow enable us to imagine what is happening to ourselves and our planet, can save us, then we must not be distracted by the things that distract us and waste our time. (On the front page of the *Rochester Democrat and Chronicle* yesterday, and on the sports pages, were a total of three large photographs of Sherman Douglas, a Syracuse University basketball player who has broken a couple of records. Three photographs of a college basketball player!) Therefore, I would cancel the entire NFL and major league baseball and NFL seasons and the PGA tour for at least this next make-it or break-it decade. (Imagine how much more time we would have to consider our approaching extinction, how much attention and effort we could direct from child's play to saving the planet's playing fields for children a thousand years from now.) I would cancel tens of thousands of other distracting and obfuscating programs and events—all Division I college sports, the Rose

Bowl Parade, the polluting Indianapolis 500 and other such races, the Olympics, space programs (we will *not* be able to escape to other worlds and NASA, for example, doesn't give a damn about a balanced and holistic life, doesn't have even a rudimentary imagination regarding the great death finding its way to Cape Kennedy as they fuck around with public relations and astronauts and rockets that have nowhere to go and that do not help us solve problems here and now though they cynically pretend to throw us a human-caring research bone once in a while). I would cancel the publication of any book (including poetry and fiction), and the showing of any film, that does not bear *directly* on the fact that all life on earth is about to join Martha, the last passenger pigeon, who died in a zoo in Cincinnati. (No more stories about Pete Rose unless the connection is made, as it can be, between his situation and Martha's, period.) I would demand that television devote itself to ecology, and metaphor that integrates our interests with final things. I would forbid the manufacture of unnecessary products. (How many millions of us use electric hair dryers every day? Thousands of human generations did without them. We could power our schools with the energy we spend drying our hair.) And since we spend more money on pet food in this country than on education, until we have a sustainable life style I would forbid pets. (Okay, okay, I'll make a big-hearted exception for some goldfish or tropical fish.) I would ban entertainers from Elvis to Sinatra to Kiss and Tom Jones and the Rockettes, would shut down the record industry except for songs that in some direct way dealt with our approaching extinction, with the fact that there might be no one alive on earth a hundred years from now to hear the great Foreigner gospel song "I Want to Know What Love Is."

I'll stop. I hear you sigh with relief, mutter with understanding. But isn't it absurd that these actions would not be absurd, that they are modest in terms of the chaos toward which our civilization spins? Pablo Neruda called Whitman a "totalitarian," but said that Walt was always compassionate, did not offend the human condition. We need to make sure, first, that there *is* a human condition a century from now. We are on the edge of a global catastrophe from which there might be no escape, and yet poets are still writing language poems and talking about post-modernism and deconstruction as though, even if intellectually a certain criticism or a certain aesthetics should help toward realizations that would contribute to our salvation, any average resident of the workaday world from engineer to janitor to corporation president to airline stewardess to small-town mayor to nurse or doctor or cop or factory worker could understand or be made to care. Poets are still meandering sloppily within personal themes while a great age of darkness laughs its way to the bank. Our poetry is an evasion, of course, but we are ingenuous, conning ourselves, convincing ourselves by way of fancy theory that we are making some kind of progress. We are fast approaching the end of all civilization, but various of us tell ourselves that our poems are valid when they are primarily about the syllable-by-syllable ongoingness of language itself, or about grandma who sewed patches on grandpa's overalls. Sure, the former poem mimics or discovers creation itself, maybe, and can lift the heart as we experience the source; sure, the latter poem might center on love and a generous non-materialistic making-do that would save us. But who are we kidding? No one is listening. We need directness now, poems that state facts and slap us with the hands of our grandchildren.

In "Dream Song" 265 John Berryman says, "I don't know one damned butterfly from another. . . ." Loren Eiseley does. He knows a swallowtail from a monarch, but knows something even deeper than this. In "The Last Butterfly" he writes that he thinks of all these creatures, in essence,

> as one immortal
> entering the winter dark
> returning always returning
> to the single
> summer plant in the world.

Berryman says "next time it will be nature & Thoreau. . . ." He says he loves "the hit-or-miss, / the mad, I sometimes can't always tell them apart. . . ." But we must know what we know, and must be able to tell the difference between sanity and insanity in art and in our relationship with the world in whose womb we live or die. The anthropologist-poet Eiseley can break our hearts and minds with his truths. In "The Desperate Man" he walks the city with a thistle in his palm looking for a place to bed the drifter down. He concludes,

> The snows will come and the rains, but what have we done
> how have we come to this:
> that someone, even I, must think, and not nature,
> thoughts for the winter sleep of the last thistledown?

Eiseley knows that because it has not been nature and Thoreau for us, we will not be staying. But perhaps we will not be able to poison all life before we leave. "And As For Man" concludes:

> This is how I shall remember New York forever:
> not by the towers touching the evening star,
> not by the lights in windows, not by lonely and driven men
> shall I recall that city, but by the weeds
> undaunted on sheer stone and waiting,
> showering their seed and waiting,
> waiting for the last train to enter the tunnel, waiting
> for the last voice to speak on the telephonic track.
> They will start to climb then, they will have had enough
> of waiting, and as for man, he will not be coming back.

We can hear, now, the desire and irony and regret of Berryman's phrase "next time...."

Is it any wonder we do not or cannot think clearly about these things? When I truly imagine, for maybe just a second or three a month, I come close to extinguishing myself in advance of the death of my species. (Poetic prophecy to the nth?) A friend said to me "When I think of these things, these inevitabilities, I want to get it over with, want it all to end right away." It *is* excruciating for us to wait for annihilations, to look into our children's eyes knowing how their children will have to look into their children's eyes. No wonder we want/need to dwell on Madonna and Mike Tyson. Three photographs of a college basketball player, while I've read virtually nothing about the Brazillian saint assassinated a few months ago because of his life's struggle to save the rain forest, his people's way of life. What was his name? I can name the starting five for Syracuse this past season. My head is filled with sludge and toxic waste. I am Goodman Brown in Hawthorne's parable: "He was himself the chief horror of the scene...."

As you know, I've been thinking about a sequence of required courses (not as a progression, but as interlocking circles) for the high school and college curriculums. When they heard my proposal, several well-meaning colleagues suggested that such courses could be team-taught. Well, maybe, I said, but said that surely each of us has to learn to teach such courses, we're too goddamned specialized, I've got to become whole and be able to teach from and learn from a range of books, a field of books, a prairie of books in one course in one integrated attempt to get past the symptomatic busted rims and axles and spokes to the force itself that drives the Conestoga hardware store and sporting goods store and chemical warehouse and missile silo over the plains, I mean I'm going crazy splintering myself off expertly in so-called "Poetry," deepening the grave my Ph.D. began digging for me, while what I need is inclusiveness, the center to which everything adheres, *poetry*, and we are all smart asses, divided against ourselves, and the unintelligibility of so much contemporary poetry for example is a result of this specialization, and it is immoral and insane, it is killing us, don't you understand, do I understand?

Sure—I've stopped raving now—when I teach *Moby Dick* I allude (though trying to stay close to the try-works of the sacred text) to Lee Iacocca, and Brahms, and Einstein, and Gregory Peck in the film version, and that great megalomaniac George Herman Ruth ("whose decorum on formal occasions I sometimes / for the health of my soul have needed to emulate" as I say in a poem) and other transcendental and historical monomaniacs in business and science and various entertainments, but these (gulp, ahem) well-rounded references are in effect just asides. I need the framework to do more. If I had a single course devoted to one of Barry Commoner's four fundamental laws of ecology, say "Everything must go somewhere," and myself and my students studied and considered Eugen Herrigel's *Zen in the Art of Archery* (what is it, what imperfections, make our shots wobble, distort our shooting and seeing?); Jean

Francois Steiner's *Treblinka* or Elie Wiesel's *Night* (technological and toxic anti-Semitism finding its embodiment in the *SS*, the power of the human spirit evidenced in the author's unextinguished sentences); Madison Smartt Bell's *History of the Owen School* (Vanderbilt University's Owen Graduate School of Management where one course on the books was/is "The Environment and Managerial Strategies") (what were the goals of these businessmen-educators, what are their desires and what are and how healthy are the current manifestations of these desires?); Walt Whitman's "Song of Myself" (infinite connections, and all of the somewhere that everything must go is here, but listen to this: "Dazzling and tremendous how quick the sun-rise would kill me, / If I could not now and always send sun-rise out of me"); Lewis Thomas's *Lives of a Cell* and/or Werner Heisenberg's *Physics and Beyond* and/or Jonathan Schell's *The Fate of the Earth* (toward what are all atoms and termites tending, what are the centers of the life source and where is it headed, what has our fear created and what are the outlets of our fear?);—if I had a single courses and kept spiralling toward integration of all texts (Simone de Beauvoir's *The Second Sex* with Adrienne Rich's *Of Woman Born: Motherhood as Experience and Institution* with Wendell Berry's *The Gift of Good Land* with Robert Siegel's *Whale Song* with Annie Dillard's *Teaching a Stone to Talk* with a study of the territoriality of the English robin or of the last six black robins in existence with Edwin Way Teale's *A Naturalist Buys an Old Farm* with the new Norton text on James Watson and the discovery of DNA and the double helix with Michael Herr's Vietnam *Dispatches* with a biography of Henry Ford or Martin Luther King with a volume of haunting collage photographs by Olivia Parker called *Under the Looking Glass* with Dr. Jacques Liebowitch's *A Strange Virus of Unknown Origin*, I could become whole and maybe help those in my classes toward wholeness. Such a course would force us to become poets, ones who *integrate*, who *connect*. And what would such poetry mean? It might mean that we could become people who realize the wholeness of the earth and tread lightly and take shallow breaths until the air is clean enough for us to breathe deeply again. As teachers and students we all have our own lists of books we've pigeon-holed into different fields but ones in whose presence we've felt the real thing, intimations of that spirit that fuses us with a cosmos that can keep creating itself if we can wise up. And we'd want to share these texts, and keep growing with them.

Then a second course on the second Commoner law of ecology ("Everything is connected to everything else"), then one on his third ("Nature knows best"), then one on his fourth ("There is no such thing as a free lunch")—all these interlocking rings of realization. We could stop lock-stepping our students from the classroom box of one course into the classroom box of another. We could begin to stop slashing and burning parts of the world (trees and minds) with which we've made no connection. We could become more than specialist pedants befuddled by rising temperature and ocean levels and soil toxicity while we conduct "pure" research into the separate slivers of what William Cullen

Bryant calls our "favorite phantom(s)." We could stop thinking of our earth as a spaceship as Buckminster Fuller does, and as the editors of *U.S. News & World Report* (Oct 31, 1988 issue) do. Their simplistic cover reads, "Planet Earth: How It Works/How to Fix it," and their lead story reduces our infinitely varied and complex and webbed and wavery and shimmering and delicately modulated mysterious world to something Megacorp thinks it can understand and dominate, another machine. They say that the Gulf Stream is "a conveyor belt" and that "the oceans act as a gigantic flywheel in the Earth's machinery," that our world has a "thermostat." The bad poetry here, the poverty of feeling, the ignorance is so great that it is almost too deep for tears, or words. In one tree in the Amazon are more than 2000 insect species living like a symphony. Is that a machine? Is the place of this tree in the forest of the world the place of a part in a machine? . . . If we could integrate our studies, we could begin to make of our educations "a music that means," what Archibald MacLeish calls a poem. . . .

Geof, during the space between these two paragraphs of mine here, my mind on the wheel of routine again, a Long Islander by the name of Hazelwood—listen to that name—fell into a drunken (if not drunken, then oblivious and irresponsible) sleep below decks of the Exxon oil tanker *Valdez* in Alaska's Prince William Sound. When I drink my morning coffee now, it tastes a little more like crude oil, the spill from the *Valdez*, we are told, covering an area the size of Rhode Island one day, Delaware the next. I've never been in a hazelwood. But my daughter has hazel eyes, and I will be thinking of Hazelwood when I look into them. And Hazelwood lives in Huntington, near Walt's birthplace. And you and I drank with Walt and Hazelwood and fell asleep with them. The old captains of Long Island left Huntington and left Sag Harbor and filled the bellies of their ships and their own bodies with whale oil. Hazelwood shipped to Alaska and filled our bodies and eyes with crude. And something in us knows that the plundering is the same, and whale oil lamps shone with a black light, and we have hated ourselves for this, and we have wanted to drink and sleep, and die, as we *are* dying. I will look into the Erie Canal in Brockport all summer and for the rest of my life and see that it is stained by the oil that covers the fishing grounds. And I will have to look into even the great *Leaves of Grass* to see if and where the oil from Alaska's North Slope stains it. And I will have to look into my daughter's eyes to try to see if I can *not* think of myself, a Long Islander from Nesconset, as Captain Joseph Hazelwood dead asleep in the belly of the *Valdez*. . . .

Francisco Mendes Filho was his name. Chico Mendes. The sane and visionary man who tried to protect the rain forest—for its own sake, for his people, for all of us. At a memorial service one of his followers said, "Chico Mendes is alive in each of us." Another spoke aloud to his dead friend: "Wherever you are, don't grieve that they have silenced your voice—your ideas exist among us." Chico achieved integration, perfection of the life and of the work. He now exists for us as an "extractive reserve," a renewable resource, a spirit of sustenance and possibility, as would a new poem, a new poetry that his people and our people could hear and take courage and direction from. Geof, I can see his face. He has imagined the end, has shaken himself out of a death-trance, has begun to visit his neighbors to tell them what he has seen, what is coming to be unless, together, they imagine extinction and imagine what can be done against it.

Trees

In the branched galaxy of *Night* when, in Elie Wiesel's words, "the world was a cattle wagon hermetically sealed," Madam Schächter began to cry her vision of the fire to come. Wiesel writes, "Standing in the middle of the wagon, in the pale light from the windows, she looked like a withered tree in a cornfield."

At Birkenau, Wiesel says, "We were so many, dried-up trees in the heart of a desert."

Later, Idek the Kapo beats Eliezer's father. "At first my father crouched under the blows, then he broke in two, like a dry tree struck by lightening, and collapsed."

The trees of *Night* wither, they are hermetically sealed, they are dried up, they are struck, and split by *SS* lightning. Tree-gallows become black crows in the poignant, helpless, tragic, despairing poetry in the dead heartwood of this deathless book.

On the eve of Rosh Hashanah, "At the place of assembly, surrounded by the electrified barbed wire, thousands of silent Jews gathered, their faces stricken." The wind seemed to speak a benediction: "Blessed be the Name of the Eternal." Wiesel writes, "Thousands of voices repeated the benediction; thousands of men prostrated themselves like trees before a tempest."

Without trees, life on this planet is not possible.

Cut from their roots in the east and buried, felled to freeze into cordwood in deep drifts, reduced to charred remains in the Reich's ovens, the Jews of *Night* are trees. They are, as Wiesel says in *Ani Maamin*, "a forest turned to ashes."

But Wiesel's books are themselves trees. They tremble and almost break in the winds of their experience, but their root systems support them, and him, and us, somehow, somehow.

Reading *Night*, when Eliezer is liberated from the camp named "Buchenwald," we wonder what his future will be, and think back to words he heard from Moche the Beadle in Sighet: "There are a thousand and one gates leading into the orchard of mystical truth. Every human being has his own gate. We must never make the mistake of wanting to enter the orchard by any gate but

Delivered at Webster University in St. Louis on September 29, 1988, during a program in honor of Elie Wiesel. Published in *Telling the Tale: A Tribute to Elie Wiesel*, ed. Harry James Cargas (St. Louis: Time Being Books, 1993).

our own. To do this is dangerous for the one who enters and also for those who are already there."

The gates of Auschwitz and Buchenwald open on/close on/open on "the orchard of mystical truth." From *Night* to *Twilight,* Elie Wiesel, by courage and prayer and devotion and intellect and intuition, would reach this Holocaust orchard where he has been speaking with the barefoot beadle of Sighet, a personage of many guises, ever since.

I'd like to read two poems, one from my book *Erika,* and one that declared itself to me as I anticipated our gathering today.

This two-paragraph prose poem is called "The Tree." As you'll hear, it's about the life and death and spirit of a village, Lidice.

> Not everyone can see the tree, its summer cloud of green leaves or its bare radiance under winter sunlight. Not everyone can see the tree, but it is still there, standing just outside the area that was once a name and a village: Lidice. Not everyone can see the tree, but most people, all those who can follow the forked stick, the divining rod of their heart to the tree's place, can hear it. The tree needs no wind to sound as though wind blows through its leaves. The listener hears voices of children, and of their mothers and fathers. There are moments of great joy, music, dancing, but all the sounds of the life of Lidice: drunks raving their systems, a woman moaning the old song of the toothache, strain of harness on plowhorse, whistle of flail in the golden fields. But under all these sounds is the hum of lamentation, the voices' future.

> The tree is still there, but when its body fell, it was cut up and dragged away for the shredder. The tree's limbs and trunk were pulped at the papermill. There is a book made of this paper. When you find the book, when you turn its leaves, you will hear the villagers' voices. When you hold the leaves of this book to light, you will see the watermarks of their faces.

I like to think that all of us together are reading and writing the book made from that tree, trying to hear those voices, even if this is not possible, trying to see those faces, even if we can see only watermarks.

This new poem is called "The Apple." It began with a few remembered words I heard spoken in the film *Shoah.* It has to do, finally, perhaps, with artistic seeing, with how we must live in order to continue to try to understand. But I'm still listening hard to the poem, feeling my way into it.

A survivor is speaking. I should say that I always want to remain aware of Mr. Wiesel's words in his essay "A Plea for the Survivors": "Accept the idea that you will never see what they have seen—and go on seeing now, that you will never know the faces that haunt their nights, that you will never hear the cries that rend their sleep. Accept the idea that you will never penetrate the cursed and spellbound universe they carry within themselves with unfailing loyalty."

The Apple

1.
In Israel at that time just after the war,
we did not have much to eat,
so when, at the beach, I saw an apple bobbing in the waves,
glistening red, far out, but an apple for sure,
I swam for it.

I did reach the object,
and, as I'd thought, it was an apple.
I carried it to shore in my bosom,
thinking of its juice and firm flesh.
But, inside, it was rotten:

it had been thrown from a boat,
or a cloud, for good reason.
Were you to eat a bit of my survivor's heart
even the size of an apple seed,
it would poison you.

2.
In Israel at that time just after the war,
we did not have much to eat,
so when, at the beach, I saw an apple bobbing in the waves,
glistening red, far out, but an apple for sure,
I swam for it.

I did reach the object,
but it was not an apple.
Unbelievable as this might be, it was an eye,
perhaps from an octopus, or a shark,
or a whale, but an eye,

translucid red, a watery gel,
its pupil black and unmistakable.
Perhaps this was the eye of the angel
of the camps. I cupped it in my hands.
I swallowed at least one mouthful, to see.

The Way: Thanks to Stafford

Since August of 1992 I've written more than 300 poems, many in a trance of process, that turn on the Custers, the Great Plains, the buffalo, and especially the Sioux mystic and warrior Crazy Horse. This morning, thinking much too deliberately of trying to write something about my old friend Bill Stafford, I was reading through sheaves of his letters, and was looking into various of his books here and there, just swerving and ambling and connecting in the Stafford way, when I found poems I'd forgotten I've known, "A Sound from the Earth" in which Crazy Horse's grandfather cries out for him as the whole bowl of the earth trembles, and "Report to Crazy Horse" in which Stafford's speaker says to the warrior's spirit, "No one remembers your vision / or even your real name." He goes on:

> A teacher here says
> hurt or scorned people are places
> where real enemies hide. He says
> we should not hurt or scorn anyone,
> but help them. And I will tell you
> in a brave way, the way Crazy Horse
> talked: that teacher is right.

A poet's work is not a body of doctrine, of course, and Stafford in so many intriguing ways taught us that a true poem will feel free to follow its own impulses, but in this poem, by way of his persona, he writes directly and unflinchingly from his moral heart: "we should not hurt or scorn anyone," for in doing so we create our enemies.

In the same way, for this was not a poet in whom perfection of the life and of the work were at war, he was extremely uncomfortable about discriminating among his own or others' poems. The soul of the world nudging itself awake, speaking itself by way or rhythm and language beyond rational audition, might be catching its breath in that apparently unremarkable or trite sequence of workshop sounds. Years ago at a reading I heard him say four little

---

Christian Science Monitor (Oct. 26, 1993). William Stafford died two months before.

words that swirled everything together for us, that challenged the scientific-industrial complexes our minds are in danger of becoming, that protested our arrogant destruction of the ecosystem, that sang out for the compassion and love that might save us. He said, "I love feeble poems."

Imagine: a poem is okay if maybe it's weak, if it doesn't feel so hot today or hear so well today, if it's a little groggy or dizzy or self-contradictory, if it seems to need a crutch, if its speech is not greatly heightened, if it is not the stunning crystallization of experience most anthology lyrics aspire to be. The poem of creation doesn't always have to exclaim "Eureka!" In a 1971 letter, he wrote me, "In general, I feel a need to figure out for myself whether I should inhibit appearance of some kinds of poems in which I grope around for achievement without conviction on my own part that the job is done, but without perception of how to redeem the gropy progress of something that still entices me to keep groping." Yes, he sometimes felt this need, as we all do—there was the activity, after all, of putting books together from voluminous writings—but other needs, more mysterious and inclusive "trajectories" (a favorite word of his), were much more important.

The poem as horse, the poet as rider. Someday, maybe, it is twilight. How much rein to give the horse on its way home? All you can—it will find the way. When I write, I feel blessed in the abiding presence of my friend who keeps finding the way before me.

Crazy Horse's real name, as Bill Stafford knew, is *Tasunke-Witko*, which might mean, I understand, something like "one whose horse dances crazy" or "one whose horse is enchanted."

Kick-Ass Cummings

Hello, I'm glad to be here. I'd like to thank Norman Friedman, especially, for getting us all together.

I've been to the New School twice before—to visit Pearl London's classes on "Works in Progress." Well, my works that were in progress at the time got done. And now, by way of our gentle directive for this occasion, I've been thinking about Cummings and just where he was/has been within me as I've been writing.

About thirty years ago, at SUNY Cortland between stints in graduate school, I taught my first class in modern American poetry. I used Cummings' long-lived Grove Press *100 Selected Poems*, and have adopted that book several times since. Way back then, a particular poem lodged itself in me. I doubt a single week has gone by in my life since then that I haven't said this poem to myself. I guess I'll say it now.

> since feeling is first
> who pays any attention
> to the syntax of things
> will never wholly kiss you;
>
> wholly to be a fool
> while Spring is in the world
>
> my blood approves,
> and kisses are a better fate
> than wisdom
> lady I swear by all flowers. Don't cry
> —the best gesture of my brain is less than
> your eyelids' flutter which says
>
> we are for each other: then
> laugh, leaning back in my arms

Delivered at the New School for Social Research (Dec. 5, 1994). Published in *Spring: The Journal of the E. E. Cummings Society* 4 (Fall 1995).

for life's not a paragraph
And death I think is no parenthesis

So, what I was thinking of doing for this brief presentation was trying to trace the various elusive ways in which this poem, by way of rhythms, images, themes, diction, etc., might have surfaced in me. "since feeling is first" has probably never occurred to me consciously while I've been in the semi-trance of writing, but how could a poem that has existed inside me for so long, as early memory, as mnemonic rhythm, *not* be part of the weave of my own lyrics?... I thought hard about this for a while, but got tired of trying to explain and x-ray. (I also realized that I have dozens of poems by other poets by heart, and this was a complication I couldn't simplify or untangle; I also realized that I've never enjoyed, or even much believed in, studies of influence.) And you know another Cummings poem, too, which makes us laugh about all these things:

mr youse needn't be so spry
concernin questions arty

each has his tastes but as for i
i likes a certain party

gimme the he-man's solid bliss
for youse ideas i'll match youse

a pretty girl who naked is
is pretty worth a million statues

In any case, and "since feeling is first," I feel like slanting in in a different way, and maybe even having a little fun.

Early this semester, in a graduate seminar, we were talking about what might be some of the aims and assumptions behind some John Ashbery poems, the aesthetics of Atocha, so to speak. We were talking about language unfolding itself in the present, about a poetics that resists closure, about the moral beauty of indeterminacy. I remember reading to the class Carolyn Forché's note on her own book *The Angel of History*: "The first-person, free-verse, lyric-narrative poem of my earlier years has given way to a work which has desired its own bodying forth: polyphonic, haunted, and in ruins, with no possibility of restoration." I also quoted from Paul Hoover's preface to his recent anthology *Postmodern American Poetry*: "Through circuitousness and obliqueness, Ashbery alludes to things in the process of avoiding them; in saying nothing, he says everything." Hoover quotes Ashbery: "religions are beautiful because of the strong possibility that they are founded on nothing," And I remember handing out to the class passages from a review by Donald Revell in *The Ohio Review* of a book of selected poetry by Edmond Jabes.

The reviewer says, "History has exposed the incorrigible criminality of language. True speech must therefore incline in one direction only: towards the unindicted future." Again, here, arose the idea that after the horrific brutality of man's history, we are all, with this current language of ours, beyond redemption and must, somehow, somewhere else, get beyond words and their assumptions, their baggage of forgetfulness and aberration.

In short, I was admiring and understanding and jiving, the class was jumping, we were being fancy and smart and even occasionally sincere about how, as we read toward the purity and freedom that postmodern incoherencies awaken in us, traditional intelligibility and accessibility are outmoded irrelevancies at best, dangerous precedents to holocaust at worst.

And then, all at once, since feeling will sometimes insist on being first and since I seem to feel several ways about anything at the same time, I grew nauseous, sick of it all, all my cleverness and the poems' deflections, deft discursivenesses, brilliant glides and flutings and leaps, the non-taking-holdness, the effortless stunning resources of the Atocha poet who was probably one of those Archibald MacLeish was thinking of when in a letter he spoke of poets who hold up to the young models of "withering heartlessness." It goes without saying, of course, that Ashbery is not heartless, but "Atocha" poetry is passionate beauty thrice removed, mirrors and refractions, hubless spokes, rootless trees, starshine from primal heavenly bodies long burnt out.

Lately I'd been reading, too, the poetry of some very direct and angry writers including Eliott Richman, perhaps the most powerful poet of the Vietnam War, whose most recent book is *Trooper, Walk On*, and Adrian C. Louis, a Native American whose address is Pine Ridge and whose *Blood Thirsty Savages* had just appeared. These poets hit hard and fast. They don't spend much time feinting and jabbing. They slash. They aren't worried about decorum or balance—if poetry is heightened speech, their speech is heightened by anger and disgust in the way that our own everyday speech, when we are passionate, takes on insistent, heavily-accented, sometimes staccato rhythms. They still believe that with available words one human being can sway another toward outrage and moral action.

I've edited two anthologies of contemporary American poets, *American Poets in 1976* and *The Generation of 2000*. Now, poets like Richman and Louis make me think about editing another. I'd call it, maybe, *Kick-Ass Poets*. "Kick-Ass" is sort of a vulgar term, of course. Before George Bush used it on the campaign trail, I think I first heard it from athletes. It smacks of piling on bodies and points, of good old-fashioned violence on the edge of the rules. Heard as verb and object as a directive, or heard with a hyphen as adjective, the spondee has already ousted the weak iambic or strong iambic that Frost said were poetry's two rhythms. The phrase is used by one athlete to encourage his teammates, by another to intimidate his opponents. Whoever uses the phrase is clear about his or her objective: to win, and to win decisively, without ambiguity, to overwhelm the enemy. No taking of prisoners. In your face. Kick-ass hears the street, is closer to rap than rapture. It's Double-Dutch jump-roping, which I heard about just last night.

As I think about this poetry, I know that Whitman is less a kick-ass poet than Dickinson. Stevens is not one; Williams often is. Eliot is not, but Robinson Jeffers sometimes is; the Frost of "Fire and Ice" is close. Marianne Moore is not, but Adrienne Rich and Levertov of the next generation sometimes are. Robert Bly, no—even "The Teeth Mother Naked at Last" has heavily romantic rhythms and undertones. Roethke, never, but Phil Levine, yes. James Wright, Charles Wright, Mary Oliver—no, no, no. Joyce Carol Oates, C.K. Williams—yes. Carruth, sometimes (and who'd like to be a kick-ass poet more than sometimes?). Barbed wire wrapped around our heads. Richard Howard, Anthony Hecht, James Merrill, no. Well, I could go on with my feelings/opinions for along time, and I probably will, if I work on that anthology and if I write a preface. Barbra Streisand: *not*; Tanya Tucker, yes. The Dave Clark Five, no; the Stones, yes. In the kingdom of kick-ass, Charles Bukowski may be furthest to the left, thematically at least.

If I write a preface, Cummings will come in as an early progenitor of this school. I don't find many whole poems in this mode—very often, as Norman Friedman has phrased it, Cummings' poems are "a compound of voices and tones." (In the *100 Selected Poems*, maybe "pity this busy monster, mankind, // not" is 80 percent there.) But listen to a few snatches from other poems for that unmistakable sound I'm talking about.

> first knocking on the head
> him, do through icy waters roll
> with brushes recently employed
> anent this muddy toiletbowl,
> while kindred intellects evoke
> allegiance per blunt instruments—

This is of course about Olaf who said "I will not kiss your f.ing flag" and "there is some s. I will not eat."

And here's an execution, kick-ass style:

> squads right impatiently replied
> two billion public lice inside
> one pair of trousers (which had died)

More e.e.:

> I say to hell with that
> that doesn't matter

And one of my favorite moments in one of my favorite poems: "jack spoke to joe / 's left crashed" and "give it him good." And the famous "it took / a nipponized bit of / the old sixth // avenue el; in the top of his head: to tell // him." I haven't spent much time tracing this Cummings through the *Complete Poems*, but listen to the beginning of this piece of rough life from *Tulips & Chimneys* (1922) that I'd have included in the *100 Selected Poems* if I'd been Cummings.

> it started when Bill's chip let on to
> the bulls he'd bumped a bloke back in fifteen.

Setting and subject are of course important. I once heard Cary Grant defend himself against charges that he was making too many movies of elegant fluff, of silk and crystal, by himself asking, "Is a garbage can any more real than Buckingham Palace?" Well, for kick-ass poets, it is, but I'm not just pointing to what we've always thought of as Cummings' tough-guy poems, but to a certain quality of vernacular voice and rhythm: "to hell with that / that doesn't mater," "jack spoke to joe / 's left crashed;" "give it him good"—torqued and heavily accented phrases sometimes seeming to be ground out or spit out. Cummings is plunging to the bottom of the page here, giving it all he's got, not pacing himself. There's a kick-ass velocity here, such poems not worried about modulation. (And an anthology of all such poems, of course, might suffer from sameness of pitch.) In an essay years ago I described Cummings as emotionally and intellectually a Transcendentalist, and believe this still, and it's hard for a Transcendentalist to be a kick-ass poet—no matter how outraged the writer might be, faithful romantic undercurrents (witness even Ginsberg) take us elsewhere, as in my own case, certainly. But Cummings' wicked genius to push voice relentlessly—M.L. Rosenthal uses the phrase "sharp and poisonous" to describe some early Cummings—surely lodged in me early, and stayed....

In my own case I know that kick-ass Cummings will be present in me on certain occasions as he was, for example, I now realize, while I was writing *Ribbons: The Gulf War* (1991).

To conclude, I'd like to read you two of the poem's forty-one sections.

2. (The Reich)

> At first during Vietnam, I didn't know squat.
> Wipe the gooks out, I said to my TV set,
> which seemed to listen & disgorge body counts.
> But I wised up fast, & marched, & wrote, but
> nothing much good: naive passion alone.
>
> The best of these poems, maybe, was in *The Nation*,
> "Good Money After Bad," about swelling troop deployments

to expand the operation & replace the poor dead bastards
leaving the jungle in body bags. "Coin of the realm,"
I called the drafted victims, & this was mild compared

to the "dogs" & "lumps of dirt" in that manual
& apogee of resistance, the "Essay on Civil Disobedience."
By the long time enough protesters' balls & breasts
clogged the war machine, there were 50,000 names
in the bank for that black marble mirror memorial in D.C.

But I was moving toward the Third Reich by then
by reason of family & reading & ambiguous dreams
in which I ran from Nazis, but with them,
slept in haystacks, but knifed them,
torched a synagogue, but died with Torah in my arms.

13.   (Conventions)

"This might be an oxymoron," says (I swear) a Pentagon spokesman
beginning to whine, "but why can't we have a civilized war?"
Meaning, I suppose, that when an American airman
bombs your neighborhood, killing maybe a few dozen
& maiming maybe a hundred in body & maybe a thousand in mind,
& he's one of the few planes hit & he has to eject,
& after you've done the best you could to drag
victims out from under debris & you've washed the blood
out of your eyes as best you could & you've captured the bastard,
you should treat him according to the Geneva conventions,
as gentleman prisoner of war, a name & rank & service number
who deserves a shower & clean clothes. You must not,
as I would, as you would, I swear, if such a technician
killed your wife & children, you must not drive steel
splinters into his eyes until they reach his civilized brain.

The Contours of Gibbs Pond: An Interview
(Conducted by David Watson)

DW: Let's start with your "Open Letter to the SUNY Brockport College Community" and your "The Host: An Address to the Faculty at SUNY Brockport."* You call on Brockport to be an ecologically exemplary institution. You start out by asking, "What if, in a hundred years. . . ." And of course this calls everything into question. You use the term "a state of reasonable dread" in discussing the ecological crisis.

WH: Yes, I took that phrase from Richard Wilbur's response to the "Open Letter." Well, this is a heavy burden to lay on people, especially young people, it seems to me, but it makes sense for us to be afraid of what is happening. The evidence of impending disaster is all around us. But talking in these terms to young people worries me. The last thing we'd want to do is to take the joy out of their lives—this would be self-defeating. As teachers, how direct should we be about these fears of ours?

And this brings to mind the same question regarding an ecoliterature: How direct can it be? How often can I yell that we're in very deep trouble, folks? But "a state of reasonable dread"? In any case, we have defense mechanisms. As many people have said, when we try to imagine extinction, our brains, our minds, extinguish themselves. Those two essays of mine began with one of those extinguishing moments that occurs a second or two a month for me, and maybe not even that long. These are intuitional moments of full realization when I grasp the possibility that there will be nobody alive on the earth a hundred years from my moment in time. When my mind understands this for just a second, I go cold, I go blank, my head buzzes. This might be the one thing we human beings are unable to think about—the possibility of extinction.

My writing was a sort of reality check for me. We've all heard the litany of forebodings. We can talk in detail about what's happening to our soil, our

---

Black Dirt 1 (1998).

* These two essays, first published in *American Poetry Review*, are included in the author's *Pig Notes & Dumb Music: Prose on Poetry* (Rochester, NY: BOA Editions, 1998).

water, our air. Now, regarding these very real crises, what can a viable literature of ecology be? How can it help us live our lives while it informs and maybe moves us to action? That's the old bug-a-bear, of course. The minute we talk about literature making something happen, we are cautioned by talk about "proletarian" writing, writing that is boring and doesn't work.

Since the ancient Greeks, people have worried about the end of the world. But our situation is so unprecedented that all our usual ways of thinking about art may have to be thrown out. Perhaps some radical new way of thinking about literature is necessary. We can't say to an artist, "Well, maybe you ought not to do this or do that." But if it is true that as a race we are fast running out of time, then maybe artists—if they're going to put their shoulders against this turning wheel of extinction—have to find ways to communicate more directly. I make this radical argument in my essay "At the Gate," taking Seamus Heaney to task for what are, in retrospect, traditional remarks about how lyric poetry works. Full of self-doubt, I read my essay now and wonder if I make sense. William Stafford says that he says things to see what the effect will be of his having said them—this is my sense of what I've done in some of my essays. But when those intuitions of extinction strike me . . .

DW: You seem to be talking of poetry that has an intent, but not a program.

WH: There's a sense in which, no matter what poem we write, that poem's subject, its heart, is ecology. It's impossible for us to write anything that doesn't connect with the world's workings, its balances and imbalances, its interrelationships. But our question now is: Do we have to lay it on the line, start talking facts, declare truths declaratively? Writing many of the poems of *Pterodactyl Rose*, I sometimes felt myself determined to be more direct. "I sit at McDonald's eating my fragment of forest." Even that might be too subtle. The poem makes a simple connection between the eating of hamburgers and the destruction of the rain forest, but the idea might still be lost. My original intention was to write a poem my brother the cop and my father the carpenter could understand, but even that poem, "Fast Food," because of my training in subtlety, evasion, understatement, all the tools of the modern poem, even that poem escaped my conscious intention. Is an even more direct poem that makes the point but is not boring possible?

Another poem begins, "At Kwik-Fill I pump ferns and turtles into my tank." There's another direct connection. The speaker of the poem realizes that the fossil fuel he's burning comes from the ancient forests, from ancient creatures. Again, is this something that my father, my brother, could connect with? Have I said something that could slow down even my own consumption of gasoline, or am I in the main delighted by my own words and sense of play, beguiled by my own images and sounds? I suppose I want to teach and preach, but in the back of my mind I always hear Archibald MacLeish saying that poetry can't go to the people, the people will have to go to poetry. This makes sense to me always, all ways. But now our situation is unprecedented. Maybe I need to reconsider everything about poetry that has made sense to me in the past. Maybe the poet must try to reach out to an audience as never before, and not to an audience schooled in critical theory.

DW: I've thought that there was more to "Fast Food" than the idea that we are destroying forests. I think what makes that poem work is that you're talking about the nature of being, you're not just talking about an inventory of being. You're not saying that based on practical or pragmatic criteria, this hamburger does not add up to this forest. You're talking about people conditioned to reduce Being to something else entirely, and that's an idea or intuition that may not necessarily be understood by your brother. He might understand the first idea.

WH: So it's a delusion, poetry as a means by which we really can reach the mass of people in America? Will poetry always be, as Richard Wilbur says, a necessary art for a small minority?

DW: I think if you go too far in trying to create a poetry with program or intent you'll undermine it because the more you try to make the gesture simple and direct, the more you're competing with things you'll never be able to outdo, like TV and movies. And their message is, even when they're environmentalists, to stay tuned. What I like about poetry and why I think there's a growing interest in it is that poetry brings you down to an experience of two people simply talking, listening. A dialogue is still going on and it continues to be reawakened each time that a poem is read, or a poem is written. A conversation occurs.

WH: Yes, sometimes it seems to me that poetry is the most radical thing we could be doing, either reading it or writing it, in terms of breaking the assumptions of a civilization that has led us to this dangerous point.

DW: W. S. Merwin calls poetry "undomesticated language"—that little bit of wilderness that remains.

WH: David Brower said (he might have been quoting Thoreau) that without wilderness the world is a cage. If everything becomes domesticated, we're in a prison. I've always believed what Emerson says, that what is needed in the American poem is wildness, and this includes its freedom to go in any direction it wants.

DW: What makes your ecology poems work for me is their vivid sense of loss. When in "Pterodactyl Rose" you look in your rear-view mirror (and that line is obviously no accident) and see the creatures going up in smoke, it reminds me of the sensibility that runs through all your work—your profound, direct sense of connectedness to nature.

WH: Recently, someone working on a thesis asked me about my inspiration for my nature poems. He mentioned as possible influences on me many writers I'd read sketchily, if at all. I thought about his question seriously for a while, and then realized that in truth, although it's not a fashionable thing to say, I'd gotten my inspiration for my nature poems from nature itself. Theodore Roethke says, "By long staring I have come to be." And when I was a kid, I stared for timeless months and hours into the ponds in the woods, absorbing, I hope, the frogness of a frog, for example. So that now if I'm lucky enough to have a frog appear in one of my poems and to have this frog reverberate, resonate, achieve some kind of dimension above and beyond itself, enter a symbolic realm, however you want to put it; if I'm lucky enough, it is because of those childhood observations of those green, glistening, slippery creatures who made those gelatinous eggs and who had big eyes that I stared into and who squatted there and who were symmetrically beautiful and asymmetrically ugly at the same time, and who had long tongues that I saw shoot out at bugs, and who I watched grow from tadpoles into these harrumphing creatures that I could see existed in different species, the leopard frog and the usual green frog and their cousins the toads. One time as a kid in Nesconset on Long Island I actually saw a tree frog, its toes like tiny cups. Imagine that, right in the middle of Long Island!

So if I get lucky in a poem, and there is some resonance regarding a frog, I think it's because of the time I spent with frogs. We don't usually say this, and many people argue (and it's largely true) that we write poems because of other poems. But I know something about frogs. I remember the ripples from a frog's throat. Sometimes you could find a frog just by looking at the ripples across the pond until you saw where they were coming from. I know something about frogs. I remember stepping on frogs with bare feet in order to smash the air out of them so that I could put them on hooks and cast out for catfish and snappers. I remember tasting a frog's blood. I remember pulling frogs apart and tonguing their legs. I remember killing frogs by the hundreds with my bb gun. And I remember dissecting frogs in biology classes in high school and college. Any sense I get into my poems of the frogness of a frog must come from all these experiences.

DW: Part of what you've just told me has been a litany of murder. It's the other side of that acute process of looking in modern bourgeois civilization, which has been classification; and with classification has always come the hecatomb. Audubon killed thousands of birds in order to record and classify them.

WH: Thoreau said that all young boys are murderers, just wanton slaughterers. When I walked through the woods and shot chickadees, the chickadees would fall and the others would come chirping around it, and I could shoot the others, too. (When are chickadees like buffalo!) And even though I felt a little sick at heart because after fifteen minutes of shooting, I had six dead birds on the ground, the next day I'd be tempted into this mindless target practice again. I liked the chickadees—what's not to love about a chickadee?—but wanted to direct my bb at these little birds and see if I could knock them down. So all young boys somehow seem to be, in our culture, murderers. But we grow up, hopefully, and out of that. And now, maybe I'm being romantic, but I like to think that when I put out a few hundred pounds of bird seed every year, and these chickadees come around, that they've forgiven me. In *The Chestnut Rain* I have a line about "the black-capped chickadee's ministry." I've just sent for a book on the whole ecology of the chickadee. Maybe I'm growing up. Maybe there's hope.

I think that one of our problems is that so many of us have only one language. I think if we have only one language, and we have one word for a creature, then somehow psychologically we feel the creature is that word, that the word comprehends that creature. Thus our one language delimits. It does not free the creature to be itself. Naming is dangerous. Maybe if we realize that language itself is terribly limited, we can realize that a creature exists outside of any human tag that would classify or explain it and therefore render it less than miraculous, and therefore expendable.

Maybe this is where poetry and song must come in.

DW: You say in *Long Island Light*, "I have the distinct impression that I can never live in the present unless I find some means of relieving the obsessions of the past."

WH: Melodramatic, isn't it? I've wanted to scratch that. . . .

DW: You have a way in a number of your books of tying history—the history of the land, the place and the natural environment—to your own personal history and your own dream life.

WH: Art is obsession, Richard Hugo says. And Stafford in so many different ways says things like, "Well, what we're always trying to do in our writing is to bring ourselves up into the present and how we feel about things now." I guess everything that I write about, whether about human ecology (and maybe my Holocaust poems are essentially about this) or natural ecology, they all go back to the obsession I have with what I saw when I was a boy growing up on Long Island. Suffolk County was the fastest growing area in the country, along with Orange County in California. I saw there, in five or ten years, what it might take one or more generations of people living in some other parts of the country to see. I saw this thing called "development."

I remember my father standing on the steps of his Nesconset Woodworking, watching all those trucks rumble by, saying to me, "Look, Billy, all these trucks going past are full, and when they come west again they're empty. One of these days the Island is going to sink." Everything in me is connected now with the ponds and the woods and Long Island Sound. My mother used to call me Nature Boy. When I think back and try to get to the truth of it, and ask myself if I am romanticizing this, I realize that my memories are accurate. I spent years by myself in the woods and at the ponds as those trucks were rumbling by on the edge of my consciousness.

The ponds were so pristine that I used to walk around them in bare feet. I didn't have to worry about beer cans or broken glass. I was the only one who seemed to be interested, the only one there. I'd have to take paths to get to the ponds. I can still trace, step by step, shape by shape, the contours of Gibbs Pond, Shenandoah, Spectacle Pond in my mind, and I often do. Sometimes I'd walk a pond counter-clockwise and sometimes clockwise. There were areas where I would have better luck catching a baby painted turtle or watching a sunfish nest or scaring up the crane that I used to see fly up out of there. I seem to want to go back to these things in my writing, in my mind. At the ponds and in the woods I felt some kind of presence, some kind of meaningfulness. I felt intimations of immortality, it may be.

DW: In your "Open Letter" you write, "From nature I knew, I know I am a spiritual being." This is in the context of a statement about trusting oneself. There's a lot of mysticism in your work, and, as far as I can tell, it seems to come from real mystical experiences you had as a young boy in the woods.

WH: Part of my dissertation was on mysticism. I've read some basic texts, and I've always read sporadically in Zen, but I've been drawn to these readings, I think, because of experiences I had as a boy. I did have moments when time stopped and the world was not separate from me. You know, we often read about these states; we read about the concept of epiphany in Joyce, about still points in the turning world in Eliot and other modernists, and can go back to Wordsworth, St. John of the Cross, and many others. But, yes, I experienced these states myself as a boy. I remember a moment under a linden tree in our backyard when I woke as though from a kind of green dream of those leaves that had enveloped me. I remember wading a pond and then standing still and then it being suddenly evening. There were many times like those, and I thought they were mysterious, but not particularly unusual.

I love poetry that moves toward the transcendental and throws me out of myself, puts me in touch with what is beyond my dailiness. Allen Ginsberg says that all great poetry has been the poetry that opens the gates for us. Whitman says his own poetry indicates the path between reality and the soul. It's always been that kind of poetry that I've loved the most, that moves from the flesh. "The flesh can make the spirit visible," Roethke says. Poetry that moves from the flesh or the tree bark or the plant stem into that other world that I always feel throbbing.

It's easy to dismiss all this as corny, and there's a kind of cynical and skeptical agnosticism that wants to diminish the possibilities of soul. But I often feel that I am not contained between my hat and my boots, as Walt says he's not. And this is one reason that lately I've been drawn to the spirit of Crazy Horse and have tried to learn what I can about this Lakota mystic. And maybe this is presumptuous of me. I'm not a Native American. But I have some sense of the vivid dream state and transcendental state, the dream time, the moment when time stands still, the moment when the other world reveals itself, the foldings and enfoldings of time. Sometimes when I am writing, by way of rhythm, a rolling image, maybe a story that keeps giving of itself, maybe certain repetitions that break the iron beat of the mind, I make my way to that other place.

Robert Penn Warren went through undergraduate school as an English major. He says he didn't realize until he got done that he never took a literature class. Every one of his so-called literature classes had been taught by one pedagogue or another and was basically a history class or biography class or philosophy class. So he began to ask a question: What is the literature of literature? What is the poetry of poetry? This is a central question. Far beyond idea, what is the essence of poetry? In *An Analysis of Poetic Thinking* Max Rieser talks about these moments that approach hypnosis, moments of semi-trance when you read a poem and become a part of its shadowy world and accent and scents, and you move into what for me is a mystical and sometimes visionary otherness.

DW: There's no better place in your poetry where this comes out than in the poem "The Snow Hen," when you're candling an egg and the two eyes are like two spots of rice and the whole world is revolving around that being. It's a powerful recognition of holism.

WH: Maybe one thing that occurs during moments of our enlightenment is that we come to see everything in one: eternity, wildflower. Whitman for a moment loafs and invites his soul to observe at ease a spear of summer grass. And suddenly, the linear world is broken. Sixty pages go by, a lifetime and more, and there he still is, not a scintillation of time older. It's as though "Song of Myself" has been a vision, a trance with voice.

I've had a rich dream life. Some of the most striking and lucid ones end up in my journal. I've written many poems about dreams, too. The trick about writing about them, I think, and I tell my students this, is to stop trying to figure out what they mean. You're lost if you think you have one nailed down, because you'd be writing from your upper mind, daylight, consciousness. You don't want to write about your dream, but want to write the dream itself. You can always go back later, get inside its spirit again, and help it get itself said. But the main thing is to trust that it's deeper than you are, to let it come to you again, and to let it be.

DW: You describe your childhood as separate from the domestic world, certainly the urban world. Yet your poetry is very inclusive; it treats nature and culture as a continuum. While at the same time you're protesting development and protesting history, you're seeing a lot of beauty in it. The image of the railroad tie, for example, in one of the sections of *The Chestnut Rain*.

WH: You know, no matter what, I think maybe in me, and I suppose maybe in my poetry, is a kind of acceptance. I mean, we live on a star; there are two hundred billion stars in our Milky Way. There are billions of Milky Ways. I want the world to go on. I want my children and children's children to experience the beauty and sense of God that I've had in nature. But I think there's an understanding in me, too, that if the earth all became ash tomorrow, something essential would still be going on. . . . But who knows what my next poem will do—maybe curse.

DW: There are times when the chestnut railroad tie contains both the sense of tragic loss, vertiginous loss, and also human history, memory. I find that you can't imagine a world without that boundary. Some poets remain entirely on civilization's side. And others—I guess you couldn't say any poet remains entirely on the side of wilderness, it would be a contradiction—but there are those who lean, perhaps, toward the wilderness more.

WH: I've always remembered reading that when Martin Luther King, Jr., was shot to death, some maniac called up his widow and laughed gleefully into the phone. And I've always thought of that tremendous darkness in the American psyche. And sometimes I've thought that a two-thousand-year-old redwood is much more important and lovely a creature than the person who telephoned Coretta Scott King. This is dangerous talk, of course, but if I had to, as God, choose between that redwood absorbing those mists from the Pacific and that racist maniac, a victim of his own education and product of a skewed culture, if I had to choose between the tree and him, I'd choose the tree.

The scariest poem in *Pterodactyl Rose* for me is "Radical American Breakdown Heartwood." It ends, "Let forest SS murderers wither under the holy trees." This was a difficult thing for me to let the poem say. I found out later that David Brower had said, "Well, jobs were eliminated when Auschwitz was shut down, too." But I couldn't just call this poem "The Trees" or something like that, although I love short titles. There's a breakdown in the voice here, maybe the speaker has gone over the edge. I've wedged so much into the title hoping I won't be misunderstood. My title is my plea for an understanding that the speaker of the poem and of the book has reached a point close to insanity and has at that point chosen trees over lumberjacks.

I don't want these loggers who are despoiling our last acres of virgin wilderness dead. Let the government pay them forever. We waste enough dough doing other things. Paying the loggers to do nothing would save us an awful lot of money. I mean, what's happening to our forests? Our taxes are going into building roads into the wilderness so that we can cut down trees and sell them to Japanese corporations so that they can make a big profit selling the logs back to us. I don't know all the details—it hurts to hear them—but our continuing deforestation is scandalous, and suicidal.

DW: That poem is very unusual for you, though. There's anguished protest, but you generally look at the lives of people, of the very people involved in making the frontier, in a different way. In *Long Island Light* you talk about the spreading of the frontier in no uncertain terms as a massacre. And yet, you honor it all.

WH: I don't know if I'd put it that way. But, you know, our emotions exist simultaneously in us. At one and the same time we can hold these—it's negative capability, I guess—conflicted feelings we have. They might even seem contradictory, but if we get lucky, we can say many things at once. As Whitman says, "I contain multitudes." I suppose our effort is always to understand before we condemn, and this in itself suggests a fusion of many feelings.

DW: The idea of collecting the poems into *Pterodactyl Rose* strikes me as a way to save things, if only memories. You're dealing with memories when you're talking about bison and about passenger pigeons.

WH: I wrote many of those poems over about a year, and also started going back to my other books to see what it was I had on this theme. I was surprised to see how much was there. I think what is odd about this book is my subtitle, *Poems of Ecology*. This is part of my attempt to be more direct. Friends told me I ought not to do that, label a book like that. It seems too limiting, and suggests a clunky view of what poetry is. As I've said, every poem in one way or another is a poem of ecology. But here I'm thinking of trying to reach an audience that might be interested in reading a book of poems that dealt directly with this theme. I think the sub-title has helped the book, has helped some people afraid of contemporary poetry pick it up and feel connected with it. You know of the complaints about the whole modern movement, how, for example, Max Eastman accused T. S. Eliot of using titles that had nothing to do with the poems. Well, my book has a strange title, but my sub-title declares the poems' general symbolic area.

DW: I'm fascinated by the way history and culture are embedded within nature in your work. In *The Chestnut Rain* you talk about the rings of a tree. That's a risky thing to do in poetry because, obviously, talking about tree rings could turn out to be pretty hackneyed. An yet, what I think is so successful about that is that you make the rings a part of the whole. The images and connections are intimate and at the same time disparate enough to give us a glimpse of the largeness of history.

WH: And again, there it is—the hands-on experience of the thing. Not only with trees and firewood now, cutting and splitting and hauling, but as a boy being in my father's lumber shed when the lumber trucks came, and for hours at a time helping unload them. And feeling the grains of these woods as I worked. And now, in many of these Crazy Horse and Custer poems that I've been writing, tree rings show up again. In one, I have one of the last buffalo inside a tree, cutting across the rings. In another, I have, come to think of it, Custer and Crazy Horse in another dimension, meeting inside the tree. But, whatever happens, my writing came from tree rings themselves and not some kind of literary or artistic source, as helpful as all the poems we know always are.

DW: In one tree ring poem, you link the death of Lincoln and other events, and yet there's a sense of your personal history; there's a sense of place, of the power of the tree as a being. You talk about the witness power of the tree in the same way you talk about, in another poem, our language entering, "as though in amber," the rings of a sugar maple. I can't think of a better image of the interconnectedness of language, culture, history, and nature. There's a tension. History has tended to devour, colonize, wreck both nature and culture, and yet there's an interplay that always leaves things open.

WH: In my Long Island memoir I quote Allen Seager who says that the trees of one's childhood are the touchstones of all later trees. Particular ones flash in my mind, two wild cherry trees beside our house in Nesconset, and white pines along our driveway, and two Norway maples that were back by my father's shop. We had a small unused orchard, and I can picture particular pear trees and particular apple trees, and there was one quince tree. Three dogwoods on our front lawn. Elms along Gibbs Pond Road.

And there was a piece of land that my wife and I almost bought in a town called Clarendon several years ago. In back of this property there was a bicentennial oak. That tree was at least two hundred years old, maybe twice that. All these trees are constantly branching in my mind. We have a bicentennial ash behind our house in Brockport. What is it in some of us that makes us love trees so much? I don't know, and I want to understand these things only imperfectly. But I'm grateful for it, whatever it is.

DW: In your case, is this because you grew up around trees? It can't be entirely this because many people who grew up around the redwoods keep cutting them.

WH: I may have an innate sense of the holiness of trees. By way of their beauty, by way of their presence as they mind their own business, by way of their support of countless creatures, by way of their mystery. Later, through books, I learned about oxygen and their breathing of carbon dioxide, so some of it is from books. But, at bottom, it is that awestruck sense of beauty I experienced as a boy.

Let me tell a story that might fit in. A few years ago my wife and I were buying a three-acre parcel in the village of Brockport, just a couple blocks from our home acre and about the last piece of undeveloped land in the village. Next to this land, a building was going up. Well, one day I checked, and they seemed to stop cutting at our line and everything was fine. The next day I went back and they'd already knocked down twenty, thirty, forty trees on our property. I told them to stop, but they kept their chainsaws going. "Stop for a while!" I yelled. And these guys, some of whom I had gotten to know, just grinned at me and said they were sure of the boundary, and waited it out. Actually, they knew what they were doing, and were clearing space for their machines and piles of dirt and materials. I got home in a hurry, and I called my lawyer. Then I called the people I was buying the land from, and I said, "Do you still intend to sell this property to me?" They said yes. "Well stop cutting trees." Right away somehow they got through to the crew and stopped them, and the whole job stopped for about a week while things got sorted out.

That was years ago. Most days now I walk over to the property, which my wife and I hope to keep green. And every time I do, I see the stumps of those big ash trees that were probably forty years old. I'm still angry about what happened. Yes, other trees are coming up. Nature is restoring herself. There's room now for a cherry tree, and I've recently found a catalpa coming up. And other trees are able to branch out more. But I'm still angry about that crew. Somebody made a decision. Some boss told some guys, "Yeah, cut down those trees." And now, for the rest of my life I'll be angry about this and miss those big trees. But also, of course, I will not continue to be angry about this, and will not miss those trees.

DW: You even talk about Long Island itself as a tree. There are a lot of references in *Long Island Light* about the cosmic tree, about the island as a tree submerged in water.

Merwin once said that intellectuals have ideas about a lot of things, but when you get down to real philosophers—I'm not sure if I'm insulting you or praising you by associating you with "real philosophers"—they have two or three ideas, or maybe, ultimately, just one idea, and they keep working the same idea.

WH: Thoreau says that to be a philosopher is to solve some of the practical problems of life. So I've practiced my philosophy, I suppose, with my wife, by trying to save a few acres of trees and meadow that make us happy, that balance our depletions. There are many chickadees over on those acres!

DW: The poems embody a sense of tragic loss, along with a growing awareness of a possibility that redemption is possible. You see it strongly in the Holocaust poems, in *Erika*. The same thing is happening in your explicitly ecological poems, and in the "Open Letter," that happens in your Holocaust poems.

WH: In fact there's a poem in *Erika* called "The Tree" about a tree that no longer exists, but does, on the site of the village that was once Lidice, destroyed by the Nazis. So there's that, too, the trees of memory. The trees cut down on the day I told you about did not have to be cut down. They were cut down because that crew needed "Lebensraum." Weeks later, I stood with the construction foreman as his bulldozer was working, and to bust my chops he yelled over to the bulldozer operator, "Hey watch out for those trees, now." I wanted to kill him.

DW: Metaphorically, there's a thread linking his indifference and that of the soldier smoking a cigarette at the edge of a pit where he's massacred people.

WH: Yes. We are all part of society. And I think we all have a responsibility for our history. But how presumptuous it would be of me to think that if I had been in the victims' shoes, I wouldn't have died without protest the same way they've been attacked for dying, or if I wasn't Jewish, that I wouldn't have been the soldier at the pit killing people and smoking in between. On the one hand, I'm part of the general human condition and often, remembering my dreams, I don't know whether I was killing Jews or helping them. Maybe I was doing both at the same time because of this fused existence of possibilities in me. I could not have done what Rudolf Hess did or what Eichmann did unless I was Rudolf Hess or Eichmann. So because of a lucky birthing in Brooklyn in 1940 instead of Berlin in 1920, I can sit back and pass judgment on historical characters? On history? If I were a Palestinian now I wouldn't know how it was that I was a Palestinian and not a Jew. And if I were a Jew I wouldn't know how it was that I was a Jew and not a Palestinian. I think the domain of art might be the domain of otherness and the domain of some kind of compassion and understanding. In any case and at the same time, I think it's proper for us to expect more of ourselves, to believe in our freedom to become more than selfish and short-sighted materialists, to desire to become people of love and charity. But it ain't never easy. I still want to choke that construction foreman. But how is it that I am not that man myself? Luck, fate, karma, genes, accident? Only poems can know.

DW: You wrote *Ribbons: The Gulf War* based on a point of view. You didn't put a yellow ribbon on your house. You didn't just sit quietly and read.

WH: Can we be engaged without being propangandists? Where is the balance, the truth? I think of one poem in the book, "Oxymoron," that mentions "civilized war," a phrase I heard from the mouth of a U.S. pilot. The poem is an attack on technicians. I did notice that the guys doing most of the damage were career people, trained technicians. It's Jean-Francois Steiner in the great book *Treblinka* who keeps referring to the Nazis as technicians. So that was in my mind as I was watching that war. This wasn't a war of foot soldiers who wondered what in hell they were doing. These were career warriors carrying out a national policy. These men trained with our taxes to be killers, and welcomed the chance to try out the latest technology. We haven't even faced the horrors of this war yet.

My favorite poem in *Ribbons* is "Gifts." Let me read it. It has its point of view, but somehow its inner movements and sounds, its poetry, may help it to keep writing itself, may help it continue to be news that stays news.

> First day of the fifth week of the war.
> "Desert Storm" there, winter storm here.
> In Iraq, the removal of bodies & body parts
> & fused lumps of unidentifiable remains
> from what we call a command bunker
> & what they call a civilian bomb shelter
>
> & which was one or the other, or both.
> In Brockport, snow outlines pastel ribbons
> in my neighbors' trees along our streets
> cleared by nightshift plows, & sanded
> as we slept. In Baghdad, women in black
> search & mourn among the blanketed dead
>
> dragged out of their devastated haven.
> Air raid sirens are still keening
> while here the snow softens everything
> in the fallen world. A White House spokesman
> informs us that human life hasn't the "sanctity"
> for their president that it does for mine,
>
> & I don't want to live, sometimes—do you?
> The blankets are not khaki, but civilian,
> in rich colors & sacred Islamic designs.
> All day across this country we'll open
> cards & heart-shaped boxes of candy.
> Happy Saint Valentine's.

In the end, *Ribbons* may be about someone wondering whether he can maintain any sense of the transcendental and the eternal and the spiritual during a time of such deep national shame. We were there because our priorities are upside down. We were there for oil, and to punish the infidels.

DW: You went to Germany when you were young. You talk about dealing with your obsessions and having to work on your past—your communal, human, historical experience and all the rest of it.

WH: I was about thirty when we went over for a year in 1970-71, but I was naïve in many different ways. There were many things I didn't know. I'm almost embarrassed to admit this, but I remember being in a beer cellar in Bonn with three other Fulbright lecturers, and one of them started talking about Horst Wessel and the *Horst Wessel Lied*. I hadn't heard of it, and by then I'd already written maybe half the poems that would come to be *The Swastika Poems*. I was ignorant about many things, but I was writing the poems because I had to write them, and I hadn't read any of the debate regarding the Holocaust as a subject matter for poetry. I was just writing out of the heart, writing things I had to write.

DW: Was there a connection between the need that you had to go to Germany to confront those issues and the war in Vietnam that was going on at the same time? You must have thought about that. I'm wondering if there's any way you could elaborate on the connections between *The Swastika Poems* and Vietnam.

WH: All I remember is being in graduate school and watching the first reports of troop buildups, and having a general feeling that, well, maybe this is the right thing, and let's go ahead and try to restore a democratic government in Vietnam. I was uneducated and didn't know anything and was busy reading English literature, writing papers about Spenser's "Epithalamion" and Thackeray's *Pendennis*, raising two kids and sweating out the Ph. D. and building a career. Once I got to Brockport in 1967 and wised up a little bit and began to get a sense of what was really happening, and people began to talk to me, and I began to read the newspapers, then I understood right away that something horrible was going on. One semester was cut short by protest at Brockport, so we had a lively community, and I think the students and administration felt politically the same way about the war. There was a collision between the townspeople and college people when we marched against the war. It got ugly sometimes.

As far as writing went, I wrote at least several poems about Vietnam, published a few. I remember that one was in *The Nation*. But when I looked at them later on, they didn't seem very good as poems. They were almost pure passion without whatever else had to go into them. In contrast, I wrote the Holocaust poems sporadically and put them into drawers for years. When I finally thought I might make a book of them they seemed to hold up for me as poems, whatever else they were.

DW: You've mentioned the Nazis as technicians. A unifying theme in your work may be your protest against the machinery of war, your suspicion of technology. In *Long Island Light* "the land smells of metal," for example, and in one of the darker poems in *Lord Dragonfly*, "The Wedding," you imagine this ceremony occurring within and being performed by a machine:

> After its great hands have held
> the two of you in the one chapel
> of its cupped palms
> for a time you've lost all track of—
>
> after the soundless music
> of your loved one's love
> has reached you
> deeper than hearing—
>
> after each of you is placed lost
> and alone in the far valleys
> of dark and are found again
> to die together in satin—
>
> after you break fast
> with wine and flowers
> and the words are told you
> from the beginning—
>
> you will walk out.
> You will kneel in the shadows of its arms.
> You will give thanks.
> You will know you are wed.

That's a very disturbing idea. It reminds me of the line in *Frankenstein* when the monster says to Victor Frankenstein, "You are my creator, but I am your master. I will be with you on your wedding night." Your line, "You will kneel in the shadow of its arms," has a sinister mix of spirituality and simulation in it.

WH: So what happens to us psychically when we dislike and distrust and even hate machines but we use them at the same time? When I start my lawn mower and smell its oil stink, and curse, but mow my lawn? And when I drive to school, knowing what it is that I'm doing? We're filled with so many different feelings at the same time. I'm glad when my machine gets me through the snow and cold to school. At the same time I hate being dependent on a car. So what is it that happens to us? With a little luck, I suppose, in our writing, if we keep ourselves free, all of those things will be part of the image at the same time. I think I got lucky in the title poem of *Pterodactyl Rose*.

Wholeness. I want the sense of the full complexity of our relationship with the machine in a poem, rather, of course, than any finger-pointing or any simplistic rendering. I want the poem to contain an image that is complex in ways beyond my ability to articulate it. And now, as we're talking, everything begins to come together.

In *The Electric Life* Sven Birkerts talks about a shocking experience he had when teaching freshman composition at Harvard. He was talking to his students about what he sensed to be a moment of fusion that occurs again and again for all of us as youngsters. When a word—for example, a word like "tree"—becomes in the mind that bark entity, that leaf entity, that branch entity, there in front of or above us. He sees this, as we all do, as an extremely important and meaningful moment when the word merges, when language suddenly merges for us with that creature, tree. What he is shocked to find out is that the young people in front of him don't have their language from the natural world, but from an electronic image. As children they'd be watching, say, *Sesame Street*. Big Bird would hold up the word tree and then maybe images of a tree would appear— photographs of a tree, or maybe a papier mache tree. Or maybe there would be a film of the whole rainforest. Nevertheless, a student gaining the word in that way is not gaining what we who learned the word "tree" from nature gained. Birkerts says we haven't even begun to assess the implications of this kind of language acquisition.

But I think we can begin to assess this. I connect it with the writing of bad poems, the usual thing coming out of the hothouse workshops. And, more important, I connect it with the destruction of our physical world. If we are at the point where a tree is just something two-dimensional, and it is not a breathing and living organism, and it has not fused in our minds in ways that our connection with nature would fuse it, then it seems to me that we can more easily get rid of the tree as a non-living entity, as something that doesn't concern us, as something we can restore by changing the channel or playing another videotape of trees. We don't need its oxygen, we think.

This also brings us back to the idea of otherness. How can I sense reciprocity with other creatures in the world, plants and animals, if I know them only by way of two-dimensional images? I can't. It's probably true that the most essential thing for us, if we're going to save the world, is to learn to revere it. How can I revere a world that only exists in electronic images? I can't. So I don't brag about it when I say, "I know frogs," but I feel fortunate. And when I hear that amphibia are disappearing across the globe—and we know, of course, that frogs are an indicator species; apparently their systems are as sensitive as women's breasts, so sensitive that they can absorb and be punished by carcinogenic toxins even if five hundred miles away from any industry—when I hear about disappearing amphibia, I see real frogs, I remember my wife's mastectomy, and I'm upset to the point where I might try to save a few acres from development.

David, the last couple days it's been raining, we've been in and out of the rain. In *The End of Nature*, Bill McKibben makes the point that the rain, for example, has been taken away from us. It is no longer autonomous or natural. Now when I hear the rain and see the rain, I don't feel it in the way my ancestors did. I wonder, for example, how much this rain has been dirtied by industry. What's in it, exactly? We know we have affected it. It is part of us now. We no longer have that sense of its otherness, no longer sense it as being healthy and necessary. And all of this is new to our human condition.

DW: But nature was already dead for this civilization a long time ago, except in pockets, like your experience. In the industrialized world most people live the great majority of their time indoors. And nature was dead when John Locke declared "undeveloped" land to be waste. In an ultimate sense, too, McKibben's wrong about the death of nature. The disappearance of whales and frogs is terribly tragic for life as we know it, but it's not tragic in an ultimate sense for the earth

WH: Not in an ultimate sense because no matter what we do, no matter what toxic stinkhole we reduce the earth to, if one algae cell survives, then eventually we'll probably have creatures like and unlike dinosaurs and whales and millipedes again, because nature has timeless time—as, within our meditations, we have timeless time in our best poems. Have you seen for sale lately one of these little self-enclosed eco-systems? They're not like terrariums or aquariums, but they're completely sealed-off plastic or glass globes in which there are tiny shrimp and snails and algae. Apparently for five or seven or ten years these little eco-systems will generate themselves. All they need is a little light and a temperature somewhere between sixty and ninety degrees. They will just keep going and going and going. On the one hand, they're lovely little instructional tools; on the other hand, it's sad to think that we in our urban apartments now might need this hermetically-sealed fragment of the world to remind us of what our oceans were once like.

DW: I guess, really, that sense of tragedy led you to question poetry in your open letter, and to say, What am I doing here? How can I make the poem do something worthwhile without doing to it the damage we do when we try to intervene in and control the rest of nature—in many cases trying to do good there as well? Obviously, there are no easy answers.

WH: You've struck the essential connection again between our poems and our lives in nature. We've already spent too much time trying to reduce the earth to a machine that we think we can change or fix any time we want. Emerson says the poet is the one who can integrate everything and see oneness in everything. I suppose this is still a voice that recognizes wholeness, that feels an interconnectedness with all things. And for better or worse, my own approach to this wholeness, at least after my first book of poems, has been intuitional. I'm absorbed right now by Crazy Horse. When I sit down and begin following a poem, rather than trying to dominate it or understand it completely, I might follow the way Tasunke Witko swings himself onto his pony, or follow the beads on his moccasins or, if he's riding into battle, the slant of the single eagle feather that he apparently wore. And the exact location of the thong over his left shoulder that held the stone—was the stone yellow, ochre?—a magic stone he believed in as medicine. And the hailstones painted on his face. If I start talking about General Crook and about the logic of political decisions made in Washington, I'll be limited, a propagandist, and out of luck.

History

     Evening. I sat at the dining room table, working with tongs, sorting a shoebox of German stamps that had reached me a few months before from Switzerland after an internet auction.

     I found dozens of glassines thickly packed with issues ranging from the 1850s to my own century's end. Below the glassines, too, were a few inches of loose stamps, used & mint. Thousands of *Briefmarken* in my horde. As I sorted, I was excited, alive. I realized that my American dollars had gone a long way.

     Sorting, I remembered as a boy spending much time with my stamps. But another childhood memory kept crowding in until I wondered why: hour after hour, I'm at my microscope, tilting its mirror to catch the indoor or outdoor light, eyedroppering pondwater onto slides, staring, surprised by the dimensions I can keep focusing into view. Just when I think I've located every organism in a particular drop, another amoeba or paramecium appears, or a grotesque & fearsome hydra that startles me....

     Time passed quickly. I was tonging various stamps into various groups. I mounted some in my albums, placed others in stockbooks, others in new glassines that I arranged in numerical Michel catalogue order in my files. There were the shield varieties of the early confederation, & many Germanias of the early empire, & a great many of the inflation issues of the 1920s, but I am most interested in the issues of the Third Reich.

     I found several of the death's mask Reinhardt Heydrich, the "Blond Beast" whose assassination led to the annihilation of a village in Czechoslovakia, Lidice, & most of its inhabitants. But of all the propaganda stamps from this period, the greatest quantity was those of the variously-sized & -colored Hitler heads....

     As I grew tired & my eyes began to cross, I hoped at least to organize all the stamps in this particular series, but it seemed that no matter how long I sorted through the glassines & then the loose stamps at the bottom of the shoebox—all this history emanating from the center of Europe—there was always another right-facing profile of the Fuhrer. Each time he appeared, he seemed smug, enriddled, immortal, not at all surprised to have reached light again, to have made his way even to America where many still celebrate his birthday. Each time he appeared, I realized I'd never be able to isolate & bring into focus all the animals in this pond.

The Pearl Museum

Included in transports from the extermination camp at Treblinka in Poland to SS headquarters in Berlin between October 1942 & August 1943, last on a roster of plunder signed (no doubt proudly, patriotically) by Commandant Franz Paul Stangl, were several thousand strings of pearls.

I know nothing of pearls in those days—just where they came from, how they were strung, how fashionable they were, how common or uncommon they might have been. Were some already cultured, grown from seed in tanks or roped-off seabeds? Were some already resin or plastic? Or were all still formed naturally in oysters' flesh as the bivalves coated grains of sand or bits of other intrusive foreign matter to render them harmless?

The Treblinka horde must have been of various quality & therefore of various worth to the Reich. They were a young girl's birthday gift; they were great-grandmother's heirloom string, lustrous for a hundred years, the silver-gray flawless beauties graduating in size toward the largest, pendant at center, & away. We don't know if the thousands of strings of pearls were classified by Stangl's jewelers, each placed in its own envelope or pouch, but, surely, they did not reach Berlin tangled like nacreous worms in a crate.

I would like to know what happened to the Jews' pearls when they reached the capital of the Reich, when they reached SS headquarters on *Prinz Albrecht Strasse.* Since only about 60 of the 1,000,000 prisoners survived the camp, & since, after the war, the dead could not demand return of (or restitution for) their stolen property, & since Stangl's list specified the far-from-precise "several thousand," did many strings that would not be missed go home that very evening to flatter the necks of beloved SS wives & daughters? In any case, most of the pearls must still be extant—one string in a safe deposit box in Rome or Lisbon or Zurich, another among a wealthy German woman's jewels in Hildesheim, a third at this very moment for sale in a shop in Montreal, two more in Manhattan windows, a sixth …

It may be that particularly rare pearls were removed from strings for fascist redeployment in other rings, tiaras, necklaces. For the sake of their & our & the victims' souls, I would like the German people to make a census of these pearls, to trace each string & each separate pearl from time of seizure at Treblinka to its whereabouts now. I would like these pearls to be collected. I would like to visit them in their own museum in Berlin, these *Shoah* syllables, tier after tier of them in arks in dimly-lit sacristies where we could remember them even with our eyes closed, where we could listen to them all night long.

Traumography

I'm a college freshman on Christmas break, 1957. I'm up front at the Fox in Brooklyn with three friends—we've driven to Allen Freed's famous rock & roll show from Suffolk County when Commack & Smithtown & Hauppauge & St. James & Nesconset are still farms, woods, fields surrounding the first few shopping centers. My chest alternately aches & empties—my high school love has shafted me, I don't sleep much, my bravado at home & with others is a strain & a lie—but I'm hyped, damned if I ain't, & I've been to Brooklyn only a few times before & then only to Ebbets Field where I saw the Boys of Summer— (Furillo & Campy, Newk & Pee Wee, Hodges & the Duke)—so I'm heartbroken but hyped as little Frankie Lymon & the Teenagers ask me why fools fall in love & Jimmy Bowen twangs "I'm stuck with you baby" as though from an echo chamber inside me & Bo Diddly weaves & hypnotizes & says that if the diamond ring he buys his love don't shine / he's gonna get himself a private eye & the Killer pounds out "Whole Lotta Shakin'" & Chuck Berry wails "Maybelline" (why can't she be true?) & Bill Haley & the Comets rock around the clock & The Platters see right through me with "The Great Pretender" & the song I'd listen to a thousand times over the years, "Only You," & I'm trying not to know that I might never get over the hollowness I feel & Lee Andrews & the Hearts sing "Oh if we only could start over again" & I'm lost but hyped up & then darkness in the huge pent-up place & then a beam of light center-stage up front & it's Little Richard.

Goldglitter heels about as high as his foot-high pompadour, earrings & scarlet-lined silvery cape, lipstick & rouge & ruffles & daddylonglegs eyelashes, fluorescent blue satin pants, who knows what else but he's just there all at once & I'm hurting but for a few seconds intermittently at least I forget as when he jumps about three feet high & slams down on the stage as though after a dunk & screams "Do you want it?" & we're all standing now & yelling *Yeah* & the cops in the aisles are bristling & he jumps again & screams "Do you want it?" & this time we all scream together *Yeahhhh* & he jumps again & almost cracks the reverberating stage & screams louder than I've ever heard anyone scream "Do you want it" & we almost bring down the building *Yeahhhhhhhh* & I know that here in this mob darkness with rock & roll already in my blood I'm seventeen & wounded & will be & I want it, want what Little Richard has, want it desperately, whatever it is, whatever sex & power & release & noise & spirit & joy & courage he's got god help me I want it.

Catlin's Flamingos

Catlin is sixty. Slogs to get to the place of this painting—South America, Argentina, south of Buenos Aires. Quaking hummocks, suckholes. "Up to our waistbands in the mud and slime," he remembers. To paint pink and pinkish-red flamingos calligraphically aswirl or, shot, plunging into that dark: the birds becoming retinal after-images we won't forget when we close our eyes to this dreamscape, the painting from now on part of our unconscious in the reds and pinks and deft touches of gray-black and white over the saline marshes.

Blam, the Colt rifle—Catlin painted this on commission from his friend Samuel Colt to show the use of these firearms in exotic settings—having done its work, no, *doing* its work in present tense here in the everything-at-onceness of our viewing. Birdshriek panic, a scene for us as of a momentary revelation of the undermind, all still but in motion, a foreboding here (one he can't quite reconcile in his composition). We must join him in his diversion, the high slapstick hilarity of the lower left corner.

But we must not misread or make too much of this. Laughter in George as he paints, yes, but not a bonefleck of derision: this is the artist who sacrificed himself to honor the vanishing native inhabitants of the Americas, whose credo was, in part, "I love the people who have always made me welcome to the best they had. I love a people who worship God without a Bible . . . . I love a people who don't live for the love of money." And as to the effect of his profuse gallery of Native Americans, we'll keep in mind this outburst by Daniel Webster: "My God, Catlin, you have shamed me. I was blind to all this red majesty and beauty and mystery that we are trampling down."

The Negro-Indian guide, his hat and body camouflaged by grasses, has been accidentally struck by the Colt's breech as Catlin fired his first round. He's frightened out of his wits, thinks he's been shot (Catlin tells us), thinks he'll be shot again. But enough cartoonish frivolity. The painter paints himself facing away from us and his painting's subject proper, as, perhaps, he'd like not to face it. We might follow his line of fire to the particular flamingo he's hit, the one just making it into our sight, then out into skeins of birds, to two or three near ones that are falling—by Catlin's accounting he shot about a dozen this morning—to a

---

Voices in the Gallery: Writers on Art, ed. Grant Holcomb (Rochester, NY: U of Rochester P, 2001).

scattering of feathers, to lower center where we sink into blasted creatures in disarray within and below the ranked fluid geometries of their nests. Here in the dead foreground Catlin has caught his own oily—how oily the green is here—and irrational and shadowy desecration of nature.

No, this painting is not of course a sermon, or an allegory, but it does brood the romantic which in its heart cherishes the natural sublime. The painter painting knows that no necessary or good thing was done here. We notice the spindly fragilities of the birds' legs, eggs in several nests, baby birds in many others. "Nests with eggs and nests with young," George tells us in his *Last Rambles Amongst the Indians of the Rocky Mountains and the Andes* as he recalls this event ten years after experiencing and painting it—the Civil War intervening with the blood of tens of thousands staining the pond at Shiloh and with the inhuman transactions of Andersonville. "The very young heads up and gaping," he continues in the rhythms of admission and wistful regret, "the older young, but without wings, pitched out of the nests or sprawling and trying to fly or to hide themselves on the ground. We replaced the little chicks in their nests as well as we could about us and left them."

Something had struck Catlin here to the depths of his being, something he couldn't quite surround: "Of all the curious hunting or other scenes I have ever seen on earth," he writes, "that scene was the most curious." Trying to apprehend what is happening here in the painter, what word or words would we substitute for the deflections of "curious?"

No, it was not a good thing that was done here in wild nature this morning, nor can a painting (or the several he did on this subject) escape this act or redeem it. And he, the preserver and rememberer of what was being lost, was this time responsible for what we won't forget as the beautiful flame of his nineteenth-century flamingos fuses in prophecy with muck and death in our souls.

As For Me: An Interview
(Conducted by Philip Brady and Daniel Bourne)

PB: At the reading last night [April 9, 2001], you mentioned that you hoped your poems about the Holocaust—in particular the poem in the voice of a Holocaust survivor—were "responsible."   What did you mean?   What makes a poem "responsible" or irresponsible?

WH: You know, Phil, I'm probably still casting about for reassurance that I haven't committed some great obscenity in writing *The Swastika Poems*, which was expanded to *Erika*, and on writing what will be another book of Holocaust poems since.   On the one hand, I believe fervently in chance-taking, wildness, writing toward breakthrough as we follow our words to get at meanings beyond words; on the other hand, I believe in being careful here: the Holocaust first of all belongs to the murdered and to the "survivors," and to insult or humiliate them, to assume we can know them and their experience, to *use* them, to take advantage of them for the purposes of art—art which is voracious and intent on itself—may be dangerous and immoral.   In the end, I keep going back to the proposition that we should say nothing that we would not say in the presence of the burning children. But we must not condescend to them, bore them, diminish them by stereotyping them.   But excessive self-consciousness is debilitating for the poet.   For better or worse—and maybe silence would have been better—during the writing of the best of the poems I've probably suspended all the questions of aesthetics that swirl in my daylight mind, or I'd never have gotten past the blank page, or I'd have had simplistic metrical moralities instead of poems, if I do have poems.

What upwells from the unconscious?   Where do the psychic maps take us within atrocity and nightmare?   The daylight mind is usually habit, convention, our veneer.   Poems may begin in this mind, but then begin listening to themselves and, by way of fused sound-image-story-rhythm, descend.   This is their process.

But I hear myself pontificating.   As William Stafford said, make believe there's a ghostly question mark after everything I say.   In fact, I really don't want to understand too much about many questions regarding poetry.

Artful Dodge 40 (2002).

PB: Robert Bly has said that most political poems are too "heavy" with personal anger to make their way into the world of public concerns.   Writing about ecology, about the Gulf War, about Native American genocide, about the Holocaust, how do you see your poems making their way into the public sphere?

WH: There's an essay in *Pig Notes & Dumb Music* that was a fulcrum point for me, I think.   I complain that Seamus Heaney's assumptions about the political dispensations of poetry will no longer serve, as they always have, because now our entire planet is on the verge of ecological catastrophe.   I argue that we need a new poetry, one somehow still evocative and interesting but one direct and filled with Truth in ways it has not been before, or else it will be less than marginal and trivial.   My essay seems to me now to be spoken by someone filled with dread.   Either, now, I've lost my edge, or I was asking for too much.   There is no way, maybe, to subvert the character of poetry as we have known it, down through time and in all cultures—its subtlety and suggestion, its complex patience, its willingness to withhold and obscure itself as teacher until the student is ready to hear and learn, which may be never.   I called for a poem that could obliterate a tank and slap a tyrant upside the head and make us all saints, and in so doing save the world.

I still believe that only poetry can save the human world.   I'm not talking about our word constructs, these lyric and other poems that we read and write, but about a poetic conception of our place here, of the earth as One, of thought as integration until we realize we must change or we will die out.   I've a feeling there's not enough time for us to learn to *accept* enough, to accept our place here and our limitations.   And the essay I mentioned wants to rush to a metapoetry that can raise us into the light by tomorrow morning at the latest.   Instant *satori*.

The public sphere?   I don't know.   Maybe our best poems keep the faith and will always be content to hang around until we're ready to have them by heart and to act by way of their song.   Maybe this is what is behind what W.S. Merwin wrote me a couple years ago (I've just dug out his letter): "What I wanted, most of my life to write was something that we would want to remember in a time of threat and crisis, to take into great peril."   This *is* that time for us now, isn't it, unprecedented in its danger for our species and for all species?   And we *do* need company, don't we, in our peril—the company of poems that can teach us what we need to know but only if we're ready for them?   Blunt poems, preachments, one-sided and blind-sided wisdom poems, only confirm our stupidity, and increase our loneliness and despair when we're with them.   What poems, what faiths, what dreams of love and meaning will we take with us into great peril, this fear of our own extinction that sometimes seems to extinguish us?

How do certain poems, in Robert Frost's phrase, become hard to get rid of and make their ways into the public sphere, if any poems ever do?   One reader, one heart at a time, I'd guess.   They're in no hurry, these poems.   I've wanted them to rush, but they can't, and won't be pressed.   It's not their fault that I've got only a decade or three left to live. They aren't *disposed* to hurry, it's not in their nature, their disposition, so in that essay of mine I might have been asking for a creature that couldn't be conceived of and born. But what do I know?

DB: I've been struck by your "long-staring" at the things of this world, your ongoing gaze toward history and toward the big stories of our time. Joyce Carol Oates describes you as a poet in whom "the 'visionary' and the 'historical' are dramatically meshed." Were you aware of something clicking in your mind at some point, something that pointed you in this direction? Or, did the poems just point themselves and you followed?

WH: When I look around, I do seem to have done and to be doing, but only on the surface, something different from most or all of my contemporaries—no value judgment here. I think that in each case I could locate some of the foreground and sources of the various books, but that wouldn't explain much. The central thing may be that in each case a generative force has to take over, and this force is something that has been building in us always so all we have to do is allow it to speak. Walt told himself that he contained enough so just had to let it out.

After it was published, I thought about the origins in me of *Diana, Charles, & the Queen*, for example. It's true that when I was a boy of eight or nine I read of the birth of a prince, Prince Charles, and as he grew up and stories about him appeared in the papers I associated him with castles and battles, kings and merlins. And it's true that when Diana appeared on the scene I was fascinated by this golden girl and she swirled in me with a thousand personal associations, and all became mixed with my graduate school English studies and with a couple trips to England, etc., etc. But when I happened to read that first book on Diana by Andrew Morton and wrote what happened to be a rhymed double quatrain in its margin, and then another, and then another, something took over as I read other books until I had over three hundred of these poems. The interesting thing to me now is not what might be said in the book about English history or the monarchy or failed love or Diana's relationship with Mother Teresa, but the ways in which, by sounds and images and associations, the whole sequence gets itself said. I mean, as Doc Williams reminds us, we can stay young in our writing only by way of this force—he uses the word "technique"—not by way of subject matter. Subject matter, as strange as it may be to conceive of it in this way, is almost incidental, is along for the wild ride of the saying, and it is always fearful, it may be, that it will lose its life, its factuality and empirical veracity. But we come to any subject matter naturally, or should. Passion won't be forced. I was deeply interested in the royals, as the poems certainly are. I wrote those poems until I had no more of their music to hear for a time. If I found them right, wrote them right, they will keep giving of themselves because, coming from visceral inchoate fens and bogs, they know much more than does the wise-ass Ph. D. who wrote them.

I see my Holocaust books, *Ribbons: The Gulf War*, *Crazy Horse in Stillness* and other books in these same ways. I become absorbed. I read. I can't not begin to write. I fall into trance or semi-trance. Everything rises and converges, sings, wails, intones, narrates. I revise in states of unconsciousness and consciousness that drift in and out. I sometimes look up from a finished poem or book and wonder where I've been while it somehow got written. Then, I want to know what I've done, want to understand, want, again, the poem or book to be responsible, intelligible, want it to communicate. But the text must protect itself from any desire in me to handcuff it and throw it into the jail of my misconceptions about it. A while ago some jerk's review of *Crazy Horse in Stillness* showed up online. He refers to the book as an endless series of tiresome vignettes, something like that. Now, there are many serious questions about my book, but a guy like this—well, I want to ask such folks to learn to *hear*, this is the whole thing, to learn to think by way of their ears. It may be that even the included brevities, what he calls those vignettes, when *heard*, yield unceasing answers to the question we put to any poem: so what? My poems' true subject matter is their sounds that carry their meanings. How boring reading must be for you if you can't sense the implications of sound.

DB: In our most recent issue of *Artful Dodge* we published an interview with Tess Gallagher, one of the poets in your the *Generation of 2000* anthology. We asked her if she thought there was any connective thread there among the poets whom she might characterize as sharing "her generation," and if there was anything to distinguish this group of poets from those who went before or who have emerged since. Have you come to any conclusions about possible connective threads in this generation, the distinctions among generational lines?

WH: From the beginning, I conceived of *The Generation of 2000* as an eclectic anthology. I don't think I had any choice. A generation is not a school, or movement. A generation of poets may best be thought of, maybe, as a group of individual voices who happen to share an approximate time period. And as I keep my eye on *2000* poets over the years, I don't think Paul Mariani has much in common with Charles Simic, Robert Morgan with Heather McHugh, Tess Gallagher with Ray Carver, Lucille Clifton with Michael S. Harper, Ai with Judith Minty, Faye Kicknosway with Stanley Plumly, Albert Goldbarth with Gregory Orr, Marge Piercy with Louise Gluck, for example. I can think of similarities between and among some of these and other poets, of course, certain themes/assumptions/ways of getting themselves said.

Mine seems to be a learned generation, I sometimes think, and the last one to have come to poetry wholly naturally: that is, we are the last poets in America to make our way forward before the great explosion of workshops and creative writing programs across the country. Were there ten such programs by the mid-'60s when I was in graduate school? Are there 300-350 now, and all producing writers hungry to break into print, to find decent jobs by way of their writing? There seems to be a factory, a production line aspect to poetry that there wasn't before. And many thousands of MFAs, for many different reasons, imperatives of body and spirit, will abandon the craft and sullen art.

In the end, maybe the main difference between a real poem, one meaningful and important, and an exercise is that we have the feeling that the former had to be written, that the poet had no choice. Much of the poetry I read these days from younger poets seems to be going through the motions, gesturing in vitiated ways toward what has already been done with more intensity. In the end, poets with fire, poets hurt into their singing will create the poems by which any generation is known.

DB: Do you know Robert Hass's statement that "the isolated lyric is no longer tenable"? He's hardly decrying lyric poetry (and he's one of our finest lyric poets anyway), but he does seem to be highlighting that lyric poetry must do more than offer the chronicling of personal experience, offer more than pretty words. This seems to be very reminiscent of your own comment about "quasi-surrealism" in *The Generation of 2000*: "It is understandable but tragic that there is so much distracting silliness and indulgence in poetry during this critical point in human history, a time when all life on earth is threatened." You've already touched on this, this dissatisfaction you feel with the state of current poetry.

WH: There I go again.... I wrote that in the early '80s. I was scared out of my wits. The ponds and woods in my mind and of my experience were being asphalted over and sprayed with carcinogens. I wanted poets to stop playing and to tell hard truths directly. I still want this, but, again, it doesn't now seem possible to me that poetry can become some kind of frank inspirational directive that can flat-out save us. It cannot become unbeautiful even in its terrors, so far as I can conceive of it. There are no advances in art, there's no progress, as John Gardner says. It is and will be at best what the ancient cave paintings are. But how can we, given our dire circumstances now, not ask more of it? I'll keep asking more of myself.

Generally, I'm not satisfied with most of what I read in contemporary poetry, but this may be my own problem. The writing I connect with—you mention Hass and I think now of Czslaw Milosz—is in-the-grain aware of devastation, exile, the obliteration of cultures, the evil behind what Paul Celan calls "that which happened." Maybe every young workshop poet ought to study the slave trade or Verdun or Hiroshima or Auschwitz or My Lai or the great killing fields of Asia for emotional grounding (not necessarily for subject matter, of course) in where we've been/what we are. Maybe. The education of a poet is mysterious. Emily Dickinson read little, except nature and her bible (while Walt read everything). *As for me* (I'm thinking of Hass's connection with Jeffers now, and Jeffers, who is more and more important for me, often uses this turn-phrase in his poems), as for me I believe there is such a thing as high seriousness beyond indulgence—not one unbroken tone of death and despair but knowledge first and *then*, if it can happen, *if* it can happen, a miraculous turn to some kind of grounding *despite everything*. The other day in my journal I wrote the phrase "mellifluous blah-blah" to describe what I thought about a couple romantic essays by a friend of mine in a magazine retrospective, good essays that I'd read years ago but that now seemed to me to be located in some neverland I recognize because I've been there, too, as will be apparent in my decades of essays collected in *Home: Autobiographies, Etc.*, being published by MAMMOTH Books.

Maybe one thing Hass is pointing to is that context is necessary. I think a single lyric remains possible but it will have somewhere in its sounds, its genetic code, the road-side dog realizations of Czslaw Milosz, of Jeffers, of Tomasz Jastrun: in your translation, Dan, Jastrun sees "A silhouette in a window / cut bread with an artificial arm"—his realizations are stark, realistic, and shock us into recognitions that may keep us from becoming part of the problem.

PB: Looking at your opus I'm struck by two things: the breadth of locations, and the intensity of concern—it seems to me that intense dismemberment is one of your themes—exploring the place where identity comes apart. I'm thinking for instance of the last lines of "Darkness" and "Simple Truths" in *Erika* and of that searing poem from *Ribbons* about the Japanese soldier.

WH: Let me try two new poems on you. The first is "Yes," and comes from the 1946 testimony of a Holocaust survivor identified for us in the book *Fresh Wounds*, edited by Donald L. Niewyk (Chapel Hill: UNC Press, 2001), as only Udell S.:

> One of my comrades was working.
> An SS man approached him with a gun
> and asked him was he was thirsty.
> Of course he replies, "Yes." So the SS
>
> called over a second comrade, a certain
> Tshernetsky from Bedzin,
> and shot him, and said,
> "Here, now drink your brother's blood."

And here is "Coal" from the testimony of a Kalman E.:

> The German said for two people
> to fill a railroad car with coal
> and for two people to lie on the floor
> and be covered. When they were covered

> he laughed at us and ordered us
> not to dig them up, they should
> swim up by themselves, and if they cannot
> they can just stay there.

Well, these are witty fellows, aren't they, these sadists? In how many ways are we dis-membered by history? These murderers are of my blood. If I'd been born in 1920 in Germany or Poland or Romania or Ukraine or elsewhere in Europe instead of in 1940 in Brooklyn I might easily have aspired to the SS and become a man of such wit. And the victims?—at least in my dreams I have often been chased by dogs & heard the sound of gas chambers' doors clanging shut like a Freiburg Cathedral bell and have been covered by night, that coal. Where is my *member*ship, where is yours? Who are we? We exist in *dis.*

These are simple poems, but can't be heard and known until the reader hears the rhymes in "Yes" of "working" and "thirsty," of "SS" and "Bedzin," for example. I don't mean simply that ideas arise from these sound like the famous "ices" and "crisis" in Eliot's "Prufrock," though they do. I mean that such sounds & echoing rhythms place us within the hypnogogic state wherein meaning and mystery reside, wherein poetry may begin to ... is this possible? ... help us to change our lives, to make ourselves *other* (which is the way I hear that last declaration in Rilke's "Archaic Torso"). Maybe we do too much talking and not enough swimming. When we give ourselves over to sounds, immerse ourselves in them, we experience, it may be, the onomatopoetic source of sound itself. An "r" or an "l" doesn't have a particular meaning, a thought-equivalent, but when these sounds are absorbed in the reading of "Coal," and when the "should"-"cannot" rhyme is heard in contrasting ways, when the "r" sounds come together, then the poem can work in us, survive in us.

But knowing what we must know, can our poems now claw their ways up into air from under that historical coal, or will they not survive, as our planet closes down on us, and just suffocate there?

PB: Those two poems are matter-of-fact, deceptively simple.

WH: Yes, straight-forward narratives with no diversion, I think. And this occurs to me: I do not break in any way and say that these events are bad, evil, but just report them as the survivors reported them, assuming that bad things were done, *inhuman* things (oh the ironies of that word), and counting on a compassionate and sympathetic listener, so if my readers are bothered by these two pieces—and not only the first time through—then maybe there is still hope for us during a time when we hear so often that murderers feel no remorse. But maybe I'm just whistling in the dark here, hoping, too, that my poems might be of some use in our evolution toward the power and order that Emerson said was at the center of the universe. But in my secret heart I might believe in what Yeats says in his modest and accepting "On Being Asked for a War Poem," that "He has had enough of meddling who can please / A young girl in the indolence of her youth, / Or an old man upon a winter's night."

DB: Are you concerned about using survivors' words?

WH: Yes, in many ways, and I'll go into this in the notes to *Shoah Train*, the new book of Holocaust poems.

DB: Do you worry about the question of "cultural ownership," of who has the right to write about certain things? I'm not just thinking about your Holocaust poems here, but about *Crazy Horse in Stillness*. You're not Jewish, and you're not Native American.

WH: In all honesty, I guess I've been concerned about this in my daylight mind, but, for better or worse, I haven't censored myself when I've been seized by a subject or character or story or sound. I don't think a sculptor or musician or artist or writer who gravitates naturally toward the Other should close himself or herself off. (The metaphor of Dutch Elm Disease just entered my mind, *fear* of invasion by an alien virus so that the tree quickly shuts itself down unto death.) That seems a kind of suicide to me. In the end, is the work sincere, genuine, responsible, enlightening? I fall back on the old verities of aesthetics. As for me, my books will be the proof of whether or not I've lusted after sensational materials or, even if well-meaning, have been a dunce when it has come to understanding the subjects that have generated the poems.

My experiences in writing have somehow been integrated ones, calming. I compose myself as I compose and as I read over, hundreds of times, what I've written. But my experience in listening to what is being said out there has often been jangling, disorienting. While one of my daylight anxieties has been that maybe a non-Jew should not attempt a Holocaust poem or book, Karl Shapiro went so far as to write that only a poet with my background could create true Holocaust poems, that I was the poet with the "right credentials" and that my poems were "unmatched." For a few minutes, I sort of felt that he solved my Jewish problems. Sherman Alexie wrote to the publisher even before *Crazy Horse in Stillness* came out because he'd seen a flyer that said this white guy born in Brooklyn was the author, and he objected. Later, we exchanged 2-3 letters. When he read the book, he said that he liked the poems but listed 11 or 13 reasons why I should stop writing about Crazy Horse and Native Americans. I wrote back, point for point, 11 or 13 reasons that his reasons seemed to me to be skewed, that he'd better not start sawing off limbs behind him that he's sitting on. He said he'd pledged to some Sioux that he'd honor their request and never again write of *Tasunke Witko*. But Leslie Marmon Silko and Joseph Bruchac spoke up for the book, and Adrian Louis, too, and for a few minutes I felt they solved my

314

Indian problems. Look, all this is very serious, and it's not. Is there any reason whatsoever that Silko or Alexie might not be seized by Bergen-Belsen and write something heartbreaking and piercing about it, something that hadn't been known and said before?—black novelist John A. Williams has a Holocaust novel, and such examples of cross-cultural art are myriad.

This may be presumptuous of me, of course, but I might tomorrow write something about the Jews of Masada—maybe they need me to express something of themselves that hasn't yet been expressed. I can almost see a man and wife with their children in a cavern where water still trickles in as, outside, the Roman ramp grows toward them. Maybe tomorrow a poem will come to me about the hailstones of paint on Crazy Horse's chest, washing from him as he rides his favorite pinto. Maybe about the catbird outside my door right now. Maybe about Martin Luther King. Maybe about passages in Raul Hilberg's *The Politics of Memory* that astounded me the other day, his *musical* conception, via Beethoven especially, of his construction of his monumental *Destruction of the European Jews.* Anything can happen, and, logically, it is easy to reduce to absurdity the argument that an artist must be limited to only certain subjects, that his imagination may be allowed to seize only ideas and stories within his own culture. Sounds are not limited to certain cultures. But, tomorrow I would listen respectfully again if Alexie urged me not to write of the Plains or Lakota again. But then I would probably dream again, and the sounds would begin.

Does only my family, or do only German-Americans, own my father, who died a few years ago? Can only we write about him or try to paint him and the culture from which he came to America in the late '20s? What if his black apprentice or Jewish apprentice in old Brooklyn had thought about him, with gratitude or revulsion, for decades, and wanted to write about him? Could we even say that *I* would have the better chance of writing a better poem than that other?

PB: Whatever the subject, how is it, do you think, that you've been so prolific?

WH: I had to laugh the other day when I was reading comments by authors in a book of photographs by Jill Krementz. Joyce Carol Oates said she just seemed to spend her time dawdling and doodling and never getting anything written! But I know her feeling of never seeming to get enough done. Ours is the generation whose parents went through the Depression, with all its attendant fears, and then WWII from Pearl Harbor to the surrender of Germany and then Japan. At ten or eleven each night, just before bed these years, I seem to get very anxious and have to calm myself—some of this anxiety has to do with feeling that another day is done, that I should have worked harder, accomplished more, found some way to make more money so that I could stay out of the poor house.

When I was in graduate school and for several years after that, I thought I was the kind of aspiring perfectionist who would publish a book maybe every five years or so, like James Wright and Richard Wilbur. I've found out that I seem to write as much as William Stafford did. New things keep showing up in my notebooks. And I've often written poems, it seems, in bursts. Once I'm where the lines are coming to me from who knows where, I sometimes can stay there while five or ten poems—maybe I have to lower my standards to call them poems—show up in a day. Once we're singing, why stop? And just as Stafford said that he has a clue to forward motion in poetry—at least a syllable or a sound suggesting another, maybe a word or a phrase, and following the poem in this way by nudge and impulse and trajectory—a complete poem will often generate another for me, and then another.

To this point, I feel I've written only two fairly long poems, "Poem Touching the Gestapo" in *Erika*, 100 or so lines, and the new "Iwo Dahlia," 168 lines. I think of *The Chestnut Rain* and *Ribbons* and *Diana, Charles, & the Queen*, for example, as lyric sequences. Other books hope for coherence and wholeness—god knows I spend an awful lot of time on their arrangement—but are basically collections of individual lyrics. I don't know. I don't want to sweat definitions, genres, the niceties of labels for these various forms we pressure into various lyricisms. Three winters ago I wrote what might become the closest for me to a single book-length poem—it seems to hover in one place instead of growing, progressing, developing. No overall narrative. It has 60-80 sections. It will be called *The Angel Voices*—from the carol, *down on your knees, O hear* preceding my title phrase—and I look forward to getting back to it once other projects are behind me.

DB: Speaking of being prolific, you mentioned that you have many more Crazy Horse-Custer poems.

WH: Yes, enough for a good-sized book again, and I've put together this book, but I think I'd like, if possible for a publisher, to integrate these new poems with *Crazy Horse in Stillness* and make one bison-sized book. Artist DeLoss McGraw has done a series of paintings in response to my Crazy Horse and Custer poems, and I'd like to have these included. In any case, I believe I'm now done writing those poems. But who knows?

PB: MAMMOTH is publishing a book of your stories, *The Hummingbird Corporation.*

WH: Yes, these stories appeared sporadically over the last thirty years or so. I've a feeling that this will be my only book of stories, ever. But who knows?

I like my brief preface. I say, in the third person, that when the writer looked over his stories, what he liked most about them was that, apparently, he hadn't known how to write them—here and there, plot complication is lacking, character motivation weak, etc.—but that there is something about each of these—

most are flash fictions—that endears itself to him. And this is the way I feel about this book. Sure, I include some stories that should be scrapped, some might not even rise to the level of fiction at all, might just be sketches, but I'm fond of this little collection of mine. The guy in the preface says, too, that his other work is not so lonely now that these stories have been published. Most of my family and closest friends—outside the poetry scene—aren't much interested in my poetry, may in fact even be pained to try to understand it, so it will be a pleasure to give them the new *Home: Autobiographies, Etc.*, and I think they'll enjoy and be relieved by *The Hummingbird Corporation*, too.

PB: You've just raised the question of audience. Do you have anyone in mind when you write? That's one question. The other has to do with the audience for poetry in this country. Are you glum about it, or hopeful?

WH: I don't know if I have anyone in mind when writing. Maybe I have the poem in mind, what it needs, how it wants me to follow it to wherever and not get in its way. In the end, maybe, only that poetry will last that will somehow deepen and ramify the *art* of poetry itself, and this art, maybe, has to do with something I've tried to express here, the transformation of subject matter into inexhaustible sources of language/story/music/spirit. But if I don't have anyone in mind while writing, when I've finished something that I think holds up, I sure do think of showing it to certain writer friends, yourselves included. But I usually don't get around to this, if ever, until a book is published. For better or worse, I don't workshop poems with friends. I've always felt that I have to become my own best reader, and, as I've said, I sure do spend much time—maybe too much time— reading my own poems over and over. But occasionally a friend or editor will help me improve a poem, as Dave Smith helped me with one called "The American Civil War" that appeared in *The Southern Review* before it got into *Crazy Horse in Stillness*, for example. In general, I'm fairly stubborn when it comes to minding my business and finishing poems myself. When I was an undergraduate at Brockport, there were no creative writing courses, and I took only one in graduate school at Ohio University, a fiction workshop from Jack Matthews. I've just been in the habit of going it alone. I'm not saying that this is the way it should be done, but this is what seems to mesh with my own personality.

Audience. It sometimes seems that there are two levels of poets in America: the famous who have been the Poet Laureate and/or have won the Pulitzer Prize and/or National Book Award, whose books sell from a large publisher with a major distributor; and the rest of us, just getting along in good faith or in desperation, lucky to find publishers so that our books will exist, lucky to get a thousand copies of a book around. The twenty-five or so stars will pack a hall, folks will line up to get books inscribed, Bill Moyers will interview them, anthologists will never leave them out. We others are the underground or compost. Some few of the famous will remain famous, most will join us as the compost of the age, some of our poets without laurels will rise into consequential identity in Time. And all is as it should be. Coming or going, always at home. The older I get, the wiser Jeffers seems to me to be who said that "If God has been good enough to give you a poet / Then listen to him. But for God's sake let him alone until he is dead; no prizes, no ceremony." Jeffers says that a poet is one who listens to nature and his own heart, and that the world's noise gets in the way of this. When this happens, "Hemingway play[s] the fool and Faulkner forget[s] his art."

As for me, I seem now to have reached a joyful equilibrium. How could I bear up under more mail, more correspondence, more friendships than I have now, how find time to stare and to live the contemplative life. I won't name poets of the generation previous to mine who seem to me to have lost much because of their fame—as Frost lost so much—because they were always on the road in one way or another, but there are many.

I'll tell you though, this question, this conception of audience in a poet's psyche—*nothing* will prove to be more complex and influential in terms of his or her life's work.

Preface

I live in a small village on the Erie Canal in western New York State. Behind my home, at the back of my one acre, I have an 8′ x 12′ cabin—Thoreau's was 10′ x 15′—under ash and silver maple, surrounded by wild rose, honeysuckle, and red osier bushes. I retired from teaching a year ago, and now get back to this hideout most mornings, usually write something in my journal, then read for a while or draft a new poem or prose piece, or work on revision in almost the same state of intense reverie. As if by themselves, books gradually form, but I have no sense of program, and little of direction. I believe that most of the writers in this anthology would say the same. In the main, we are not journalists, scholars, political scientists. We're often not sure how our writing gets written, or if we'll be able to do again what we've just done. We compose by way of what Emerson called "the flower of the mind," and can only hope that our text, in the end, by way of its interfused music-image-story-thought, knows more than we do and will continue to be evocative and meaningful.

Just before noon this past September 11th I left the cabin and came inside. I turned on the television. My mind still elsewhere, I saw a plane flying into a skyscraper. As did countless others, I thought I was watching a clip from a new disaster movie, then wondered if this could be a hoax updated from Orson Welles. But I recognized the anchor's voice, and began to absorb the events of that morning.

At 8:45 a hijacked passenger jet out of Boston had crashed into the north tower of the 110-story World Trade Center in New York City; at 9:03, another hijacked liner crashed into the WTC's south tower; at 9:43, a third hijacked plane hit the Pentagon in Washington; and between the total collapse of the south tower at 9:50 and the north tower at 10:29, a fourth hijacked plane crashed in Somerset County, southeast of Pittsburgh. The scenes of death and devastation—thousands dead, including hundreds of firefighters and police, sixteen vertical acres of people and buildings in smoking ruin, a section of our military headquarters burning for days—were overwhelming as we tried to comprehend what had happened.

September 11, 2001: American Writers Respond, Ed. William Heyen (Silver Spring, MD: Etruscan Press, 2002).

Thoreau once said that the news is always the same—a fire somewhere, a sultan's wedding somewhere, a war somewhere—and this was all the more reason for us to mind our own business, even to hide out. But he and the other American transcendentalists, if they were listening, if in their afterlives they were sensing the violent upheavals of this material world, must have lost their immortal breath that morning. Their faith was, as Emerson said, "that within the form of every creature is a force impelling it to ascend into a higher form." And even cataclysm could translate, eventually, given time, given sufficient perspective, to beauty, to soul. But it seemed to me that the trauma of this day would abide, soul-deep in our village and across the country.

A few days later, I was asking unfashionable questions in my journal about what our creative literature, given the magnitude of these iniquitous events, must and surely would now become if in the future it could hope to be of any practical use or relevance or moral value. I cautioned myself against optimistic over-reaction, reminded myself of America's accelerating amnesia when one headline event takes the place of another (as now these attacks would at last displace months of gossipy reports about a U.S. congressman's relationship with a missing intern), but I continued to feel that the events of September 11th had awakened us and shaken our senses of identity and security. I proposed this book to Etruscan Press. A day later, I withdrew my proposal, afraid that such a project was untenable for creative writers who, as William Butler Yeats says in "On Being Asked for a War Poem," cannot set a statesman right and who are only meddling when they try to do more than please "A young girl in the indolence of her youth, / Or an old man upon a winter's night." I guessed that others might be feeling the same contraries, the same paralyzing complexities that I felt as the desire for art disintegrated with the prodigious symmetries of the Twin Towers.

But I changed my mind again, and soon wrote to a wide-range of potential contributors. (Later, too, by the e-grapevine, word would spread and I'd receive hundreds of submissions, including some of the strongest in this book.... Poet Philip Brady wrote me and put into words what was my hope for the eventual anthology, that as a whole it be instrumental in "focusing the diffuse but immense powers we bring to our separate works every day."

But who has any right at such a time to say anything at all? What person who was not there or did not lose a family member or friend has a right to talk personally? I doubt that there will be a contributor to this book who has not asked himself or herself this question. Writing anything at all can seem like an obscene indulgence to us, and we remember Theodor Adorno's famous declaration that "*Nach Auschwitz, ein Gedicht zu schreiben ist barbarisch*" (to write a poem after Auschwitz is barbaric). His is the ultimate argument for silence, and much of my divided self nods assent to his injunction. But—and this anthology will exist by way of this *but*, this *con*junction—as Czeslaw Milosz says in *The Witness of Poetry*, "Whoever invokes genocide, starvation, or the physical suffering of our fellow men in order to attack poems or paintings practices demagoguery."

Where are we? What is the state of our union, or disunion? William Stafford, a conscientious objector during a vastly-different WWII, reminded us that "justice will take us millions of intricate moves." And as millions of new flags appear along our streets, on our baby-strollers and bikes and gasoline-powered vehicles, in our advertisements, and on our bodies as tattoos, these symbols themselves must remind us that the result of blind patriotism is always, in Robinson Jeffers' words, a blood-lake: "and we always fall in."

But, too, as our writers try to have their say (I'm thinking of Walt Whitman musing in his old age that he was content because he'd had his say), whatever their say and however they say it—in the end, of course, the way something is said *is* what is said (this being the secret heart of all creative writing)—we must understand that the September 11th hijackers were filled with such hate for American aspirations and were of such fanatical (from the Latin *fānāticus*, of a temple, inspired by a god, mad) fervor that they would with a sense of great fulfillment have killed all 280,000,000 of us, every man, woman, and child, if they'd been able. Theirs was not the flower, but the hellfire of the human mind. Such mania evokes new dimensions of fear and realization and commitment in us, disrupts and challenges the romantic American imagination as perhaps never before, and demands from us a different retaliation, an intricate move toward world justice for each star or stripe on every Old Glory now or to come.

Brockport, New York
September-October 2001

As the book you are holding in your hands was coming together, I dreamt I was driving a bus along the edge of a cliff. At the bottom of the abyss was chaos, madness, trauma, death. But the bus was filled with all the writers here, and all together they leaned the opposite way, toward that other life we all hope for, and kept us from plunging into the void. How could I, how could any of us ever thank them enough?

The Verities

Soon after September 11, 2001, it was my privilege to be in touch with many writers from across our country as an anthology I was editing for Etruscan Press on our responses to the attacks was coming together. You've heard the litany of our reactions to that day, and have experienced many or all of these emotions yourself: grief, rage, shock, disbelief, confusion, disgust, fear, hate, even an amorphous guilt. I needed community, the community of creative writers—I was listening to many television and newspaper reporters and retired generals and congressionals and editorialists—and I felt that I wanted to catch our first, naked reactions to events, even if reacting so fast makes poets and fiction writers suspicious and uncomfortable. Long ago poet William Wordsworth talked about the necessity of the poet's emotion being "recollected in tranquility." But as contemporary contributor James Longenbach from New York says, "Art traffics in risk."

It seemed to me at the time that my hoped-for anthology demanded a certain dispensation from my usual consideration of art, of aesthetics. Certainly, I found and included the best things I could. But I kept in my mind the truth that beauty might include ugliness and fear, too, disjointedness, twisted cursive steel and carcinogenic dust. Never did I so clearly understand, it may be, the Beat aesthetic, or poet William Stafford's mind-blowing admission of allegiance, "I love feeble poems." Philip Brady from Ohio writes, "Sometimes language just takes off and I get that knot in the pit of my stomach, thinking, we will never land alive." This is often the language of my 125 contributors. I wanted the sub-conscious take-off, whatever the landing, & wherever. Ralph Waldo Emerson's one most insistent demand of the American poet was for "wildness." Where else could the truth be except within the rhythmic and passionate and intuitive pressure of words fusing into form beyond politics? I've always loved Theodore Roethke's "When I raged, and I wailed, / and my reason failed, / that delicate thing, my soul, / grew a new wing." I wanted art, of course, and there is much artistry in this book, but given these horrendous and in some senses unprecedented events, so

---

This essay grew from talks given in 1992 and 1993 at Roberts Wesleyan University, C. W. Post University, Keystone College, SUNY at Brockport, Miami Book Fair, Kutztown University, and John Carroll University.

what if a poem had a broken pelvis or shoulder or a sui-generis prose piece raved toward incoherence?

The writers in the anthology were writing *in medias res*, even before our assault on the Taliban in Afghanistan, but whatever our political or religious leanings, didn't we all feel that we'd experienced some kind of reality check—the alien, deadly thing itself, whatever it was, finding us out in our American home, intensifying our American light? At first we thought, as John Updike writes—he lives in Massachusetts but was visiting the Apple that day—at first we thought that this "could be fixed; the technocracy the Towers symbolized would find a way to put out the fire and reverse the damage." But this, of course, was not to be, and we had to stare into that which almost blinds us. Karen Blomain from Pennsylvania who was at a melting-pot flea-market when she heard the news writes, "We shaded our eyes against the glare for a glimpse of what had happened"; Joanna Scott, from western New York, drives to the perimeter of Ground Zero and says "There was too much sunlight." This reality reached us here, under our breastbones; here, in our minds. Poet Judith Minty from Michigan writes, "The events of September 11 were an attack on the American psyche." Yes, sandstorms and ash deserts were close to us now, the inner and outer oceans did not seem as vast. Richard Foerster from Maine writes, "The events of September 11 have redefined the boundaries of neighborhood on a global scale. Our resolve to set things right at home and in the world had better build on that realization."

Hugh Ogden from Connecticut was listening to a Brahms symphony on his car radio when he heard the news of the Twin Towers. He speaks of "the end of pure harmonies, flames replacing music/until the radio was awash with fear and bafflement." Trying to hear what was going on as I read hundreds of submissions and scanned 9-11 websites, I heard this disruption of what had been an essentially romantic conception of ourselves and our nation. At the heart of our American experience, it may be, we've always believed in ourselves as progressing toward, evolving toward … what?: the shining city on the hill where peace and justice and prosperity would prevail for all. But how does Emerson's "power and order that lie at the [universal] heart of things" compute with 16 acres of smoking ruin in Manhattan, the struck wing of the Pentagon, the hijacked airliner that crashed in a Pennsylvania field—"Let's roll"— with the thousands murdered in one day at the beginning of our new century?

Suddenly, ours became a different estate: Aliki Barnstone from Nevada writes, "for me, consciousness itself changed on September 11." David Watson from Michigan says, "I, too, seemed to be saying farewell to some previous life." David St. John from California writes, [After September 11] every writer I know was asking himself or herself 'Where now do I fit, where do I belong, against this horrifying landscape'" Joanna Higgins from New York says, "Before is over. Now is now. And here we are. And it's … hard. Harder, maybe, than wherever we've been before." The very title of poet Stanley Plumly's essay—he's from

Maryland but was in Italy on that day—is "The Morning America Changed." H. L. Hix from Ohio writes, "nothing the same for us, in us, ever again." Ray Gonzalez sent me his essay from Minnesota. After September 11, he says, ours is a world "where it seems like each tiny thing we do has now been amplified by fear and fire." Just how myriad and domestic the changes are is registered in this brief poem, "Her Very Eyes," by Kimiko Hahn of New York City:

Her Very Eyes

A friend's sister, my daughter reports,
cannot close her eyes,
and I interrupt, it must be asbestos irritation—
until she adds,
she sees bodies falling from the sky,
she sees bodies breaking through the glass atrium
or smashing onto the pavement,
she sees one woman, her skirt billowing out like a manikin's,
and a suited man plunging headfirst.
And she hears them land in front of her
but cannot turn away when she closes her eyes.
And she doesn't know what to do.
This is what my daughter reports
upon coming home from school
last Tuesday.

Yes, what have these indelible images done to our children? But—and this is a huge but—many writers ask us to imagine what life has already been for others. Listen to novelist Denis Johnson from Idaho: "I think we sense," Johnson says,

but don't care always to apprehend—the reality that some people hate America. To many suffering souls, we must seem incomprehensibly aloof and self-centered, or worse. For nearly a century, war has rolled lopsidedly over the world, crushing the innocent in their homes. For half that century, the United States has been seen, by some people, as keeping the destruction rolling without getting too much in the way of it—has been seen, by some people, to lurk behind it. And those people hate us. The acts of terror against this country—the hijackings, the kidnappings, the bombings of our airplanes and barracks and embassies overseas, and now these mass atrocities on our own soil—tell us how much they hate us. They hate us as people hate a bad God, and they'll kill themselves to hurt us.

I say in my brief preface, which I wrote before receiving more than maybe a dozen usable contributions, that if they could have, these particular hijackers would have killed all 280,000,000 of us in this country. (After the book appeared Californian contributor Sharon Doubiago wrote me that I was mistaken to say this, and that my saying it was destructive.) I don't know whether I'm right or wrong, and will never know. On the one hand, these strikes were meant in part to be symbolic: against our economy at the WTC, against our military at lthe Pentagon, against the seat of our government at the Capitol—that Pennsylvania plane was probably heading there, or to the White House. On the other hand, we've seen the eyes of those hijackers. Would they not have punished every man, woman, and child on our continent? I don't know. My statement in the preface, though, seems hopeless. Sharon Doubiago is more faithful, and asks for understanding and love.

And then, in a complex concluding sentence in my preface, I say that "Such mania evokes new dimensions of fear and realization and commitment in us, disrupts and challenges the romantic American imagination as perhaps never before, and demands from us a different retaliation, an intricate move toward world justice for each star or stripe on every Old Glory now or to come." As do many writers, I ask for more than what was surely coming, as surely as death and taxes, a massive military response. I've always remembered something Henry David Thoreau says in *Walden*, that there are a hundred people hacking away in the *branches* of a problem for every person getting to its *roots.*

In any case, listen to this strange ballad by Rosalynne Carmine Smith— I can tell you now that I am she, that stanzas of this poem came to me in a balancing dream—which, at its end, necessarily complicates all my perhaps paranoid simplicities, and speaks, perhaps, for a better person than the one who labored on his preface.

The Poison Birds

A robin whispered in my head
I want you dead I want you dead
Though you're a man or child
I want you dead

A grackle screaked in my head
I want you dead I want you dead
Black white yellow brown or red
I want you dead

A bluebird sliced into my head
I want you dead I want you dead

You're Christian agnostic Buddhist Jew
I want you dead

A hummingbird blurred in my head
Farmer teacher nurse and cop
Mick and kraut and spic and wop
I want you dead

A passenger pigeon extinguished my head
I want you dead I want you dead
Women who show your public face
I need you dead

An eagle taloned in my head
In Texas Maine or Tennessee
L.A. Detroit or bluegrass country
I want you dead

Who taught our birds Osama's song
Towers of fear fall all year long
Feathers of ash could they be wrong
I want you dead I want you dead

Let me try to be clear about what I am trying to say here: during the ballad, during the sounds of the song, questions deeper than national and political ones rose in me; I came to wonder just what built "Towers of fear" and loosed "Feathers of ash." I'm glad this poem found me, found the writer of my preface. As contributor Richard Deming from Connecticut writes: "These are times that must be defined by a necessary complexity of thinking and feeling: such complexity must be kept possible in order to offer a multiplicity of approaches and responses. One can feel as I do: that I *am* an American, full of grief and anger, but that is not all nor is it enough. The personal act, the act of looking, is where ethics and politics come together. If this confluence is only academic, then the twisted steel girders and debris that bear mute testimony aren't the only wreckage that confronts us now."

Denis Johnson continues:

On Thursday, as I write in New York City, which I happen to be visiting at the time of the attack, the wind has shifted, and a sour electrical smoke travels up the canyons between the tall buildings. I have now seen two days of war in the biggest city in America. But imagine a succession of such days stretching into years—years in which explosions bring down all the great buildings, until the last one goes, or until bothering to bring the last one down is just a waste of ammunition. Imagine the people who have already seen years like these turn into decades—imagine their brief lifetimes made up only of days like these we've just seen in New York

Johnson keeps telling us to *imagine.* Contributor Jay Meek's essay—he's from Michigan—is titled "Imagination As a Democratic Principle."

So, where are we? What can we say, what do? Let us mourn the dead of September 11, 2001. Let us mourn them without qualification. They were mostly Americans, but they were also from dozens of other countries, and they were murdered. And our hearts go out to their families, friends, lovers, colleagues. We mourn the dead, and must not use them for political agendas they might not endorse. They lived among us, we knew them, we'll remember them and the day they died as best we're able, as best we're able despite our capacious ability to forget. Emerson mourned what he phrased the "evanescence and lubricity" of the human condition even as we try to hold to something as piercing as grief.

The dead all knew, during their last seconds alive, what was most important in being human. We can hear eight of them in a remarkable poem by Fred Moramarco of California called "Messages From the Sky: September 11, 2001." The poet draws on farewells reported in the *New York Times.* We can hear what may be the only essence of ourselves that we can take with us to our graves. The poem concludes with summary and then the simple cell phone words of Daphne Bowers:

> To mothers and
> wives, to husbands and friends, to
> fathers and lovers, to brothers and
> sisters, to aunts and uncles, to the
> inert tapes of answering machines:
> Love from the towers, Love from the
> planes, from the towers and the
> planes, Love and again, love,
> "I love you Mommy, goodbye."

Yes, we knew this, didn't we? And now it is seared into us, this fragile being of ours, with love as our hope and our bulwark. We mourn the dead. And many writers tell us that they will try to live better, deeper, because of "that day"— we'll always refer to it as "that day."

But—and how I love the word "but," its complications, its realizations that there is more to this—and how I love the word "maybe"—educational institutions should cherish these words—but maybe there is such a thing as responsible commemoration, too. Our mourning is simple and sincere, but we must come to realize that it is not enough just to shout "God Bless America" and go about business, *business* as usual. We are subjected to so much claptrap and nonsense, so many platitudes, that we can lose all sense of balance. Thoreau called for an "austere accountability" in our lives. Something is wrong, something is so obviously wrong that we may all perish of it. Black novelist John A. Williams from New Jersey writes, "These days my soul feels like lead. I don't know how many times those television pictures rerun of their own volition through my memory. Sometimes my eyes grow tears and my soul groans in pain, tells me quite distinctly, *"You know this didn't have to happen! How many* next *time, stupid? All you have to be,* must *be, is fair!"*... His *soul* tells him this, and he has the whole history of slavery and oppression in his mind. *How many next time, stupid?* he asks. I'm sure that you, as I do, fear that a whole football stadium of people will be wiped out, or a car bomb in a tunnel will bring a river down to drown tens of thousands. All our tanks and soldiers, be they as numerous as sandgrains on a beach, cannot prevent this. Only our sincere desire to help others (and we *do* often show evidence of this desire—as we wish to raise people's standard of living, and to free women, for example), and our ceasing our exploitation of them for oil and money, can prevent this.

And here's writer David Watson from Michigan: "The September 11 cataclysm risks becoming the iconic estheticization of American disaster and suffering in a world where the disaster and suffering of others are not only daily affairs, but in fact, essential consequences of imperial economic plunder and military domination from which American elites, and to some lesser degree the majority of people of the advanced industrial world of the West, benefit." "…. our claims to innocence, justice, and reason are deeply flawed." "Iconic estheticization"—I had this phrase in mind as on evenings surrounding the first anniversary of 9/11 I viewed an art show in response to the attacks, and took part in a candlelight procession. Do we do these things, in part, to try to balance the disgust many of us feel over an increasingly decadent lewd thug/pimp/gangsta/porno culture we are forcing down others' throats? Jack Matthews from Ohio finds this culture largely responsible for "that great infamy of darkness that fell out of the sky on September 11th." But he says, "With thoughtfulness, determination, and luck, we might reverse time and become more like the *early* Romans, leaving behind the decadence, vulgarity, and moral entropy of their final centuries as they rotted into fecklessness and desuetude."

Love in us. And the need for, desire for, *justice* ... in our souls, our consciences, our genes. Love and justice, those verities. When I was in the 6th grade I was standing quietly in line waiting to go out the classroom door to lunch when there was a commotion behind me. A teacher I loved came over and cuffed the back of my head and told me to be quiet. How fast tears broke out in me, how angry and upset I was. As a lesson to me, I'll never forget this brief childhood moment of injustice, a key moment in my life. Imagine much greater, consequential injustices going on for generations. Writer Douglas Unger from California who since the 1998 downing of Pan American Flight 103 over Lockerbie, Scotland has served as memorialist and spokesperson for Syracuse University, which lost so many, offers this general definition of terrorism, one that every high school and college class should study and debate and filter and add to in terms of the world situation now:

> Terrorism is a tactic of desperation directed against what is perceived to be an inflexible, powerful authority, without appeal to law or any existing social contract, in the perceived absence of any forum for expressing real grievances with a voice that will be heard. Terrorism is a form of violence of last resort, born of rage and frustration, arising from the conviction that there is no other choice.

"Born of rage and frustration," Unger says. And perhaps born of what *else*?—religious fanatacism, another brand of oppression: witness the Taliban. Religions—always the sand in the gear of my thinking, and I consider myself a religious person. Contributor Philip Appleman from Indiana and New York reminds us:

> So we now live in a world where Catholics are killing Protestants (and vice versa) in Ireland, where Muslims are killing Hindus (and vice versa) in India, where Hindus are killing Buddhists (and vice versa) in Sri Lanka, where Muslims are killing Christians (and vice versa) in Egypt and Algeria and Azerbaijan and Nigeria, where Roman Catholics are killing Orthodox Christians (and vice versa) in the former Yugoslavia, where Sunni Muslims are killing Shiites in Iraq, and Shiites are killing Baha'is in Iran—to name only a few examples of contemporary religious bloodshed. And now, of course, the lethal faith-based initiative of September 11, and our retaliatory bombing, with its increasing numbers of the inevitable innocent victims.

Douglas Unger adds this warming: "The current crime and punishment response to fight terrorism can only lead—as it almost always has in modern history—to a further spiraling of violence and more terror, which is precisely the reaction the terrorists themselves wish to achieve." Sharon Doubiago writes of Jesus:

> He wasn't a Christian. He didn't say
> God Bless America. God bless our might.

> He said blessed be the meek. He said
> blessed be the merciful. He said
> blessed be the peacemakers.

She tells us that during the weeks after September 11, before we started bombing, she read the "Sermon on the Mount" again for the first time since she memorized it as a girl. "How profoundly, like from a trumpet," she says, "those words seemed directed at our so-called Christian government preparing for 'a long, difficult war.'"

But these of course are subjects for four years of study, a lifetime's study, and not for my brief talk … Wendell Berry from Kentucky points out that we have "several national military academies, but not one peace academy. We have ignored the teachings and the examples of Christ, Gandhi, Martin Luther King, and other peaceable leaders. And here we have an inescapable duty to notice also that war is profitable, whereas the means of peaceableness, being cheap or free, make no money." … Why shouldn't our educational institutions, whatever we study, become peace academies?… Terry Tempest Williams from Utah says: "Seismic shift. A shift in consciousness. Is this too much to imagine? Do we have the strength to see this wave of destruction as a wave of renewal?… This is my prayer," she says: "to gather together, to search freely without judgment, to question and be questioned, to love and be loved, to feel the pulse, this seismic pulse—it will guide us beyond fear."

One contribution came in that made me laugh until I cried. Al Hellus is from Michigan. His brief essay may be the one moment of comic relief in these 450 pages. September 11 was his birthday. He woke up that morning, cut his foot in a freak accident, then heard the news. Even while he wrote his piece, he says, workers were "cleaning up the debris and identifying corpses and body parts." His reaction, too, speaks for what many of us felt that day:

> Nor do I mean in any way to make light of the horror
> perpetrated here by, no getting around it, no other words in my
> personal vocabulary for it, some goddamned crazyass genuinely
> twisted sons-of-bitches. I know, as a poet, I'm supposed to be
> more elegantly articulate than that, but sometimes there's
> nothing for it but the talk of the streets, the bars and alleyways.
> And there's poetry in that, too. And I find myself with nothing
> quite as elegant and articulate to say than: Fuck Them. And I
> mean that from the bottom of my broken heart.

Hellus concludes, "And I'll tell you what: I'm damn well moving my birthday to an undisclosed location under an assumed name."

How moved I was, too, to read Naomi Shihab Nye's contribution—she's from Texas—her letter "To Any Would-Be Terrorists." She describes herself an

"Arab-American"—her father was a Palestinian— and tells aspiring terrorists that she is "humble in my country's pain and I am furious." She reminds them that "Many of the people killed in the World Trade Center probably believed in a free Palestine and were probably talking about it all the time." As the terrorists' cousin, she begs them to listen: "We can't understand, unless you tell us in words. Killing people won't tell us. We can't read that message." She asks them to "make our family proud."

Tammam Adi is from Oregon, is a Muslim married to an American. He says, "I am a Muslim from the George Washington Mosque!" He says, "I am a Muslim from the Thomas Jefferson Mosque!" Listen to his *inclusion*, the love and justice here, as he echoes even the Beatles!

> I am an American Muslim.
> I believe in God. Allah is God.
> The God of peace and justice.
> I believe in Moses, Jesus, Muhammad and all the prophets.
> I believe in the Torah, the Gospel, the Quaran and all the scriptures.
> Thomas Jefferson believed in God.
> But he knew that despots always used the clergy.
> I believe "there is no god but God."
> It means "be free and help others be free."
> It means "no clergy in government."
> It means "get rid of monopoly and oppression.
> I am a Muslim from the Thomas Jefferson Mosque….
>
> I love the star-spangled banner.
> A star for Texas, a star for Iowa, a star for New York,
> A star for Iraq, a star for Iran, a star for Afghanistan,
> A star for Palestine, a star for Israel,
> A star for Russia, a star for China.
>
> A star for Jesus, a star for David, a star for Muhammad.
> A star for Buddha, a star for Krishna, a star for the Great Spirit.
>
> A star for Abraham Lincoln, a star for Mahatma Ghandi,
> A star for John F. Kennedy, a star for Robert Kennedy,
> A star for Martin Luther King, a star for Malcolm X,
> A star for Yitzhak Rabin, a star for Anwar Sadat,
> A star for John Lennon.
>
> A star for 9/11.
> A star for you and me.

We need a bigger flag.
We'll make a bigger flag.
Come together, right now, over you.
We'll all shine on. Like the moon and the stars and the sun.
On and on and on.

Norbert Krapf from New York invokes the ghost of the greatest American poet, Walt Whitman, who labored as a nurse during our Civil war, who saw piles of amputated limbs outside a surgery tent at Fredericksburg. Krapf fully understands how September 11 threatened/threatens to obliterate the spiritual, the transcendental in our lives. As he communes with Walt, his is a prayer for the same unitary experience that Adi asks for:

Come back to smoking Manahatta, Father Walt, where you walked the streets
with immigrants from many lands and rode the onmibus and listened
    to Italian opera
and American folk songs and applauded the singer and ferried back to Brooklyn,
convince us the lilac will blossom again and release its fragrance into the air,
help us believe the mockingbird will trill and caper and the hermit thrush sing
and children will smile, shout and play in these streets and parks again.

Come back, implore the wounded moon to pour her mysterious
    ministrations on us,
petition the splendid silent sun to come out and shine long while wounds heal,
teach us a language that rises into prayer as we lift one another,
help us not to fear our grief as we remember the thousands lost,
look over us as we read the poem-prayers that inform our resolve
to become larger than before, open-hearted, strong, wise, patient,
keep waiting for us in the grass that grows beneath our boot-soles.

I'll conclude with these inspiring words from writer Scott Russell Sanders from Indiana:"We are all now more deeply acquainted with the night than we were at dawn on September 11. The night is real, it is powerful, it is frightening, but it is not the final truth. Every good impulse in your heart tells you that life is larger than death, that love is stronger than hate. Cling to that knowledge, and carry it with you as medicine for your wounds."

The Colon

March 19, 2003. On the day we begin our second war against Iraq, I read something in the newspaper that is new to me: "The Colossal Colon—a 40-foot crawl-through model of the large intestine—has begun its 20-city nationwide tour."

After months of national and international debate, from the left and from the right & from who-knows-where-else, after the protests & rallies of support & poets' peace websites & email campaigns, tens of millions of us are worn out with sadness &/or frustration / patriotism / rage / resignation / disgust / confusion / pride / fear & a sense of Yogi's déjà vue all over again. What is responsible citizenship now as our pilots and our laser-satellite guided missiles dispatch dictator Saddam & his cohort & countless innocent collaterals to hell in a *Götterdämmerung* of flaming oil & blood?

A dozen years ago, on sabbatical & watching television, I wrote *Ribbons: The Gulf War*, a sequence of 41 poems. I've read this book a few times since. I probably can't be a disinterested bystander, but it still seems to hold what I have inside me to witness, &, as the cranky master of Walden insists, the news is always the same. In the 10th section I report,

> I walked out into the Brockport woods & vomited.
> We are killing Iraqis by the thousands,
> burying them with bombs, blowing their limbs off.
>
> Only transcendent poetry is not deluded,
> its karma perfect, but no one, today, can write it,
> not Whitman, or Rilke, or Rumi, or Mirabai—only God
>
> in God's spacelessness & timelessness says
> moment by moment whether any life still lives
> in us, the slaughterers, or in our slaughtered.

Long Shot (2004).

"Its karma perfect," I say. Transcendent poetry. Maybe the Colossal Colon is the agent I've been waiting for. Now beginning its nationwide tour, it "depicts Crohn's disease, diverticulosis, ulcerative colitis and polyps in various stages." I would like to crawl through this large intestine. I would like my president & the Iraqi dictator & the French & German & Chinese & Russian & North/South Korean & Indian & Pakistani purveyors of weapons of mass murder & all fanatics of all persuasions—Reverend Falwell who blamed 9/11/01 on homosesuals, Osama bin Laden who could have used his enormous wealth for education & health care, extreme right-wing Israelis who will not stop building settlements in disputed Palestinian territories unto conflagration of the entire Middle East, Islamic fundamentalists who would continue to attack Israel even should Israel withdraw from Gaza and the whole of the West Bank, the Catholic/Protestant adversaries of Northern Ireland—I would like them all to crawl through this colon to see these karmic diseases in action. I would like us all down on our hands & knees steeped in human cess, feces & gristle, as the corpse-odor of greed & righteousness & war is pumped in. We're told that "the Colossal Colon spares nobody's sense of propriety or comfort: the exit includes hemorrhoids the size of the visitor's head." Coming out into light & fresh air again, maybe we'd be visited with a sense of global community, resolved to ingest healthful foods & the clear water of decency/forbearance/understanding. Maybe we would purge ourselves of the vicious gods in our minds & innards.

Frogress

Someone writing a thesis wrote to ask me if my nature poetry had been influenced by writings ascribed to Hermes Trismegistus, by Jacob Boehme, and by other occultists, hermeticists and mystics I'd only read sketchily, if at all. Because of certain experiences I've had since childhood, I've always been interested in mysticism, and read in graduate school William James' *Varieties of Religious Experience*, Saint John of the Cross, Rudolf Otto's *The Idea of the Holy*, Evelyn Underhill's *Mysticism: A Study of Man's Spiritual Consciousness*, and other related books, so I thought seriously about the questions, but then wrote back as best I could to say that I thought my nature poetry had actually been influenced, primarily, by nature.

The question of influence is of course complex. Each of us has his or her language-vision from myriad sources—a parent's voice, an angle of architecture, morning light on room furnishings, the shape and timbre of our own body as we grow, the smell of oatmeal or woodsmoke or leather jacket, a green troll under a bridge pictured in a grammar school reader. But in my case, all came together, I believe, with my experience in the woods and especially at the ponds of my boyhood Long Island. I spent months of hours staring, always staring, always on the verge of seeing, sometimes seeing. At the ponds, I first realized whatever my later writings, by way of their language (which in poetry is the fusion of rhythm, image, intuitional idea, sound, etc.), come to discover or suggest about nature, about human and natural relationships.

I believe that when I grabbed my net and fishing pole and biked to Gibbs Pond in Nesconset in old Suffolk County—I was seven-eight-nine-ten-eleven—I lived almost primally, almost wordlessly, virtually forgetting about school and my stucco home a couple miles away. I lost myself, lost my self in hypnotic gazing, in pondwater and plant creatures, insect creatures, fish and reptile creatures, loving the excitation of my fear and awe, of my human solitude. I was thrilled. My head and heart filled with the profusion and balance and perfection of so much being, so much beauty.

I mention my own experience not to report my virtue or special sensitivity, but my luck. Walt Whitman's "There Was a Child Went Forth" is his early testimony of communion, of absorbing and being absorbed. If I feel what he describes, it is in large part because I have had his experience: "And the fish suspending themselves so curious below there, and the beautiful curious liquid, /

And the water-plants with their graceful flat heads, all became part of him." In *Wisdomkeepers*, a book of photographs of and interviews with Native American elders, the Seneca Corbett Sundown, falling into a trance says, "Things come into me.... The falling leaves ... the stars ... I watch them move ... they come into me." However much I sometimes now because of the dead ends and blind alleys of my western education lose the essential, as child I realized and knew and inhaled that buzzing and blooming and breathing life beyond my own ego. If somehow I sometimes get lucky and a frog or pike or snapping turtle or dragonfly in my poetry concentrates and vibrates in dimensions beyond the linguistic and empirical, it is not because I've read Emmanuel Swedenborg on amphibians or seen a photograph of the Sioux warrior Crazy Horse's shield cover on which there are two dragonflies—though such readings or sightings can spring poems loose for me—but because by long-staring into nature's eyes I came to an emotional knowledge that abides in me and that pressures the exhalation of my saying.

I was seven or eight years old just before mid-century when the first television, a 10" black and white Philco, came into our house. I saw "Howdy Doody" (with the silent clown Clarabelle who could only honk, and with the Indian Princess Summer-Fall-Winter-Spring). I saw the news with John Carmeron Swayze, saw some boxing and Charlie Chan mysteries, saw the Lone Ranger series with faithful Tonto, always watched "Crusade in Europe," laughed with Milton Berle and Red Buttons and Groucho Marx, saw the Ed Sullivan show when Elvis sang "Loving You," but my vital life was still lived outdoors, even in winter when I walked the woods killing black-capped chickadees and sparrows with my Daisy rifle, then feral cats and squirrels with my .22. I grew away from that stupid and basically motiveless killing—it was just play-acting and target practice—because it made me feel sick-at-heart. Without words for it, I knew I was destroying something that should have belonged to itself, to that mysterious presence felt in nature, imbued with that same spirit I felt in me in this Nesconset on this fish-shaped island that we inhabited.

In *The Primal Mind: Vision and Reality in Indian America*, Jamake Highwater argues early on, and this is the basis for everything he says in this luminous book, that "if someone does not experience an aesthetic relationship to what is before him or her, all the information and education will not permit that person to cross the distance that exists between different peoples and, for that matter between different individuals of the same technological society." This "aesthetic relationship": perceiver (poet) with perceived, reader with the poem that embodies aesthetically-felt nature. (Is *being there* absolutely necessary, direct personal sensory experience? No: we know that imagination and/or dream and/or even intense reading sometimes evoke the authority and authenticity, the believability we insist on in the poem.)

But now listen to this stunning experience that Sven Birkert recounts in his *The Electric Life: Essays on Modern Poetry*. He describes something he learned while teaching a freshman writing course at Harvard:

I was talking about language, etymology, and the ways in which a poet's use of language differs from that of other users. I observed that all of us, however subliminally, have a charged feeling for certain primary words, and that each of these words represents an original "breakthrough" experience. There was perhaps a moment, I said, when the word-sound "tree" first fused meaningfully with our perception of the branched and bark-covered entity in front of us. At this point I noticed that a number of hands had gone up. One after the next they nodded and confirmed me: Yes, they knew what I was getting at. They could remember Big Bird on *Sesame Street* bringing them the images and names of the things in their world. Further questioning seemed to confirm it: A substantial portion of their language acquisition had been by way of television. They had not learned the names of many of the things in the so-called real world; they had learned the names of the images of those things.

Surely it is apparent that for any society to nurture its children's inborn love of the beautiful—and I assume here, Romantic that I've been, though it sounds a shade too utilitarian and anthropocentric, the validity of Emerson's seed-bed assertion in *Nature* that "nature exists to satisfy the soul's desire for beauty"—that society will require more than what television or other imaging technologies can give us.

Highwater says that the most complicated lesson of his life has to do with words and the ideas they convey. Realizing—making real for ourselves—what needs to be realized, he says, is especially difficult if we grow up "insulated by a single culture and its single language." For example, growing up Indian, colliding with and being impelled backward by the dominant white culture, he learned the confusing fact that the creature signified and living for him in his word "meksikatski," a word used by the Blackfeet people for thousands of years, had a different sound and word in English, "duck." Highwater doesn't elaborate on the sound-poem "meksikatski," but it must of course be onomatopoetic in ways that "duck" is not, must hold countless generations of life experiences within its syllables. Our "duck" goes back to Old and Middle English, and I can hear in it a swift breaking of the surface of water, and even comical quickness, but "meksikatski!"... What experiential sensory fullness there must be in this word! As Emerson says, in the beginning every word was a poem, and there must be a primal symphony in this one. And the creature signified is in turn by this word assumed to be, imagined to be, created to be a more meaningful and complex and living part of our world than that signified by "duck." It's not that every Blackfeet word would have an English or French or German word beat—European words, too, of course, go back into a natural pre-history—but, in this case, Highwater's whole sensibility was obviously the richer, and the world the more honored, and his relationships with nature more complex, for the poem "meksikatski."

Maybe the fact that my parents spoke German and I was often around other German-speaking relatives helped me at least a little to stay awake to the otherness of the world. If a turtle was a *Shildkröter*—a shell creature—and if there were apparently other words for it in other languages, I must have sensed that the beings I saw at the ponds were not completely pinned down and summed up by such sound-designations but were what I saw and felt and smelled—O how even baby snappers just out of their leathery eggs smelled—them to be. Throw in some Latin and Spanish in high school—courses I did poorly in—some reading of French in graduate school, and non-linguist that I am I'm still intellectually and soulfully sure now that these life forms are not aware that they are "turtles," that what I call turtles are mysterious beings far beyond any human culture's ability to capture them decisively and thereby limit them with a name. I have seen Iroquois box turtle rattles six-eight centuries old, but do not know what the Iroquois called these yellow and brown-black plated wanderers. But in memory when I stand still in the woods, I can hear a box turtle foraging among bracken and leaf-litter; when I stand still for long enough at Gibbs Pond, I can hear and see a painted turtle climb back onto its log; when I reach a stick toward a big cess-smelling snapper that I've dragged to shore, I can hear it hiss as it strikes, its neck unfolding outward much further than I'd thought it could. The Blackfeet "meksikatski"— the memories and ideas in a word, the poetry, cannot be exhausted. But you, Jamake Highwater, must learn to speak in a civilized manner if we have to fire our words into you with a Gatling gun: *duckduckduckduckduck.*

I know that my response to that thesis writer smacked of impatience and petulance, as do my paragraphs here, but imagine, then, what has happened to us if we come to our language not by way of sense experience in the woods and at ponds or in the forests or on the plains or on city streets, but by way of television and computer screens where the word "tree" refers to a picture. How much is lost to us? Birkerts says, "We can't even begin to assess the deeper psychic implications of that information," but surely we can. Language divorced from our experience of the physical world will not enable us to live in a way, to conceive of reality in such a way that we will be able to continue to exist as a part of nature. We will destroy our home without realizing what we're doing and how we're doing it. In this old poem of mine, I seem to come near to something that has been in my mind since I was a child.

The Meeting

Long Island Sound, Crane's Neck
the horizon behind me, I drifted
by rowboat to trenchline: creation
indented the seafloor

to further than anchors could fathom:
my heaviest sinkers were feathers,
my wire billowed outward but down
to something below me I wanted.

Line, hook, & squidweight
arcing away from my sight
into water so green it was black,
into time when the Island was born

when my bait was struck
as though by a swimming rock
that swept it under my boat
to the cave of the glacier & back,

but I reeled my fear with the line
upward in blood when I cut
a wristvein by whipped wire,
but won the visible meeting

& hauled the six-foot killer
into an oarlock
where its jaws ground metal to blood,
& teeth broke, & my set hook

snapped.... The creature rolled over
in surging water, & blended,
turned its walleyes upward,
almost milky, almost opal,

but black-flashed, empty,
almost translucent, blank,
nature's gaze without language,
our eyes lit by the same sun,

as our stare went wild
from glacier to brain, & back, until
I touched my blood to the oarlock
in respect, & the shark descended.

"Nature's gaze without language," the poem says. There seems to be a
realization here, human eye to nature's eye, that our most primal experiences must

be wordless, but there must be *contact*. And I wish I knew the right word, the inclusive word for my "respect" in the last line: my speaker feels regret, awe, recognition, some kind of primal sympathy. Maybe my phrase "in respect" should be "in memoriam."

Meanwhile, in a SONY television commercial we see a television set perched on a ledge over the Grand Canyon. The image on that imaged television's screen is what we see behind it, the Canyon itself (which presumably exists somewhere in nature). Now parents with their young son (or, rather, images of parents with their young son) enter stage center and sit down in front of the television, their backs to us, to stare at the Grand Canyon on screen while the Canyon itself becomes—we can be sure—unreal in or disappears from their imaginations. The commercial implies that the screen image is as appealing, as vivid, as awe-inspiring, as necessary, as *real* as the tangible/palpable world, and perhaps preferable to the geologic *Ding an sich.*

Whole dimensions are missing on that television screen. Most of the time, we sit slack-jawed and eyes-glazed-over in front of it. To associate the word "frog" with a photograph or film of a frog, or a TV actor in a frog suit, is to be unaware of the slippery glistening frogness of that amphibian's skin in your palms and fingers, the glop of its jump, the way it hides itself in a trail of silt as it returns underwater to shore. Much is lost when we dissect one of those formaldehyde deadnesses in biology lab, but even this study adds to the depth of the signifying frogword for us. Sometimes I knew a frog was hiding near the notch of a lily pad just by the tiny ripples emitted by its throat-pulse. Countless times, I've watched a turtle chew on a frog. I've smashed frogs with my bare feet to get the air out of them so that they'd sink, and baited hooks with them, and dragged big bullheads and snappers to shore with them. I've dipped my hands into their gelatinous spawn. I've tasted a frog's blood—it tastes cerise and salty and 160 million years old—frogs have probably been around this long, were eaten by and crushed underfoot by dinosaurs. After cutting off a frog's legs, I've run my tongue into its sinews. And still there were hundreds, thousands of them yelping everywhichway as I waded the ponds. What does a child have of the world when he or she sees on television the printed word FROG and then the image of a stereotypical harrumpher? Not much. Nothing of its pond-life, its winter sleep, its long tongue that plucks flies out of the air, the leech under its armpit, the film over its underwater eyes, its asshole, the countless shades of its green, its weight, its twilight croak when it survives through pollywog stages (that word *pollywog* seems to wiggle as the creature does as it swims) to become one of the big ones. What to make of that parable of the bored frogs in their Edenic pond who prayed for divine visitation until they were granted first a log—too passive—and then, in perverse answer to their long entreaty for a deity more forceful and dramatic, a voracious crane, unless we've been among the population boom of hatched tadpoles and the leg-growers upward in their evolution in our minds until we associate with them or impose on them some of our own desires and restlessnesses and stupidities so that we can laugh at ourselves, instruct ourselves, warn ourselves by way of them even as we know that frogs are frogs are frogs and in the saying know that the word is a useful and perhaps mnemonic and suggestive and expressive sound, sure, while the named creature itself is myriad with secrets as it breathes with Time and the spheres?

Frogress: I watched an hour-long television documentary on amphibians of the world, and this was instructive; I've seen various frogs in the various zoos, including, in a rain-forest exhibit in Germany, a bright blue beauty whose skin was deadly, and I've retained more from this close-up seeing; I caught one tree frog from a catalpa leaf when I was a boy on Long Island, touched it and stared at it before placing it back on its leaf where it immediately disappeared, and this experience was better still; I've handled thousands of pondfrogs and this was best.

David Day's *Vanished Species*, a book first published in 1981, reports the extinction of two species of the frog family. One was the Palestinian Painted Frog which was "obliterated through large-scale land-reclamation by the Israelis." The Painted Frog "was ochre and rusty coloured above and greyish-black below, with numerous white dots around its glandular orifice." It was only discovered in 1940, the year I was born, and we know little about it. Apparently active at night, it spent the day burrowed in sand with its head just protruding from water, adapting to shallow swamps now filled for crops and homes.... The second of these, the Vegas Valley Leopard Frog, was last seen in 1942 and was declared extinct in 1966. Its illustration looks like one species of frog I knew, but it "differed externally from other Leopard Frogs in its very faint (or absent) spotting, and in the absence of the usual white jaw-stripe." Las Vegas needed its water.

When fossil fuels have gotten me to that sleepless desert city to play poker, I've enjoyed Vegas water in many ways, have watched pirates in front of the "Treasure Island" casino fight above waves of it, have showered in it and have soaked in tubs of it. I am not disconnected from the extinction of the Vegas Valley Leopard Frog, but responsible, a participant, and I didn't do the Long Island frog species any good, either. I am poised here, and lethal, me with my suburban home and SUV that can get me to my childhood ponds—those that have not been asphalted over—or to the Grand Canyon in the first place, between frog and water.

I've been trying to hear, to appraise, a poem of mine, written fifteen or twenty years ago. Ezra Pound called for poetry that is "austere, direct, free from emotional slither." In "A Jar" I seem to try to begin objectively, with factual recounting, but then color my plot in romantic ways that interest but worry me.

A Jar

Each noon, at the construction site around the corner
from my own wooded suburban acre,
I checked progress: the bigger trees—almost all ash,

a few maple, one white oak—chainsawed, dragged out
by dozer and chain; then dozer back in for clearing brush;

then dozer, backhoe, and ten-ton roller to cut
foundation-, drainage-, and sewer-pipe patterns
into subsoil and clay, to pack dirt so it would never shift.
Day by day, in drizzle or shower, hot sun
or one sudden out-of-season jet stream shift to chill,

the men widened the site's geometric margins
to where, in one corner, piles of trucked-in-sand
diminished a twenty-foot puddle filled for weeks
with thousands of tadpoles just beginning
to grow legs and lose their tails. The time would come,

of course, to fill this last swale. Meanwhile,
the polliwog population prospered in this lukewarm
algae-sweetened pond of their world....
And then was gone, all at once, their birthplace leveled
with sand and a few inches of good topsoil

over which we walked. That was that, except
for this, the one thing, the thing in itself:
how, at about this time, our species began to document
amphibians' disappearance across the globe;
how marshes and swamps were growing silent;

and how, an actor in our sentimental elegy, one worker
placed in his tool chest to take home at quitting time
a jar filled with muddy water and a host of tadpoles,
little blips of sperm-shaped black light. To catch them,
he must have knelt and cupped them in his palms.

The speaker of my poem tells us that a construction worker has gathered
some tadpoles to take with him, probably to show his kids, we suspect. It seems
to me that "A Jar" may primarily be about not the fact of the disappearance of
amphibians, or about development, or about that worker—though it is about all
these—but about the sentimental construct the speaker creates from/imposes on all
of this. Just what is "the thing in itself" for him? He uses the word "host" to
describe the tadpoles, calls them "little blips of sperm-shaped black light," and
imagines that the worker, "To catch them, ... must have knelt and cupped them in
his palms." Is his last sentence insipid with reverence? (The reverentially insipid
is a tone I've noticed in some contemporary nature poetry.) He calls our whole

relationship with the fact of our diminishing world a "sentimental elegy," but then, it seems to me, participates, by way of his language and story, in this same conflicted way. Does he know that he does this? In my non-austere, emotional rush, I didn't consciously sense this softness when I wrote and first published the poem. Many of my poems may be jars of tadpoles I've knelt to gather. Shown to children who are absorbed by polliwogs within the transparent water of television, they will surely perish. Meanwhile, what continues is "the one thing, the thing in itself," whatever that is, probably the whole complex of themes in my poem's book, its pond, *Pterodactyl Rose*.

Consider the species of frog whereof I speak. I like the way it can croak and jump at the same time. Consider its ungainly symmetry and the way it wedges itself into its element when it swims, its front legs just trailing, its back legs strong, its toes webbed to a miracle of evolved efficiency when it pushes back, closed when it draws legs back to body. Consider the holes in the roof of its mouth—I've felt these holes with my fingertips—into which its eyes roll downward when it swims. Consider that frogs are not allegorical signs, standing for maybe this or maybe that for the inexperienced mind. Consider that inside each frog there are mountains and temples, glints of nebulae. Consider that they are, of course, what ecologists call an indicator species, now warning us, by their demise around the world, of what is in store for us. Consider how it will be as rare for the coming generations of our own species to see a frog in its natural habitat as it is for us now to see a tiger in the wild. Consider how it will not go well for our poetry/for us unless it goes well for the "meksikatski" whose body, apparently cannot sufficiently filter out the human-produced poisons that are killing it.

Fana Al-Fana

How could it be that my older brother, my childhood protector and lifelong friend, no longer exists? How could it possibly be that if I drove to Mountainhome, Pennsylvania, in the Poconos where he lived I would not find him in his home and be able to talk with him? Werner, a prodigious smoker, died of cancer on April 16, 2003. He was 65. I'd seen him in his hospital bed in Scranton about two weeks before. I thought I'd see him at least once more. A line by John Berryman keeps ringing in me: "All the bells say: too late."

My wife and I had spent April 14-15 at Lawrence Academy in Groton, Massachusetts, where I'd met with students and faculty and given readings. On the morning of the 16th, we were driving south to Mountainhome when we heard by cell phone that he'd died a few hours before. We veered east to Long Island to break the news to my old mother, spent three days with her. Werner's widow, Barbara, arranged for a memorial service for him in Hampton Bays. Werner had retired from the Southampton Town Police Department, and many of his friends were there. He was laid out in his lieutenant's uniform. I knew, saying goodbye to him, to his mortal remains, I'd break down. I waited to kneel at his coffin until almost everyone had left. And then I was lost in the ancient wild lament of death.

Our father had died six years before. And I'd grieved the passing— "passing" is a faithful word, one that suggests movement from one mode of being to another—of publisher and close friend William B. Ewert in 2001, of Brockport poet friends Al Poulin and Anthony Piccione in 1996 and 2001. But it may be that for each of us there is one death that is *the* death, and for me this death, so far, has been Werner's. All the old consolations of religion that have been veils for me since I was a boy now console very little. One morning I found myself in a sudden gust of weeping during which I was repeating to myself, "He really loved me, he really loved me, he really loved me." I was mourning, of course, for myself as much as I was for him and his family. I've never forgotten the lesson in Gerard Manley Hopkins' sermonic "Spring and Fall." Whatever we believe the source of our earthly sorrows to be, as the seasons pass it is ourselves we mourn for. Yes, it was Werner's brother Bill I was grieving, the decades that had wisped

---

An update of the 1989 essay "Home" for Gale Research Company's *Contemporary Authors: Autobiography Series* (2004).

away from him as he sped toward his own death. But, too, I really loved/love Werner.

Since retirement from teaching at 59 in 2000, I've been that cliché, a retiree so busy that he wonders how he ever had time to work. I've been catching up with myself: three new books have appeared in 2003, three more will appear in 2004 including a collection of thirty years of essays called *Home: Autobiographies, Etc.* and a book of stories with one of my best titles: *The Hummingbird Corporation*. This is a time of harvest for me. I miss teaching not at all, though I do think about the money I could still be earning, money my wife and I can get along without but which could have gone into college accounts for our four grandchildren. But their parents are doing well, and I was getting sappy from classes and busywork and quit at the right time. At the end, even when about to meet with a dozen of Brockport's best students in an advanced poetry class, students who would go on to MFA programs at NYU, George Mason, Eastern Washington and elsewhere, I still wanted out of there. Well, I began teaching when I was 20. In addition to my regular classes over the years, I'd read or lectured at about 250 other universities and elsewhere. And I had a writing life that more and more created and defined the person I had become.

But for this son of a blue-collar worker, retirement was *still* a difficult decision, psychologically complex, mixed in with feelings of unworthiness and failure and the fear that I'd be lost and might for one reason or another find myself with only blank pages in front of me. I wrote to poet Phil Levine about this. In maybe the most helpful letter I've ever received he replied, in part, "There's no way someone else is going to write your poetry or you're going to stop writing it. By now it's obvious: you're in for the long haul."

If I hadn't retired, I'd have been beginning classes again in the fall of 2001. There's no chance I'd have been able to edit *September 11, 2001: American Writers Respond* which appeared in 2002 and which gathered raw and immediate reactions from 125 creative writers to the events of that watershed day in our history. The psychic disequilibrium at that time, especially among poets, seemed almost palpable to me, and necessary, and right. My thoughts had been inchoate about poetry and politics for years, I'd gone as far as I could on this theme in an essay on Seamus Heaney in *Pig Notes & Dumb Music* called "At the Gate" in which I argued (no doubt protesting too much) that poems *must* come to be able to stop tanks, I'd written whole books of poetry on the Holocaust and the Gulf War and ecological degradation and the collision of cultures at the Battle of Little Bighorn in 1876, and had wondered why more of my contemporaries weren't similarly disposed to enter and engage history as best they could. Now, seemingly all at once, the climate was as poet David St. John in his essay for *September 11, 2001* described it: [After September 11], "every writer I know was asking himself or herself 'Where now do I fit, where do I belong, against this horrifying landscape?'" Some writers declined my invitation to contribute, some said they would contribute and then for various reasons didn't or couldn't. From across the country, I could hear teeth grinding and brains short out from the shock emanating from Ground Zero in New York City and from the Pentagon and from that field in Pennsylvania where heroes died who kept their death plane from obliterating the Capitol or White House. What could poems and fictions contribute, reveal, warn, prophesy? Could there be a *new* literature of some kind, one *not* relying on the dispensation Heaney assumed to be the very soul and saving grace of poetry? Reading several hundred submissions to my project, scanning poetry web sites devoted to September 11 where I found little beyond the trite and boring, the soporific and the blindly patriotic, I was immersed in questions of aesthetics. I wanted the truth that exists beyond careful thought, beyond what scholars and journalists can give us. And, almost struck dumb myself by the enormity of what had happened, I needed the community of creative writers. I worked hard for months on the anthology, but in the end it has given much more to me than I gave to it.

Segue to another anthology, this one edited by H.L. Hix and called *Wild and Whirling Words: A Poetic Conversation* (2004). It includes a new poem of mine:

Andes Flame

Other sacrificed maidens are found, chipped
from graves in the sacred mountains,
but this one cannot be accessioned,
&, as she thaws, disrobed, a few stitches

at a time. This one remains beautiful, frozen,
my pottery set around her—black & red,
zigzag designs. I chose her, revered her,
died within prayer when I lost her,

but now we are almost gone
to that distance where heat from dead stars
still seeks her beneath my breastbone,
but cannot reach her, ever, love of mine....

In the outer world, skyscrapers flame and fall, the Balkans and Africa and Iraq and the so-called Holy Lands seethe with bloody discontent, corporations run governments by way of their own greed—I am a participant in this as I root for my own pension fund, of course—and sports stars become idols who can get away with rape and murder. But in the end, whatever the poet does with these events is determined, it may be, by his or her deepest personality which in turn is formed by experiences that remain mysterious and which themselves generate such a poem as "Andes Flame." I'd seen a television documentary on such a sacrificial burial as I sketch here. As I wrote the poem—there were many drafts—memories of my high school girlfriend who'd cut herself away from me when we graduated took hold of me. I'm not sure what my poem, in the end, does—maybe it creates its own inviolable place where the speaker's memory leaves the maiden inviolate.

Karin was born in Norway. There's a poem by Norwegian poet Rolf Jacobsen, translated by Robert Bly, called "The Old Women" that begins, "The girls whose feet moved so fast, where did they go? / Those with knees like small kisses...." They've become old now, perhaps even ghosts, but the poet cautions us to be kind to them: "Bow clearly to them and greet them with respect / because they still carry everything with them, like a fragrance...."

Karin and I separated to attend different colleges in 1957. The Dear John letter came—actually it was a phone conversation that still leaves me shaken for that vulnerable boy—over that Christmas vacation. I was heartbroken for a very long time (and sometimes, almost fifty years later, still dream of her). This melodrama continues: I saw her only once more, at a high school reunion on Long Island in 1997. We spoke for just a minute. She'd been married to the same man for thirty-eight years, she said. She'd lived in California. She said she knew I'd become a college professor and a writer, and congratulated me. Self-effacing, she said she'd become only a kindergarten teacher. I remember her blue dress of that occasion (as I remember the dress she wore on our first date when I was sixteen), and I've wondered if she was buried in that dress, for just a couple years ago, surfing the web, I learned that she'd died in 1998 at the age of fifty-eight of lung cancer—did she smoke? did her husband smoke?

I snail mailed and emailed her husband—I'd have liked to have a program from her memorial service. No answer. No matter. I'd even sent 2-3 holiday cards to her and her family in the years after the reunion, but no one took the time to write me a note that Karin had died. No matter. She belongs to them, yes, but belongs to my poem now and to other writings including, in oblique ways, the entire book *Diana, Charles, & the Queen* (1998) sparked by her.

Diana is a book of rhymed double quatrains, 321 of them, three to a page, written before Diana's death. For a long time I've felt that several poets of the generation preceding mine, poets I've admired, had gone soft, had let their lines and whole poems slacken, had begun settling too easily for the easy effect, predictable closure, that their free verse had become too free, that they had lost their passion. I try to guard against this entropy in myself, and it may be that this concern for abiding intensity and control drives the *Diana* poems, this and the sheer fun I was having in using some of my old graduate school English lit book-learning that as I wrote fused in sounds with castles and kings of my childhood imagination and with reading I'd been doing about the current Royals. I'd like to elaborate on this in another essay, but for now, to have it keep "Andes Flame" company, want to show you sort of a vulgar poem, "Diana," that arrived to me 3-4 years after the book it could have been part of was published.

To expiate, once & for all, my own golden girl,
I wrote a poem, & then another.
Soon, I had a couple hundred on the royal single,
her husband, & her husband's mother.

What lies we tell to tell the truth!
I wrote a poem, & then hundreds more until
Di lay back on my bed like a cheerleader
I'd fucked to death.

The heart does not keep time or place, Long Island or California or London. My poems are zig-zag patterns and designs that sound sources I'm afraid to locate entirely in case poetry itself might stop in me.

About five years ago I wrote a love poem, and include it here to try to remind (or maybe convince) myself that I have, in fact, grown up since high school. It traces an experience that might serve in essence as the curve of my whole spiritual life.

Fana Al-Fana

Islamic mystics' *fana al-fana*,
the passing away of the passing away,

as when, last night, my wife of thirty-five years
held me & told me she loved me:

at first, I was afraid, our decades only
rootless light from dead stars,

but then my soul received her words,
& the passing away passed away.

"The name of it is Time, but you must not pronounce its name," says Robert Penn Warren. Yes—a stark realization of our brief span on earth can shock the system. But during our clearest moments, it may be, we realize that timelessness, eternity, too, is obvious, and the fear of death, by way of love, may pass from us.

My brother dead, my old flame dead, but I remain in luck, for now, happily married for more than forty years, children and grandchildren healthy (knock wood), my body still making its way up and down the basketball court two or three times a week. I've slowly begun typing the diary-journal I've kept since 1964—400 single-spaced pages so far, and I'm only into the fourth of thirty-five or so blank books. Despite my best efforts over the years to conceal my lack of admirable character, this personal writing often reveals me to be callow, gauche, naive, petty, and sometimes unfair, at best. But I'm glad that these millions of words of mine exist, and I hope eventually to publish them entire, keeping in mind Walt Whitman's belief that the only obscene book is an expurgated one.

(2003)

About the Author

William Heyen was born in Brooklyn, New York, in 1940. His graduate degrees are from Ohio University. He retired in 2000 from SUNY at Brockport where he was a Professor of English and Poet in Residence. A former Senior Fulbright Lecturer in American Literature in Germany, he has won prizes and fellowships from the NEA, the Guggenheim Foundation, *Poetry*, and the American Academy and Institute of Arts and Letters. His books are listed in front of this volume. His work has also appeared in hundreds of anthologies and in such magazines as *The Southern Review*, *TriQuarterly*, *The New Yorker*, *Harper's*, *The Ontario Review*, *Ploughshares*, *The Ohio Review*, *Kenyon Review*, *American Poetry Review*, and *Michigan Quarterly Review*. He and his wife, Hannelore, live in Brockport near their two children and four grandchildren.

LIVING WITH TEXTILES

LIVING
WITH
TEXTILES

ELAINE LOUIE

MITCHELL BEAZLEY

To Anna

Living with Textiles

by Elaine Louie

First published in Great Britain in 2001 by Mitchell Beazley,
an imprint of Octopus Publishing Group Ltd,
2–4 Heron Quays, London E14 4JP

Copyright © Octopus Publishing Group Ltd 2001

Executive Editor **Mark Fletcher**
Executive Art Editor **Vivienne Brar**
Editor **John Jervis**
Designer **Lovelock & Co.**
Picture Research **Jo Walton**
Production **Nancy Roberts**
Proof reader **Sue Harper**
Index **Hilary Bird**

Text for pp130–139 by Janie Lightfoot
Colour artwork for pp134–139 by Amanda Patton

ISBN 1 84000 387 1

A CIP record for this book is available from the British Library

Set in Stone Sans

Colour reproduction by Sang Choy International PTE LTD, Singapore
Produced by Toppan Printing Co. (HK) Ltd
Printed and bound in China

CONTENTS

INTRODUCTION

Textiles, of both ancient and modern times, make our lives warm, not only physically, but also emotionally and aesthetically. They provide sensuous essentials to our lives. We use textiles to wrap our bodies, to cover our floors, even to canopy our beds. What is a tent, after all, but a home made entirely of textiles? And what is a canopied bed but a tent brought inside?

Whether a textile is densely woven, like a tapestry, or nearly transparent like the finest, most delicate silk, it will enliven and animate our homes. This book, *Living with Textiles,* focuses on textile pieces as drama, art, delight – and function.

Banish the idea of floors covered with grey industrial carpeting, the concept of windows framed by thick brown drapes, or monastic beds dressed with just two pillows and austere woollen blankets. Instead, think of floors covered with ancient 150-year-old hand-woven rugs dyed from madder, the orange-red colours slowly fading, consider windows with curtains billowing in the wind, imagine beds lavished with not two but six cushions covered in printed Indian cotton, perhaps with a quilted covering, or comforter, of the same beguiling print.

Above Here, a quartet of Indian women stand on carpets which are placed around and inside a pavilion and are woven to resemble gardens. A textile hanging around the edge of the pavilion's roof serves as a sunshade, while a carpet is carefully draped over the steps. Textiles play the part of furniture in the pavilion and add the grace note to the outdoor scene.

Left This sculpted gentleman, possibly from north-west India, hardly looks Greek or Roman, but the antique drapery and the graceful folds of cloth hanging on the beam behind him, are decorative motifs of Greek and Roman sculpture. In statuary of rooms, thrones, men and women, not only are the people dressed in cloth, but fabric also appears as canopy, awning, or a throw over a chair or throne. In art, as in life, textiles have a softening influence.

Textiles are treasures of other civilizations that, simply by existing and being positioned on your wall, bed, or floor, enrich your life as the owner. The function of textiles within society has varied widely over the centuries. The earliest known textile, a heavy cord twisted from three two-ply fibre strings, was found in the painted caves of Lascaux, France, and dates from 15,000 BC. According to Elizabeth Wayland Barber in her book *Women's Work: The First 20,000 Years* (W.W. Norton, 1995), people used cords such as these, which were made from the inner bark of a plant, to guide themselves "down the dark and treacherous passage from one gallery of the cave to the other."

Ancient peoples made strings, cords, baskets, and string skirts from wild plants such as flax, hemp, ramie, sisal, elm, and willow. And then, with momentous effect in the history of textile development, by 5,500 BC came the invention of the weaving loom. When the Egyptians built pavilions to shade themselves from the heat and glare of the sun, they made airy mats for the sides of the structures so that breezes could blow through and they wove textiles for the roof.

The Egyptians were weaving linen by 5,000 BC. Two thousand years later, Indian weavers had discovered cotton. And when the Babylonians, in 700 BC, spoke of "trees bearing wool," it was probably a reference to cotton.

Below In this medieval setting, a cluster of women are gathered in a room lavishly decorated with elaborate textiles. Woven hangings warm the walls, with some of them woven with a fleur-de-lys pattern alternating with those designed with a diagonal harlequin pattern. The canopied bed, right, is extravagantly draped with a fabric decorated with a lacy star pattern. The floor is covered with a rug, while the bed, at left, is not canopied but covered with a textile whose warmth entices a tiny dog.

Above Count Dimitri Tolstoi (1823–89) was a reactionary. In Russia, he was the minister of education, where he prohibited revolutionary ideas from being taught, and later, approved the censorship of books. In his country home, he lived as the typical Russian aristocrat. The house, with an inlaid parquet floor, was furnished in cosmopolitan European, Renaissance Revival style. The lavish lace window treatment let in light, provided some privacy, and was a show of expensive material.

Then people discovered animal fibres – wool by around 4,000 BC, and silk around two thousand years later. Both materials proved to be more practical than plant fibres, in that they insulated the wearer better and they accepted dyes more readily, a characteristic that allowed still greater scope for creativity and exploration. Chinese mythology tells the story of a princess, Si Ling-Chi, who was drinking tea outside, when a silk cocoon fell into her teacup. The heat of the liquid enabled her to unwind the unbroken filament of fibre and she eventually learned to process silk.

These new textiles of wool and silk offered further artistic possibilities and stimulated a wealth of creativity and exploration – rugs, tapestries, and bed coverings were created for functional and decorative purposes; people made banners for war, and banners to hang over doors. In France and England, they created screens which they covered with textiles to ward off drafts blowing between one room and another. In Persia, Turkey, and Afghanistan, rugs were draped from the wall over divans and onto the floor. In Nepal – a country without a long tradition of sophisticated furniture – some of the vendors at the open market in Kathmandu sit or squat on rugs, not chairs. Throughout the world, people weave textiles – bridles, harnesses, and saddles – for their animals.

Textiles were not only functional, but they were also a conspicuous sign of wealth and status. They often comprised a proportion of a girl's dowry and, in Palestine, girls first learn to embroider in readiness for this, as young as six years of age. In India, Hindu brides wear red wedding shawls, which the family either embroiders themselves, or, for the intricate work in particular, they instead often employ skilled local artisans.

In China in 1562, Yan Song, a former Grand Secretary, had an inventory made of all his worldly possessions. The textiles alone included 14,331 lengths of fabric (not yet made up into clothing) and 1,304 items of dress. And what could he possibly do with these thousands of pieces of silk satins, gauzes, velvets, and brocades? Silk was currency. Silk was gold.

Textiles do not have to be precious and spun of gold thread to have a universal appeal today. The remnants of a *kilim* can be transformed into a half-dozen cushions, and make even an ordinary divan look exotic. A quilt with a drunkard's path design may be too old to keep you warm, but when hung on the wall, it suddenly takes on a visual dynamism. Grandma's quilt becomes Op Art.

Living with Textiles is intended, above all, to inspire the reader to interact and play with fabrics and textiles – to toss them blithely over sofas, to frame them, even to wrap an entire wall with them. Textiles create mood, they envelop us, and they stimulate our sense of touch. A home, after all, is an idiosyncratic nest.

Below In 1919, Walter Gropius, the German-born architect, became the director of the Bauhaus – the school of design that nurtured ideas of International Modernism. In the mid 1920s, the Bauhaus moved from Weimar to Dessau, where Gropius designed the buildings, including the study shown below. In keeping with the Bauhaus aesthetic, which was anti-historical, Gropius showed off the modern wares – the carpets and wall hangings – produced in the school's textile workshops.

MODERN

When the twentieth century ushered in Modernism, leading architects such as Le Corbusier and Walter Gropius believed that form should follow function. They called for the suppression of ornament and historical allusions and styles. They wanted honest materials used economically, and Le Corbusier famously defined the home as "a machine for living in." The modern home, as it has evolved over the last hundred years, is usually one composed of clean, spare lines and filled with natural light. Walls are often white, floors often of of gleaming wood, and windows plentiful. Homes have become visually simple, hygienic, and pristine.

"It all became cold and boring and repetitious," according to Kate Carmel, Director of Operations at Phillips Auctioneers in New York City, and a former acting director of the American Craft Museum. "So to make a point of who you are, you could bring in a textile. Wall hangings led the way." Weavers like Anni Albers and Gunta Stolz experimented with textiles. "They made textiles for the modern vision – a wall hanging as a piece of art," she continues, "they put in raffia, cellophane, and metallic threads."

To the all-white, modern room, textiles add texture, density, and often colour. They can make a cold room look warm, but they can also focus the eye. Since few of us live by the strict dogma of the Bauhaus, we can use nearly any kind of textile to enhance a room. Consider using, for example, cushions, bolsters, wall hangings, or curtains. Textiles can articulate a space and give shape to walls, windows, and ceilings.

Previous page Why should a white curtain remain white, when it can glow pink, lavender, or any other colour? Lights have been tucked within the window frame, and are covered with coloured gels, which can be changed according to whim. An ordinary room suddenly becomes a stage set, with you as the production designer. A woven rattan chair and a clutch of silk-covered pillows tossed on the floor provide an intimate gathering place in front of the romantically lit windows.

Left The colour red brings life to this austere white bedroom. The pillows against the headboard have a thin, red horizontal stripe, and in front, the crimson and gold striped cushions are arranged just so, for perfect symmetry. What softens the room, however, are not only the colours, but the silhouettes of the cushions, bedspreads, and the towels neatly folded at the foot of the bed.

Opposite This pure white-on-white room is a serene reminder of early Modernism, when architects banished decorative details in rooms. Here, only the textiles – the black and white cushions and hanging – and the golden built-in rectangular perch carved from the centre column provide colour.

TEXTURE, SCALE, AND COLOUR

In a Modernist minimalist room, big accents from textiles, whether a wall hanging, curtain, or rug, are usually more successful than small ones. Although a white living room or bedroom is not an art gallery, its neutral, monochromatic design makes it a perfect background to display something that is dramatic, eye-catching, and alluring. Bric-a-brac is lost in a stark, austere room. Think with grand gestures, and decorate with a view to creating a sense of veiled mystery. In the ubiquitous all-white room, sheer textiles in particular add soft textures and layers. By veiling a corner of the room, a window, or a sculpture, you can create layers of transparency and surprise. Objects become oblique, hidden, and exotic.

Be fearless about colour. When light comes through a sheer textile, whether it's emerald, cobalt, or ruby, coloured shadows are cast onto the

Below A trio of gossamer panels of fabric, two white and one yellow, work as soft, tactile room dividers. The central yellow panel is a bright, light shot of colour, a vertical ray of sunshine. The sheer fabrics contrast with the flower-sprigged fabric, left, which offers privacy and enclosure. The fabrics are carefully chosen. In this white environment, they provide colour, texture, and pattern.

Above What could be more sheer, weightless, and airy than this corner tableau of a brilliant magenta swath of fabric, with its delicate pattern filtering the light, and the equally transparent bamboo birdcage? The magenta warms the corner of the room, and the fragile tracery of the pattern echoes that of the tree outside. Like the magenta curtain, the birdcage appears lightly suspended in air.

Right The white curtain, with an opening in the middle, has just the right amount of translucence to create a little bit of mystery. When closed, it veils the view outside, and also gives a deceptive appearance that the circle is the sheerest part of the woven fabric itself. When the curtain opens, the circular window is revealed. Note, too, the use of the round chair for a simple reiteration of shapes.

Previous page The beach cabana comes indoors. Semi-circular cabanas of boldly striped canvas divide the shower from the dressing table, and of course from the bedroom. The vertical stripes contrast with the horizontal stripes across the ceiling, but the mixture isn't dizzying. There is brilliantly lit space between the tops of the cabanas and the ceiling.

Opposite All stripes point to the sea. The black and white striped awning and runner are textile signs, canvas arrows whose direction is clear: they make people focus on the water in front of this beautifully sited terrace. The striped canvas also features on the chairs, and even wraps, in candy-stripe fashion, the horizontal pole supporting the awning.

Above right In this living-room setting, the huge quilt on the wall and the smaller cushions all have wide, strong horizontal bands. The colours on each piece are tone-on-tone. The quilt is blue shading to lilac and pearl grey, while each cushion shades from one tone to another, from green to gold, fuchsia to pink, red to gold. The rectangular silk cushions against the navy sofa are a smaller scale reflection of the large rectangles against the blue background of the quilt. But the silk cushions reflect light, while the quilt appears matte.

floor, which change in tint and shape, depending on the time of day. There is movement too, in the slow dance of light and colour across walls, floors, and ceilings.

When working with textiles, consider yourself to be a graphic designer. Think of the power and visual impact of checks and stripes, circles and squares, and treat them in a modern, free way. After all, you are liberated from the constraints that the craftsmen of antique weavings were obliged to conform to when they produced their textiles for particular uses. Prayer rugs were used for prayers, door hangings belonged over doors. In the modern idiom, you are free to put what was an Indian floor covering on a wall, a Bedouin blanket on a chest, or a Persian tent hanging on a bed.

When you want to display more than one textile, group them so that they are visually related by either colour, texture, shape, or culture. A collection of a dozen Thai silk pillows, each in a different colour, is more powerful than displaying just two. A valance draped with one piece of fabric may look sparse, so why not add more?

Opposite In his Manhattan home, the artist Izhar Patkin set the bed frame on legs which are metal vases turned upside-down. The bed is covered in a blue and gold brocade, which was supposedly woven for the King of Morocco, and the chandelier was assembled from parts of other chandeliers by craftsmen in Bombay. "Nothing is lost," Patkin said, "Everything is transformed."

Left Architect Jonathan Leitersdorf's loft in Manhattan's SoHo. The industrial exposed beams and bricks are juxtaposed with the gleaming silk bolster and fringed satin bedskirt.

Below Pattern upon pattern: the colours of the folk-art rug – yellow, orange, cream, and caramel – are repeated in the painted stripes of the floor. The result of the layering is simple light-hearted charm.

Freddie Leiba, a stylist in New York City, has a collection of Indian elephant blankets, in ivory, magenta, and saffron. All are lavishly embroidered, some with mirror work. He uses these ornate blankets as bedspreads and, to make the bed even more inviting, he casually drapes a Hermes cashmere throw at the foot or corner of the bed. What unites the cashmere throw and the blanket is colour: he may put a chocolate cashmere throw on an ivory elephant blanket, or a crimson cashmere throw on a magenta blanket. The Indian elephant blanket is exotic, brilliant, glittery – the cashmere is familiar, soft, cuddly. The vivid embroidery contrasts with the solid colour, but when the textiles are layered on the bed, they make the bed doubly inviting and luxurious. By combining textiles, you are creating soft, tactile still-lives that not only draw the eye, but the hand too.

Just as Freddie Leiba layers his bed, so too can you layer the floor, the walls, or the divan. When a home is minimal, or stark and stripped down – like an industrial loft, an old weathered barn, or a sterile high-rise – textiles become even more essential. The careful juxtaposing of highly sensuous fabrics, like cashmere, silk-satin, lace, hand-loomed rugs, against plain backgrounds, can result in a striking, unexpected, and seductive atmosphere. An expansive loft with soaring

Opposite This room is pure minimalism, but without hard edges. What softens the white-on-white look are the fabric-covered walls, which add texture and sensuality to what could be a starkly austere space. The bed is white-on-white, too, but the fat puffy comforter and two plump pillows make the bed alluring rather than monk-like.

Right The theme of blue and white predominates in the corner of this room, in the boldly striped fabric which hangs lightly on the wall, the striped fabric on the small white chairs flanking the table, and in the pinstripe on the sofa. The flower-sprigged cushion is a contrast in pattern to the stripes.

ceilings, old brick walls, and scuffed wood floors is airy and spacious, but hardly cosy. Textiles make spaces friendly.

A floor is a giant canvas, and invites the layering of rugs, a small one on a big one, a floral one on a plain one. At Olives, a new restaurant at the W. New York Union Square Hotel, the Manhattan architects, the Rockwell Group, created a patchwork rug made of remnants of crimson-coloured Oriental-patterned rugs and *kilims*. The architects had the pieces stitched together, laid the rug on the wooden floor and, to frame it, they used copper paint and stencilled a border of tendrils onto the floor. The lacy filigree border contrasted with the density of the rug, the paint with the fabric – "hippie chic," as David Rockwell called it.

PATTERN AND SHAPE

Textiles on walls perform the same function as paintings and photographs. They become a soft, changeable art. Strong, large-scale patterns, like woven plaids, stripes, and dots, will stand out better against a wall than small patterns, such as little paisleys. A huge woven tapestry, one rich with texture and loops and curls, will add a three-dimensionality to a wall. If it is large enough, it becomes a wall by itself. A textile that is a solid colour is almost synonymous with an abstract colour-field painting, only the textile invites you to touch it. Any piece of fabric large enough to hang from ceiling to floor can stand alone.

A shorter or smaller piece, however, may be more dramatic when it is part of a still life. In the Renaissance, people often hung a tapestry on the wall, put a table directly in front of the tapestry, and a sculpture on the table. You can improvise on the Renaissance tradition, and

THE HOUSE BOOK

FARM

Left In 1972, Jack Lenor Larsen, the American textile designer, created this Laotian ikat fabric, seen on the chair on the left and hanging at the window, as a homage to Jim Thompson, the American architect and entrepreneur who revived silk weaving in Thailand at the end of the Second World War and then disappeared, perhaps kidnapped to China or Cambodia, in 1967. When Larsen designed the ikat, he persuaded the Thai weavers to make bolts 36 metres (40 yards) long, rather than the traditional skirt-lengths.

create your own altar. Substitute a loosely woven shawl for a tapestry, hang it above a plain birch occasional table, and add a framed photo on a stand.

Another kind of still life is a grouping of similar textiles. Hermes scarves, for example, when framed, and hung together across an expanse of wall, or above each other in a square format, can have the same effect as a group of botanical prints, or silk-screen prints by Andy Warhol. Textiles also hide architectural flaws, like an uneven wall, or provide some privacy. Fabric-covered walls can help muffle sound, so that the sound isn't as sharp as when walls are bare.

When you go to the theatre, the great swath of velvet curtain hangs before you, signifying suspense and drama. A home is a private theatre, where all sorts of antics take place, and the use of textiles as room dividers, in place of doors, can be equally dramatic. They are silent and mysterious, and create suspense as they open and close, reveal and hide. They provide visual, but little acoustic privacy, and can be used when total privacy isn't required.

Textile dividers work nicely around dining areas, kitchens, living rooms, but less successfully around bedrooms, bathrooms, or home offices where privacy is preferred. When you introduce great lengths of fabric to a room, from floor to ceiling, as a series of dividers, hangings, wall art, draperies, or curtains, the fabric lengths should be the same, or very closely related. The modern look is an uncluttered one, of clean vistas and planes.

In large spacious homes, whether drafty seventeenth-century buildings or modern industrial lofts, heavy textile room dividers can help keep the heat in one room, and make a particular room cosy and enveloping. "Before there was central heating, people lived in a few rooms in the winter," the Manhattan interior designer Mario Buatta said. "They used heavy linen curtains lined with blankets to keep out the cold."

Opposite White fabric in three different lengths performs many functions here. The fabric is a drapery for the windows upstairs. It also performs the work of walls and doors, dividing one area from another, upstairs from downstairs, staircase from dining room. The double-length curtains, which hang from the top of the second floor, are so dramatic that they resemble theatre curtains.

Above On this open veranda, the panels of sheer white cloth control light and air. They blow in the breeze, while shading both the veranda and the glass-walled interior from the dazzling, even blinding, sunlight. The plain fabric is suspended from the overhang, which is designed as an open gridwork. The light casts shadows of the grid onto the curtains, making the fabric take on subtly shifting and changing patterns.

Right Like an enormous sail, the huge swath of fabric, loosely hung from a point above and then billowing out at the sides, controls the light in this white-on-white room. The fabric shades the room, while letting brilliant light pour through the uncovered windows. Light and shadow are in constant play, with the grid pattern of the window wall shown both magnified (through the fabric) and minimized (on the floor).

In Maine, Lucinda Lang, a real estate agent who rents out summerhouses on her property, uses double-sided linen drapes, pale chartreuse on one side, taupe on the other, to flank the sitting room, surrounded by glass windows on three sides. In the summer, she leaves the drapes open, but in the winter, she closes them off, so that the chill from the exposed sitting room doesn't penetrate the centre of the house.

In the summer, huge swatches of a sheer, lightweight fabric, a plain cotton sheet, a length of canvas, can keep out the bright summer light, and shade different rooms and patios. But rather than limply hanging the textiles at the sides of the windows, hang them in panels, or as great billows of cloth. When fabric is hung in panels, with space in between, a peek-a-boo effect is created, of alternating clarity and opacity.

'NOOKS', OR 'ONE BIG TEXTILE, ONE SMALL SPACE'

In Manhattan, Michael Pierce and D D Allen, of Pierce Allen Architects, designed a home where they flanked the two open sides of the dining room with lined velvet cloth, dark bottle green on one side, and a soft rose on the other. The drapes give the room an aura of mystery, of stepping into a special place. When the drapes close, the room becomes intimate and, since the view of the city is obscured, the illumination is primarily by candlelight, with an overhead electric light set on a dimmer switch.

Textiles, used dramatically, transform plain spaces into dramatic ones, small ones into intriguing atmospheric nooks. Roman shades, balloon curtains, and swags are the vocabulary of the interior designer, but can be appropriated by anyone. When a Roman shade is pulled up, it pleats horizontally, with soft edges. When a balloon curtain is pulled up, it has a voluptuous excess of fabric that puffs out. A swag is

Opposite No room should lack drama – not even the bathroom. In the home of Peter Steake, a London fabric designer, the bathroom, the most private, intimate, and often forgotten room, has been given a stunning entrance. The designer has hung a voluminous amount of fabric in front of the capacious shower, and tied it back with plump fringed tassels.

Right No plain pull-down window shade for this room. Instead, a glowing shade in magenta, pink, and yellow stripes hangs over the window. The sheer stripe is semi-translucent, and allows a glimpse of the foliage outside. The sunlight pouring through the shade is tinged pinkish-gold. The cushions below are similarly brightly coloured.

Left Helene Verin, a Manhattan designer of wallpaper, furniture and shoes, once said that all big pieces of fabric were potential throws. So it follows that all big scarves could be possible banners that can hang vertically or, in this case, horizontally, and ripple in the air. The fringed gray cloth, perhaps a scarf or simply a length of fabric, is suspended on poles, and contrasts with the peach-coloured cloth hanging behind it.

Opposite Silk and rusticity marry in this dining area. The table, chairs, and bench couldn't be simpler, but a casual use of textiles – the table runners and the silk cushions – add a touch of sophistication. The pink-red cloths are laid across the table, a departure from the usual table runner laid lengthwise. The silk cushions add colour, texture, and, above all, comfort.

draped fabric, caught back usually with some kind of tie, like a corded rope. It is a luxurious way to treat a window, or an opening to a room.

Simple lengths of fabric, draped along a corridor of windows, can look highly dramatic when there is an excess of fabric, so that it trails onto the floors, catching dust, of course, but also adding to a full, generous look. It's the same effect in a curtain as the train on a wedding dress.

For strong but minimal window treatments, consider using a length of large-scale printed fabric as a shade, rather than using plain white vinyl. Huge stripes, polka dots, checks, or flowers at a window in a plainly furnished room will have the same powerful effect as a big piece of art. Or, on consecutive windows, you could make shades of fabrics in primary colours, red, yellow, blue in sequence.

There is no aspect of a room that cannot be warmed by a textile. The table can be covered with a tablecloth of linen, damask, or lace, and napkins of silk, seersucker, or batiste. Placemats come banded in ribbon, sisal, and raffia. But consider the table, like the wall, as an empty canvas that can also be delineated with large, bold strokes of textiles. Any long strip of fabric – a Chinese silk table runner, perhaps, or a length of lace, a bolt of ruby velvet, a paisley shawl – can dress a plain oak table, by running lengthwise down the centre. A bench is another hard surface asking to be warmed by a textile, perhaps a fragment of an oriental rug.

The ceiling is a place from which to suspend fabric as if was sculpture, a mobile caught in air. Some people hang kites from their ceilings, their shape and vivid colours suggesting flight and the outdoors. In auditoriums and concert halls, acoustic engineers and architects sometimes suspend textiles from the ceiling to control the sound, and to create a sensual, sometimes rippling effect.

TEXTILES AND LIGHT

Textiles provide a sensuous and evocative means of modulating light. When a room is lavished with natural light, sometimes it can be too much – the light can be harsh, even blinding. Translucent fabrics, such as thin silk pongee (a thin, plain-weave, silk fabric), tissue paper-like taffeta, cotton voile, muslin, and lace, filter light while veiling the view, whether it's a brick wall outside, or simply the sight of the neighbouring room. Sheer fabrics work like theatrical scrims, adding mystery, so that what goes on behind the curtain can be guessed at, but not necessarily seen clearly. Textiles make the light soft and intriguing. The more sheer the fabric, the more light pours into the room, but as the natural light enters, it is shaded and tinted by the colour of the textile.

Red, yellow, and orange curtains – or any other colours in this spectrum – transform white light into warm golden pools of colour that dance across the walls, floor, and furniture. Along with sheer fabrics of natural fibres like cotton and silk, there are also sheer synthetics, like metallic fabrics woven of polyester with copper, stainless steel, or aluminium. Sunlight (or artificial light) glints off the metallic surfaces and adds sparkle and sheen to a room. When a view outside a window is enticing – a steepled church, greensward, or fields of wheat – a sheer textile is all you may want at a window. But if the view is ugly – an airshaft, a factory spewing smoke, an all-night diner with bright neon lights – an opaque fabric becomes a screen, letting in light but hiding the view.

Right Primrose yellow sheer panels make the light especially sunny and cheerful in this room. An intriguing shadow play of the mullions on the fabric and the chairs adds movement and drama. In this white room, the yellow textiles are banners of colour. Hung at intervals, they provide privacy and also a glimpse of the outdoors.

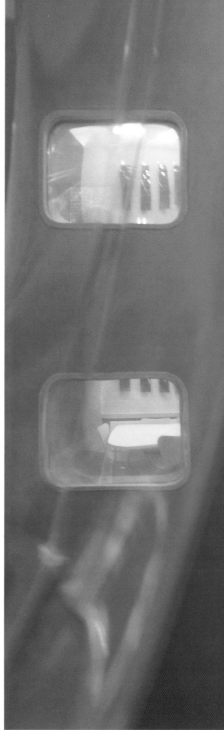

Above Layer upon layer. Two sheer panels of white fabric hang at the entrance to a dining room, serving as a room divider. The fabric at left veils what appears to be a solid blue screen whose openings afford a peek into the room. The sheer fabric also mutes the colour of the screen.

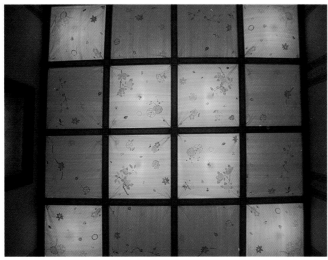

Left The ceiling was low and ugly, the light harsh, so Lucretia Moroni, the Manhattan textile designer, suggested, "Why not do a lighting design in textiles instead of glass?" She designed sixteen panels of hand-painted silk, eight dark and eight light, through which the light glows mysteriously. She has framed the panels in a wooden grid that has been stained brown.

Right Fabrics in three colours, red, white, and blue, have been stitched together to make these curtains, and frame the window in a flag effect. The curtains become a bold graphic statement in a stark, white, angular room. The impression is also of a white cross set against a blue and red background.

JAPAN AND THE FAR EAST

The use of Eastern objects or motifs in Western interiors today – a futon on the wooden floor of an erstwhile industrial London loft, or a Chinese Ming chair in a nineteenth-century Manhattan townhouse – is a practice that originated many centuries ago. As early as the sixteenth century, European collectors embraced Chinese and other Asian artefacts, including textiles, with enthusiasm, whether they were chairs inlaid with mother-of-pearl, blue-and-white porcelain vases, gleaming lacquered bowls, or Chinese and oriental rugs and silks. Such pieces evoked exoticism, far-away mysterious lands, and led to the Chinoiserie style in decorative art, where Western textiles, ceramics, furniture and other artefacts were decorated with Chinese or pseudo-Chinese ornamental motifs and designs.

In 1854, Commodore Perry of the United States opened the ports of Japan to diplomatic and commercial relations with the West. When Japan showed textiles, lacquers, and ivories at the international exhibitions in London and Paris in the 1860s, 1870s, and 1880s, the Europeans were delighted, and thereafter *Japonisme* became an important influence on the decorative arts in Europe and the United States.

Westerners discovered traditional Japanese architecture and interior design at the same time, with its system of sliding wooden screens covered with opaque paper, tatami mats of rice straw covered with woven rush, an absence of chairs, and a minimal yet effective use of textiles.

Previous page Woven textiles, arranged in different grid patterns, envelop this Japanese courtyard. The colour palette is subtle, soothing, muted. The curtains hanging in the doorway are called *noren*, and are traditionally used in the doorways of shops and restaurants, though they can also be used in homes, as here.

Right Although formal heraldry was abolished in Japan after the Second World War, the crest is still found in Japan, on kimonos or transformed into logos. Here, curtains the colour of cinnabar bear the temple crest of Zenko-ji Temple in Naga. The curtains billow, and the crest is the focal point.

Opposite The Japanese make some of the most sophisticated, technologically advanced textiles that can incorporate copper, steel, and aluminium. These metallic textiles shimmer, catch, and reflect light, and startle the purist who may insist that textiles be woven of natural materials. These translucent textile screens, dividing the dining room from the living room, appear to be made partly of copper.

Below The Japanese often use asymmetry in their design, in the belief that nature is asymmetrical. The curtains shown here, in a room in Kyoto, are designed with a black and white crest, and there is a pleasing asymmetry to the design on the panels blowing in the breeze, with the crest, left, and calligraphy, right.

CURTAINS, SCREENS, AND BEDS

Noren are the little curtains, usually made of linen and cotton, which traditionally hang in the upper part of restaurants and stores in Japan, and their presence indicates that the place is open for business.

Noren, however, were first used in the home as long ago as the twelfth century. On hot summer days, the Japanese hung large *noren* in the open doorway of a house, where they provided shade, visual privacy, and allowed air to circulate. *Noren* are not only decorative and graphic, but also soft and warm as you brush against them when entering a restaurant or shop. When made of handspun thread, they have a lovely, somewhat uneven texture, which adds to their tactile quality. The curtains are made in single woven panels, but in such a way that each panel matches up with the next, so that the motif appears almost seamless, running from panel to panel.

Although there are traditional uses for *noren*, they are also sold in Japan as souvenirs, portable curtains that translate effortlessly and serenely into Western homes. They add warmth to a long, dark, narrow

Left In this minimal London flat, curtains flutter in a hallway and add bold graphic design, movement, and colour to a serene white home. Although the curtains have the name of a movie written on them, in the context of a Western home they are pure decoration, while at the same time giving a cosy, intimate scale to the hallway.

Below In this atelier in Kijoka, Japan, these beautiful, almost transparent hangings are placed where indoor and outdoor meet, so that the birds seem to be taking flight. Toshiko Taira wove the cloth of *basho-fu*, or banana fibre cloth, a light fabric that allows air to circulate. This atelier has been designated a Living National Treasure.

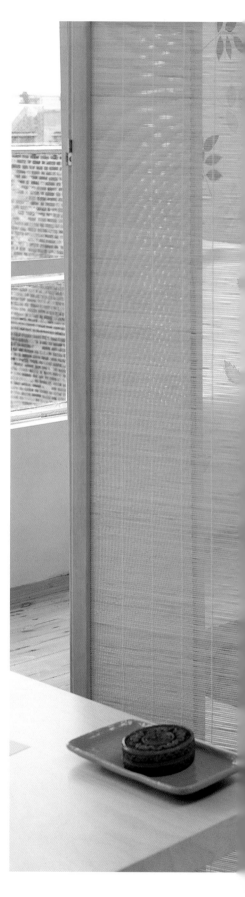

Previous page In this bedroom in Casa Kimura, a huge swath of patchwork fabric is draped over a chest. The patchwork is arranged in a carefully conceived pattern, not a random collection of scraps. A floral-patterned cover lies on the futon.

Left Calligraphy possesses a graphic strength, whether or not you can read Japanese. Here, the white characters have an aesthetic force that leaps off the fabric, and there is an undulating motion in both the calligraphy and the way the fabric drapes.

Right This is a blithe evocation of a Japanese room. The futon is on the floor, as in a traditional Japanese home, but the canopy is simply a swath of a leaf-printed sheer. At the foot of the futon are *geta*, outdoor shoes, with high platforms, which would be left outside in Japan.

hallway. Hung in front of a kitchen that adjoins the dining room, they shield the pots and pans from the eyes of people sitting at the table. When you enter the kitchen, you are not faced with the effort of opening a door, but simply glide between the panels of fabric. They can separate indoors from outdoors, and are also softer, more pliable alternatives to closet doors. They can be made as long as you'd like, and of fabrics that are not too stiff, but are not necessarily cotton or linen. Sheer or opaque, they can be printed or painted. They can be just a few panels, or many. *Noren* can be silk, cashmere, or canvas, so long as they feel good when they brush against the skin.

Screens, with their solid frames, however, provided the greatest privacy. The traditional Japanese home, which was designed to cope with the hot summers (but not for the very cold winters), had sliding opaque screens so that the air could circulate, but privacy could also be protected when necessary. The interior of a Japanese home was often quite dark, the light diffused.

Modern homes can have screens made of silk, lace, or muslin. A screen does not have to be the architectural necessity it was in a

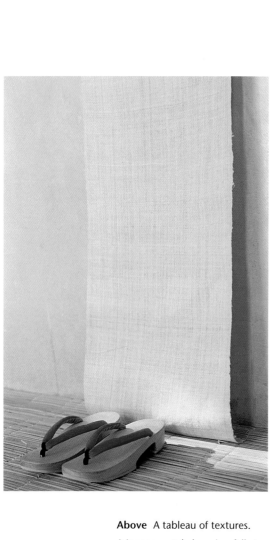

Above A tableau of textures. A Japanese-style hanging falls to the floor, creating an interplay of colour and texture, white fabric against cream-coloured walls and blond wooden floors. The Japanese sandals appear to be waiting for someone to walk by and slip their feet into them.

traditional Japanese home. A screen can be decorative, and as sheer as a theatrical scrim. It can be a graphic statement – plaid banners gently moving in the breeze.

If the sun is so bright that it casts a glare, the use of opaque screens or panels of cloth can filter the light. If a gentle, intimate ambience is intended, then diffuse light, perhaps brightened by candles or lamps on a dimmer – or a combination of both – produces this effect.

To achieve this muted look, use textiles like linen, ramie, jute, or bamboo, which have been worked so that they are either translucent or have openings in the weave or structure that lets light peek through. Or choose the most modern textiles, like those invented in Japan in recent years, which are sometimes synthetic and have astonishing properties.

Just as *noren* and screens can be appropriated for the Western home, so too can the futon, the Japanese bed. In the Japanese home, bedding is taken out only when needed and, in the absence of furniture, a bed is simply a layered series of textiles, carefully placed on the floor.

The ancient Japanese did not sleep naked. They put down padded quilts on top of the tatami, and tucked themselves in, wrapped in clothing, and covered by an roomy padded kimono-shaped robe, which often had an extra panel sewn in, so that it wouldn't be constricting. Sometimes there was yet another silk quilt padded with silk or cotton. Multiple layers of soft, padded cottons and silks, then, formed their bed.

The traditional Japanese way of sleeping – close to the floor – has been adapted by Westerners in search of a less austere way of sleeping. What is a platform bed, after all, but a futon taken off the floor? Keeping a bed low, although not directly on the floor, makes a low-ceilinged room feel bigger. If a room has windows that are so

Left A Japanese-style bedroom in a Western home has a typical spareness, serenity, and diffused light, which comes through the *shoji*-style screens. But the bed has been raised and given a headboard for greater comfort. The bedspread has clean, unobtrusive lines. As in a Japanese interior, no object in this room shouts for attention.

big as to end just above the floor, you might want to sleep on a low bed for reasons of privacy and to maximize the view.

At a recent Modernist show of decorative arts in Manhattan, one of the dealers showed a burlwood Art Deco bed and headboard whose platform was less than half a metre (twenty inches) from the floor. Was this an Art Deco designer's reinterpretation of sleeping on a futon? No, the dealer said that someone had simply cut off the legs. But the juxtaposition – Art Deco Japonisme – was delightful. The gleam of the burlwood had its own sophistication. The languorousness of a low bed was alluring – for what is seduction but the act of gently and inevitably pulling the observer down and close to you?

COLOURS AND OBJECTS

To the Japanese, "colours speak with a loud voice; they should make themselves heard only for short periods," according to Eleanor von Erdberg in *Japanese Folk Art: A Triumph of Simplicity* (Japan Society, 1992). In the Heian court, during the tenth and eleventh centuries, the Japanese nobility judged a woman's elegance and taste by the colour of her kimonos, which were worn in layers. Did the scarlet top layer look right over the plum colour beneath? They understand the harmony between colours, with one peeking out from beneath another.

The Japanese layered their clothes to represent the beauty of a flower, or of a particular season. They understood the nuances of colour within nature. They named colours after nature, like pale pink cherry blossom, the first snow of the season, and even barren fields. Their colour spectrum imitated that of nature. It could be bright, but it did not shriek.

In a Western home, bedding can be changed according to the season, not just from winter to summer, as people often do. Contemplate

Above In this study of natural textures against a background of industrial brick, delicate, translucent shades, with an irregular weave, filter the light. The amaryllis, a bright orange note, is placed in a bamboo container, one of a group, each cut diagonally at a different height.

Right For a tabletop, consider the possibility of using block-printed fabric as a runner and, along the table, place old wooden printing blocks that have been transformed into candelabra. Tiny glass saucers filled with oil have also been lit here.

Opposite The Vienna-born American architect Rudolph Schindler (1887–1953) worked for Frank Lloyd Wright in 1918, and in 1921 moved to Los Angeles, where he designed houses, first of concrete, then with timber frames and stucco finishes, and, later, with plywood panels. In this house in California, with its timber beams, he has created a muted interior with natural materials, including a table runner, probably a silk *obi-age*, the under sash of an *obi* (a broad Japanese sash), which is decorated only at the end.

Right Carefully layered white and beige textiles dominate this airy dining room facing a harbour view. Dramatically swagged white fabric frames the view, while the trio of beige shades is embellished by lavishly fringed tassels. White linens cover the table in two layers, while the chairs are covered three times over. From bottom to top, each chair has a white slipcover, a beige fringed shawl, and oversized white napkins.

Left Like goes with like. Here is a casual homage to Mariano Fortuny, the Spanish painter and stage and dress designer. In 1906, he began designing textiles, and is famous for his technique of pleating silk with heated ceramic tubes. He also printed cottons and silk velvets with designs inspired by the Italian Renaissance and oriental textiles. At left, his lampshades hang, lantern-like and lavishly tasselled, on a spiral frame, while the printed pillow on the chair is a Fortuny-type pattern. A calligraphy scroll hangs on the wall, and a photo rests on the table.

Opposite Molly Hogg, a collector of and dealer in exotic textiles from China, Thailand, and Japan, mixes and matches textiles, masks, and baskets in her London home. Eclecticism lives easily in her dining room – a Chinese silk robe, possibly made by the Yao people in southern China, is displayed over the mantelpiece.

spring, with the bottom sheet the colour of ivory crocuses, the top sheet the pale green of a young leaf, and a duvet cover the dark green of clover. Or make your bedcoverings resemble the spring colours of an azalea plant, shading from palest to deepest pink. Come autumn, a bed could have a bottom sheet that is peach, a top sheet in a Kraft paper beige, and a duvet cover of chocolate velvet. When the maple leaves begin to change colour, you could emulate their colours, which range from scarlet to deep orange to a muted ochre.

THE NEW TEXTILES

The textile designer Junichi Arai has produced fabrics that are extraordinary and startling. He has made a white textile that resembles a spider's web, and consists mostly of air. Is this man-made spider's web textile art, or a new type of lace? He has also made a textile partly of aluminium, which is white with hints of ice blue and looks like the wings of a butterfly. Pliable, lightweight, translucent, and waterproof, the fabric might make a nice raincoat, he once said. It would weigh only 115 grams (4 ounces) – and would make the wearer feel like a butterfly. The designer Reiko Sudo stitched nylon tape onto a soluble base fabric in a loopy kind of plaid, then dissolved the base fabric, so that all that is left are the bands of nylon, curling and twisting across a background of air.

There are soft cottons that pucker, linens that have been dyed so they shade through a spectrum of indigo, from dark blue to almost blue-black. These new, innovative textiles can be hung on walls, as panels in front of windows, or laid on tables as runners. They can billow under a ceiling, or be framed as screens. The textiles are not necessarily made of natural fibres, but they are nevertheless alluring.

Whether you are using natural textiles like silk or those spun of copper or aluminium, you can create a soft, gentle atmosphere. Choose textiles that are somewhat pale or sombre in tone, rather than bright. It is an austere look, but has more warmth than the contemporary minimalist look.

SMALL TEXTILES

When you transpose Eastern artefacts to a Western home, you do not have to create an entire look. But the design trick is the same, regardless of what you collect: consider the scale. If the piece is large like a futon or a kimono, it can stand on its own. But if the objects are small, group them together. Small textiles, like antique Chinese silk insignia badges, hats, or purses, can be framed and grouped. When textiles are only fragments and no longer complete, they can be salvaged and displayed. When Japanese collectors have only fragments of a beautiful kimono, they mount them on a folding screen so they appear as if they draped over a rack.

Left Classic Chinese chairs surround the round dining table, with a beautiful panel of fabric running across the centre of the table, its lustrous, figured design adding colour to what would otherwise have been a dark dining area.

Opposite Sinuous serpents writhe the length of the fabric, a lavishly embroidered hanging that is treated as wall art. The pairing of the lively serpents and the shooting flames in the fireplace animate the hearth, and add a visual and physical warmth to the room. Imagine the candlesticks lit, too, late at night.

Left Antiques meet sleek Modernism: Calvin Tsaim a partner at Tsao & McKown Architects in Manhattan, collects antique textiles and refuses to cut them up. "There's and integrity to antique cloth," he said. In his New York city apartment, he placed a Javanese wedding skirt, made of cotton richly embroidered in gold threads, over the chaise. It's one of a collection of similar tube-shaped skirts, and he transforms the others into bolsters, sliding pillows inside the cloth.

ROBES AS ART

In Japan, as in all cultures, clothing is status, a tactile form of conspicuous consumption. In the seventeenth century, when Tokugawa Ieyasu, a shogun, died, he left 3,000 robes. The Japanese so prized clothing that they had fashion contests for women, some of which have become legend, fable, or mere gossip. Each woman tried to outdo the other. There is one story that the artist Ogata Korin (1658–1716) was hired to advise a rich merchant's wife for a competition. He dressed her in a completely plain black robe, making the other women's outfits appear over-elaborate. Because the Japanese did not necessarily distinguish between the fine and decorative arts, the finest artists like Ogata Korin painted on paper or silk screens – and even directly onto silk robes. The robe could be a work of art, along with being a statement of social status.

The Japanese took the Chinese robe and transformed, adapted, and reinvented it into what we commonly think of as the kimono – the rectangular T-shaped robe – although there are specific names for many of the robes. The *kosode*, for example, is a small-sleeved robe. Costumes for actors in the No theatre have their own names, too. It is clothing that conceals the body, but

Above Although the Japanese usually store their kimonos folded flat and carefully put away in chests, they also have a tradition of displaying them on a rack, as here. The sight of a kimono hanging over a lacquered rack can be seen as a kind of titillation, raising the question of who has just taken off the robe. Here the kimono is displayed as a work of art.

Left An eastern jacket hangs lightly on the wall, above a spare yet alluring still life of table, photograph, statue, and potted orchids. This tableau makes an often forgotten space – a corner by the staircase – a place to stop and linger.

Right The big black wooden-framed sofa dominates the room, which would be austere and sterile were it not for the sprays of greens in the vase and, more particularly, the red kimono. Hung on a frame, it is a *furisode*, or a young woman's kimono. Its pattern, brightness, and softness warm the room.

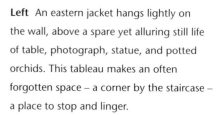

moves with the body with extraordinary grace. The Japanese made robes from silk, cotton, ramie, and crepe. They embroidered the robes, and applied gold and silver foil onto the fabric. They created designs that swept diagonally across the back of the robe, or were of beautifully aligned patchwork. They plucked motifs directly from nature, whether animals (birds, tortoises), plants (bamboo), or elements of the landscape (mountains, lakes, and streams). Some robes are embellished with family crests, such as chrysanthemums, wisteria, or butterflies, which decorate the top of the front, back, and sleeves.

Japanese robes can be stored folded and flat, but in the Nara period (710–794), clothing racks were introduced from China. In cold, drafty castles, a kimono hung on a rack became a screen, a partition to ward off the chill. Today, in Japanese department stores, some kimonos are displayed flat, while others are shown on racks. Occasionally, a family might display a kimono on a rack in their own home, usually a wedding kimono on which they may have spent a great deal of money.

These robes lend stark, graphic shape to a room. They are textiles as sculptures, and can be displayed much as they were in the Nara period – as screens. Because most of them are flat, the silhouette is clean and strong.

Above The corner tableau is focused entirely on the kimono, whose black and white theme is repeated in the chair, placemats, and porcelain. The floral design begins only on the bottom third of the kimono and then seems to tumble extravagantly onto the ground. Real flowers in a green vase are a happy juxtaposition to those on the kimono.

57

GLOBAL

Previous page In a house in New Mexico, a North African rug is the focal point of this austerely beautiful, subtly monochromatic room. The entire room – walls, carved wooden door and furniture – are earth shades. The rug is a muted terracotta, a few shades brighter than the rest of the room, so that it adds a glow. It is set on a diagonal, and is aligned with the fireplace, rather than the wall.

Left Pattern upon pattern. An Islamic hanging is displayed on the wall behind the ornate divan, which is inlaid with glittering mother-of-pearl. Layers of cushions and a custom-made seat cushion make the carved divan appear inviting. Octagonal carved tables, also inlaid with mother-of-pearl, rest on a Persian kilim. The curtain is tied back, so as to let light in and avoid making that side of the room oppressively dark. Masses of cushions line the shelves. What keeps the room from feeling claustrophobic is the bright white of the walls, ceiling, and floor, and the play of light from the windows, lamps, and chandelier.

Right In this house in Northamptonshire, an Indian *toran*, or embroidered frieze, sparkling with mirror work, hangs above the hearth. In the state of Gujarat in India, people hang the *toran* above the doorway, and the pennants represent mango leaves which are believed to bring good luck.

Around the world, from India to Central Asia to Africa, people have woven rich, glorious textiles for use as beds, rugs, wall hangings, and animal blankets. From India, there are lavender silk saris glittering with mirror work that were made to be worn by women, but can be turned into tablecloths, throws, and curtains. From Central Asia, there are *suzanis*, hand-embroidered textiles, usually made in shades of red, that were used as wall hangings in Uzbekistan – and can perform the same function in modern homes. From Africa, there is kuba cloth, made from raffia by men, and embroidered by women, which can be nearly 9 metres (10 yards) long. The cream and black cloth is made to be worn as skirts, but can do powerful graphic duty as wall hangings. Textiles from around the world, from a clutch of scarlet, cobalt, and cream coloured kilims cut down to cushion covers, to turquoise *dhurries* bordered in emerald, are often richly textured and coloured. They are an antidote to white-on-white minimalism.

COLOUR AND PATTERN

Textiles from far-flung countries – India, Persia, Afghanistan, Central Asia, Russia, and Africa – are a way of adding colour, pattern, and exoticism to a Western habitat. They allow you to escape into an imagined environment, an escapist fantasy many thousands of miles from where you actually live.

Textiles can also play the role of furniture. They can take over a room, so that furniture becomes incidental. In Nepal, Erich Theophile, an American architect, lives as the Nepalese do – without much furniture except for a drafting table, dining table, and some chairs. In traditional Nepalese homes, the façades of the buildings are ornately carved, but the interiors are bare, often without tables, chairs, or sofas. Theophile entertains his guests on the floor, and everyone sleeps on the floor, on futons. What gives his five-storey house in Patan beauty, warmth, and comfort is his brilliant use of Indian, Tibetan, and Bhutanese textiles. "Textiles give you colour and design – but without objects," said Theophile, who is the executive director of the Kathmandu Valley Preservation Trust, which restores historic temples, palace buildings, and pilgrim rest homes. What unifies the designs in his home is that they are all from the same regions, so that the patterns on the different pieces are culturally related. When he has particularly dazzling colours, like red and gold, he groups them together.

Below Cushions can be collectibles. In this wooden trunk each one of the cushions in this treasure trove is appealing. The one in the left foreground has a three-dimensional quality, the red one is designed slightly asymmetrically, leaving a red border at the bottom, while the orange patterned one behind it is banded in the middle.

Opposite A passageway is usually neglected, wasted space, often left plain and simply lit. Sometimes, it is treated as an art gallery, a place to hang a series of photographs, botanical prints, or posters, so that passing through is a visual treat. This carefully lit passage is a gallery devoted to textiles. A Tibetan carpet runs the length of the floor, and laid across it is a bolster covered with an Uzbekistan fabric. A peony-patterned woven textile wall hanging stretches from ceiling to floor, and at the far end, a *portière*, a curtain hung in front of the doorway, keeps drafts out of the passage.

Seat cushions have striped yellow silk covers. A futon covered in a sturdy Nepalese white cotton takes the place of a sofa. On the floors are thick sisal rugs, made in Nepal. The futon in the guest room is covered with a red cotton quilt from Gujarat, India, and the cushions, also from India, are lavishly hand-embroidered with huge dots. He has covered his own futon with a cherry-coloured sheet edged in a geometric pattern of rust, rose, teal blue, and lime green. The navy duvet, a sole touch of Americana, is rolled up and placed at the foot of the futon. The duvet's origin, however, does not jarr with the surroundings. It is an anonymous solid colour, and not a shriek of Americana, like an Amish quilt. The occasional solid colour block – the white sofa and the navy duvet – are calm focal points, amid the bright colours and patterns. Textiles not only play the role of furniture, but also of art. Theophile designed a case with wooden dowels to display lengths of silk-embroidered cotton from Afghanistan, raw silk from Bhutan, nineteenth-century silk from Bali, a blanket from Tibet – most in red and gold. Textiles are functional, decorative, and mutable. "You can change them by the season, or when they get dirty," Theophile says.

What Erich Theophile has done in Nepal can be extrapolated anywhere. The trick is to unify the textiles. If you like the lavishness of glittery, gold-threaded, mirror-worked Indian textiles on brilliant backgrounds of red, green, and gold, then stay with them, or with textiles from adjacent cultures, which have related motifs and palettes. Do not mix them with, say, American Indian blankets, or African kente cloth. They will clash. Textiles from China, Japan, and Korea will work together. So will those from South America, or from Central Asia. Choose a corner of the world, and roam free within those rich boundaries.

Below In a house in Gloucestershire, a *suzani*, an embroidered textile from Uzbekistan, modulates the light by the raised window platform. In Central Asia, the largest *suzanis* were used as wall hangings or bedspreads. Small *suzanis* would cover a low table above a charcoal brazier, and people would sit there, slipping their arms and feet under the textile. In contrast to the *suzani*, a sheer wide-hemmed fabric hangs in the foreground, letting the light through. The wooden chest is also wrapped in fabric.

Opposite In the same Gloucestershire house as the picture on the left, the bed and divan are placed low so that the views through the windows are maximized. As is the practice in the Middle East, the fabric is draped over the divan and continues onto the floor. Since the ceiling is exceptionally high, panels of fabric hang on the wall and make the scale of the room more intimate. White curtains by the bed modulate the light, as did the *suzani* in the other room.

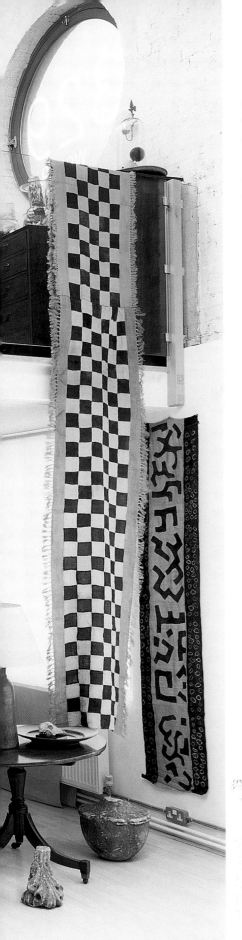

Left Textiles delineate the functions of this loft room, which is suffused with light pouring in from the clerestory and round window. White curtains canopy the bed for privacy, while great lengths of kuba cloth, originally skirt lengths, hang at intervals. The great lengths of the cloth accentuate the height of the loft.

Right This tableau is a study in black, sepia, and white. The darkness of the wooden furniture contrasts with the muted tones of the rug, and the strong, simple line of the furniture is echoed in the rug's design. Had the furniture been placed on a wooden floor, the shapes would not have stood out.

AFRICAN TEXTILES

Some African textiles, like kuba cloth from Zaire, with bold black embroidery on a cream raffia background, or kente cotton and silk cloth from Ghana – slender strips often of red, green, and black on a gold background – are such bold, strong, and lively designs that they demand centre stage and can become the dominant motif of a room. They are not subtle and do not fade away. Other cloths, like yellow mud cloth from Mali or striped cottons from Senegal may have more subtle designs, and won't take over a room.

When the textiles are quiet, although rich in texture, they can be used in profusion, just as you would use any other muted cloth. Use them for upholstery, bedspreads, or cushion covers. The less bold the design, the less attention they call upon themselves. The largest kuba and kente cloths are irrepressible. Kuba cloths, which can be as long as 9 metres (10 yards), and take up to a year to weave, are usually only two colours, black on a cream ground. But the size and scale of kuba cloths, many of which were woven as skirts for both men and women, make them graphically powerful. They are an ancient kind of African Op Art, and have a sense of motion in their design.

Since the kuba and kente cloths are so strong and graphic, they should be used with a bold, spare hand. They do not mix with American Indian textiles, for example. Instead, consider working with kuba, kente, and mud cloth in the same room. Their geographic proximity travels well

Previous page A length of kuba cloth hangs at the window. In the Congo, this fabric is beaten with a mallet to make it soft. A hand-sewn, commercially-made throw is tossed over the fluffy duvet, for a contrast of textures and cultures.

Opposite In the Provence region of southern France, a wall hanging with an abstract design is the sole pattern in this simple yet inviting room. The yellow cushions seem to borrow the sunlight that pours through the window.

Left In a safari lodge in South Africa, the vivid colours of the kente cloth bedspread and drapes stand out against the dark, rustic architecture. A mat of kuba cloth is on the floor, by the side of the bed, to warm the feet in the morning.

to a Western living room. The kuba and kente cloths, when handwoven, are painstakingly made. Once the men finish weaving the kuba cloths from softened raffia (palm-leaf fibres), and have beaten the fabric with a mallet to soften it further, the women take over the decoration. First, they embroider the fibre, which, when finished, feels smooth like a heavy embroidered burlap, but without that fabric's flexibility. Strictly speaking, embroidery means stitching on a fabric after it is taken off the loom. It's not restricted to what your grandmother made you do on doilies and napkins. Sometimes women also transform the fabric into a cut pile, or what is called kesai velvet, by inserting very fine raffia fibres, one at a time, through the interstices (weave) of the fabric. To create an even pile, the women's final task is to cut the fibres short, even, and flat. Designs are not necessarily balanced or symmetrical. Instead, they are exuberant. They make the eye move.

Ghanaian kente cloths, made from slender strips of fabric sewn together, are electric. The geometric patterns, whether rectangles, squares, or crosses, appear to vibrate in front of your eyes. They are worn as clothing for men, women, and children, and are also used as hangings over tents, or as liners for palanquins. They are still often given as gifts. Like kuba cloth, they are available as handwoven or machine-printed fabrics. Clearly the handwoven ones have more texture and character, but the mass-produced ones, the printed ones, have the same visual zap.

Opposite Eccentricity rules in this foyer, which defies all normal conventions of interior design. Africa meets classical Greece meets modernity. The wall framing the door is covered with two related kuba-style patterns arranged asymmetrically. The door is flanked by modified Corinthian columns, while the foreground is painted in crisp, bold stripes which are painted the same width, but in slightly differing colourations. The foyer, however, is not optically dizzying, because the door, ceiling, and floor are neutral areas where the eye can rest.

Left The same rules of eccentric design apply to this room as to the one opposite. Busy, nearly frenetic patterns can cover a wall or floor, as long as there are areas of visual respite, like the painted wall, ceiling, and door here. The lace tablecloth is short, so that the prancing horses – the feet of the table legs – are visible. Even the furniture depicts movement.

Kuba and kente cloths work as wall hangings (in place of art), as bedspreads, and as curtains. They can be draped over chairs, sofas, or chests. They are strong against solid-coloured backgrounds, whether white, mustard, beige, rust, or ochre, colours that speak of the palette of the earth. They are also successful in a simple, rustic environment with beamed roofs, or walls of panelled wood or bamboo. The lively cloths can also use some air around them – a clean, non-patterned space above, below, or perhaps on either side – so that they don't overwhelm you.

African textiles don't have to be handmade to have visual impact. Throughout Europe and the United States, there are shops selling both handwoven and printed kente and kuba cloths, as well as mud cloths from Mali and patterned cottons from Senegal. Stark Carpet, a company in New York City, makes carpeting in patterns inspired by kuba cloth. African textiles marry well with European furniture. Aline Matsika, an interior designer originally from the Congo, owns two home furnishing shops in Paris and one in Manhattan. She shows African fabrics upholstering European-style furniture, like a curvy chaise longue upholstered in a Senegalese cherry and white striped cotton. A pert square ottoman, and a Louis XVI-style sofa, are covered in kuba cloth, the finish of which is so fine that it feels like linen.

She also sells African textiles as tablecloths, runners, and place mats. To show off the patterned cloths, she has painted the walls of her loft-like shop in a pale cream, and hung the huge windows with sheer lengths of fabric, some cream, others chocolate. The effect is stunning and exotic, yet sophisticated and livable.

USING GLOBAL TEXTILES

Just as Aline Matsika mixes European furniture design with African textiles, so you can upholster European furniture in textiles from any other country. You can also single out one room, perhaps the bedroom, which is the most intimate and seductive room in a home, and make it a homage to a memory of visiting the Taj Mahal, or sleeping in a tent on a safari in Kenya. When you don't want an entire evocation of another culture, you can use one large piece as a wall hanging, or a collection of small pieces, grouped together for visual interest, simply to enliven a wall – any wall.

The more exotic the textile, the more alluring the still life. Take a somewhat unused space – the wall on a stair landing, behind a bookshelf, in a bathroom, a hallway, a foyer – and hang a textile. If you put the fabric at an accessible height where people can touch it, the textile, whether a length of kuba cloth or a fringed

Left The Indian cottons covering the cushions and coverlet, tossed in a *déshabille* manner here, are not luxury fabrics, but the mix of patterns (all in the same bright colourway), and the largesse of cushions make the bed very inviting. If a bed could speak, this one would say, "Hop in."

Right The pink walls capture the light, and appear to glow in this romantic room. An electrified candelabrum (far more seductive than an ordinary lamp) is at the head of the bed, which has been made up with a double layer of pillows and a thick duvet. The base of the bed appears to be wrapped in fabric. The armchair and hassock are other notes of comfort. Placed by the foot of the bed, they invite intimate conversation.

Opposite This skylit landing has been transformed into a place of quiet reflection. A bark cloth hangs on the wall, and a cushion and seat cover make a metal-framed chair comfortable. Sunlight from the windows make this small space a miniature greenhouse, ideal for someone who wants to be alone and bathed in sunlight.

Left This stair landing has been transformed into a place to contemplate a few, intriguing objects. A red textile catches the eye; a wooden door goes nowhere. But it's the ceramic pots in front of the door which make a person pause. They are charming obstacles.

Below "When you visit someone in the Congo, you bring a seating mat, a kuba cloth square, as a symbol of hospitality," said Mark Shilen, a rug dealer and expert in New York City. kuba mats hang on the wall here, and are juxtaposed with the striped cushions on the sofa.

Kashmir shawl, will invite people to stop, stroke it lightly, and wonder what it is and where it came from. It is a way of sharing your passions with your friends.

Textiles can be used architecturally. Large pieces can cover an entire wall, hanging from floor to ceiling. They can also be used to mask architectural flaws. A series of African, Central Asian, or Indian cloths, hung side by side, can obliterate an uneven wall or a window that looks onto an ugly view. A textile can substitute for a door, and gossamer panels of block-printed cotton gauze can become the entrance to a closet, a room, or a pantry. Why open a door, if just nudging a panel of soft fabric is easier?

Textiles can also colour cue a room. You can be seduced by a Persian floor-sized rug, in shades of soft dusky blues and greens, embellished with a scroll and vine motif, and those colours can suggest the muted blue-green palette for your walls and ceiling. Helene Verin, a Manhattan designer of fabric, furniture, and shoes, remembered that when her son, Ryder Ripps, was little, his favourite book was *Goodnight Moon*. And what were the colours of the child's room in the book? Red and green. So she replicated those same colours in his room, starting with a red and green Scottish tartan

bedspread. Then colour-cued by the bedspread, she painted the walls green, and the mouldings red, leaving the ceiling white, so that the room didn't become cave-like. Look to your favourite textiles, whether a Navajo blanket, a beige, brown, and black striped Moroccan bedspread, or a red and magenta Indian sari, for the colours you want to live with.

The eclectic room has no global boundaries, no rules of decor, other than to avoid creating a hodge-podge. Robert Homma, a partner in Dimson Homma, a home furnishings shop in Manhattan selling wares such as Chinese antique furniture, Venetian glass, and Japanese silk scarves dyed from natural materials, lives as he sells. He has furnished his penthouse studio apartment with the same mixture of textiles and furniture that he sells in his shop. He has chosen blue as the leitmotif for the textiles in his 600 foot-square apartment. Blue is in the Tibetan rugs, and in a French quilt on the bed. "Some people think blue is cold," he said, "but I think it's calming." His use of blue can be imitated in limiting yourself to shades of green, russet, gold, sustained through rugs, sheets, pillow cases, and duvet covers or quilts. The rugs could be Chinese, the quilt American. Or, a rug could be Moroccan, and a duvet cover Scandinavian. The unity would lie in the colour.

Han Feng, a fashion designer, mixes textiles – Thai silks and plain muslin, linen and organza – in her Manhattan loft. She has sixteen windows, and filters sunshine through white muslin curtains, some hung straight in extra-long panels, and others are swagged and draped like theatre curtains. The duvet cover is white cotton, and the pillows are covered in linen edged with a deep band of silk organza. The high canopied bed appears to float above the floor. Although the bed looks ethereal, and pale, she sets her dinner table with bolts of colour: place mats and napkins of iridescent Thai silk, in magenta, gold, emerald, cobalt, and turquoise.

Left Molly Hogg, a London textile collector and dealer, displays fabrics from Indonesia, Thailand, India, and China throughout her London home. She stitches fabrics to linen stretched over a frame, and hangs jackets from bamboo poles, which she then suspends from a picture rail with transparent fishing line. Here, she has covered a wall with a huge swath of kente cloth.

Left Red in its many shades dominates this seating arrangement, where there is tomato, madder, and oxblood red. An Indian cotton covers the divan, while a new Turkish kilim lies on the floor. The way the red shades from bright red-orange to madder makes the seating arrangement vibrant and warm, but not garish. What unites the textiles is not only the colour but also the geographical origins of the patterns. Most seem to be from South-East or Central Asia, or the Near East, and marry happily.

A SENSE OF ENCLOSURE

A modern use of exotic textiles is to suggest far distant habitats – Moroccan souks, Bhutanese temples, Brazilian fishing huts – but not to create exact replicas. In fact, you can do what Andy Warhol, the artist, did in his townhouse on the Upper East Side of Manhattan.

Jed Johnson, the late interior designer, worked with Warhol to create each room in a different style. One salon was French Art Deco, with lacquered furniture made by Jean Dunand, and decorate objects made of shagreen. Silk upholstered some of the chairs. One bedroom was American Victorian, with touches of red velvet. Another bedroom was Early American, with a fisherman's net strung across the four-poster bed, as an airy, rustic canopy. To walk through the house was to enter a different culture with every few steps – the formal swagged character of Victoriana, the sleek sharp lines of French Art Deco, and the homespun nature of early Americana. What gave the house even more of an escapist quality was that Warhol, the ultimate self-promoter, did not have any of his own art in the house. The only photographs were those of American Indian chiefs, taken by Edward Curtis.

Left The idea of a Moroccan room can be transported anywhere, as in this eclectic room. The divan is covered with printed textiles and lavished with layers of cushions, inviting people to recline. It is recessed, with chairs pulled up close, creating an intimate ambience.

Right This room at a Rajvilas resort in Jaipur represents romance and escape. The canopy of block-printed cotton is airy yet voluptuous. Brilliant orange cushions embroidered with mirror work reflect the sunlight and glitter on the bed. White curtains feel cool in the tropical heat, and contrast with the dark wood.

Left Tiny altars, special places to display a photograph of a saint, guru, or ancestor, can be created anywhere in a home – in corridors, niches, or on top of chests, or mantelpieces. Framing a picture with a curtain, as shown, bestows importance on the altar. The tieback – with its gold ropes and orange tassel – is pure ornament.

Above Sunlight pours from the clerestory through the sheer mosquito netting, making the canopy appear even more diaphanous. The feather-light canopy falls like a bridal veil from a tiara, and tumbles onto the floor. Sleeping under mosquito netting is both romantic and functional. You are sheltered as well as safe from insects.

If there is one textile that is particularly evocative of the rural lifestyle, it is probably the quilt. The quilt conjures up images of thrifty women winnowing dresses into dishtowels, and finally into patches, that would be worked into quilts, that would serve to keep them warm on cold blustery nights. The process of quilt-making suggests groups of women sitting around a table, painstakingly creating a tactile, subtle folk art, stitch by patient stitch. In Colonial America, people learned that textiles were precious, and the cost of imported textiles from Europe was marked up by as much as three hundred per cent. Transforming flax from the plant into usable linen took sixteen months in total. Scraps of fabric were to be hoarded, and reconfigured.

Although most quilts found at antique dealers and flea markets date from the nineteenth and early twentieth centuries, the art of quilt-making is, in fact, an ancient one. The oldest known quilt – a quilted robe – was found in Egypt, and dates from as far back as 3,400 BC. A surviving remnant of a Mongolian quilted floor cover dates back to around the time of Christ. In India, quilts were being fashioned from as early as the sixth century onwards. From the eleventh to thirteenth centuries, knights in the Crusades wore quilted fabrics as an extra layer under their armour to protect themselves from harm, as well as from the cold.

People have slept on top of quilts, using them as bed mats, as well as under quilts, using them as bed covers. People have worn quilted fabrics as robes in Japan, and as skirts in America. But primarily we are used to thinking of quilts as reflections of rural lives, where they were used as blankets, year after year, until red calicos faded to pink, and white backgrounds slowly turned yellow.

Left When you can't afford a quilt, consider a quilt top. A quilt top won't keep you warm, but it is a decorative piece of textile, full of patterns and lovingly made. They are best used on tables where you aren't going to dine, like this writing table.

Previous page Shabby chic, in the country where it was invented: England. Here, a quilt is tossed on the seat of the sofa, while another piece of faintly related fabric (the red) wraps the sofa like a shawl. A clutch of soft cushions is the finishing touch.

Above In this room in the Sheldon Hawkins house in Deerfield, Massachusetts, the quilt is museum quality. It has a bold, sophisticated design, and fine needlework. Antique white cotton night shirts and night gowns are treated as decor.

Opposite In Menorca, a simple flower-sprigged fabric has been turned into a tablecloth. Perhaps it was once a drape, or a summer slipcover. Although the paint on the furniture is flaking off, there is a sweet, unstudied charm to this room, scented by wild flowers, and warmed by the ad hoc tablecloth.

QUILTS AND COUNTRY TEXTILES

These days we treat old quilts differently. If they are precious, they can be put on stretchers and hung on walls. A somewhat fragile quilt, with a backing sewn on, can even grace a table, but not one where you eat. It can go on a side table by the bed, or in a hallway. If you insist on eating on it, shield it with a piece of glass cut to fit, said Blanche Greenstein, who with her partner, Thomas Woodard, sells antique textiles in Manhattan. Sturdy new ones or even some old ones in good condition can perform their original function and be used as blankets, bed covers, or throws.

Antique dealers caution you to beware that many countries make new ones to look old. The Chinese, for example, make Amish-style quilts in solid colours, and wash them many times so they look muted. Know the difference between a new quilt made to look old and the authentic piece, as the price difference is enormous, and don't pay the price for an antique when you're buying a new quilt.

Quilt covers, where the pieced cloth was put together, but never backed and quilted, are also charming. But quilts aren't the only textiles that look particularly apt in a country home. There are new and old blankets with Indian motifs. Rolls of old chintz, dating from the 1930s and 1940s and printed with cabbage roses, can be cut into tablecloths and curtains. Some people collect only printed tablecloths from the 1940s, with clusters of apples, grapes, and bananas printed on a white cotton background, and often bordered in red. (Similar tablecloths are also made new.) These fruit motifs look homey. Fancy they are not.

At flea markets, jumble sales, and street fairs, look too for old nightgowns, bed linens, pillowcases, rag rugs, and samplers. Nightgowns can hang in a room, just as a reference to times past. (Maybe you could even wear one.) Some of the most beautiful pillowcases have openwork, or hand-crocheted edges. Samplers can be framed and grouped on a wall.

Above This fringed textile, which in another life could have been a shawl or a tablecloth, now hangs on a mantelpiece. In this white-on-white room, the blue stripes add a horizontal dash of colour, while the fringe adds a breezy, lacy texture. The fabric proves that almost anything you find at a flea market – a lace tablecloth, a piano shawl, a bolt of unused chintz – can have multiple lives.

Overleaf The use of white paint on ceiling, wall, floor, and the white textiles makes this eaved attic feel spacious, bright, and clean. Gone is the muskiness associated with an attic. A flower-sprigged textile lies at the foot of the bed, a colour contrast to the white quilt.

Above A white-on-white room, always looks clean, bright, and summery. It is surprisingly easy to create with fabrics, especially from flea markets, which can be great sources of antique linens, from flat sheets to pillowcases with openwork.

Opposite This wooden bench is proof that you should never miss a fabric sale. The green, yellow, and blue fabrics are the same design, as if the owner went to a sale, bought the last yardage in each colour, and draped them over the bench – adding the fourth, non-matching fabric, as a lark. It works.

Hooked rugs, sometimes depicting dogs, cats, and ships, can also be framed and hung, or find their natural place on the floor. When you buy old textiles, especially fragile ones like linens and laces, hold them up to the light and look for holes. If there are holes, then the fabric probably won't last long.

In the city, go to discount fabric houses, where famous companies and designers sell the few last remaining bolts of fabric. Buy the same design in two or three different, harmonious colourways, in pieces large enough to cover a bed, a bench, or the back of a sofa. Or buy a striped chintz in blue and white, and a flowered one in the same colours. This way you have fabrics that can relate to each other in the same room. Think large when it comes to inexpensive textiles at flea markets or discount houses, because it's easier to find a use for big pieces than small.

Collect textiles with colour in mind or, in the case of white-on-white rooms, the total absence of colour. The white-on-white room speaks of summer, of feeling cool on a warm and sultry day. Regardless of the temperature outdoors, a white-on-white room looks and feels clean, pristine, soothing. It's also a look that requires a nearby bottle of bleach and a washing machine.

Peri Wolfman, the vice president of product design at Williams-Sonoma, the retail chain and mail-order catalogue, shares a SoHo loft with her husband, Charles Gold, a photographer, and three dogs. The living-room furniture is covered with white Marseilles spreads. Do the dogs shed? Yes. Do the dogs' paws make the white

Opposite In this bedroom in Gloucestershire, the canopy is artfully casual. The floral fabric, lined in pearl pink, has been suspended from a rod, and gently draped over the ends of the bed. The same floral fabric is hung as draperies, while another textile, a cheery patchwork pattern, covers the bed, pillow, and the chair seat. What unites the two differently patterned fabrics, both from Osborne & Little, is the pale palette.

Right As in the room featured opposite, the same hues, red in this case, link the different fabrics. Here the red in the flower-sprigged fabric-covered screen relates to the red in the checked cushion on the chair. There is an interval of a solid colour, in this case the white chair, which makes the mix of flowers and checks delightful, and not discomfiting.

spreads dirty? Yes. Do people spill wine? Yes. And what does Ms. Wolfman do? She whisks the fabric off the furniture, and tosses them into the washing machine. Voilà. Pristine whiteness.

Peri Wolfman is not alone in her love of white. Mallory Marshall, an interior designer in Portland, Maine, has two houses on the Maine coast. Each time she finds a piece of furniture, whether it's a bureau, a table, or a chair, she strips the old paint and repaints it white. But a white-on-white country room, with its wide floorboards, beamed ceilings, and wicker chairs, doesn't feel cold and austere as does white minimalism in an urban setting, where every surface is bare and smooth. In the country, a white-on-white feels more natural, and less self-conscious.

The canopy is not restricted to a formal urban setting. In the country, a canopy can be made of the simplest fabrics, like mosquito netting, white cotton sheeting, batiste, fish nets, crewel, or lace. Antique lace tablecloths can be draped on the wall behind the headboard, or suspended as curtains on the rods of a four-poster bed.

Left An Amish quilt, Goose and Gosling, with a Geese in Flight border design, dominates the room. The Goose and Gosling motif is repeated on the cushions, and the colours of the quilt are carried through in the throw. The quilt is a bold, graphic background for the chaise, whose upholstered comfort make it a place where you would want to settle down with a book.

Opposite Finally, Grandma's crocheted afghan blanket has a place of honour. In the sun porch, cooled by a ceiling fan, and shaded by old-fashioned louvred blinds, the furniture has been haphazardly covered with assorted fabrics, ranging from two afghans to a flat-woven rug, and metres of red cloth. The brightly coloured textiles, however, stand out against the quiet grey-green of the room.

Right A Variable Star quilt in a subtly electric combination of green, lavender, and pink, vibrates on the wall behind the chest. The photograph stands out against the quilt, while the placement of the quilt – behind the chest – keeps the textile protected from wear. Quilts like this one and the Bow-Tie variation, shown above, seem to capture optical movement, a graphic liveliness.

One of the small pleasures of country living lies in visiting the flea markets, jumble sales, and garage sales that so proliferate at the weekends – an activity that proves that shopping can be an addictive hobby, especially on rainy days, and yet shoppng in these places is relatively inexpensive. Focusing on textiles as collectibles is a natural, easy thing to do – textiles are all around us, in all their faded delicacy. Although some may be in need of repair (or at least a good wash), they often need a little care and attention, and only a bed, a pillow, or table to bring them back to life once again.

In the United States, flea markets can be not only sources for old quilts, but also items such as chenille spreads, lace curtains, Beacon blankets, Hudson Bay blankets, ruffled satin spreads, antique white sheets, and pillow shams (large, over-sized pillowcases). A fun way to shop can be to begin to focus on a single kind of textile, so that it can proliferate in a home. Renny Reynolds, a floral and party designer in Manhattan, has covered windows in his country home, in Bucks County, Pasadena, with mismatched lengths of antique lace. The sun filters through the fragile lace and moves across the room, sometimes in filigreed shadows.

To bring colour to a rustic home, consider covering all the beds with a variety of boldly coloured American Indian-style blankets. They come in vivid shades of red,

Below An all-white room in the country (or even in the city) is the answer to salvaging old and tired furniture. Several coats of white paint make uneven walls, crumbled corners of brick fireplaces, and splintered beams look smooth and of one piece. White paint also makes a room look clean. An antique white fabric is tacked on the wall behind the headboard, and acts as the suggestion of a canopy.

Opposite This enchanting nook is a window seat, an extra bed, a secret hideaway. The bed rests on boards which are wide enough so that the platform can also be used to hold flowers, a cup of coffee, a newspaper. White cotton batiste hangs on wires, and can be drawn close for privacy. The bed is made up of Indian cottons and, although the fabric is inexpensive, the massing of cushions gives the bed a feeling of extravagance.

Right An American flowered quilt, probably from the third quarter of the nineteenth century, is the focal point in this bedroom. The biggest antique quilts, which were made between 1840 and 1860, when beds were made to be raised high and wide, fit king-size beds today. The tablecloth is white-on-white appliqué.

Above Textiles can be less expensive than cabinetry. In this bathroom, white cloth with a scalloped hem has been gathered and fastened to the front of the sinks. The textile is both decorative and functional. It adds a softness to the room, covers whatever is underneath the sinks, and allows room for the feet.

Left The big quilt wall hanging contrasts with the hard surfaces and textures of the refectory table, the metal chairs, and the angular ceiling, in this austerely beautiful room. The grid of the mullions is repeated in the grid of the chairs. There are grace notes, apart from the quilt, in the table runner, the slender candlesticks, the flowers with their delicate trailing vines, and the seashells.

Opposite The great piece of fabric, decorated with flowers, foliage, and vines, and casually tossed over the armchair, is a piece of crewel work. It is a kind of embroidery using a worsted wool yarn on a plain weave fabric. The fabric can be used as bedspreads, hangings, and, in this case, as a very large and luxurious throw. The pale pink flowers in the hearth are the same delicate colours as those on the embroidered fabric.

Above A sheer figured net, dyed in kingfisher blue, veils the arched windows, making the view mysterious. The transparent curtain has been carefully hung, tied at four points, so that it drapes softly and trails along the floor, like the train of an evening gown. The panel is a gentle jolt of colour and a modulator of light.

cobalt, turquoise, emerald, with patterns of Indians, buffalo, horses, or graphic designs of stripes, diagonals, and diamonds. The blanket will become the focal point of a room, and add jolts of colour, pattern and warmth to the space.

Barbara Schubeck, an art director in Manhattan, once owned a house in Cutchogue, New York, with her husband, Ronald Barrett, an artist and author. For their kitchen, which faced the water of Long Island Sound, Ms. Schubeck collected only one kind of textile: 1940s and 1950s red and white cotton tablecloths, dish towels, and runners. The crucial design element was that the colour red featured somewhere on the cloth, whether it was in the bunches of cherries, in the dishes of strawberries, or if there was simply a red border. The red of the cloth, coupled with the red-painted knobs on the kitchen cupboards, gave coherence to the room – and also made finding hostess gifts easy. (This was in the 1970s, when the red-patterned textiles were authentic designs of the 1940s and 1950s. Now, the same patterns have been revived and are being made anew.)

FOLK ART

QUILTS AS

One person might treat his quilt as a coverlet to tuck a child in, on a cool autumn night. Another, who has just paid thousands of pounds or dollars for an early twentieth-century Amish Centre Square quilt, with a glowing violet square bordered by bands of forest green and russet, will have it stitched to linen, and attached to a wooden frame. That quilt will never wrap a squirming human body. Instead, it will be art, to be looked at and admired, just as you would peer at a painting by Josef Albers, Mark Rothko, or Kenneth Noland.

New quilts are made throughout the world, from Haiti to China, for export to Europe and the United States. The hand-made quilt is still being made, but is no longer an inexpensive example of women's handwork.

Quilts have visual power. They are also tactile lessons in history and folklore. Just consider the names that quilts bear. There are the simple, literal names – Maple Leaf, Tulip, Fruit Basket. There are animal names – Flying Geese and Wild Goose Chase, Sea Shell and Clamshell. Drunkard's Path, a zig-zag pattern, is also known as Country Husband, and Rocky Road in Dublin and California. What you do with your quilt is a private decision. It certainly doesn't have the warmth of a duvet stuffed with goosedown. But a quilt can delight the eye.

Above The orange and white quilt is the focus in this white room, where delicacy seems to be the design rule. The moulding is very refined, as are the lacy metal bed frame and the pedestal holding the flowers. The orange design on the quilt is refreshing.

Left In this tiny, eaved attic room, the dark wood of the sleigh bed and the window frame contrast with the white ceiling and walls. Here, as with the room on the opposite page, the orange pattern on the quilt and the piece of fabric draped over the foot of the bed, is bright and cheery. The quilt perks up a small, quiet room.

Opposite A collection of blue and white quilts hang on this enormous rack. The quilts are similarly bold, graphic, and lively. On the rack, they seem to have a three-dimensional quality about them. They ask to be touched, examined, compared, and contrasted. This collection is based on a colour palette, but a collection can start with any inspiration, the urge to have only Amish quilts, Tree of Life quilts, or baby quilts, for example.

Left A floral quilt in this clearly feminine bedroom covers the wall next to the bed, while another quilt, whose floral motif is far more spare, covers the bed. Fresh flowers in the vase add to the femininity of the room, which, however, is not cloyingly sweet.

FORMAL

Previous page This room, with the red-orange canopy suspended from a gold crown and the dark walls, is a dramatic, theatrical nod to the French Empire style.

Below Bath as theatre. The fringed curtains are a *portière*, and keep out drafts when the door is open. But they also transform the function of bathing into a sybaritic ritual, of stepping through curtains and languishing in a bathtub lit by a candelabrum.

Using textiles formally is to use them sumptuously, and with exquisite attention to detail, to create a spectacular, almost theatrical, effect. The formally dressed room makes people feel like kings and queens, ruling over their domains, even if it is a town apartment or a loft. It is the choice and treatment of textiles, whether it's a satin coverlet, silk canopies, or damask-covered chairs, that makes a room feel lush, sybaritic, and escapist. The formal room borrows elements from aristocratic life, and interprets them on a domestic scale. In all cultures – African, Indian, Chinese, French, Greek, English – textiles represent status. The more magnificent a person's tents, clothing, coverlets, wall hangings, rugs, and canopies, the more exalted his or her status. As John Morley writes of medieval European interiors in his *The History of Furniture: Twenty-Five Centuries of Styles and Design in the Western Tradition* (Thames & Hudson, 1999), "Mattresses, cushions, valances, and draperies succoured the seated body and shielded it from draughts. Bed-covers were 'glistening, shining, shot with gold, with stars gleaming on them'."

Furniture lagged behind. Courts travelled to maintain their authority, and with them came portable, sometimes rough, wooden furniture, that they would cover in lush fabrics. Textiles were placed over buffets and tables. When castles and grand houses were designed with suites of rooms lined up in a row, with doors that faced each other, it was called an enfilade. If all the doors were left open, strong drafts could blow down its length. So the French designed the portière, a curtain, which was sometimes a tapestry, which they hung over an open door to keep out the drafts. In today's homes, the portière adds formality to a room.

Opposite "The husband didn't want curtains," said Lucretia Moroni, the Manhattan textile designer. But the wife did, although she didn't want to lose any light. So Moroni produced these hand-dyed, hand-printed gauze curtains, so sheer that they are nearly transparent.

Opposite Mario Buatta, a Manhattan interior designer, says that rooms which are suffused with red, pink, or peach light, as they are here, make people's skin glow. The use of textiles here is extravagant. The canopy is dramatically, asymmetrically designed, and the headboard is lavishly upholstered.

Below This could have been a window seat, but instead the recessed space has been transformed into a secret hideaway, with curtains that draw, cushions that invite reclining, and purple window shades to keep out prying eyes.

CANOPIES AND HANGINGS

In ancient Greece and Rome, canopies, wall hangings, and awnings were originally functional, utilitarian textiles. The canopy was first a portable sun shield, to protect kings, queens, and armies from hot rays. A velarium was an awning, a huge swath of fabric, hung outdoors to protect people, whether at home, or at an outdoor theatre, from the sun. Canopies sheltered thrones, couches, beds, offering a real or suggested comfort, while signifying aristocracy. Antique draperies and wall hangings added warmth and softness to homes. At Versailles, there is an elaborately canopied bed where Louis XIV ostensibly slept, drawing panels around him, so that he could have an iota of privacy. But he actually slept elsewhere. A secret door, made to blend into the wall of the bedroom, led upstairs to a far more intimate room with solid walls, which was more private and, because it was small, much warmer. Even the cradles of royal heirs were often canopied, and put on display as cradles of state. In today's home, warmed by central heating, a canopied bed or tented room doesn't have to ward off drafts. Instead, such features can give architectural shape and interest to a room. "A tented room or canopied bed focuses the bed," according to Ronald Bricke, a Manhattan interior designer, "It changes the height of a room." For a room that had a double-height ceiling, and one, rather low window, Renzo Mongiardino, the late Milan-based architect, whose

Right This bed is ornate, with its turned spindles and carved asymmetrical headboard. The lace has been carefully draped over the headboard to suggest the lightest, softest canopy, not unlike a bridal veil. The antique lace cushions are also limp, fragile, and delicate, and contrast with the carved wood.

rooms were stunningly theatrical and voluptuous, created a double-swagged tent. Inspired by an eighteenth-century Turkish tent, the designer started the tent at the ceiling, and allowed it to drop in a double fall. A chandelier hung low under the tent. The tent obliterated the dark corners in the high part of the room, and collected light from the large window during the day and from the chandelier during the evening. A canopied bed or a tented room is synonymous with romance, seduction, and tactility, and make us feel pampered, cossetted, and rich. A canopy is a memory of fairy tales, sybaritic luxury, and romance. "Canopies are under-appreciated – especially by men – until after you actually sleep under one," said Mario Buatta, known for his transplanting of the English country style to the United States, and for his subsequent nickname, the Prince of Chintz. Once, Buatta designed a canopied bed for a married couple, transforming the bed into a cocoon by hanging four side curtains on a valance. "The husband came home from work, tossed his coat off, looked at the bed and said, 'Do men sleep like this?'" Buatta said yes, left the house, and tried to call them over the weekend to find out how they liked the design. Each time he called, there was no answer. Friday came and went. So did Saturday and Sunday. Finally, it was Monday. The wife called Buatta and said that they had fallen into the bed on Friday, and never got out of it until Monday. It was the most romantic bed they ever had. But alas, a bed does not a marriage save. They divorced eight years later, and the husband took the bed with him to his new wife.

For canopies and wall hangings, use textiles that drape naturally, like silk charmeuse, silk satin, taffeta, canvas, wool suiting, and cashmere. Silk, of course, reflects light, and some textile manufacturers, such as Osborne & Little, weave heavy silks that are two different colours, like red on one side and magenta on the other, or emerald on one side and turquoise on the other. When light strikes these two-toned fabrics, extraordinary colour changes happen.

Opposite Like stair landings, the corners of rooms can be forgotten places. In this room, a corner becomes a gallery of textiles. A thick rope with plump tassels ties back a length of curtain, which looks especially voluptuous trailing onto the floor. More textiles – a red brocade, a black and white check – are draped over a screen (which in itself is interesting) and onto the floor.

STAGE SETS

Renzo Mongiardino designed theatrical, atmospheric rooms and palaces, villas, and castles, as well as the Caffè Florian in Venice. His rooms took you out of the present and into places of beauty and fantasy, inspired sometimes by ancient Greece and Rome. Mongiardino understood that rooms can be theatre sets. Of all the rooms in a home, the bedroom is the most likely room to lend itself to theatre. After all, the bedroom is designed for acts of intimacy, of dreaming, and of revealing both flesh and fantasy. It is here that our bodies are naked, and highly attuned to the feel of fabrics, like silk, linen, velvet, and Egyptian cotton. Think of your favourite play, movie, novel, or exotic locale. "Rooms that are stage sets are great for guest rooms," Ronald Bricke said. "It should be unlike any room you've ever been in. It could be in the casbah or the Taj Mahal." You can cover an entire wall with fabric, in the antique drapery style of the Greeks and Romans. Or, as Mongiardino did, cover a wall in red damask and then drape it in white fabric, so that the red wall peeks through at the top. In a bathroom, he shrouded the walls with thick white terrycloth, edged in gold-coloured fringe. In Ronald Bricke's Manhattan apartment, he has a collection of forty different paintings, sketches, and etchings. To show them, he placed them on several adjacent walls, and then designed opaque white curtains – two for each wall – to cover the pictures. "You pull open a curtain and you see just two pictures," he said. When an entire room is covered in fabric, sound is muffled. "It's like when you're on the streets of New York, when snow is falling."

When you do not want to use a full canopy, or cover an entire wall with fabric, you can use fabric on just one part of a room. Ronald Bricke collects textiles, and he uses huge pieces of

Right The fabric has been meticulously stitched, gathered, and stretched to create this sunburst effect. The soft fabric contrasts with the lacquered headboard, matte against sheen, textile against wood. In another juxtaposition of textures, the roses, with their silky petals, are placed next to a gleaming metal lamp.

Opposite This bed is not designed for reading the Sunday papers. Dimly lit, it's clearly a soft and seductive love nest with fabric draped, swagged, gathered. What is splendid about this room is its excess, the swag on top, the lavishly fringed tie-backs, and more swags on the ceiling and on the walls. The bed is triple-layered in textiles, so that climbing into bed would be a series of exquisite sensations against the skin.

Previous page Classical draperies. White fabric has been lavishly, extravagantly draped across the walls, in the Greek and Roman style. "Drapery adds vertical lines to a room," said Ronald Bricke, a Manhattan interior designer. "The cowl-like drapery is very sculptural."

Right In this exceptionally tall narrow bedroom, "the use of pattern on pattern makes it cosy," said Mario Buatta. There is a rich interplay of pattern. The walls, curtains, and bed appear covered in the same design, while the walls are bordered in a second pattern. The floor is intricately patterned in two different designs.

Left To transform this carved wooden canopied bed into a place to sit, and not to automatically fall asleep, the designer layered cushion upon cushion, each in a different fabric, shape, and colour, on top of the custom-made mattress.

fabric, like five metres (5.5 yards) of poison-green damask, or the same amount of brilliant lavender Indian silk, as throws, bolts of colour tossed over the back of an all-white sofa in an all-white room. "It may be the only fabric in the room," Bricke said. "You could have five different saris, and change them during the seasons. You could use the saffron yellow one over the sofa in the spring, and use ice blue or lavender in the summer." He likens the use of textiles to the use of flowers. "You have yellow tulips one week, and pink hydrangea the next." Fabrics can be transient elements of decor, to be brought out and put away, rotated according to whim. In a formal bedroom, textiles not only cover the bed, and maybe the walls, but also the floor and the lights. The sybarite shouldn't have to put his or her bare feet on a cold floor. Rugs can be layered on the floor. Light is most appealing when it is diffused through shades of silk, paper, or glass. The bed frame can be a focal point. It can be a Chinese bed, designed almost as a room within a room. Some come with three wooden sides, others so that silk hangings can be drawn tight around the sides. Peggy Guggenheim commissioned Alexander Calder to make her a silver metal headboard, with sculpted fish. A bed can have four posts. But what softens these angular beds is an extravagant use of textiles: velvet duvet covers over fat, down comforters, four pillows rather than two, and curtains that can be tied back, swagged, or tumble to the floor to mute the light.

Above A vaulted ceiling and arched windows give drama to this room, as do the transparent white curtains on the four-poster bed. The gossamer white curtains are almost weightless to complement the slender posts of the bed. The bed skirt is crisply tailored. A golden light shines through the gathered fabric shade.

Opposite A Napoleonic travel tent, traditionally striped, goes indoors, complete with collapsible campaign furniture. Although the tent is made of cotton canvas, this is a formal use of an informal fabric. The stripes have been perfectly matched where the canopies meet the fabric on the wall and ceiling. The tented room has a tailored but romantic ambience.

Since ancient times, military leaders, whether in Persia, France, or England, have used textiles lavishly in their tents. Persian tents combined flannel and silk that was cut and appliquéd. In Mogul hangings, decorative motifs included roses, poppies, and lilies. Henry VIII of England hung his tents with gold and silver brocades and tapestries. A typical travelling tent, however, was striped and often made of a sturdy plain fabric, like a canvas. But, tents do not have to be relegated to the outdoors. Indoors, a completely tented room provides a cocoon-like architectural structure without built walls. Sleeping in a tented room gives you the illusion that you are camping outdoors, but in the most self-indulgent way. In fact, Todd Dalland, an architect at FTL/Happold, a Manhattan firm specializing in tensile designs, said, "If people embraced modern technology in home construction as enthusiastically as they do advancements in airplanes, computers and fabric for clothing, housing would look like tents... Shapes would be curved, so the body language would be different, more sensual. Tents use less material and are lighter in weight." Tented buildings and rooms could be translucent. In Tokyo, Noriyuki Asakura, a Japanese architect, topped the house where he lives with his wife, Sachiko, with a tent-like roof made of resin-coated fibreglass. In Manhattan, the architect Gisela Stromeyer designed a conference room for the Click modelling agency that is part fabric, part curving fibreglass wall. The room is under a skylight that pours light into the room, and plays on the translucent fabric.

Above Stripes on stripes. There are three striped patterns at work here, all going in different directions. The multiple stripes add architectural definition to the wall, and because one is horizontal while the other is vertical, the stripes are visually interesting without being fatiguing to the eye. The striped curtain adds colour and especially softness to the space.

Left Stairwells, along with stair landings, tend to be forgotten places. Here at Rajvilas, an Oberoi hotel in Jaipur, India, a textile with a zig-zag pattern hangs on the wall of a stairwell. The textile is lively enough to distract anyone going up and down the steps and make them stop and pause.

Right Enormous red and white striped quilts hang on the wall and cover the bed, emphasizing the height of the room, and adding graphic punch. The tapestry is hung from the same height as the quilt, creating a visual balance. What unites these slightly disparate textiles are their weightiness and scale.

To create a wholly or partially tented room, or simply to warm the walls you can choose textiles from weighty, heavy tapestries to embroidered silk hangings to translucent polypropylene, stretched taut on frames. Tapestries are portable wall hangings, and sometimes depict stories and myths. From the Middle Ages into the eighteenth century, tapestries have been considered as important works of art, and have been commissioned and collected by royalty. Charles VI, the Holy Roman Emperor, commissioned a series that commemorated his military campaigns. Louis XIV had an extensive tapestry collection, and Henry VIII owned more than 2,000. Tapestries were also considered worthy as high art, and Raphael and Rubens designed cartoons for tapestry weavers. Tapestry production was in decline by the second third of the eighteenth century. The rich began to collect and display paintings, cover their walls with Chinese wallpaper, and were better able to heat the interiors of their homes, making tapestries less essential as a source of insulation.

At the other end of the textile spectrum are sheer fabrics, exquisite laces, gossamer embroidered silks, and hand-printed cotton gauzes. These fabrics can frame a window, flutter over a bed, or divide a room. New technologically derived textiles, like polypropylene or the Japanese polyester fabrics woven with aluminium or copper, can also be used formally, as swooping canopies over beds, as coloured veils over windows, or as hangings at the sides of a bed.

Sometimes the inspiration to live in a more formal space is simply maturity. As we get older, and the children leave home, the desire to live a slightly more formal life may overcome us. And sometimes that sense of formality is as simple as wanting to surround ourselves with extraordinary textiles, from the sheets on our beds, to the coverlets, pillowcases, rugs, and upholstery.

Left Many shades of peach. This corner tableau is a palette of peach tones which makes the room glow. The flowers on the hanging are peach, the walls are coral, and the stripes on the fabric lampshade are a deeper red-orange.

Formality can be as simple as allowing yourself complete indulgence in textiles – just as when we grow older we choose to wear cashmere sweaters rather than Shetland wool, or silk shirts rather than cotton.

Begin, then, with the bed. Sheets come in cotton blends, pure cotton (the higher the thread count, the smoother the fabric), and linen. The luxury of tucking yourself into a freshly laundered and pressed fine cotton sheet is exquisite. On a hot summer night, a linen sheet can be positively seductive.

In the formal bed, the number of pillows is seldom as few as two. In *Shelter* magazine – and in real homes – four pillows for two people show up frequently: two regular pillows and two European squares. Sometimes there are up to eight, including neck rolls. An abundance of pillows signifies luxury. The extra pillows may be superfluous for sleep, but they possess a sense of extravagance, of blissful excess. They can be covered in cotton or linen, and are often embellished with handwork like faggoting, embroidery or cutwork. The very fragility signifies formality.

Opposite The brief for interior designer Laura Anson for this London flat was to "make it eccentric." So Anson covered Gothic-style chairs in yellow, purple, pink, and red velvet, and used a fire-station pole to support a dining table. The tapestry hanging above the chaise came from an auction. The anaesthetizing unit, far left, is to become a drinks cabinet.

Right In this bathroom in a Derbyshire farmhouse, the heavy brocade curtains are an unexpected addition. Brocade is usually a fabric reserved for living rooms or canopies – but in bathrooms it is rare. Nevertheless, the luxurious fabric frames a rural view, and a carefully arranged collection of seashells – while at the same time providing privacy.

Left "If you take out this gossamer veil, it's all hard edge," said interior designer Ronald Bricke of this room. The beautifully shaped curtain, hung asymmetrically and caught at the side, modulates the light in a mysterious fashion, and lets it sweep across the bare floor. The shape of the curtain is modern, in contrast with tbe furniture, and provides semi-privacy.

Then there are the bed covers, one for winter, the other for summer. For winter, consider a duvet cover made of velvet, linen, or embroidered wool. Duvet covers also come in cashmere, silk or damask, or lavishly tasseled, with buttons, or silk ties.

Come summer, white matelasse has a rich texture, and just a bit of weight. White lace stitched onto an ecru spread, or ecru lace on white, would make an elegant spread for summer. Linen edged in organza, or the reverse, is crisp and cool.

Where bare polished wooden floors once sufficed, consider collecting carpets. There are beautiful silk rugs, old and new, which have a soft, beautiful light-catching quality. They tend to be fragile, but they could be used as the top layer of a wool rug in a bedroom, or positioned by the side of the bed. There are rugs which are designed like mosaics, abstract art, or Op Art. They can be bordered in silk, hand-painted linen, or lavishly fringed. A floor is a blank canvas, and a carpet can be a functional piece of art.

You can apply that same formality in thinking to your window coverings. Instead of using blinds, consider layers of fabric like silk, cotton, linen, lace, and pongee floating at your windows. Excess can be appealing, like having curtains trail onto the floor by a few extra inches. They can be overly full, so when they are tied back, they form lush, voluptuous folds. They can be hung asymmetrically, or centred where they are gathered together in the middle, and tied with thick tasseled cords. Formality is a coming of age.

Opposite The sheer yellow curtains perform a multitude of design tricks here. They divide one room from the other, provide a modicum of privacy, and filter the natural light from the living room into the dining area in a sunny way. Since the curtains are almost ethereal, they don't distract from the heavier textiles used in the living area.

RICH FABRIC

NEW USES FOR

Although tapestries fell out of favour towards the end of the eighteenth century, they re-emerged as a vogue in the late nineteenth century with the enthusiasm for weaving introduced by the Arts and Crafts movement. Twentieth-century weavers such as Anni Albers, Sheila Hicks, and Jack Lenor Larsen created modern, one-off tapestries, as distinct from the pictorial pieces of the Renaissance as the architecture of Mies van der Rohe was from that of Palladio. What all tapestries possess is exceptional tactile presence. If they are figurative, they are a story told on a gigantic, floor-to-ceiling, scale. Tapestries are thick and heavy, and can dominate a room, whether on a wall, behind a bed, above a table, or in a corridor. Tapestries should not, however, be used for movable drapery. Because they are weighty, they are difficult to open or close. Ronald Bricke, a Manhattan interior designer, recommends that if you want to hang heavy fabric around a four-poster bed or canopied bed, do so, but layer it with a lighter-weight sheer or opaque fabric. Then, if you want to draw the fabric around you, and snuggle within the soft cocoon, you will be tugging only the light-weight fabric. An

Left Chairs wear slipcovers, and are sometimes wrapped and tied in sheets, so why can't they also wear burnooses (long hooded cloaks with a hood)? "It's a sculptural way of dealing with a chair," said Ronald Bricke, the Manhattan interior designer.

Left To medieval European aristocracy, tapestries were movable art – as they were to the Marquis de Sade, who even hung tapestries on the walls of his prison cell. In this dining room, a tapestry fulfils the same original function.

Above What is appealing about this dining area is the amassing of heavy, natural textures in one room. Each object, from the tapestry to the table, chairs, basket, and flower pot, is sturdy and tactile. The flowers add a bright note against the tapestry.

exquisite rug – a Chinese silk rug, for example – would be too beautiful and possibly too fragile to be placed on the floor, so treat it like a tapestry and hang it on the wall. Pretend you're Rembrandt who, in his paintings, placed rugs on the table and on the wall, but not on the floor. Textiles can dress up chairs. Ordinary wooden-framed chairs can be covered, from top to bottom, with brocades, damasks, cottons, linens, and glistening rayon satins. Those slipcovers are not the party designer's prerogative. They are on sale everywhere. In 1999 in Manhattan, at Dining for Design, one of the benefits for Design Industries Foundation Fighting Aids (DIFFA), one company sponsored a table, and the chair's upholstered touch – a pashmina shawl neatly folded and draped over the back of the chair – was also the souvenir, the take-home gift.

M any textiles are in various states of repair or fragility when they are first acquired by their new owners. They are also very often dirty or dusty, which in itself can often contribute to fabric deterioration. Any cleaning of textiles that you decide to undertake yourself should be carried out with care. If you are in any doubt about the condition of your textile, consult a professional textile conservator who will be able to advise you with specialist cleaning or conservation issues, and who will also have access to the appropriate specialist tools – such as variable suction vacuums – and professional cleaning methods. Specialists can also advise on the kinds of fabrics that you will need to purchase to use in conjunction with your textiles, for example underlays for your rugs and *kilims*, or backing fabrics for textiles that you wish to hang.

The range of fabrics that are available for presenting and displaying textiles is vast. It is important to choose one that is compatible – visually and practically – with your textile, and which is also easy to handle. Most decorative textiles are made from natural fibres, and so presenting them with a natural fabric will often compliment them aesthetically.

Below A specialist textiles restorer in a workshop uses distilled water to carefully clean each individual strand of the fringe of a large decorative textile.

Right When laying rugs and carpets, the use of a good quality underfelt is very important. Here, the drugget protection is rolled back, as is the corner of the carpet, to reveal the wooden rugstop and the hair underfelt.

 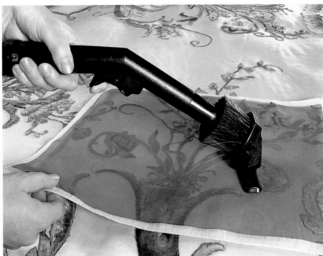

Above A conservation cleaner works on a bedspread. The delicate embroidered surface is painstakingly cleaned with a low-suction mini vacuum – a specialist textile restorer's device. A nylon monofilament is used to protect loose threads from being caught up, snagging the delicate fabric and distorting the intricate pattern.

Above The conservation cleaner protects the embroidered surface of the bedspread, this time using a low suction mini vacuum with a crevice tool, and a nylon net to remove surface dust.

Cotton and linen are often the best backing fabrics to use for lining hanging textiles – they have a weight to them that helps the material to hang well. The grains of these fabrics are also normally straight, making them easier to cut. If you are using silk as a backing fabric, choose one with body; if it is too thin it will be difficult to cut and sew in a straight line.

If you decide to work with textiles at home, it is vital to invest in good quality equipment. A pair of large, sharp cutting scissors is essential and a small pair of needlework scissors is useful. A long tape measure and a carpenters tape are also helpful. Brightly coloured cotton can be used for temporary tacking stitches, and tailors chalk may be used to mark on the backing fabric (but never to the textile itself). Also, remember that different types of pins should be used with different fabrics – fine pins should be used with silk, as thin fabrics tend to snag very easily. Glass-headed pins are available in different sizes and lengths to suit most weights of fabric.

Textiles tend to be fragile and sensitive pieces – conservation and careful maintenance are vital to preserve them and to prolong their lifespans. Avoid placing them in direct sunlight, as it will cause the colours to fade and the fibres to deteriorate. Do not display them directly over radiators, or in damp locations, because both extremes will cause warping. It is also important to always try to use acid-free materials, such as woods and boards which are inert, and won't damage the fabric structure.

Lining a Hanging Textile

Hanging a textile is an excellent way of displaying larger, stronger pieces, such as tapestries, crewelwork, and ancient rugs. It is important to use the right support heading and backing fabric, so that the weight of the textile is distributed correctly. Incorrect hanging will be look wrong and can damage the fabric.

There are several ways of heading a textile for hanging. A safe means of hanging heavier textiles, is to create a sleeve for a baton, which can be attached to a wall or suspended from the ceiling. Most hanging textiles have a fabric backing to help protect them, and to which the baton heading is attached. The process of backing or lining a textile is similar to lining a curtain. An interlining with a cotton domett, or a slightly heavier cotton interlining can be added if needed. Choose a fabric that is strong enough to support your textile – for example, a good strong linen for a tapestry or a soft cotton for lighter textiles.

The textile should also be given a false hem, so that the backing fabric will not be hemmed to the base of the textile itself. The false hem is a fabric strip that is sewn to the bottom of the textile, to which the backing fabric will be secured.

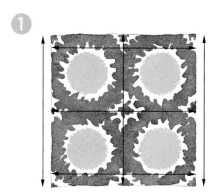

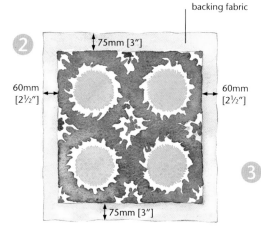

backing fabric

75mm [3"]

60mm [2½"]   60mm [2½"]

75mm [3"]

It is useful to remember the following seam allowances: 60mm [2½in] for turn-in on the side seams, and 75mm [3in] for turn-in on the top and the bottom seams. If you are joining your fabric in the centre, allow a further 12mm [½in] each side for a seam allowance.

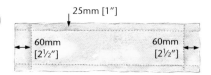

25mm [1"]

60mm [2½"]   60mm [2½"]

1 Measure the textile from corner to corner and through the centre field. Older textiles will vary considerably in dimensions, as the corners and edges may stretch over time.

2 Before cutting the textile, always lay the fabric completely flat. Make sure it is square and cut on the line of the weave, so that it will hang correctly.

3 The length of the sleeve to be attached to the backing fabric depends on the size of the textile, but it should be 150mm [6in] deep. Allow for a 25mm [1in] seam at the top and bottom, and 60mm [2½in] at each end.

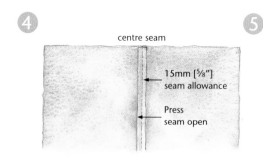

centre seam

15mm [⅝"] seam allowance

Press seam open

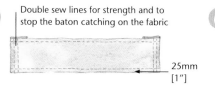

Double sew lines for strength and to stop the baton catching on the fabric

25mm [1"]

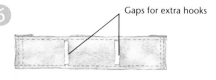

Gaps for extra hooks

4 If you are preparing a large textile, you may need to join the backing fabric in one or more places. Press the centre seams flat.

5 When preparing the fabric for the sleeve, Turn in the top and bottom edges to the correct width using a sewing machine. Sew 12mm [½in] from the edge. Turn in each side edge by 25mm [1in], so that the sleeve is approximately 50mm [2in] shorter in width than the textile. This prevents the baton from being seen when the textile is hanging.

6 If the textile is very long or heavy, leave gaps in the sleeve at regular intervals so that hooks can be attached to the baton to take some of the weight, preventing the baton from sagging in the middle.

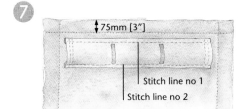

7 Place the sleeve on to the backing fabric 75mm [3in] from the top, with the open seam facing down. Pin the sleeve onto the top edge and machine into place. Stretch out the sleeve and mark the line of the bottom edge. Pin the sleeve 12mm [½in] above this line so that the sleeve gapes slightly, enabling the baton to fit easily, without distorting the front view of the textile.

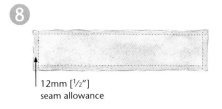

8 The false hem is sewn separately to the bottom of the textile. This allows it to hang without bagging at the hem and helps to protect the bottom from dirt and dust. Again, the length of this piece depends on the size of the textile. Allow a seam of 19mm [¾in] on all of the edges.

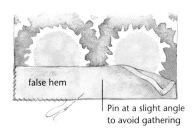

9 Hand sew, with a slip stitch, the false hem to the textile, taking care that the stitches do not show on the front side of the textile.

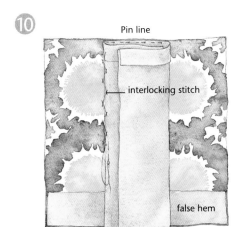

10 Lay the lining on the top of the textile with the sleeve at the top. Fold the fabric 5mm [¼in] above the sleeve line and position this onto the top of the textile. Straighten out the lining.

Most textiles will need a couple of rows of a loose interlocking stitch, running the height of the textile. Divide it into 3 sections, and working from the centre, pin the centre third.

11 Fold back the lining towards the centre of the textile at equal distances from both edges and interlock. This secures the lining to the textile. Straighten out the lining and continue to pin the rest of it into place, turning the edges in. Sew the rest of the lining to the textile using a slip stitch, apart from the bottom hem.

12 Sew a support stitch under the sleeve to stop the textile from separating from the lining when the baton is inserted. Above the bottom of the textile, sew a 25mm [1in] long button hole chain stitch every 150mm [6in] at 35mm [1½in] to stop the textile billowing out.

The textile is now ready to hang.
Insert the baton through the prepared sleeve. Secure hooks to the wall and suspend the baton from each end, or support at regular intervals if needed.

Mounting Flat Objects

Whether you decide to finish your mounted textile with Perspex, a picture frame, or left with no cover at all, the process of mounting the textile will be the same.

fabric or paper

When measuring the textile, lie it onto a piece of cloth or paper to visualize whether you would like a border around the textile, or whether it would look better without. Make a drawing with the measurements of the textile and the border. The textile needs to be measured from corner to corner and across the centre field. (Take into account the size of the border if you are having one.) Your textile will probably have some stretch in it, so allow some room for this and for attaching the fabric to the board.

Choose a backing fabric that will compliment your textile. It needs to be strong enough to take the weight of the textile, so that it will not sag at the bottom over time. Smaller textiles can be mounted straight onto a flat board if they are going to be framed. An interlining will give the textile a light padding and protection.

① interlining board glue

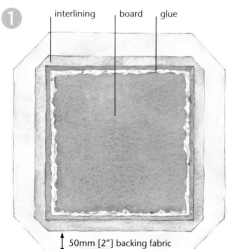

50mm [2"] backing fabric

② Mitre corners flush with each other

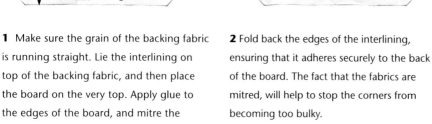

③

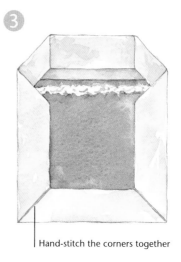

Hand-stitch the corners together

1 Make sure the grain of the backing fabric is running straight. Lie the interlining on top of the backing fabric, and then place the board on the very top. Apply glue to the edges of the board, and mitre the corners of both the backing fabric and the interlining.

2 Fold back the edges of the interlining, ensuring that it adheres securely to the back of the board. The fact that the fabrics are mitred, will help to stop the corners from becoming too bulky.

3 Fold back the edges of the backing fabric, making sure that it also adheres to the board and securely stitch together by hand the mitred corners. Turn the board over. You now have a backing on which to mount your textile.

Ideally, larger textiles need a stretcher under the board to prevent it from warping and bending. Wooden stretchers are available from art stores. Many art stores and framers stock acid-free materials, try to use these when ever possible. If not, use a foil barrier between the frame and the fabric, such as Gator board or Melinex.

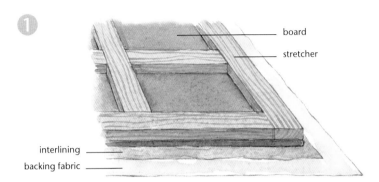

board

stretcher

interlining

backing fabric

1 Fix the board to the wooden stretcher with an adhesive. The method of mounting the textile is the same, but instead of glue, the interlining and backing fabric should be stapled to the stretcher frame. Begin stapling from the centre of the side of the frame out towards the corners. Then move to the opposite side and do the same. The mitred

corners are to be sewn by hand. Make sure that the weave has stayed straight on the front of the stretcher and that there are no creases.

2 The backing fabric is now prepared, so that the textile can be sewn, by hand, directly on to it.

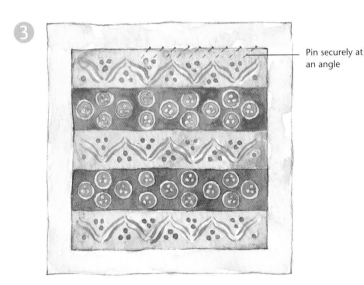

Pin securely at an angle

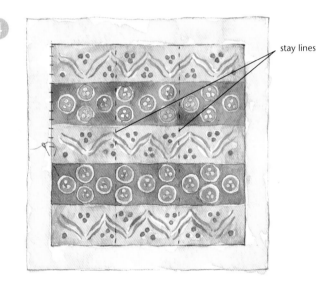

stay lines

3 First, pin the textile into place, leaving as much of the backing fabric to appear as a border as you wish. Gently pull out the textile to create a tension, this will prevent the fabric from sagging when it is hanging. When the textile is secured into place, the pins will be replaced with stitching. The stitches should be straight and at regular intervals on the top side of the textile. You may find it easier to use a curved needle.

4 If the textile is very heavy, the bottom stitching can be left unsewn, to help the textile hang without sagging at the bottom. Stay lines can also be loosely sewn to help support the the weight.

The textile is now ready to be framed professionally. A slip, mount card, or fabric-covered mount should be used so that the glass or does not touch the textile. Alternatively it be displayed in a Perspex case, or even hung without a projective cover using the same method as for hanging pictures.

Free-standing Displays

Many textiles, such as costumes, Chinese and Japanese robes, kuba cloths, embroideries, ecclesiastical textiles, Tankas, or double-sided textiles can be displayed suspended – using hanging poles – or free-standing. Three-dimensional objects, including beaded objects, purses, hats, fans, and other accessories can look quite sculptural, whether free-standing or presented in Perspex display cases (depending on the fragility of the piece).

1 When hanging a robe, it is best to suspend it from a covered, padded wooden pole to avoid creasing and fold lines. Padded poles can be used to display other textiles such as quilts, palampores, and the kuba raffia cloths which are often too long to display entirely. The pole is padded to protect the textile from the acids in the wood. Leave a small amount of the wooden pole bare, so that it can be suspended. If the robe is open at the neck, the colour of the padding should compliment the rest of the robe. In the neck area of the robe, the padding can be taken down to fill the neck of the robe.

2 The pole must be strong enough to take the weight of the robe. Many thicknesses of polyester paddings are available. You will need another fabric to cover the padding – silk works well with Chinese and Japanese textiles. Cut the polyester to fit around the pole. If you are padding the neck, then cut this at the same time. To achieve the thickness required, use a few layers but avoid making it too thick.

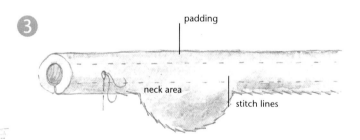

fold line

neck area

3 Place the padding around the pole, pin into place, then stitch. Use long stitches but do not sew too tightly. For the top cover, cut the same shape as the padding, remember a seam allowance of 25mm [1in] all around. Pin into place over the padding and sew using a small invisible hemming stitch.

padding

neck area

stitch lines

4 To finish the padding at the sleeve ends, cut a circle of fabric, with the same diameter as the end of the padding, with an allowance of 12mm [½in]. Cut a hole in the centre for the pole to go through, and clip the edge to enable the hem to turn in flat. Sew with a small running stitch. Place over the pole end and finish the outside seam in the same way.

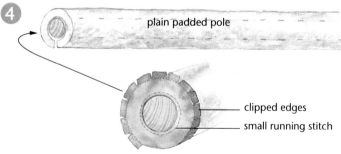

plain padded pole

clipped edges

small running stitch

Displaying a Three-dimensional Textile

Displaying three-dimensional textile-related objects is a pleasing way to view them and to see them in their entirety. A good support structure is needed to display any of these objects, Perspex is ideal for this – it is unobtrusive and elegant. Most good picture framers work with Perspex or will be able to put you in touch with someone who will make up display stands and cases.

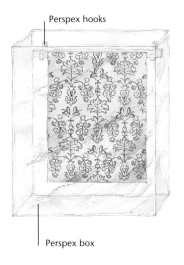

Perspex hooks

Perspex box

◄ Tankas and other similar textiles can be suspended in a Perspex display case. Many Tankas already have a pole at the top for this purpose. A clear thread can be attached to each end and fixed to the top of the case, or Perspex hooks can be made. If a sleeve is needed, use the method described in *Lining a Hanging Textile* (pp134–135). Alternatively a freestanding support can be made.

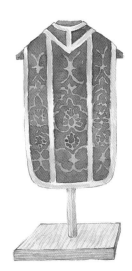

◄ This style of display stand can be used to support a double-sided piece such as Chinese chair back, or ecclesiastical textiles. Make sure that the stand size is in proportion to the textile. The pole diameters should be wide enough so that they do not bend or break under the weight. Padding can be secured to the top pole; this can be made to fit the shape of the article or garment that is being displayed. Cover the padding with a fabric to compliment the textile.

To display hats, or other accessories, a display stand made from Perspex similar to the one above can be used. The stand size needs to be in proportion with the size of the hat.

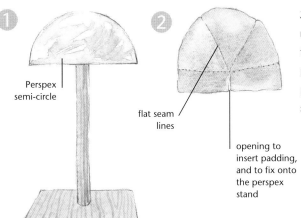

Perspex semi-circle

flat seam lines

opening to insert padding, and to fix onto the perspex stand

2 The padding should be firm enough to stop creases forming, but soft enough not to strain the seams of the hat. Insert the top of the stand into the opening at the bottom of the pad and stitch it together on the underside. Cover the support pad with fabric to finish it. The support is now ready. By changing the shape of the padding on the top support to suit the object, many kinds of textiles can be supported in this way.

1 The shape of the top support should vary, according to the kind of object you wish to display. For a hat, it should be a half sphere. This can be padded, depending on the condition of the hat. To make a the support into a hat shape, first make a pattern of the inside of the hat. Use soft cotton or calico and sew together with a flat seam. Leave the bottom unsewn, as you will need to stuff it with polyester padding and attach it to the Perspex stand. Take care to ensure that the shape of the hat is not distorted.

INDEX

AUTHOR'S ACKNOWLEDGMENTS

I would like to thank the curators and experts who gave so generously of their time. In New York City, thanks to: Kate Carmel of Phillips Auctioneers, and former Acting Director of the American Craft Museum; Lynn Felsher, curator of textiles at the Fashion Institute of Technology; Annie Van Assche, curator of education and textiles at the Japan Society; Gillian Moss, curator of textiles at the Cooper-Hewitt, Smithsonian Museum of Design. The interior designers Mario Buatta and Ronald Bricke were generous and funny with their ideas. Thanks to Blanche Greenstein, Doris Leslie Blau, Mark Shilen, Lucretia Moroni, Tracy Turner, Helen Verin, and Robert Grossman. In Washington D.C., the staff of the Textile Museum were extremely helpful, especially Sumru Belger Krody, associate curator, Eastern Hemisphere, and Claudia Brittenham, assistant curator, Eastern Hemisphere. And in London, I want to thank the team at Mitchell-Beazley who made the book possible: Lynn P. Bryan, Mark Fletcher, John Jervis, Jo Walton, Hannah Barnes-Murphy, John Round, and Mary Scott.

PHOTO ACKNOWLEDGMENTS

The Publisher would like to thank the following for their kind permission to reproduce photographs in this book

KEY

t top, b bottom, l left, r right

AvE Andreas von Einseidel; **CP** Camera Press; **CQ** Carolyn Quartermaine; **EW** Elizabeth Whiting/www.elizabethwhiting.com; **HW** Henry Wilson; **H&G** Homes & Gardens; **I** Inspirations; **IA** The Interior Archive; **II** International Interiors; **IPCS** IPC Syndications; **JB** Jan Baldwin; **LE** Living Etc.; **RM** Ray Main/Mainstream; **MF** Michael Freeman; **N** Narratives; **O&L** Osborne & Little; **RHS** Robert Harding Syndication; **RB** Richard Bryant

Front cover RM; **Back cover, l** Fernando Bengoechea/IA/Owner: Tracey Garrett; **Back cover, r** AvE/Alistair Little, fabric: O&L; **Endpapers** RM; **1** EW; **2–3** Polly Wreford/N; **5** AvE/Designer: CQ; **6 b** Musee Municipal, Sens/Erich Lessing/AKG; **6 t** British Library/AKG; **7** British Library/AKG; **8** State Historical Museum, Moscow/AKG London; **9** AKG London; **10–11** Designer: Boris Sipek/Wolfgang Schwager/Artur; **12** JB/N/Roger Oates Design; **13** JB/N; **14** Galatea: Liberty Furnishings/O&L; **15 l** Nicolas Bruant/IA/Designer: CQ; **15 r** Polly Wreford/LE/IPCS; **16–17** Designer: Peter Romaniuk/Dennis Gilbert/View; **18** HW/IA/Designer: Anouska Hempel; **19** Wayne Vincent/IA/Designer: Jackie Llewellyn-Bowen; **20 t** Verne/Architect: Jonathan Leitersdorf; **20 b** RM; **21** Verne; **22** JB/N; **23** Nick Pope/LE/IPCS; **24** MF/Architect: Jun Tamaki; **25** MF; **26** Verne/Architect: Robbrecht & Daem; **27** Dieter Leistner/Artur/Architect: Eugen D Merkle; **28** Tham nhu tran/H&G/IPCS; **29** RM; **30** Adrian Briscoe/Ideal Home/IPCS; **31** RM/Designer: Kate Blee; **32** JB/N; **32 r** RM; **33 t** Fatto a Mano, by Lucretia Moroni Ltd; **33 b** Deidi von Schaewen; **34–35** William R Tingey; **36** Jim Holmes/Axiom; **37** Lu Jeffery; **38 l** Hiroshi Kutomi/Axiom; **38 r** RB/Arcaid/Architect: Gale & Prior; **39** Masayuki Tsutsui/Bashohu textile by Toshiko Taira; **40–41** MF; **42** William R Tingey; **43** Steve Dalton/LE/IPCS; **44 l** Fair Lady/CP; **44 r** RM; **46** MF; **47 l** Tom Leighton/H&G/IPCS; **47 b** RM; **48–49** HW/IA/Designer: Anouska Hempel, Owner: Lady Weinbeg; **50** Max Jourdan/CP; **51** RM/Designer: Kelly Hoppen; **52** Andrew Wood/IA/Title: Asian Elements; **53** Andrew Wood/IA/Title: Asian Elements; **54–55** RB/Arcaid/Architect: Tsao & McKown; **56 l** HW/IA/Designer: Albrizzi; **56 r** William R Tingey; **57 t** Spike Powell/EW; **57 b** Masayuki Tsutsui; **58–59** MF; **60** Fritz von der Schulenburg/IA/Designer: Rima el-Said; **61** Lu Jeffery; **62** Deidi von Schaewen; **63** Chiswick by Liberty Furnishings/O&L; **64** Mark Bolton/Red Cover; **65 l** Deidi von Schaewen; **66** Simon Upton/IA/Owner: Simon Upton; **67** RM/Designer: Ellis Flyte; **68–69** Brigitte/CP; **70** JB/N; **71** Schoner Wohen/CP; **72** Fernando Bengoechea/IA/Owner: Deborah Fine; **73** Fernando Bengoechea/IA/Owner: Bengoechea; **74** Fritz von der Schulenburg/IA/Designer: Anokhi, India; **75** Fritz von der Schulenburg/IA/Designer: Rima el-Said; **76** Trevor Richards/Abode; **77 t** Fernando Bengoechea/IA/Owner: Tracey Garrett; **77 b** JB/N; **78** Max Jourdan/CP; **79** Philip Bier/View; **80 l** Deidi von Schaewen; **81 l** RB/Arcaid; **81 t r** Mark Luscombe-Whyte/EW ; **82–83** David George/Red Cover; **84** Eduardo Munoz/IA/Designer: Gonzalo Anes; **85** MF; **86** Brock/Abode; **87** Adrian Briscoe/Inspirations/RHS; **88–89** Designer: Sasha Waddell/Paul Ryan/II; **90** Ianthe Ruthven; **91** Deidi von Schaewen; **92** AvE/Alistair Little, fabric: O&L; **93** Sussie Bell/I/RHS; **94 t** Dennis Stone/EW; **94 b** Deidi von Schaewen; **95** Peter Woloszynski/IA/Property: Southern Style; **96** Jakob Wastberg/IA/Property: Fidenas; **97** Brigitte/CP; **98** Designer: Mary Blanchard/Paul Ryan/II; **99** Pia Tryde/H&G/IPCS; **100–101** Designer: Kathy Gallagher/Paul Ryan/II; **102** Lizzie Orme/I/RHS; **103** Nick Carter/EW; **104 t** Spike Powell/I/RHS; **104 b** Designer: Marjolyn Wittich/Paul Ryan/II; **105 t** Fritz von der Schulenburg/IA/Designer: Jasper Conran; **105 b** AvE/Alexandra Stoddart; **106–107** Ianthe Ruthven; **108** Pia Tryde/H&G/IPCS; **109** Fatto a Mano by Lucretia Moroni Ltd; **110** HW/IA/Designer: Emma Kennedy; **111** AvE/Amanda Eliasch; **112** EW; **113** EW; **114** RM; **115** AvE/Red Cover; **116** Deidi von Schaewen; **118** Deidi von Schaewen; **119 l** Alan Weintraub/Arcaid/Designer: Candra Scott; **119 r** C&C, Milan; **120** Deidi von Schaewen; **121** AvE/Designer: Timney-Fowler; **122** RB/Arcaid; **123** Ian Parry/Abode; **124** Max Jourdan/Abode; **125 l** Cecilia Innes/IA/Designer: Lucy Eady; **125 r** Lu Jeffery; **126** Minh & Wass; **127** Masayuki Tsutsui; **128 l** AvE/Charlotte House Hotel, fabric: Mulberry; **128 r** Spike Powell/Ideal Home/IPCS; **129 r** Lu Jeffery/EW ; **130** C&C, Milan; **132, l** Blickling Hall NTPL/Rob Matheson **132 r** Kingston Lacy, NTPL/Ian Shaw; **133 r** Kingston Lacy LNTPL/Ian Shaw; **134–139** artwork © OPG/by Amanda Patton; **141** Polly Wreford/N; **142** Tom Stewart/LE/IPCS; **143** RM/Designer: Oriana Fielding-Banks